Please read before you proceed.

This book is designed **ONLY** for those who are seeking to be better today than they were yesterday. This book belongs in your hand and on your nightstand. It isn't your typical kind of book; it has an atypical format in that you could read it backwards or forwards or start from the middle if you really wanted to. It's also unique in the stories that it shares and in the quotes and philosophies that it seeks to brand in your heart, and the empowerment that you'll find on the page—not just by my pen, but by yours.

Yes, by yours. If you've picked up this book, if you're reading this now, my educated guess is that you've got an open mind and/or you're looking to do better and be better at something in this thing called "*life.*" You'll find that there is extra lines and spaces in this book for you to contribute with your own thoughts, your own responses, and for the realization of your own DSTV—your *dream*, your *struggle*, and your *triumph victory*.

Proceed with caution as you read and be sure to maintain an open mind so good things can fall in. For you avid readers, I caution you to be careful not to get hung up on the punctuation, writing style, grammar or ALL CAPS usage to where you miss the overall message of the content. This format was done intentionally for a specific purpose. This book was written primarily with the "*non-reader, social media people*" in mind, and it also can offer some great value and insight for you too if you are willing to give it a chance. Although some thoughts in this book may come across as being a bit edgy or pointed, it's important you keep in mind that the purpose of this book is not to criticize, complain or condemn and tear down, but to encourage, inspire and build up a hurting humanity.

Furthermore, as you read in the days ahead be careful not to slowly allow yourself to build up an immunity to the positive messages herein. Read a little bit at a time, then put it down to allow the thoughts to marinade and digest before reading more. This will help you to avoid what I call "*positive burnout.*" Allow the contents of this book to feed you a regular dose of motivation, inspiration, empowerment, education and positivity in the days ahead. Also, feel free to use it as a reference guide of sorts and refer back to it from time-to-time to help stimulate your thought processes in the future. A *keyword* for each section has been provided for your convenience.

Please understand this book is not meant to be about "*me*" but more about the "*process*" that I've gone through and the lessons I'm continuing to learn that may also be beneficial for you. I truly believe that experience is the best teacher but wisdom gleaned from the experiences of others is just plain-ole smart. I invite you to claim it today. Make this book your own. It is for you, specifically and individually. And starting now, we're writing it together.

Embrace the "*process*" during your journey through this thing called life. Carpe diem (*seize the day*) and let's use these breadcrumbs of lessons and wisdom to make it GREAT!

Bread Crumbs
to
Making
it
GREAT

Lessons to living your
best life everyday.

by
Cedric R. Crawford

First published 2012
by **Cedric R. Crawford**
Bread Crumbs to Making it GREAT
©2012 Cedric R. Crawford

Cedric Crawford, Inc. or
3rd Born Inspiration, Inc.
9530 Hageman Rd. Ste. #222
Bakersfield, CA 93312
www.cedriccrawford.com/

Cover Design by Gregory Grecia
Cover Photo: Autumn Marler
Cover Background Photo: John Witherspoon
Book Editor: Emily Freeman & Karen Ice
Book Layout Designer: Ramesh Kumar

ISBN-10: 1480192317
ISBN-13: 978-1480192317
Printed at Createspace.com (United States of America)

To inquire about Cedric speaking or partnering with you or your organization at an upcoming event, please log onto **www.CedricCrawford.com** and click on the "**Book Cedric**" link, or send an email to **Crawford@CedricCrawford.com** (Subject: *Booking Inquiry*)

"There are no excuses for not staying focused and accomplishing your goals if you have this book by your bedside."

My Mom and Me in 1983

This book is dedicated to my Mom, the glue that kept it all together.
Mrs. Geraldine Allen-Crawford
April 4, 1949 – May 9, 2008

My Mom and Me in 2004

Table of Contents

Acknowledgments

To my parents, Bennie E. Crawford and the late Geraldine Allen-Crawford (*April 4, 1949 - May 9, 2008*), who taught and told me in their Texas Southern words, "*All money ain't good money,*" meaning that money has absolutely no value if you have to compromise your integrity and honor to get it. This is a belief that I hold dear and have subsequently passed on to my kids.

To my first pastor, the late Superintendent Leonard Fields of Greater Mt. Olive C.O.G.I.C. in Dallas, TX, whose best message preached was the one he delivered with his life's actions. A true man of integrity after God's own heart (*Sept 1925 - Feb 7, 2011*).

To my three brothers, Bennie B. Crawford, Zimbalis J. Crawford and Patrick J. Crawford, who have been the catalyst of my competitive edge and staunch supporters of all that I do.

To my four beautiful children, Monique, Cedric Jr., Chance and Chayse, who have become the reason why I want to be a better teacher, mentor and Dad. Their acceptance and level of inspiration for me knows no bounds.

To my beautiful wife, Karen Ice-Crawford, who is my best buddy and biggest cheerleader. She's sacrificed so much in support of my dream and her level of commitment is unparalleled. Thanks for taking one for the team babe. I love you even more than a huge scoop of butter pecan, Haagan Dazs ice cream ☺.

To my friends, family, business associates and anyone who had anything to do with making this book a reality, I extend a heartfelt, sincere, "*Thank You*" from the deepest part of my being.

Finally, to my Creator, who I am told loves me in spite of all my shortcomings, flaws and imperfections. Thank you for giving me, among many other things, a stable, sound mind and free will to choose. I choose to serve you by being in service to others and make this life GREAT. May others see my life works and actions and want to know He who empowers and inspires me to do what I do.

Introduction

As the author of this book I feel compelled to offer a disclaimer in advance to all of those who have received a copy. As an author, I run the inherent risk of appearing as if I may think that I *"know it all."* Let me be clear that this is definitely not the case. I am a self-proclaimed *"Work in progress,"* never to be completed. This entire book was birthed and inspired from all the lessons I've learned and continue to learn on my personal journey from ghetto broke to a *"wildest dreams life,"* to almost losing it all and then rising again with a new vision to model servant leadership and create an undying legacy for the world to see and thereby be inspired.

This book is anything but your average, everyday, run-of-the-mill book with a bunch of fluff and no real substance. This book contains some nuggets, take-aways, epiphanies and *"Aha"* moments I developed during the roller coaster process of change I've experienced. The overwhelming majority of the entries in this book came from the many inspired writings in my personal journals over the period of the few years during my process of change. It bears repeating that this book is not meant to be about *"me"* but about the *"process"* and the power of positive change.

This book is a compilation of conversations, special events, life lessons and defining moments that were captured throughout my everyday experiences from obscurity and insignificance to embarking on a journey of creating a life that really matters for the world. It also contains many entries from those who have followed me along this never-ending journey. I'm confident that any reader will find something that's useful and beneficial from the content contained herein.

May this book instill hope in those whom hope is of short supply, and faith in those whose faith is diminishing, and give encouragement to those who are growing weary on their unpopular journey. **This book is based in my *"Subjective TRUTH"* from my perspective and opinions based on my personal experiences from all that I've learned from reading, listening and participating in business and the business of life.**

Studies show that babies have REM sleep activity in the womb, which means that we start dreaming even before we're born. Studies also show that at a certain point in most people's lives, they stop dreaming of what *"could be"* for them and start living a life by default and routine. It is my sincere desire and intent for this book to Inspire, Motivate, Encourage, Educate, Entertain, Uplift and/or Empower the readers to continue to discover their purpose, pursue their passion, chase their dreams, find their gift, expose their God-given talents and grow them to their full potential.

My sincere desire is that this book will be a tap on the shoulder for many to remind the readers of what it means to *"Live your best life today."* I apologize in advance for any comments that may be offensive to someone for it is not my intent to offend, but to inform, encourage and uplift. My prayer is that the reader will be empowered to take the necessary steps to rise above their current undesirable circumstances and pursue a life of significance and ultimately make a positive impact in their respective communities and/or the global community at large. I could only hope that this book will take on a viral personality of its own and positively infect millions, if not billions, of others around the globe and spark a global shift in the direction of *"Service to many"* and *"Servant leadership."*

I've found that a life committed to this cause is definitely worthy of my greatest of efforts and I will not disappoint. This book is the first of many. I would love to hear your thoughts and feedback and stories of overcoming and becoming something new and amazing. Feel free to post your comments on my blogs and website or mail or email them in to be possibly used in upcoming books in the series. I hope to see you at one of our future events and I'm looking forward to developing a healthy relationship of mutual encouragement with you for many years to come. *Carpe diem* and let's take these breadcrumbs and make it GREAT!

Contact me:

Mailing address:	9530 Hageman Rd. Ste. #222
	Bakersfield, CA 93312
Email:	TheBook@CedricCrawford.com
Channel:	www.YouTube.com/CedricCrawford
Website:	www.CedricCrawford.com
Facebook:	www.Facebook.com/CedricCrawford
Twitter:	www.Twitter.com/CedricRCrawford

Suggestions for the reader:

Over the years I've come to realize we're all somebody else's answer to whether or not they can overcome their challenges and adversity in life. As we win and achieve success and milestones in our lives, I believe we have a duty, in fact an obligation, to share our stories of triumph with those who dare to dream of what *"could be"* for their own lives. I'm sure that someone desperately needs to hear your story of how you managed to overcome some of your challenges and become a new person in the process. Don't let your opportunity to share your story pass you by.

I designed this book to be consumed in small bits and pieces and to act as a daily thought type of devotional or an occasional revisit for enlightenment, encouragement, empowerment, motivation, inspiration and/or mental stimulation for the hour, day, week or month. Even though the days are numbered by the calendar based on certain entries and events, feel free to jump around during your journey through the book. This book was also designed to serve as a reference guide with keywords to make it easier for you to find specific areas of entries on various topics.

This book was created from the best parts of me and my experiences, conversations, *"Hallelujah defining moments of clarity,"* and epiphanies over the last 41 years of my life. All the quotes listed above each entry were all created personally by me. Feel free to post your favorite and/or most inspiring quotes to your respective social media groups and forward them to your friends and family and encourage them to do the same. Just don't forget to refer them to this book and/or website, **www. CedricCrawford.com**, from time to time so that they may be able to experience and enjoy the daily benefits of inspiration first hand for themselves. My intent is to grow a family of *Goal-Getter, Dream-Driven, Purpose and Passion-Pursuing* individuals that are all looking to encourage each other along the journey of life to accomplishing our respective goals and dreams. This book is the start of a global phenomenon and movement to inspire the world.

This is indeed an elite club that is comprised ONLY of those who are looking to be better today than they were yesterday in every way. We all embrace a new reality that we do not fit into the category of *"Most people"* or the *"Average"* person. We're also willing to be *"Good for nothings"* from time to time in service to others, meaning that we will choose to do *"Good"* and expect *"Nothing"* in return. We refuse to be defined by words like *Typical, Normal, Usual and Ordinary*. We understand that our service is the rent we pay for the life we live in this moment and we shall not be delinquent.

It is my sincere hope and prayer that this book won't be the one sitting on the shelf collecting dust, but sowing into millions, if not billions, of lives for many years to come.

Be blessed as you read on and don't forget to smile and show your teeth as you use these *Breadcrumbs to Make it GREAT* while *living your best life everyday*.

Comments from Readers

Joan M.D.   *The first thing I do each day is check your quotes... Each one is amazing and I love sharing them. Thank you…*

Henjathang T. S.   *I went through your profiles today. And I was indeed blessed just reading your posts and articles, your albums convey a lot of God's grace in a person's life. I myself have experienced God's abundant grace in my life, from insignificant to a respectable person in my society. But as of the moment I'm going through a phase, which only the Lord knows. The past few months have been really difficult for me, just getting up from my bed in the morning was an ordeal. I believe its God's plan, even though it's only on Facebook, that we met because going through your page, it really motivated me a lot. I was all this time content in living a life of mediocrity. I always knew there was more to life than just merely existing. Your words, "Conceive it, Believe it and Achieve it," really stirred me up!!! I really acknowledge your presence in my list of friends and I look forward to hearing more and being motivated through you. God bless you my friend.*

Nita T.   *Cedric! I love reading your posts, you're always so positive and you always enlighten things on the positive side and simple things in life! I honestly look to your post for positive insight on what I struggle to say. Oh, and I did get myself completely enrolled in College today and I am ready for this journey to began. If I never told you, it was your words speaking on self improvement that made me want to make change in my life. Thanks! J*

Pamela R. C.   *Cedric~ YOU ARE AMAZING!!!!!! I just spent the last half hour READING everything I could get my hands on!!! I am so thankful I found someone like you! Your wife and children are BEAUTIFUL! Your home, your love for people, your desire to help us all reach OUR GOALS is INCREDIBLE!!! I pray that with mentors like YOU, I can reach MY goals.... My kids are raised, and I raised them by myself no child support. Rough road but my kids turned out great. I am a daughter of a FOOTBALL COACH so I have lived with a MOTIVATOR all my life! I am 56 and work with the Special Olympics with a very dear friend of mine, I Love my work but I want so much to be financially free, to never *NEED* a man (financially). I need to make some MAJOR changes and I know that now that I have found someone like YOU, I feel energized and praising GOD for you. When you* *talked about your beautiful Mom, you made me tear up. POW-ERFUL STUFF inside YOU Cedric!!! God bless and thank you for writing me, it blew me away!! Take Care, my friend.*

Laurel D. H.   *Cedric ~ I just want to say THANK YOU again for all of your inspirational messages! I can't even begin to tell you how many times, on any given day, they have been exactly what I needed to hear. Blessings to you!*

Laura K.   *Cedric...You truly have a gift! Keep putting that GIFT to good use 'brother' and continue to share, inspire and educate. The world needs YOU!*

Trisha P.   *Love it Cedric! Woo Hoo! You are such a gift!*

Bernadette F.   *You make such an impact on everyone's day, especially MINE! I look forward to reading your daily posts. Thank you!*

David C.   *Cedric I am captivated by your words of wisdom.*

Donna M.-V.   *Excellent my brother! Not many of us can give useful advice to others that can be taken and used by ourselves and I commend you on your honest, integrity and goal-oriented personality. I think that it's great what you're doing and "HOW" your doing it! Keep up the good work because the words of knowledge and wisdom you share will touch others for generations to come.*

Vicki R.   *You are such a blessing! Thank you for inspiring me every day!!*

Howard C.   *You are a magician with words, or maybe inspired.* ☺

Before you get started, I invite you to watch the following video at www.YouTube.com:

<u>**Search Code:**</u> Cedric R. Crawford – (20)

Without further ado, here we go!!!!

January 1

COMMITMENT

New Year's Resolution vs. Commitment

*"Eyes straight ahead with laser focus on our desired goals
coupled with proper action in the new year makes success not
only possible but highly probable."*

- Cedric R. Crawford -

Happy New Year to all who have been graced with yet another day above ground and another chance to pursue bettering your best in the new year. I say to you today that we all must not make the common mistake of starting this year or any year off with making a traditional *"New Year's Resolution."* I'm told that many studies show that new year resolutions are almost always broken, however, new year commitments made publicly to a group can increase your chances of sticking with the plan. Also, the bigger the group the commitment is made to, the higher the probability of following through.

So, let's all commit to truly make this year different by daring to make those commitments publicly or to a few accountability partners. Write them down and post them visibly so we can visit them often. What happened last year is gone never to return quite the way it happened before. Eyes straight ahead with laser-focus on our desired goals coupled with proper action in the New Year makes accomplishment and success not only possible but highly probable. So, let's all make it a GREAT day and an AWESOME YEAR!!! Our limitations exist only at sky level.

January 2

INSPIRATION AND MOTIVATION

Daily Dose of Deodorant

"Motivation and inspiration are like deodorant and antiperspirant.
They both start to wear off after being exposed to a little bit of heat."

- Cedric R. Crawford -

Well, I've been doing that *"thinking"* thing lately and I invite you to consider the following parallel that I've recently realized:

Metaphorically speaking, it seems to me that motivation and inspiration are like deodorant and antiperspirant. They both start to wear off after being exposed to a little bit of heat. Yes my friends, the heat from life can both literally and figuratively make you sweat and become offensive to others. That's why I encourage you to crack open this book or tune-in to my website and/or Facebook and Twitter page to get a small, healthy dose and application of motivation and inspiration daily. It usually has a welcoming aroma and it won't cost you a dime, just a little bit of your time to flip a page or two or twenty.

I caution you to not be like some who miss their regular application and walk around with funky attitudes, stinky behaviors and offensive comments. And, just like deodorant and antiperspirant, feel free to use this *"motivation"* and *"inspiration"* generously and often, because the last thing you want to do is offend your co-workers, neighbors, friends and family members.

So, feel free to tune-in, wash up and clean-up both inside and out on a daily basis. A page or two a day keeps the funk away is what I say. Let's all give our best efforts and take these breadcrumbs and make this good life, a GREAT life.

www.CedricCrawford.com
www.Facebook.com/CedricCrawford
www.Twitter.com/CedricRCrawford
www.MrBreadCrumb.com

January 3

COMMITMENT

What's your Level of Commitment?

"In pursuit of your goals and dreams, may you have the commitment and focus of a suicide assassin."

- Cedric R. Crawford -

It has been said that the toughest assassin to stop is the one who's willing to sacrifice his own life in exchange for accomplishing the goal of taking out his target and getting his kill. This extreme level of commitment places failure in the *"Not an option"* category and dramatically increases the chances of one's success. I believe a very interesting parallel exists here as it relates to our goals and dreams in life.

Making the necessary adjustments and commitments in life is absolutely necessary for those who are serious about winning and succeeding. Your weapon or vehicle of choice is also very important so please be sure to take your time and choose wisely. Focus your sites on the goal and practice daily on the disciplines that it will require for you to take down your target and achieve your ultimate goal and objective.

"A man is never really living until he's found something worth dying for" is a very true and powerful statement that's been echoed down through the ages. So a good question today is, have you found your *"To die for"* cause yet? No need to answer out loud, just make me proud, and no need to raise your hand, just hear and understand and make your plan then take your stand.

So I say to you today, for those of you who are in hot pursuit of that well-defined, worthwhile goal or dream, may you have the commitment and focus of a *"Suicide Assassin"* until you succeed and WIN!

Let's all continue to focus clearly on that ever-elusive, worthwhile target, goal or dream and keep it centered in our crosshairs in the days ahead in this New Year like never before and settle for nothing less than success.

Let's renew our commitments and make it a GREAT YEAR you *"Suicide Assassins!"*

Karen B.   *That's some serious commitment...Cheers to making those Excellent Choices!*

Let your Creative Juices Flow

"The size of our hands is not in demand in this land. It's what we decide to do with them that matters most."

- Cedric R. Crawford -

My beautiful niece, Shelby Rene Ice is celebrating her 18th birthday today. She's a senior in high school and one of her physical markers that she uses to describe herself in her bio-profile is *"Five-foot-two with the smallest hands in the world."* I've checked her hands out myself and although they are very tiny, they're definitely miles away from being the smallest in the world.

I took the liberty today to give her some unsolicited assurance that it's not the size of our hands that matters most in this world, it's what we decide to do with them that will define how big we really are. Simply put, the size of our hands is not in demand in this land. It's our ability to create with that thing between our ears that matters most.

Undoubtedly, some of the greatest creations and ideas on earth were birthed and created by some who had small hands and even some with no hands at all. Our intellect, knowledge and ingenuity can be the ticket to making that dream on the movie screen of our minds eye a reality. What will you dare to create with your *"hands"* today? Hmmmm… No need to answer out loud just make me proud and stand out from the crowd as you attempt to make it GREAT!

Shelby

illustration by Shelby Ice

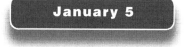

DREAM

Sacrifice the Dream?

"Share your dreams with your kids and they'll drag you out of bed and push you out the door daily."

- Cedric R. Crawford -

I was blindsided this morning with a realization that I never knew what my mom's dreams were. As of May 9, 2008 at 6:00 a.m. (CST) she took her last breath and left her physical body behind and escaped to another world. I'm sure she had dreams, but she never took the time to share them with me. I realize that like most moms, she sacrificed her dreams so that she could provide for her family in hopes that we wouldn't sacrifice our dreams. So I guess the reasonable question today is, *"With which generation does the dream sacrifice stop and the dream pursuit begin?"* Hmmm…

I invite you to seriously consider the answer to this question in the days ahead. As I consider this question, the term *"balance"* comes to mind. Yes, there is a way to balance dream pursuit with family focus if we let our creative juices flow.

Looking back over my childhood, I truly believe that the best thing that my mom could've done for me and my three brothers in terms of goals and dreams was to share her goals and dreams with us kids and include us in them. I submit that if we as parents make the choice to do this today, our kids will drag us out of bed and push us out the door daily. Then, what better example could we have set for our kids by doing this? No need to answer out loud, just make those kids proud. Continue to lean forward and make it GREAT!

Karen B.	*Wow, that one hit home Ced…I've been raising kids for 34 years!!*
Cedric R. Crawford	*The structure of life as we know it in this world will make it such that this quote will hit home with millions, Karen. My prayer is that it will make Mom's and Dad's alike, "Think," and thinking was and is the start of everything big.*
Jennifer A.-C.	*This made me cry! I've been a stay at home mom for 20 yrs, I gave up so many dreams by choice, no regrets but choosing to live my dreams now is making me "selfish" I hope one day my boys will see what you see, because the reality is we revolved our lives around our children but they do leave home and when they do? Who are we? Our identity is gone! I encourage women when your kids turn old enough to be 15 or 16 and drive a car? Let go, and they will figure it out, because you have to find "you" again or you will die inside! Let go let God!*
LuTrina S. W.	*Never did that! But bet I will tonight!*
Tiare F.	*Cedric - that is so true and I think women sacrifice because we saw our mothers and their mothers do it. But as women I think we need to stop and look to see if our "Dream" would in the long run truly benefit our family vs. take away from our family… Love ya lots and appreciate all your thoughts that you share. YOU are making a difference in a lot of lives!!*
Chris P.	*I think living the dream is being able to lay down my life for those I love. Perhaps your Mom would say that she gained more from you than she ever gave to you. Good question, one I've pondered.*
Sandra K.	*Maybe your mother lived her dream, maybe her dream was to have a family and home filled with love. Maybe your mothers dream was to have a son like you! I am certain she thanked God everyday for YOU!!*
Cedric R. Crawford	*"Maybe" you're right Sandra… ☺*

January 6

Daily Disciplines

"Tell me about your daily disciplines and I can tell you about who you are and who you're becoming."

- Cedric R. Crawford -

I came up with a funny yet interesting life scenario this morning and wanted to share it with you. A good friend of mine got caught by his boss behind his desk secretly engaging in one of the oldest stimulating activities in the *"Book."* His stated reasoning for his behavior was that this activity improves his work performance and the companies overall bottom-line.

Now even more interesting than that is the fact that the boss's secretary and a co-worker were caught red-handed a month earlier engaging in the exact same act. After reviewing company records, his boss had no other real answer for why production was up over the last few months. So as a result, his boss decided to start regularly engaging in the same activity himself and he even started to encourage others in the company to do it too. Hmmmm. What is this activity? Well, it's called *"Prayer"* and *"Meditation."* Not a bad daily discipline to be found guilty of, huh?

My number one formula for being all you can be in this *"Life"* thing is simply called *"D8."* Doing Daily Disciplines Daily Develops Dominance and Determines Destiny. If you tell me about your daily disciplines, I can tell you about who you are and who you're becoming.

Question: If you were caught doing your daily disciplines, would it make you smile with pride and joy or blush with embarrassment and shame? No need to answer out loud or raise your hand, just hear and understand and make your Daily Discipline Plans my friend. This is one of the most important breadcrumbs to making it GREAT!

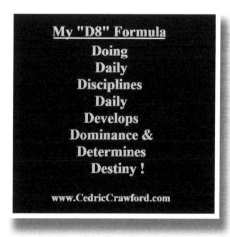

Melissa G.   *My daily goal is to go to bed at night proud of my actions of the day.*

PSA(Public Service Announcement)

We're at WAR !

"We're at war against society's unacceptable version of a life of comfort and safety which bears no fruit for the generations to come."

- Cedric R. Crawford -

I would like to issue a Public Service Announcement (PSA) for the benefit of putting us all on notice. We are at war today. At war against the unacceptable status quo. At war against living a life cemented in mediocrity. At war against society's acceptable version of a life of comfort and safety which bears no fruit for the generations to come. This war and battle is forever ongoing and is one that never ceases in our day-to-day respective lives. We must refuse to be duped and fooled by the alluring pleasure of comfort and safety. As the great speaker Les Brown has been known to say, *"There is no 'safe' position in life, you can't get out of this life alive."*

We're all exposed to different types of dangers everyday and we have to be willing to take some risk in this life thing. So our choice is either going through this life ducking, dodging, hiding and shooting for a goal of comfort and average, or boldly attacking our rapidly unfolding future with a ferocity and fervor of intentionality and making it *"Great"* not just for our own family but also for our communities and generations that will come after us. *"Most people"* only contribute their time, talent and treasures for the benefit and concern for those inside of their own four walls. How about you? Hmmmm…

I wrote this book based on these principles that I've learned in life and have felt the overwhelming need to offer the content herein as a reminder of what is possible and what *"could be"* for our lives if we dare to stretch past the point of comfort and endure the uncomfortable process of positive change so that we may inspire the next generation. Yes, the *"process"* is necessary to become much better tomorrow than we are today in every way and share our wins with our fellowman..

Please hear me today and choose to embrace this message of hope and join the fight against a life based in just doing for self. The worst thing anyone can do is to allow themselves to build up some sort of immunity to a positive message and say, *"Ahhh, I've heard that before."* It is my sincere prayer today that you will be encouraged and re-energized for your journey ahead as you attempt to defy the laws of average and make it GREAT!

Life Lessons

I Blame You Dad

"Do something about it or just shut up."

- Cedric R. Crawford -

Today is a good day to assign some positive blame. So, here it goes...

Although it was several years ago, I remember it like it was yesterday. Growing up in the mean streets of west Dallas, Texas, six of us lived in a small, 650 sq. ft., three bedroom and one bath home. I was embarrassed and in many ways ashamed of our home. The house was sandalwood brown in color with the paint peeling, the roof sagging and the lawn was poorly manicured. I was in the eighth grade and I remember I used to ride the school bus home from E. H. Cary Middle School. The bus conveniently ran down my street during the normal route through my neighborhood so I would always ask the bus driver to drop me off in front of my house. Coincidentally, the nicest house on our block was directly across the street from our home so I would act like our neighbors house was my house.

Our neighbors, the Gibson's, were a retired couple whose house was white in color, trimmed in forest green with a car and pickup truck to match parked in the gravel driveway. The lawn was always perfectly manicured and the front hedges that lined the chain link fence were always nicely trimmed. As I would exit the bus I would always open the front gate to the Gibson's fence so that my friends would see what I was doing and have no problems believing the lie. I would slowly walk up the walkway toward the door looking back over my left shoulder as I waved to my friends as they drove up the street, around the corner and out of sight. Once I was sure they were out of the line of sight, I would immediately turn around and quickly exit the Gibson's property and cross the street to my home hoping that the Gibson's didn't see me.

Well, this plan worked well for my reputation and ego for a while until that fateful day in the spring of 1985. I was following my usual routine and as I crossed the street and stepped through the front door of my house I noticed my dad standing looking out the kitchen window. This window gives him a full view of everything that happens in our front yard and the Gibson's house and yard also. To my surprise, he had seen everything. I put my books down on the floor and began to make my best effort to act as if nothing out of the ordinary had happened. He immediately looked at me and asked the question, "*What were you doing over at the Gibson's house?*" At this age I had already developed the ability to lie with a straight face at the drop of a hat or at least bend the truth a bit without batting an eye. So I said, "*I was going to tell them something but I changed my mind and I figured I'll just tell them later.*" Standing five feet, nine inches tall and about 350 pounds, my physically intimating dad had also developed a skill at detecting whenever I was lying. So true to form, my Dad made what I call the "*Ultimatum statement,*" which was, "*Boy, I'm going to ask you one more time and you better tell me the truth.*" This meant that the *jig* was up and I had one last chance to tell the truth or I would have harsh consequences to face when the real truth was dragged out of me. So I dropped my head to my chest, slumped over and stammered a bit. Before I could get any words out, he said, "*Are you ashamed of this house?*" I stammered some more and then finally was able to mutter the word, "*Yes.*" He then said the following words that have stayed with me all of these years and have been the catalyst for the drive to succeed I've had in my life. He said, "*Then do something about it.*"

As a result, I have to blame him for planting that seed of action inside of me that solidified the belief in me that if we don't like something about our life or situation, it's up to us to "*Do something about it,*" or shut up and tolerate it. To date, I don't spend much time complaining about things unless I'm taking action steps to change them. I also don't make for good conversation when it comes to talking politics and bashing elected officials and things like that because of the same reason. I've found that it's really not a bad philosophy to adopt.

Don't like what's happening or where you're at or where you're going in life, then "*Do something about it.*" Don't wait to make it GREAT!

January 9

DREAM

Dream Stealers

"Most 'Dream Stealers' don't even know they're committing a crime, but ignorance of the law is no excuse."

— Cedric R. Crawford —

I've been doing that *"thinking"* thing again today and I've come up with another truth that I'd like to share with you. It seems to me that the most common crime in the world is the theft of someone's dream. The most interesting thing about this violation is that the robber usually shares the same last name as the victim, yet the crime is almost never reported. The even more interesting fact is that most robbers don't even know they're committing the crime. But, I've also heard that ignorance of the law is no excuse. Or is it? Hmmm...

Well, for those of you who are reading this entry today, you can no longer plead *"ignorance"* of the law for you have been hereby *"put on notice"* of the negative effects of such dastardly deeds. We must be careful of what we say to others because I believe we can and will be held personally liable for any and all goals and dreams that we play a part in robbing or stealing from those unsuspecting individuals that are relying and counting on our support for them to win and succeed.

So I say to you today, for all of you who have a goal or dream that you're in hot pursuit of, be sure to protect your dream from those would-be robbers who are quick to shoot down your dream with a reckless comment or partial truth or opinion that's not based in fact. Be advised that they may mean well but they're doing more harm to you than good. So, forgive them in advance for they know not what they do.

In any cause that is noble and just, we must choose to use the negative comments from the naysayers as fuel to propel us forward in our quest for victory. So I say to you dreamers today, be encouraged and boldly move forward with confidence and delete the negative comments from those nasty naysayers and dream-stealers and press forward as you attempt to make this good day a GREAT DAY!

Jabo B. *Sadly, I have been both the victim and the violator...but by taking responsibility for the hurtful things I may have said in the past , I can turn a new page and 'edify' those I have negatively tarnished. And in the power of asking and receiving forgiveness...We ALL are healed and dreams re-ignite! :)*

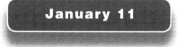

January 10

FOCUS

Focus on the Good

"Everyday is a great day when you're walking among the living."
- Cedric R. Crawford -

Woke up with a big smile on my face this morning. No sun shining through the clouds today but no worries, I know it's still there. I've come to realize that everyday is a great day when you're walking above ground among the living. This simply means we still have a chance to do something positive in this world for others while we're still here. For those who might say, "Well, I'm too old to be getting involved and trying to change the world," I would caution and encourage you to reconsider. I truly believe that if you're still here, that means your work here is still unfinished.

Today for those of us who aren't feeling so good about our current situation, it may be because we're focusing on what's bad in our life and what we're lacking. I invite you to consider the following tip.

Start to focus on the good and what you're grateful for having and try to do it with a smile on your face and watch what happens. The results are almost magical. Today is indeed a good day and we will bound out of our respective beds and enthusiastically press forward in an attempt to make it GREAT because we're STILL HERE! Make it a GREAT DAY!!!

Judy M. *I have a Big Smile too Cedric!*

January 11

FOOD FOR THOUGHT

A Year in Review

"Only a fool will try to take 'it' with him."
- Cedric R. Crawford -

The strangest thought paid a visit to me today as I was looking back over this past year. I couldn't help but to consider the question of if I were to die tonight, could I honestly say that I was satisfied with the contribution that I've made to the planet thus far. At this very moment in time as I am writing this entry, I would have to answer that question with a disappointing "No." In fact, my answer would be more of an "*ABSOLUTELY NOT*."

Out of all the money I've made over the years from my wife and me building a once massively successful real estate investment business and building and developing dozens of properties for people, that contribution is short-lived at best. Making a more worthwhile contribution from a mental and spiritual perspective to the world and the billions of people that are in it will definitely prove to be a much more arduous and laborious task. This type of contribution can never burn up, fall down or rot away. It is for this reason I am convinced that this task is definitely worthy of my best efforts.

Looking back at the great history of mankind, I realize that the great Pharaoh's and Kings of Egypt hadn't quite figured it out. They had it all wrong as they foolishly attempted to take their best servants and worldly possessions with them at death.

My message to you today is to continue to remember that we entered this world with nothing and we take the same with us when we leave, "*nothing*." However, we can leave our positive mark with the message of our life's actions. The knowledge and wisdom that we are able to successfully pour into those souls that occupy this great planet of ours is a gift that will undoubtedly keep on giving.

So, let's commit today to share our time, talents and treasures with the world while we're here as if one day we won't be here, because the simple truth is, one day we won't be here. Continue to lean forward in this new day and make it GREAT!

January 12

MARRIAGE

Know When to Shut Up

"Sometimes the best words or actions are actually no words or actions at all."

- Cedric R. Crawford -

I was having a discussion with my wife this morning in one of our most popular discussion rooms, the bathroom. During the discussion, she made a certain statement. Before I responded, I thought about whether my response would lead to something good or not-so-good. Ultimately, I decided to say nothing.

It's taken me some time, but I've finally realized that knowing when to "*shut up*" is an art form and skill that is often overlooked by most. The harsh truth is that in marriage sometimes the best words or actions are actually no words or actions at all. Concession, compromise and compassion are your allies more often than not. I'm getting better and better at this one everyday. Just a little "*food for thought*" for you today. Eat up and enjoy this little breadcrumb to making it GREAT.

Laurie A.	Smooth, very smooth... Sometimes in order to win the war we pick our battles. When we realize that most battles are not important we really fight fewer wars. Now if we could just translate that to the powers out there in the world. There would be peace.
Lois C. K.	I usually follow with a prayer, "Lord, help me to work on me when I am tempted to concentrate on others' flaws."
Meredith K. P.	I'm still learning that one!!
Lisa M. F.	OMG I did the EXACT same thing at lunch with family today!! I didn't think I could do it... I just knew I had to say something. I passed the test, and decided to save it for later-patience!! I feel like an adult!

January 13

BELIEVE

A Compelling Case for Victory

"Don't give up on that Dream of yours because someone is secretly counting on you to WIN."

- Cedric R. Crawford -

May I be so bold as to give you some unsolicited words of encouragement today. Don't give up on that Dream of yours because someone is secretly counting on you to WIN! You just have to *"believe"* you can accomplish that goal you've set for yourself. Don't have a goal today? Well, you should always be reaching for something that requires you to be better and do better as you grow because if you're not growing, you're dying.

So go ahead and set your goals and recalibrate those dreams and push on. Our best days are indeed still ahead of us, so be encouraged again and again and again and instead of giving in and conceding and settling with excuses, be sure to make a compelling case for your inevitable victory at each bench mark.

Let's make a solid commitment today and everyday here forward to let others know that we can be counted on and not counted out. The "*you*" of the past is no more, this is indeed your "*now*" and your new normal. Go ahead and breathe in the moment and carpe diem as we all continue in our efforts to make this good life a GREAT LIFE! THIS IS MY NOW !!!

Please view the video on:

www.YouTube.com

<u>**Search Code:**</u> **Cedric R. Crawford – (28)**

Laura K.	*WOW...I loved this! I can feel your Positive Energy over the internet! Way to go Cedric :))*
Vicki R.	*There's no way to watch it without smiling! Loved it!!!*
Judy M.	*I can feel the LOVE in this video Cedric! You're The Man! Game on!*
Jack W.	*Well done video Cedric, inspiring music too. Go get'em big guy!*
Harold F.	*Bring it Ced! Making your dreams a reality while helping others. Gotta love it !*
Paris B.	*Very well done Cedric.*

Bonus DAY 1!!!

Average Little Boy

An average little boy was born several years ago.
His average parents told their average friends because they wanted them to know.
Quite average was the little boy, ten fingers and ten toes.
Two eyes and two ears and an average little nose.

The average length and weight, really nothing outside the norm.
His head was even average size and his body just average form.

By all accounts this little boy was as average as could be.
Would he too grow up to lead an average life like his parents? I guess we'll see.

At the age of five he started school which is the average age to begin.
The first year he did about average, even made some average friends.

By his teenage years the system was learned and nothing had seemed odd.
He knew the goal was to get an education and graduate, then go out and get a job.

At high school graduation he got his diploma and a slightly better than averge score.
So he thought, *"Maybe I'll go to college to get a degree so I could make a few dollars more."*

Well, all was done as all was said, he got his degree and his accolades were read and he found
him a good job like they all had said.

His dream was to work at a job where he could make a better than average living.
But he too found out that time at a job outside of his passion and gifts is not worth giving.

A nice house, two nice cars, four kids and a beautiful wife to boot.
But he didn't like his job nine hours a day and that's not counting the commute.

*"Man, oh man, I wish I would've followed my PASSION and purpose avoided this unbearable
strain. Well, I guess I'll just have to hang in there for a few more years and something is bound to
change."*

One year passes, two years pass, year three, four, five and six…
Still nothing changed, it all stayed the same, and he exclaimed, *"OH FIDDLE STICKS!!!"*

He hoped the government would change or his boss would change or his luck would change
for the better.
He created a list of demands and signed petitions with his friends and even wrote his Con-
gressman a letter.

'Till that fateful day, in the month of May, he heard a short, little, simple rhyme.
"If CHANGE is to be, it's up to ME." You catch that? Well, I'll say it one more time.

"If CHANGE is to be, it is up to ME." Not him or her, he or she.

But, if it's to be, it's up to ME…

From that day forward he started his journey to discover his purpose and follow his true Passion. He realized he could never find these things without his commitment to consistent action.

The generational cycle of working outside of one's passion will continue, yes it's true.
But the cycle can be broken and a new course can be taken but the first step starts with YOU.

Yes my friend, if it is to be, it is up to ME. That's my rally cry you see. Dare to change the way you think and pursue your passions and you too can be FREE, this I decree. *"Choose to follow that passion so you too can be FREE!"*

Oh, by the way, that *"Little Average Boy"* was me…

by Cedric R. Crawford

> **Please view the video on:**
>
> **www.YouTube.com**
>
> <u>**Search Code:**</u> **Cedric R. Crawford – (13)**

> **January 14**

LOVE

The Best Things in Life

"The best things in life aren't actually 'things' at all, they're intangibles."

- Cedric R. Crawford -

One of my most fascinating discoveries of the 21st Century is realizing that the best things in life aren't actually *"things"* at all. *"Intangibles"* is what I call them and if you give it a bit of thought I'm sure you would agree that this is true.

It should come as no surprise that sitting at the top of the list of intangibles is that famous four letter word *"love."* Fill your heart, soul, mind and body with this one and I'm sure you'll find that everything else will start to fall into place as your priorities start to shift and your focus becomes clearer.

It also appears that the more love we give away the more we will get back in return. So I encourage you today to go ahead and give until it hurts. You'll absolutely *"love"* it and you won't regret it, I promise. Let's all continue to live life loving and leaning forward. This is definitely an important breadcrumb to making it GREAT! *"Got LOVE?"*

Got Love?

www.CedricCrawford.com

January 15

DREAM

I Have a Dream

"Bullets from the gun of a homicidal opposition may kill a noble and just Dreamer but it takes much more than that to kill a noble and just Dream."

- Cedric R. Crawford -

On this MLK Monday I'm reminded of the irrefutable reality that bullets from the gun of a homicidal opposition may kill a noble and just *Dreamer* but it takes much more than that to kill a noble and just *Dream*.

What was this dream you may ask? Well, it was a dream for equality as I understand it. A dream without fear of ridicule or retribution I'm told. A dream of compassion and understanding I'm sure I read somewhere. A dream of a union and consolidation into one race, called the "*Human Race*."

The irony is the "*Dreamer*" died during his quest, fighting for all to have the equal right to pursue their "*Dream*." No, this man was not the first to have such a dream and he most definitely won't be the last. Dreamers exist in all shapes, sizes, colors, creeds and kinds and I'm proud to say that I'm a member of the "*Dreamers Club*" too.

A great man once said that you're never really living unless you've discovered something you'd die for. If this is true, then to put one's self in harms way for a dream and belief should be considered the most noble of all, especially when that dream is selfless instead of selfish.

So, the big question today is, for what dream or cause are you willing to die for? I invite you to find the answer and get to living. I invite you to join me today in dreaming a BIG dream in honor of the "*Dreamer*." I'll go first.

I have a BIG Dream that one day having a BIG Dream and chasing that BIG Dream won't be looked at as being taboo. Also, when it comes to pursuing that BIG Dream, may those doubting friends and family members willingly cancel their memberships in the "*Discouragement Club*" and become #1 supporters in the "*Encouragement Club*."

Maybe one day this BIG Dream will come true or maybe I'm just dreaming. Hmmmm… Dream a BIG Dream and let's work to make it GREAT!

Blake M.	*Here Here!*
Harold F.	*DREAM ON! WORK ON! Life is about how WE finish. More great WORKS coming from Cedric R. Crawford.*
Chris P.	*That's a great dream, but I think I'd miss some of the growth if everyone who I expected to support me actually did. It's like grabbing that last rep and no one is spotting, but God's got His pinky on the middle of the bar and I can't see it, but I can feel it, and that bar is moving up. But man, that is a sweet dream. If you know someone who's buying the memberships in the Discouragement Club, I've got plenty of phone numbers for cold call leads. LOL.*

NOTES

Write down Goals   - share w/ girls
Motivate & Inspire others
Don't settle for Average
"Do Something About It" - make a
plan & take Action
Focus on the Positive - embrace
God's blessings in my life
The girls are counting on me &
watching what I'm doing
Find my passion
Love - give it away, make others
feel loved and love yourself
Dream - "Go Diamond"
My dream

January 16

Balance your Action Book

"Don't let your words write checks your actions can't cash, because "InSufficient Funds" in the action account can make you look silly."

- Cedric R. Crawford -

I was talking to an old friend today. This old friend of mine is notorious for making big claims of what he's going to do but lacks the commitment to follow through. As he was explaining the details of his plans I swear I heard the sounds of "Blah, Blah, Blah, Blah, Blahhh" coming from his mouth. It was hard for me to focus on what he was saying and take his words seriously because his life is built around, *"I'm gonna, I shoulda, I woulda and I coulda,"* but almost never *"I'm doing and I did."*

After letting him speak, I then explained to him that history has shown his actions and his words have always been at odds with each other. I also stated that he would have trouble convincing me or anybody else that he has changed and this time he was serious and was prepared to start the process and see it through. After a few moments of awkward silence, he relented and said. *"You know what, you're absolutely right. I needed to hear that. We need to start hanging out more so you can hold me accountable."* Know anybody like this? Hmmm…

So I say to you today, please don't let this be you. We can't ever get caught letting our words write checks that our actions can't cash. Bounced checks are inconvenient, but *bounced words* are just down right embarrassing.

If there is no commitment or serious intent to follow through on what we say, it's best to just shut up or just talk about the weather or something. FYI, *"insufficient funds"* in the action account can make us look silly. A little harsh today, but I speak the truth out of love. ☺ Let's make this *"life"* thing GREAT with our actions!

Emad B.	*Hey.....real is real....Tough medicine is good too.... Keep'em coming sir.*
Tiare F.	*Great words to live by Cedric!!!*

Christy N.   *We say stop shoulding on yourself.... :)*

Elizabeth Ann C. *Greeeeeaaat pic, Cedric!! Great attitude!!*

January 17

PERSONAL DEVELOPMENT

A Better "YOU"

"A Better Business, Better Performance, Better Income, Better Job and a Better Life starts with a Better 'YOU.'"

- Cedric R. Crawford -

I had the good fortune and privilege of speaking to a group of local business men and women about some important principles yesterday. The thought of the day was, a Better Business, a Better Performance, a Better Income, a Better Job and a Better Life starts with a Better "YOU." I'm confident that the buffet-style event left them with more than just a full belly, but also a full mind for change and what's possible for them.

If we commit to work on ourselves twice as hard as we work on our respective jobs, we automatically will make ourselves more valuable in the marketplace. So, I guess a good question for the day would be, *"What can you become better at?"* Hmmm… Give it some thought as you continue in your efforts to make it GREAT!

David B.   *Cedric that was very inspiring and motivational yesterday... Thank you sir.. I jumped out of bed this morning at 6:15am ready to get my day started..*

January 18

GRATITUDE

Happy Birthday!!!

"Birthdays are good for you and can extend your life by several years because the more you have, the longer you live."

- Cedric R. Crawford -

I was lying in bed this morning with my eyes closed and the sun on my face. I couldn't help but overhear the conversation between my eight and ten-year-old in the dining room. They were both arguing over crayons while eating waffles, sitting in comfortable chairs, in a warm and toasty house, in a nice, safe neighborhood. Ahhh, in addition to it being my birthday today, I have soooo much to be thankful for. Also, I've heard that birthdays are good for you and can extend your life by several years because the more you have, the longer you live.

These past 41 years have been good to me and I promise that I will pour all I have into the next 41 to give back and pay it forward. Don't forget to make your best efforts to maintain a consistent attitude of gratitude, which in turn opens us up to receive only the best things that life has to offer. I'm grateful for life, good health and the strength and sound mind to do whatever I believe is possible. Let's make this day GREAT!

    Moses S.   *Thanks. For a long time I have focused so much on what I do not have forgetting what God has blessed me with like good health while someone now is in ICU or been in an accident even though they may have all the money but can't help them in some circumstances. God bless you Cedric.*

    Cindy L. H.   *AMEN Cedric, may your day be blessed and filled with family, laughter and good food! Enjoy!*

January 19

PARENTING

How Do You Spell "Love?"

"The most important thing is not how hard we W-O-R-K or how much M-O-N-E-Y we make, our kids spell 'Love,' T-I-M-E."

- Cedric R. Crawford -

When it comes to parenting and raising solid, respectful kids one of the most important words I've learned to say is *"Yes."*

As a father of four beautiful kids I must admit that years ago I used to spell *"Love,"* W-O-R-K and M-O-N-E-Y. I used to be quick to say *"no"* when it came to doing the simplest of things with my kids like playing basketball or curb-ball or rough-housing. I would justify my answer with the fact that I was "*too busy.*" Well, thank God years ago I eventually realized that "*too busy*" was just a common scapegoat that demonstrates our real priorities in life.

I'm happy to say that one glorious day I had the good-fortune of overhearing a conversation a couple of my kids were having with my wife and it suddenly hit me like a ton of bricks that the most important thing is not how hard we W-O-R-K or how much M-O-N-E-Y we make, our kids spell "*Love,*" T-I-M-E.

No wonder there are countless stories of multi-millionaires and billionaires the world over that have failed to create the proper bond and connection with their kids due to the lack of T-I-M-E invested with them. The biggest factor in our kid's lives is not the school teacher or the BFF or the babysitter or the TV or the video game. The biggest factor in their lives should be "*YOU*" and your ability to say "*yes*" to the time investment in the simple things that they're interested in that shows them they're important.

So, here's a brief reminder for you today. In this life we have many, many mistakes to make but we don't have to make them all ourselves. I invite you to learn from my mistake and take time to tune out of the business that life can bring us and tune in to those little ones around us both young and not-so-young. And, remember we only get one time through this "*life*". No do-overs on this one, so let's get it right the first time through.

Be encouraged today and be sure to say "*Yes*" as you choose to invest your T-I-M-E wisely with those who are counting on you to show them how to win and succeed. The unfortunate reality is that most people won't even have time to read this post today, they're "*too busy.*" Hmmmm. Don't let it be you.

Let's make it GREAT!

January 20

POSITIVITY

A Virus Called "*Positivity*"

"May our spoken and written positive words take on a viral form and positively infect millions, if not billions, of people around this great planet of ours."

- Cedric R. Crawford -

VIRUS ALERT!!! I feel obligated to advise you that I have been severely infected by an airborne and internet driven virus of *"positivity,"* and I am highly contagious. The National Center of Disease Control has advised me that there is no known cure for what I have and I'm perfectly ok with it. Strangely enough, I am proud to be known as the host carrier for this aggressive virus and I've come up with a fascinating idea.

I figure that with all the unsavory characters out there in cyberspace trying to negatively affect and infect our lives on the internet, my mission is to take this indestructible virus of *"positivity"* and push it to epidemic proportions and cause worldwide positive panic and pandemonium. I readily admit that I am already guilty of infecting thousands so far and have an ambitious goal to positively infect billions on this great planet of ours before the time of this world is up.

My dream is to create a worldwide community of positively infected people both young and not-so-young that are committed to dumping more and more positivity into this world to balance out all those brokers of negativity. I fully understand that negatives develop in dark areas so I intend to shine a positive light for the world to see in some of the darkest areas. I'm absolutely convinced that my mission is noble and just and will undoubtedly make this world much better today and tomorrow than it was yesterday.

I had a blood test done at my doctor's office not long ago and I found out that my blood type is B+ (*be positive*). So I guess I can really say that *"being positive"* really is in my blood. LOL ☺ For you B- (*be negative*) and A- (*a negative*) people out there, please keep your distance unless you're ready for a complete transfusion and overhaul. If you're A+ (*a positive*) person, then I'd love to welcome you into my circle of friends. Feel free to become a member of our positivity club on my website right now at: **www.CedricCrawford.com.**

There's no stopping us now for this movement has taken on its own viral personality and more and more severe cases of infection are being reported daily. YAY!!! Again, don't get too close to me or you'll definitely get sprinkled too.

This book is only one source of the infectious disease. I have sooooo much more currently in production for this community of positively infected individuals, including events, CDs, DVDs, MP3s and FREE Audio-Jots and Video-Jots made available on our website, Facebook, internet channels and other mediums.

If you ever see something you like, I invite you to please feel free to share it with friends or even better, have your friends connect with me directly. This is definitely the start of something big and I can't wait to see where this activity takes us.

Our team is committed to creating valuable content that will inspire, motivate, encourage and educate you and get your personal development juices flowing. We're on our way and we'd love to take you with us. So, let's make it GREAT TOGETHER!

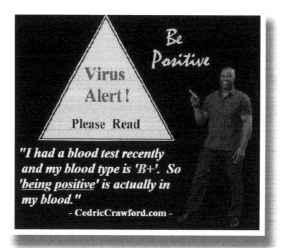

Jabo B.   *Quick! Infect me! :)*

Nita T.   *Cedric! Your words are so comforting! Being on certain online sites are so depressing, almost like being in a bed of thorns and when I come to your page, it's like I am cushioned by your kindness. Cedric makes the pain go away. Stay pure and stay GREAT!!!*

ADVICE FOR LIFE

Need a Breath Mint?

"Allowing someone else's actions toward us to negatively affect our mood and day is nobody's fault but our own."

- Cedric R. Crawford -

If you have a *bad taste in your mouth* about something someone said or did to you, or didn't say or didn't do for you recently, let me give you a small *breath mint of advice*. What people say or do, or don't say or don't do, for us is not what matters most in this life, it's how we choose to respond to what people's actions are toward us that matters most.

We're charged with the exclusive responsibility of controlling how we allow ourselves to feel. Yes, allowing someone else's actions toward us to negatively affect our mood and day is nobody's fault but our own. When it comes to our feelings, we do have a choice, so it's in our best interest to choose our feelings wisely. I trust that you will make the right choice today.

Enjoy your breath mint, Altoids are one of my favorites. Let's stay in control of our feelings, attitude and emotions as we continue in our efforts to make it GREAT!

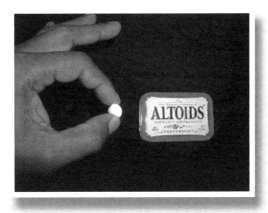

January 22

FOCUS

Stay the Course and Bring a Friend

"The venom from the 'snakes of well-intention' can be extremely immobilizing."

- Cedric R. Crawford -

Throughout my life I've often times heard the phrase, *"Do nothing out of selfish ambition."* This phrase is extremely powerful in terms of its attempt to keep the *fleshy focus* from doing what comes naturally to us. This fact is demonstrated as early as infancy where the focus is strictly on us and our wants and needs and no one else's. Breaking the *"selfish ambition"* tendency doesn't happen by accident, it takes practice.

We should always offer to bring others along on our journey to success and significance in our respective endeavors because the top of the mountain can be really cold and lonely if we concede to go it alone without others. So, as they say, *"The more the merrier."*

In addition, don't be discouraged if others don't want to join you in your quest because not everyone is capable of drafting from your vision. Just continue to love on them at a safe distance so as to protect your vision from the *"snakes of well-intention."* I've heard the venom from such snakes can be quite immobilizing. What are *"snakes of well-intention,"* you ask. Well, snakes of well-intention are those people who mean well but their comments can be slashing, condemning and venomous.

Feel free to adopt one of my personal phrases if you will, *"Some won't, some will, so what's the big deal, NEXT!!!"* or *"Some will, some won't, some quit but we don't."* Stay the course and others may join you as your level of success and commitment starts to exceed their expectations. And, make sure that your goals and ambition are driven by your willingness to help others. Remember to always *"Lift others up while climbing,"* and make it GREAT!

January 23

Struggle is Necessary

"The 'Struggle' always comes before the after."

- Cedric R. Crawford -

W ARNING! I've recently discovered that the phrase, *"Before and After"* is missing a very important word. The omission of this one word has undoubtedly been the kryptonite and main reason why so many people fall short of their goals. Yes, many have been ambushed, accosted and victimized by this short, eight-letter, two-syllable word that rhymes with *"trouble."* What is this word you ask? The word is, *"STRUGGLE."*

I was talking to my buddy Wayne today about the achilles' heel of those who seek to succeed and win in any endeavor and we both agreed that it's the lack of a healthy appreciation and respect for the *"struggle"* in between the goal and the dream. To know Wayne is to love his spirit and passion for helping others succeed in accomplishing their respective goals too. Many may see his *"after"* results today, but it carries little or no weight unless you are fortunate enough to see his *"before"* results yesterday. And even more so, to hear his story of the *"struggle"* in between gives you even more of an appreciation for his accomplishment.

I caution you today and every day here forward to beware for the *"struggle"* always comes before the *"after."* The *"Struggle"* is what brings about the change that is necessary to achieve the *"After."* The struggle is what adds the intrinsic value to the goal and dream that's realized after the dust of the struggle has settled.

So my good word to you today is to be sure to welcome the struggle and embrace the process, and on the other side of the struggle will stand a better man or woman, guaranteed or your money back. ☺

Let's continue to lean forward on our journey through this thing called life as we attempt to Make it GREAT.

Before **After**

Struggle

"The Before & After, and the Stuggle in between."
www.CedricCrawford.com

Elizabeth O. *Without the Struggle there would be no Wisdom to share After.*

January 24

Conversations with Iko

"Getting to know your enemy might just make you a friend for life."
- Cedric R. Crawford -

There may be a lot of things I take for granted in this world, but my regular conversations with my 4 foot, 10 inch tall, 88 pound, 76 year old, Japanese Master Tailor Iko is not one of them. She is a wealth of knowledge and her many true stories make me laugh, cry and sit on the edge of my seat with anticipation. I am often guilty of taking shirts over to her to be tailored just as an excuse to hear more of her awe-inspiring stories.

With her five pound, seven-year-old, apple-head, Chihuahua named Plum in her arms, she smiles as she recalls the events from her past. She was born as an only child to an unwed mother who was a concubine of sorts to a rich inventor of the Japanese Saki-making machine. Raised in Japan in the early 1930's and 40's, she remembers vividly the year of 1942 when she was just eight years old. Her nightly routine was being led by her single mom into the pitch black caves of the mountainside to avoid the bullets and the air-bombing raids from the American enemy. *"The bombs were so loud and the caves were so dark that I couldn't even see my hand in front of my face. We would not dare light a match or make a fire for fear of being detected by Americans,"* she said. Even now she's unsettled by loud noises because of her experience as a child.

After the war, the Americans set up base in an area of her rural town and as a teenager she caught the eye of a young American military gentleman as she was walking to the market. He was obviously smitten by her and she thought he resembled the handsome, great movie actor Robert Wagner, but she was very careful to ignore any and all advances from him. She was in college during this time and could only make it back to her rural town every six months or so. Ironically, one day she found out his name was also Robert and he asked a local clerk to ask her if she would meet him for lunch. After a few declines she finally reluctantly gave in and met with him. She explained, *"That first meeting was so awkward. I did not speak English and he did not speak Japanese. I got up and left after being there for only a few minutes."*

This language barrier did not prevent him from pursuing her and showering her and her mother with flowers and compliments regularly. After a long while he won her and her mother over. Despite her only knowing bits of English and him only knowing bits of Japanese, she managed to fall in love with *"the enemy."*

He made several sacrifices over the years to continue to see her and ultimately he convinced her to go with him to the American Embassy to get married. Several months later she ended up in America were the bullets and the bombs came crashing down on her again, but this time it was the bullets and bombs of racism and discrimination.

In Iko's words, *"I was determined to make something of myself in spite of all the bad comments and bad looks people would give me. I was a good sewer-seamstress, so I eventually got a job sewing and tailoring at Macy's. The head tailor was an old man that was pretty mean and impatient with the other workers,* but he took a liking to me. Over the years he eventually taught me everything he knew and I listened good and learned. That was years ago and after he died, I eventually became the best tailor and seamstress at the large Macy's store in Las Vegas. I worked on the clothing of many rich people including movie stars and entertainers. I learned that if you do top-notch work, people can sometimes put their racism and discrimination aside and respect you. I was good at what I did and took pride in my work and people loved my work because I was always good and honest about their look. I soon became the person that all the other tailors and seamstress would bring their most complicated jobs to."

Iko and her husband Robert had three boys and she's so proud of the men they have become. Despite the many ups and downs over the years, she credits her successful life today with the ability to be resilient and not give up when times were rough on her. Getting to know your enemy might just make you a friend for life, and that's exactly what she found in her husband Robert who's now deceased. "There's not a day that goes by that I don't think about Robert. My little Plum (dog) was his last gift to me. He was a good man to me. My life is so much better because I knew him," she says.

Although she has long since retired from Macy's, she still enjoys her passion which is sewing and tailoring clothing. "It helps me to relax during the day. I don't do it for the money. I just love doing it and I'm pretty good," she said as she beamed that big smile of hers. When asked what is the key to becoming a Master Tailor she quickly responded, "The key to becoming a Master-Tailor is to never become a Master-Tailor. Stay always a beginner, always learning." When asked what advise she would give to others to live a good life, she said, "Follow your heart and passion. Do what you love."

Wise words for all of us to live by from a very wise woman. She's definitely making it great so let's continue in our efforts to do the same. Thanks Iko.

January 25

LEADERSHIP AND ADVERSITY

Why Me?

"Challenging times are just a creative way for our Creator to groom us for leadership while staying anonymous; he doesn't want to blow his cover."

- Cedric R. Crawford -

When going through the fire of struggle many ask the question of, "*Why me?*" But, I would ask an even better question of, "*Why not you?*" or "*If not you, then who?*"

Troubles, trials and tribulations are designed to test our level of commitment to our cause. The struggles, strife and strain of life is absolutely necessary in order to fashion us into who we need to become to succeed on the road ahead.

I've discovered most untested leaders are ill-equipped to handle the heat of the big battles in the moments of adversity and crisis. For this reason I'm convinced struggles, sufferings and challenging times are just a creative way for our Creator to groom us for leadership while staying anonymous; he doesn't want to blow his cover.

During these times it's best to just know something special is coming for you up the road ahead and now is the time to show you can endure through hardships and cling to your faith and belief during moments of uncertainty. Understand all things great and significant are obtained only on the other side of the struggle, adversity and fear.

So I say to you today, "*Why not you?*" and "*If not you, then who?*" Be encouraged and press on yet another day friend and be not dismayed or discouraged. Know someone is secretly counting on you to win. Yes, someone is anxiously waiting to be inspired by your story of triumph and how you overcame.

So understand today that there's a lot more than just you riding on this life. We all only get one time through this "life" thing, so be sure to give it your best effort and make it GREAT!

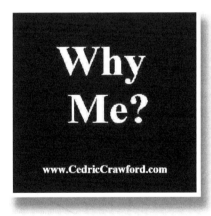

Scott B.	*The words of a champion....thank you!*
Chris P.	*10+ Bro! I think it's an honor to be chosen and tested. Especially by the Lord, because He knows how we will perform, He's just giving us a chance to see what ability He has given to us. Also, as you know, some things in life can only be learned one way. Keep it coming!*
Ron H.	*Thank you for this post !*
Robert M.	*Thank you Cedric. I was down and with these words I remember and focus on the happiness that is right there for me.*

January 26

PARENTING

Actions vs. Words

"Say what you mean, mean what you say, then do what you say."
- Cedric R. Crawford -

*Y*our actions speak so loudly that I can't hear the words you're saying. We must consistently practice what we preach and be careful of what our actions are teaching those who follow us. Over the course of my life I've learned the most important things we learn from our parents or guardians will be *"caught"* and not *"taught."* Yes, they will learn most from what they see us doing.

We can't go through our lives living hypocritically. We must make sure our actions match up with our words, or over time we will risk losing all influence over our kids. The person who lives by the motto, *"Do as I say and not as I do,"* is living in a fantasy world at best. So we must make a point to say what we mean, mean what we say, and most importantly, do what we say, or just shut up.

Nobody's perfect, including me, but I think you get the idea. Commit to becoming a great role-model for the runway of life and let your actions speak so loudly that it drowns out the words you say. Make it GREAT!

January 27

PERSONAL DEVELOPMENT

Hot Stock Tip

"My hot investment stock pick of the week is, 'YOU,' so invest wisely."
- Cedric R. Crawford –

I was recently looking over my stock portfolio and retirement investment accounts to make sure I was on the right track. Nice to see the Dow Jones and the NASDAQ bounce back after so many months. Then all of a sudden I was blindsided by this *"Aha!"* moment or what I call a *"Hallelujah moment of clarity."*

Years ago as a securities broker, I would give clients info on different stocks and mutual funds. Each time I would have to give them a prospectus and make recommendations and give them investment advice based on things like their age, experience and risk tolerance. I now realize with all the risk out there in the different markets, the only sure-fire investment that has absolutely no risk and we can never lose on is an investment in ourselves. The best stock I can purchase shares in is "Cedric R. Crawford, Inc," *(ticker symbol "CRC")*. As a result, instead of putting my extra money in the risky market, I'm committing to make more regular investments in furthering my own education by purchasing books, CDs, MP3s and event tickets for things that will enrich me and increase my knowledge in things I care about. Increasing my own knowledge will automatically increase my stock value. Not a bad concept, huh?

Dare to join me and stay on the right investment track? My hot stock pick of the week is "YOU," so invest wisely and make it GREAT.

Nadine L.   *Really good thought! And even if people are trying to destroy or control you, continue to BELIEVE in "you." :-)*

Please view the video on:

www.YouTube.com

<u>Search Code:</u> **Cedric R. Crawford – (7)**

January 28

FOCUS

Rearview Mirror vs. Windshield

"Success is not a destination, it is a journey and a continual, progressive realization of a well defined goal or dream."

- Cedric R. Crawford -

Success will show up when you commit to the journey. For success is not a destination, it is a journey and a continual, progressive realization of a well defined goal or dream. Have you started your journey yet? On the road of success avoid all distractions from things and people who may attempt to pull you off your course. Stay alert and focus so as to avoid those lesser things that will make several attempts to compete for your affection and attention.

Don't be surprised if one of your biggest distractions is a goal that you accomplished in the past. Be sure to avoid the irresistible urge to look back too often to relish in that past accomplishment. It's OK to glance back from time-to-time for inspiration or motivation but make a point to stay focused on what's ahead. I've found that there's a specific reason why the rearview mirror is much smaller than the windshield.

So, eyes straight ahead, hands on the steering wheel at ten and two, and foot on the gas. In the words of the famous country singer, Jerry Reed, in his hit song from the 1980's movie "Smokey and the Bandit," *"East bound and down, loaded up and truckin'. We're gonna do what they say can't be done."*

There are several things we can be good at, but we choose to be GREAT at *"this one."* So, what is your *"this one"* today? No need to answer out loud just make me proud as you continue to make it GREAT!

January 29

AFFIRMATION

Stubborn as Heck

"Stubbornness is a good thing if you leverage it for a good cause."

- Cedric R. Crawford -

If *"stubborn"* is one of the qualities that best describes you, then let me be the first to give you a *"high-five"* and *"pat on the back"* in advance for your inevitable victory and success. If you're in hot pursuit of something positive and significant for the world in this life, this intangible quality will definitely come in handy and separate you from *"most people."* Being stubborn enough to stay the course in spite of the negative comments from the nasty naysayers around you is imperative for you to win at anything you do.

So I say to you today, don't be so quick to try to eradicate this controversial trait and characteristic. Just be sure to focus it in the right direction and you'll soon find that it will see you through some of the most difficult and challenging times. Yes, *stubbornness* is a good thing if you leverage it for a good cause. Follow that passion of yours and be as stubborn as heck. Here's your *high-five* in advance for your inevitable success you stubborn go-getters. Continue to make it GREAT!

Stan B.	*In my mind, the difference between "Stubborn" and "Determined" is whether or not I agree with your effort.*
Danny S.	*Thank you for this positive affirmation!!!!*
Dawn S.	*Stubborn Swede over here… ;)*

January 30

Parenting a Winning Team

"Too many rules can squeeze the life out of life."
- Cedric R. Crawford -

You can pick your cars but you can't pick your kids. Good or bad, happy or sad, glad or mad, your kids will always be your kids. Out of all those who complain about some of the members of their family, I'm not one of them. I actually feel I've been dealt a pretty good hand. This little rag-tag team is full of personality and no two are alike, but they do have at least one thing in common, they're all dreamers.

My assistant coach/wife, Karen, is award-winning when it comes to keeping this team on task, including me. After eighteen years of being together, she still has not lost her fire and drive for making herself better in every way. I'm pleased to say I'm still her biggest fan. Apart from each other we would struggle, but together we can't be beaten. We have a habit of enjoying the moment because tomorrow is never promised and as adversity rears its ugly head, we prepare to dig in to overcome and become even stronger on the other side. Perfect? NO! A team? Absolutely YES and by choice!

Yes, our team is indeed a force to be reckoned with and we continue to steamroll ahead as we fight to maintain our battered and scarred but still undefeated record. Together we cannot and will not lose. Come what may for the day, we are committed to remain a team and each player knows their roll and is getting better and better at living it out. A well-oiled machine we are with an occasional hiccup that resolves quickly like most great teams do. We are committed to continue to bring our best to the table because it's then and only then that the scoreboard becomes obsolete.

I challenge you today to make sure that your team is not just on the same page but also reading from the same book. Formulate a game plan in advance so that steps for overcoming challenges and adversity will be already in place. Regular team meetings conducted at the dinner table to vent frustrations and concerns appear to prevent a lot of undue heartache, stress and strife. Picking the right battles and not sweating the small stuff can make a BIG difference too. Always remember to never forget we only get one time through this *"life"* thing and we don't want to experience *"death by rules."* Too many rules can squeeze the life out of life, so LIVE OUT LOUD!

Finally, don't forget to have some pure, unscheduled, random, spontaneous, senseless, unadulterated, legal and ethical FUN! We can all be more intentional about making this good life GREAT, so let's whip that team into shape and make it GREAT!

www.CedricCrawford.com

January 31

CHANGE

Enough is Enough !!!

"One of the most compelling statements in the English language that initiates change is 'Enough is Enough.'"

- Cedric R. Crawford -

Three of the most important life-changing phrases I know of are, *"I'm sick and tired of this!," "I've had it!"* and an emphatic, *"Enough is Enough!"* I believe some of the greatest events, ideas and accomplishments in the history of this great world of ours have come on the heels of one of these phrases. The speaking of one of these choice phrases definitely signifies one's discontent with the status quo and need for immediate change.

So, the question today is quite simple, *"Has the time come for you to use one of these phrases and head off into a new direction?"* Give it some serious thought over the next few minutes and decide if any of your discomfort is intense enough for something drastic to happen next. Someone may be secretly counting on you to scream out in frustration and make a change for the better today so you may inspire them for their tomorrow. So, don't let them down, not this time around. Let's go make it GREAT!

Joan M. D.   *The first thing I do each day is check your quote, each one is amazing and I love sharing them. Thank you and have a blessed day !!!*

> ## Please view the video on:
> ## www.YouTube.com
> ## <u>Search Code:</u> Cedric R. Crawford – (6)

> ## My Viral Quotes
> ## Feel Free to SHARE

"Success is just the byproduct of succeeding in the collective moments."

"In life it's not the fewest mistakes that matters most, it's the fewest repeated mistakes that's most important."

"The harder you work the harder it becomes to say "I quit," and the more you get up, the tougher it becomes to keep you down."

"We time" is just as important as "me time."

"Sweet nothings may be good, but sweet somethings are absolutely GREAT."

"Good intentions are a penny a pound, a nickel a six-pack, a dime a dozen, and a quarter a case, but actions rule the day."

"In life if you don't have problems, you've got a huge problem."
   - CedricCrawford.com -

"Great leaders understand the importance of being willing to suffer opposition so that others may be inspired to do the same."
   - CedricCrawford.com -

Feburary 1

Service Before Self

"Be a blessing and be blessed applies to us all, big or small, short or tall, hair or bald."

- Cedric R. Crawford -

THE SMELL OF OPPORTUNITY IS IN THE AIR!!! This New Year will be whatever you make it. How dare we complain about the things we don't have in this country when our poorest of the poor rivals the world's middle class. In this New Year I will seek not more money and material possessions, but more skills, tools and knowledge to propel me closer to my goal of motivating, encouraging and inspiring the masses. This is my true goal and I now have come to understand wealth and service have a direct relationship. The more people I can source and serve with my time and talents, the more my personal needs will be met. What's your story?

I've heard it said this way, *"The more people you help to get what they want, the more you can have what you want."* This law was created by our Creator and I sincerely believe it is so strong that you don't have to be a *"believer"* to take advantage of it. Be a blessing and be blessed applies to us all, big or small, short or tall, hair or bald.

So, eyes off of self and eyes on service is a fantastic way to start this New Year. Let's keep leaning forward as we attempt to Make it GREAT!

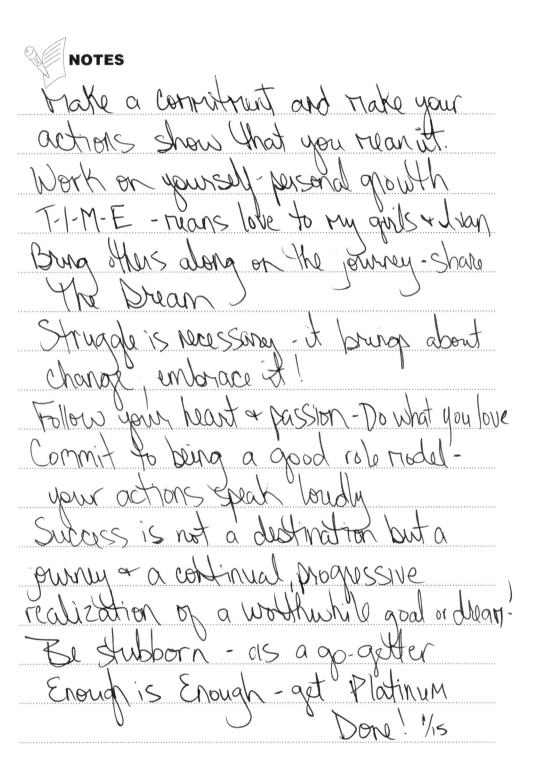

NOTES

Make a commitment and make your actions show that you mean it.

Work on yourself - personal growth

T-I-M-E - means love to my girls + Ivan

Bring others along on the journey - share the Dream

Struggle is necessary - it brings about change, embrace it!

Follow your heart + passion - Do what you love

Commit to being a good role model - your actions speak loudly

Success is not a destination but a journey + a continual, progressive realization of a worthwhile goal or dream!

Be stubborn - as a go-getter

Enough is Enough - get Platinum

Done! 1/15

Rage

When Rage Rules, Rage Ruins

"For some, the metaphorical light at the end of the tunnel is not a happy day, it's a Big, Fat TRAIN!"

- Cedric R. Crawford -

Like a fourth brother to me, he was not just the tall, dark and handsome type but he also had the natural athletic ability like none other that I've seen to date.

Blessed with the superpowers possessed by many animals in nature, he was fast as a gazelle, strong as an ox and tough as a razor-claw badger. But being stubborn as a mule and angry and uncontrollable as a bull would ultimately lead to his demise and undoing.

Stanley was his name and his story is a textbook example of how when we let our *"inner green hulk of rage"* rule and run our lives, it will ultimately lead to our ruin.

As a kid I vividly remember Stanley started coming around our house in the rough neighborhood of west Dallas, Texas. He was a delightful guy, one year older than me and always looking to do something fun and adventurous with me and my brothers. He instantly bonded with the four of us and ultimately became like my dad's fifth son. It didn't take long after that for his true colors and anger and unwavering need for control to rear its ugly head slowly over time.

A product of a rough upbringing, he was quick to defend his position and even quicker to release his pent-up rage on individuals who crossed him. If you were a good friend of his, your battles became his battles and I have several memories of him offering his unsolicited and unwelcomed aggression and rage in moments of tension and frustration in an attempt to solve a dispute or problem.

Football and Track were two sports that he excelled at and pound-for-pound few could match his speed and abilities on the track and on the gridiron. But as it were, not even the track or the aggression and controlled violence of the football field were enough to satisfy and quench his combative, confrontational thirst and pent-up rage. His chronic, uncontrolled *"anger"* was only one letter away from *"danger"* and his inability to submit to authority and heed advice of others was propelling him down the wrong way on the tracks of life. His metaphorical light at the end of the tunnel was not a happy day. It was a big, fat TRAIN.

Ultimately his unbridled pugnacious and vicious behavior coupled with a few bad choices and decisions not only led him to lose a full scholarship to a Southwest Conference Division-I University, but it also resulted in him eventually losing his freedom and having to spend several years in a box called "prison." There he learned quickly that eventually the "buck" has to stop with someone, somewhere. Everybody has to eventually answer to somebody and the further you allow your uncontrolled rage to take you, the more freedoms you're destined to have stripped away from you.

But thank God that his story doesn't end there. Stanley managed to eventually put a period at the end of that paragraph of his life, turned the page and then started a whole new chapter free of the debris of rage. If you asked him today he would tell you that being locked up with a ton of time to himself to think about what was most important in this life was probably one of the best things that led him to getting his life together and his attitude and rage in check. The box of confinement slowed him down just long enough for him to take a good look at his redeeming qualities, and ultimately he became submissive to his faith and the laws of an omnipotent and just God.

Today those who knew him from years past would be shocked and completely amazed to see the kind of man he has become. I know I am. His life and his story is a testament to show that positive change can happen to all of us if we're willing to seek it out and fully embrace the process. But we have to be willing to commit to making the change, and it all starts with "*You.*"

We can't use our brawn to belt, battle and bully the weak and mild, meek and docile into capitulation and compliance. We must refuse to allow our "*green hulk of rage*" to pulverize and punch our way out of our problems and we can't yell and scream others into submission. Uncontrolled rage can be like trying to kill a fly with a sludge hammer, you're bound to cause way more damage than intended. So be sure to check yourself before you wreck yourself because it's definitely bad for your health.

I don't know what the future holds for Stanley. His story is to be continued but he is definitely on a great track to making his story GREAT with his current productive position in society. If a change is needed in your near future, don't wait for all to be stripped away. You can start today. I encourage you to make the difficult right choice over the easy wrong one today and choose to make it GREAT! Stanley did. ☺

Feburary 3

Leading an "*Average*" Life?

"Comfort breeds average and mediocrity."

- Cedric R. Crawford -

With which word would you like your life to be described in your absence: *typical, ordinary, common, normal, usual, fair, so-so, run-of-the-mill, not bad or mediocre?* "*Most people*" would be disappointed if any of these words were spoken in the same sentence when describing their life's legacy after their death. The hard truth is all of these words are synonyms of the word "*average.*" Yep, this word equates basically to a life of "*nothing really ventured, nothing really gained,*" and the unfortunate reality is most peoples lives end up categorized this way.

I believe each and every one of us was created and designed to be and do something great, but somewhere along the pathway of our life we settle into "*comfort*" which breeds a life of "*average*." A life of "*average*" is okay but I believe we have too many people making "*average*" and "*good*" the goal. Some people will even become upset and defensive when they're offered the notion of reaching for higher heights and going further to do something outside of themselves and their family for the betterment of others. It appears they in some way feel they need to justify their desire to stay on a life-path of mediocrity. Hmmmm… I caution you today to not let this be you.

Many will concede to a life of "*average*" no doubt, but not us. Many may consider settling for a life of "*so-so*," but not us. Many will yield and surrender their ambition over to a life of "*mediocrity*," but not us. Many will resign themselves to leading a life of "*normal*," "*usual*," "*typical*," and "*ordinary*," but definitely not us.

I invite you to consider the possibility of living a life of thriving and not merely surviving. A life in service to others and not just our own brothers. A life trying to better the world and not just raising our own boys and girls. In a world where most are pushing and striving for "*average*" and good, let's renew our commitment to do what it takes to make it GREAT!

ANYTHING BUT AVERAGE!!!

Feburary 4

LAZINESS

Unwanted Rescue

"If laziness was a criminal offense, some people would be hung from the gallows."

- Cedric R. Crawford -

I pulled into an ARCO Gas Station not long ago and I was getting ready to fill up my tank when I noticed a gentleman approaching me with an "*I need some money*" look on his face. I'm sure you know the one I'm talking about. But unlike "*most people*," I actually like these opportunities to see what the person's story is.

"*Sir, would you happen to have some change that I could use? My truck ran out of gas and I need to get me and my wife home*," he said. It was about 10:00 p.m. that night and I noticed his beat-up, black, gas-guzzling pickup truck over at another pump with his wife in it. So I peppered him with a few other questions like where specifically did he live at, how many kids he had and what was he doing on this side of town knowing that he was low on gas? I cautioned him ahead of time that I would be checking all of his answers with his wife in the truck to make sure that he was being truthful.

To my surprise he obliged me. Among many other things in our conversation he also stated that he had been looking for work but had been having trouble finding anyone who would hire him. Feeling a bit pleased with his comments and answers, I moved the conversation over to his wife and after confirming that his story matched up, I proceeded to run my debit card through his pump and told him to fill it up. He and his wife were most grateful and verbalized their sincere appreciation over and over again.

It was obvious that he had neglected his hygiene for a while and his hair was matted and his clothes were tattered. So, one hundred dollars later, I figured it was a good time to express to him the importance of his first impression and maintaining a level of pride in himself no matter what his situation, circumstance or condition is. I then beamed one of my signature, big, toothy smiles at him and he returned the same. I told him to pay it forward when he gets back on his feet. Then I gave him my card and advised him to call me the next day before noon because I may have something for him. I also told his wife to make sure that he calls me and she insisted she would.

I got home that night and was quietly excited about the opportunity that was before me. I started thinking about several ways that I could assist him in getting back on his feet and headed in the right direction for a new outcome starting with a new outfit and a new outlook.

Well, the sun came up the next day as usual and noon came and went with no call. To date, I have yet to receive any calls or messages from Kenneth. I've thought long and hard about what could've possibly happened, but I have fallen short of any plausible scenario other than him being a victim of what I call *"Laziness Syndrome."* I'm convinced that if laziness was a criminal offense some people would be fried in the electric chair, paraded before the firing squad or hung from the gallows.

Many have been inflicted with this disease for so long that their sincere desire to find a cure for their situation and circumstance has left them and they find it increasingly more and more difficult to participate in their own rescue.

My good word for you today is we can't help those who refuse to help themselves. We must move on quickly to those who are able, willing and ready for a cure and answer to their situation and circumstance. So, gather no moss as you roll on to your next neighbor in need and share a few breadcrumbs to help them make it GREAT!

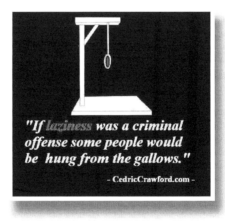

"If laziness was a criminal offense some people would be hung from the gallows."

– CedricCrawford.com –

Feburary 5

HEALTH

Mind vs. Body

"My body has been enduring physical abuse from the bad food choices made by my mind for many years and now it's starting to send my mind a visual signal of discontent every time it looks in a full-length mirror."

- Cedric R. Crawford –

ears ago I heard the phrase, "*Nothing tastes as good as good health or as good as being fit feels.*" I've never forgotten this phrase. At the tender age of forty-one, I now understand. I've come to realize these bodies we occupy are counting on our minds to make the right choices and decisions when it comes to taking care of them. Our bodies can do absolutely nothing for themselves. They can only take specific instructions from the control center which is our minds. Hence, whatever our bodies look like today is a direct result of the choices and decisions made yesterday.

I've found my biggest problem to be my mind thinks certain foods like CHOCOLATE really taste good, and those sneaky little taste buds have a way of transmitting a euphoric signal to my mind every time I shove specific food in the mouth of my body. As a result, my mind continues to tell my body to keep shoving the bad stuff in. It just so happens, those specific foods that transmit the best taste signal to my mind are void of nutrients and minerals and loaded with sugar and fat and empty calories.

My body has been enduring this abuse from my mind for many years and now it's starting to send the mind a visual signal of discontent every time it looks in a full-length mirror. As a result, my mind is now more intentional about its specific instructions to the body of what to put into my mouth. My mind is learning that a taste compromise is necessary from time-to-time to keep the body looking good and feeling good. My mind is also getting better with portion size and time of day in which food is allowed into the mouth of my body. Lastly, my mind is even making my body get up and work itself out on a regular basis.

What is your mind telling your body lately? Hmmm… Chew on this question for a while and let the thought marinade. Continue to make those good choices as you make it a GREAT day.

Feburary 6

TUNE OUT

Siesta

"Our laptop computers, desktop computers and head-top computers work so much better when we reboot and refresh them regularly."

- Cedric R. Crawford -

Sometimes the single most important activity we can do in our day-to-day life is actually nothing at all. Yes, that's right, no activity whatsoever. There are times when we need to just sit down in a chair in a quiet place, lean back and just stare at the ceiling. Turn off the TV or radio, unplug the phone, put the kids in storage for a few minutes, and just tune out so we can tune in to complete nothingness. Close your eyes and check your eyelids for cracks and you should find that there are none.

I've noticed *most people* think they have to caffeinate their bodies and speed them up in order to trick them into performing, when in actuality, they should be listening to their bodies and slowing their bodies down. This will then allow the natural recharge and refreshing of the body and mind resulting in the productivity they seek. Large areas of the Asian culture have had this truth figured out for many years. Many of the Asian business communities even have desk pillows and napping rooms on sight to facilitate and accommodate siesta activity.

I believe you too will find being still in the darkness behind your eyelids daily will definitely give you the elusive boost that you seek. Simply put, our laptop computers, desktop computers and *head-top* computers will work so much better when we reboot and refresh them regularly. A mid-day fifteen or twenty minute siesta session of silence can yield huge dividends over time. So don't be afraid to budget this time into your schedule just like you do all the other important things, because refreshing your own batteries should definitely be one of the most important activities of the day. It's actually my favorite. ☺ Let's make it GREAT!

Lisa M. F.   *You got an AMEN! Most definitely a crucial part of a day. It shows in my spirit when I don't make this quiet time.*

Feburary 7

How's Your Stress Level Today?

"Never let someone else's stressful day ruin yours."

- Cedric R. Crawford -

For those of you who are in positions of authority, please be sure to check your stress level from time-to-time to avoid taking your frustration out on other harmless individuals. As an ex-peace officer myself, I understand that there is a distinct difference between the *"Spirit of the Law"* and the *"Letter of the Law."* I've found that often times high stress levels can tend to push a person to the side of the *"Letter of the Law"* when it may not be warranted.

I was driving home late a few nights ago from hanging out with my group-home boys for the day. It was about 10:00 p.m. and I was traveling on a major road with no other civilian vehicles. I pulled up behind a CHP (*California Highway Patrol*) vehicle at a stop light. The light turned green and I switched lanes and then continued on and watched in my review mirror as the CHP officer got in back of me. I watched carefully to make sure that I didn't go too slow or too fast. The posted speed limit was 50mph and my speed was fluctuating between 49mph and 52mph. After about a mile or two the officer yelled at me over his bull-horn, "STOP SPEEDING! YOU'RE DRIVING TOO FAST! SLOW DOWN AND DRIVE THE SPEED LIMIT!" I must admit that I was surprised to hear this, considering the speed I was driving at and the surrounding conditions. I actually felt kind of like I was being scolded by my father. LOL.

As a result, I immediately decreased my speed by 2mph to prevent from endangering the general public. Then it hit me. I suddenly remembered that even CHP Officers are human and have to deal with stress too. I thought to myself that maybe he was headed home from a hard, stressful day at work out on the freeways and interstates and he felt that my actions in his presence was an act of some sort of disrespect. Whatever the case, I wasn't going to let his bad day ruin my GREAT day. So, I smiled and waved and drove on singing my song.

This event prompted me to issue this gentle reminder. We must check our *"stress level"* often and keep ourselves in check. We should also be sure that we never let someone else's stressful day ruin ours.

Stress-free for me. How's your stress level today? No need to answer out loud or raise your hand, just hear and understand and make your plan to keep that stress level in check. Let's continue to make it GREAT!

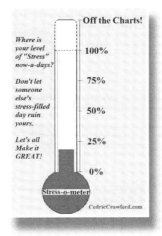

"*Power-Chats*" with Allies

"Power-Chats amongst allies can keep the noise of negativity and drama in check."

- Cedric R. Crawford -

I was talking to a friend a short while ago about some new developments in her life. She had just received word about a couple of individuals who had resurfaced in her area and had been known to cause drama in her life in the past. She was a bit frantic about the idea of them colluding together to find her and her husband so that they could work in concert to exact some more drama into their life.

"What do you think we should do?" she asked. I politely responded, *"If drama makes an attempt to find you, just be nice. Be nice until it's no longer appropriate to be nice, then ask for help from the proper authorities. In the meantime don't start freaking out and let hypothetical and potential problems of the future negatively affect your joy and happiness in the present."* Simply put, don't waste time worrying in advance about future negative possibilities that may never become reality.

I further reminded her that *"worry"* is a cunning, sneaky, professional thief that is highly proficient at accosting individuals and robbing and depriving them of their joy and happiness in the present moments of life. She immediately voiced her understanding and gratitude and agreed to hold on to her happiness in the moment.

Honestly, it's conversations like these that really fire me up and get my juices for life flowing. These types of conversations serve as a reminder for me as well. I call them *"Power-Chats."* I sincerely believe that power chats on a regular basis with other individuals that are *"goal-getters"* and *"dream-driven"* and are looking to better themselves is an absolute must to keep your edge and focus in this *"life"* thing. Trying to brave the storm of life by yourself can be a daunting task to say the least.

Life has shown me that the constant noise of negativity and drama of the world around us can beat us up and cause severe damage to our psyche if left unchecked by an occasional *"power-chat."*

So, have you been experiencing some undue stress and worry lately? Hmmmm… I invite you to consider forming a strategic alliance relationship with several like-minded, quality friends and family members that can serve in the role of mutual encourager. A relationship where you both are mutual champions of each other's success and wellbeing. A relationship that mutually nourishes and uplifts and affirms each other in the best of times and the not-so-best of times. When it comes to combating pervasive drama and negativity there's definitely safety in numbers.

So let's grow our strategic alliances and leverage the potent power and possibilities of the prolific "*power-chat*" on a regular basis. Now you have no excuse not to make it GREAT! So buddy-up and make it GREAT!

Feburary 9

WISDOM

Learn from Others' Mistakes

"*Yes indeed, the second rat always gets the cheese or the greasy bread.*"

- Cedric R. Crawford -

Ever heard the phrase, "*The early bird catches the worm?*" I define this as being ready for opportunities when they arrive. But, have you heard the phrase, "*The second rat always gets the cheese?*" This phrase suggests you can learn from the mistakes of those who have gone before you. Experience may be the best teacher, but why ignore the wisdom in the books of those who have already bravely blazed the trail?

I remember as a kid, growing up in the poor part of west Dallas, Texas in the 1970's and 80's. When the winter months rolled around we would always have rats that would come out of the vacant fields and into our home for food and warmth. After seeing one or two in the house, we would immediately get the rat traps out because we knew that usually meant we had an entire clan in the house. We would bait the traps with a greasy piece of bread because we didn't always have cheese. The next day we would check the traps and would almost always find a dead rat on the trap, but the bait was usually missing. I could never figure out why the bait was missing until my adult years. Yes indeed, the second rat always gets the cheese, or in our case the greasy bread, at the expense of the mistake made by the one who came before him.

Don't miss this message. We can definitely learn a lot from those brave men and women who have dared to go before us fighting for what they believed in. I believe we would be two kinds of foolish and three kinds of crazy if we chose to ignore and turn a blind eye to what others have done to make our respective goals more attainable. So, let's mentor up and/or grab a good book, CD, DVD or MP3 and absorb that wisdom that's all around us as we continue in our attempt to make it GREAT!

Please view the video on:

www.YouTube.com

Search Code: Cedric R. Crawford – (22)

Feburary 10

LEADERSHIP

Rebellion Can Be a Good Thing

"True leaders are the ones who aren't afraid to rebel against the status quo or the rules when change is needed."

- Cedric R. Crawford -

I must admit as a kid I always had that little part of me that wanted to rebel against the rules and the status quo, especially if I felt something was unfair. Now as an adult, I freely admit I still like the frosted side of my mini-wheats, so there's still a part of that little kid inside of me.

Surprisingly though, over the years I've learned true leaders are the ones who aren't afraid to rebel against the status quo or the rules when change is needed or when they truly feel an injustice is being done against themselves or people around them. Actually, I believe true leaders by nature are non-conformist, but they may choose to conform for the betterment of the team and society except in the face of injustice.

So today I choose to applaud and salute you *"true leaders"* who have refused to stand by and permit injustice however large or small around the world. Martin Luther King Jr. once uttered the now famous words, *"An injustice anywhere is a threat to justice everywhere."* This timeless quote still resonates and reigns true today. So I say today to the *"true leaders,"* rebellion can sometimes be a good thing. Let's continue to make it GREAT!

Feburary 11

Set Your Number High

"How many 'no's' and failures and losses are you willing to
accept before you get your 'yes' and succeed and win?"
- Cedric R. Crawford -

For those of you who are striving to accomplish some type of big goal or dream, I encourage you to *"stay on the right track"* as you consider the following questions today:

How many times are you willing to fail before your success shows up? How many losses are you willing to endure before you get your win? How many *"no's"* are you willing to hear before you get your *"yes?"*

Yes my friends, these are indeed the tough questions that we all must answer with a high number before we can obtain that significant goal or dream in our lives. So I say to you today, be sure you're ready to tackle these questions with an unshakable resolve to endure until you succeed and WIN.

So exactly how many setbacks and no's and no-shows are your goals and dreams worth? Hmmmm… No need to answer out loud, just make me proud as you stand out from the crowd.

Be sure to set your numbers HIGH as the distant sky as you continue to move forward in your attempt to make this good life GREAT! *"Stay on the right track."*

Feburary 12

That's My Seat

"It's black history month and I would like to thank Mrs. Rosa
Parks for standing up for human rights by sitting down."
- Cedric R. Crawford –

I spent the day hanging out with my favorite little nine-year-old, Chance, on a bus trip to Pioneer Village. I distinctly remember the last time I road a school bus, I had to fight a boy with two first names (*Brian Keith*) for my seat. I only had to endure a couple of harsh stare-downs to get these choice seats this time around. Boy, have things changed. I made several new friends and also increased Chance's popularity now that his friends think he has *"a cool, black dad with BIG muscles in comparison to theirs."* I definitely won't soon forget this classic experience. No more sitting at the back of the bus in this day and age. Thanks to that first incident with Mrs. Rosa Parks in December of 1955 in Montgomery, Alabama.

This black history month I would like to thank Mrs. Parks for *standing up* for human rights by *sitting down*, sparking the statewide boycott of Montgomery's transit system which over a year later resulted in a complete eradication of the law of segregated bus seating sections.

I didn't miss my *chance* today to hangout with *Chance*. Don't miss your *chance* to make some cool memories with your little ones and be sure to capture them on video or photograph. Those memories will definitely come in handy when we're old and grey and sitting on the porch. Let's make it GREAT.

Bonus DAY 2!!!

LEGACY

Leave a Legacy

There once was a man whose hair was all gray.

Who sat on the porch in a rocking chair all day.

He spent most of his days just crying alone.
Because all of his kids had grown and moved on.

His wife had passed away a few years before.
And the future for him he didn't know what was in store.

He'd spend most his days thinking of what he should've done.
And the quality time missed with his daughters and sons.

His mind was overflowing with thoughts of regret,
And what type of example he had managed to set.

He didn't have the time to see his kids at their games,
And he never once knew their closest friend's names.

He was always too busy to do family events,
Because on his job was where most of his time was spent.

He really thought he had his priorities in order,
But he lacked a proper bond with his sons and daughters.

He thought about his job and worked all the time,

But the words *"Legacy"* and creating *"Memories"* had never crossed his mind.

W-O-R-K was the way he spelled Love you see,
But his kids chose to spell it, T-I-M-E.

What a shame some will say when this story is told,
But it's all too common for those of us who grow old.

It's amazing to see what some value the most
The nice house, fancy cars or other luxuries we boast.

It's OK to have nice things but don't let them be your vice,
Or prevent you from playing an active role in your kid's life.

You see, this old, gray-haired man had realized all but too late,
That creating a *Legacy* and making *Memories* is not up for debate.

He finally started to see that he was reaping what he sowed,
And for expecting family visits, his kids never showed.

Success on a job can never make up for failure in the home,
So take heed to this message before your kids are grown and gone.

And if they're already grown and gone and you never took the time,
Be sure to give them a framed copy of my short little rhyme.

Work as you must to live and faithfully carry the torch,
But participate in those little lives so later you can smile on the porch.

So from this day forward think of what you must do,
And remember in life we only get one time through.

Pay close attention to what you do and how you behave,
And be sure to create a *Legacy* that makes you smile from the grave.

So when your name is mentioned by those who remain,
They'll smile and remember only positive things.

When the time comes for you to draw your last breath and check out,
May your loved ones say, *"He/She knew what leaving a legacy was all about."*

by **Cedric R. Crawford**

Please view the video on:

www.YouTube.com

<u>Search Code:</u> **Cedric R. Crawford – (8)**

Feburary 13

One Life to Live

"At the end of my days may my words be, 'been there, done that, bought the t-shirt, shorts and hat.'"

- Cedric R. Crawford -

Breaking News: A few years ago I realized if we are content with spending our years playing it safe and tip-toeing through life, we will eventually get to the end of our days and look back only to say what countless others have said down through the years after reaching the end of their life's journey. Our words wouldn't be far from the rest in saying *"I only wish I would've, could've, should've, but I didn't."* It now makes sense to me that it wouldn't be smart to get to the end of my life only to look back like so many others and make an inconsequential *wish.* I want my words to be, *"Been there, done that, and bought the t-shirt, shorts and hat."*

We truly only have one life to live and one body to do it with. So let's not spend our lives doing things that take us further away from our passion and purpose and into the arms of deceptive comfort. We must be careful to take care of our dreams and our bodies and in our later years our dreams and body will take care of us. And remember not to forget that most people's last wish isn't that they wanted to spend more time at their job. We only get one time through this *"life"* thing so let's continue to lean forward and invest our time wisely and do what it takes to make it GREAT!

Feburary 14

Valentine's Day

"Found yourself without a special someone or with a someone that's not so special on this special day?"

- Cedric R. Crawford –

Now everyone's gone home and you've smiled enough and you find yourself sharing company with the man or woman in the mirror. Beware, for this is the time you may find your negative self-talk emerging to keep you company. Take heart this Valentine's Day those of you who find yourself without a special someone or with a someone that's really not that special.

Be encouraged and realize that you alone are enough for now. When this truth settles in with you there's a good chance that special someone will then magically appear if you're open to receive them. The key is realizing that happiness is an inside-out job. We have to truly find it within ourselves before we can truly enjoy it and share it with a special someone.

So be encouraged today and continue in your efforts to make it GREAT!

Feburary 15

Using Your Gifts?

*"If you're working in your area of passion, you'll not only
enjoy your life more, but you'll also look forward to Mondays.
TGIM!"*

- Cedric R. Crawford –

Today I invite you to consider the following ideology I've learned over the years. Whatever job or profession you choose to spend your life doing, make sure at the end of the week you have much more than just a paycheck, because if it's just about the money, your life will be void of any real feeling of accomplishment or satisfaction. History continues to prove that money is not a constant or consistent motivator.

When I was in high school we took a field trip to a local black hair product manufacturing company. While touring the factory, I had a chance to meet the head engineer who had designed and built all of the production machines in the factory. He stated he had completed most of the construction of the machines at home in his garage. He also stated that as a professional electrical engineer, he made an incredible amount of money. I was overwhelmingly impressed at all he had accomplished and the amount of money he was making, so I decided right then and there I wanted to be an electrical engineer.

After finishing high school, I entered college on a student-athlete scholarship at the University of Utah and immediately declared a major in the area of electrical engineering. After the first few months of the math series, I realized I wasn't going to like that field at all, in fact I hated it. As a result, I changed my studies from an area that was money-focused to something I had a passion for, which was communicating and connecting with people. In hindsight this was one of the best choices and decisions I've ever made, for it was directly in line with my passion, my gifts and the *"law of service."*

I've now learned that to achieve greatness and significance and live a fulfilled and meaningful life, we must find a way to use our talents and gifts to be of passionate, meaningful service to others. If you're working in your area of passion, you'll not only enjoy your life more, you'll actually look forward to Mondays.

Simply put, if you do what you love you will love what you do. So be sure to live a life doing what you love in service to others and watch what happens. Thank God I found my area of passion and greatness and it sure feels GREAT! Found your's yet? No need to answer out loud or raise your hand, just hear and understand and make your plan friend. Let's all continue to Make it GREAT!!!

NOTES

The more people you help get what they want, the more you can have what you want.

Live a life of thriving, not merely surviving

The bodies we occupy are counting on our minds to make the right choices + decisions

We must check our "Stress level" often + keep ourselves in check - never let someone else's stressful day ruin ours.

True leaders are the ones who aren't afraid to rebel against the status quo or the rules when change is needed.

Take the no's, so you can eventually get your yes + succeed + win

Use your gifts to pursue something you enjoy + are passionate about!

Feburary 16

G6-Formula for Success

"Define, Plan, Write, See, Say, and Move."

- Cedric R. Crawford –

I had the opportunity and privilege to hang out with over 800 students, teachers and administrators today at a Junior High School. I gave them my secret formula for Success: $G6 + dS \times B = Success$. I find that the Junior High School age is a perfect age for developing the foundation for a BIG Goal or Dream and the G6-Formula can help anyone achieve any goal they "*Believe*" is possible for them.

The survey shows that 98% of the teachers and students polled liked the presentation and would love to have a follow-up event. The students left that day feeling much more empowered to *focus* in the classroom and *believe* they can achieve great things by using their ingenuity and intellect to come up with new ideas and ways to create value for the marketplace and the world.

I just had to share this snapshot of a creative way to positively influence the future generation. What can you do to make this world a little bit better today than it was yesterday? Hmmmm… Give it some serious thought then take some serious action. No action is too big or too small, just choose to make the call and get involved. I need a little help to make our future GREAT!

Mary C. K.   *Way to go Cedric!!!*

Ryan S.   *Dude....that is awesome. ..They'll be changed for life!*

Feburary 17

CHANGE

Is Change in the Air?

"Times of crisis forces us to excavate, eradicate, renovate,
rejuvenate, re-educate and innovate so we can celebrate and
make it GREAT."

- Cedric R. Crawford -

There's nothing that can cost us more in life than a closed mind or clinched fist. The reality is, we can't give or receive with a closed hand or clinched fist. Also, if our minds are closed to new thoughts, ideas and ways of doing things, the cost of not changing can be astronomical. So I invite you to consider always keeping your mind and your hands open so you can give and receive that which you want and need in the days ahead.

As I've said before, it's times of crisis that force us to take a hard look at what changes we need to make in order to maintain the same quality of life. Times of crisis and uncertainty forces us to *excavate, eradicate, renovate, rejuvenate, re-educate* and *innovate* so we can *celebrate* and make it GREAT. Necessary *"change"* is always in the air waiting for somebody to embrace it. So, be sure to breathe it in when it's your turn. Let's all be willing to go at least one step out of our way if necessary today to make someone else's day GREAT!

Feburary 18

ACTIONS

Waiting for your *"Good Things?"*

"Choose wisely as if the quality of your life depends on it,
because your quality of life depends on it."

- Cedric R. Crawford -

All my life I've heard the saying, *"Good things come to those who wait."* But over the years I've found that those who are waiting without taking action are doomed to have to fight over those things that are left behind by the people who are taking action now.

I believe that *some* good things may come to those who wait, but success never does. We have to go get it. Success only comes to those who get off their butt and pursue their *"good things."* We must be careful not to think that prayer and faith alone will move mountains. I believe our Creator intends for us to move our feet and hands in the direction of our mountains and with prayer and faith, he will give us the strength and the appropriate tools to climb. If we're not willing to move, then we will just have to settle for picking through leftover scraps. The choice is and always has been ours and ours alone.

So be sure to give it some deep thought and choose wisely as if the quality of your life depends on it, because your quality of life does depend on it. Let's choose to move toward our "*Good Things*" and make them GREAT THINGS!

Blake M.   *Nice Cedric. Yeah, I believe He hands us the shovel!*

Kristine D.   *Ready-set-gooooo!! It's on....:)*

Feburary 19

MARRIAGE

Stubborn as Heck

"Billy's secret to 58 years of marriage; Faithfulness, Honesty and being Stubborn to Stay."

- Cedric R. Crawford -

After fifty-eight long years of marriage, she still loves like they met just yesterday. She's seventy-six and he is eighty-three years young. Billy says that many years married to Russ hasn't all been marital bliss, but one day she tallied up the good and the bad and the good came out shining like the sun and smelling like a rose.

Four kids and seven grandkids later she's now enjoying her retirement years and knowing that her kids and grandkids are all outside of the prison system makes her smile from ear to ear. As she shared her story with me, I asked her to what can she attribute her marital success thus far and she without hesitation pointed out three things. The first two "*faithfulness*" and "*honesty*" are pretty common, but I have to admit the third one caught me a bit off guard. She said, "*The most important thing is, you have to be 'stubborn as heck,'… Stubborn to stay.*" I thought about it a brief second and couldn't help but to agree with her 100%.

Stubbornness in marriage in this case is actually a good thing. It appears to me that most people appear to be stubborn to the point of leaving as opposed to being "*stubborn to stay.*"

What a concept and philosophy. Adopting this attitude may preserve more unions down the road of marriage. Well, I guess it can't hurt. Thanks for the tip, Billy. It's amazing the type of stories and wisdom you can stumble onto if you just say "*Hi*" to a person in the hot tub at an In-Shape Fitness Club.

So, what's your story? No need to share it here, just make sure someone hears it. Let's all make it GREAT and be stubborn as heck in those relationships that are worth the fight.

Sandra K.   *Billy is a smart woman. I always say it is too easy to get out of a marriage today. When the going gets tough, work harder....the rewards are worth it!*

Donna M. V.   *Wow Ced! Tell Mrs. Billie thanks for that advice because I asked that question two months ago when I married my teenage sweetie! Ced I believe she is right too because as teens my hubby and I were separated by our parents and I never thought I'd see him again. Twenty years later he shows up (pure stubborn) and wants me to marry him! And get this, he surprised me with a ring he bought for me in 1991 that his grandma kept for "his wife." It makes me thank God Ced for this "stubborn" man!*

Feburary 20

SUCCESS

Are you Attractive

"Don't pursue success for it will be fleeting. Attract it by becoming an attractive person."

- Cedric R. Crawford -

Do you consider yourself an attractive person? As a kid, I always found that it was a lot easier to attract animals than it was to catch them. Running after them almost always resulted in failure as they would always run away. Such is life in terms of success.

True success is not to be pursued for it will be fleeting, but attracting it dramatically increases your chances of succeeding. Be careful not to confuse this form of attractiveness with your physical outward appearance, for the emphasis should be placed squarely on how you look inside and how you think. After going through the mental process of becoming an attractive person, success will automatically follow.

This is a simple truth that can actually make all the difference. Let's commit to make this day soooooo great that yesterday gets insanely jealous. Stay attractive. ☺

Karen B.   ⟡ *Personal Development = Priority #1*

Laurie A.   *Sooooooo truuuuue... It flows when you grow.*

Feburary 21

PERSISTENCE

Two Wrongs Gets You Closer

> *"We must be willing to be wrong and wrong and wrong again until we are right."*
>
> *- Cedric R. Crawford -*

ever heard the phrase, *"Two wrongs don't make a right?"* I've learned that this is true, but during the innovative and creative process, two wrongs can get you two steps closer to a *"right."* So, we must continue to be willing to risk being *wrong* or failing until we're right and successful in our respective endeavors.

The great Thomas Edison is famous for stating he found thousands of ways of inventing a light bulb that didn't work and continued to persist until he found the one way that did. He succeeded because he was willing to fail his way to success. He was willing to be wrong and wrong and wrong again until he was *right*.

I feel that it is my civic duty to inform you that we have received unbridled permission from our Creator to frequently fail forward fast and furiously toward our goals and dreams. Our applause is guaranteed to come sooner or later if we persist and don't quit. So stay the course for one more day. Just another small breadcrumb to make it GREAT!

Dennis S.   *And we'll call this one Sunday's Best.*

Lisa M. F.   *That is good! "A just man falleth 7 times and rises up again!"*

Feburary 22

WORDS

The Spoken Word

 "Speak it, Believe it, Take proper Action and Achieve it."
- Cedric R. Crawford -

If the spoken word is really as powerful as they say it is, then, *"What say you?"* What words do you choose to speak over your life daily? A great man once said, *"The spoken word brings into existence that which did not exist before."* So if this is true, then we must choose today to SPEAK UP for what we want in our lives. My favorite book advises us to *"call those things that are not as though they* were." This infers that the words we choose to speak over our situations and circumstances do matter.

We must have an unwavering belief and certainty that whatever we want out of this life is absolutely possible and couple our belief with proper consistent action. If we do this properly, then over time we will start to see changes in the direction of that which we seek. Good or bad, our spoken words have power in them and with that power comes responsibility. So what words are you responsible for today? What words do you choose to speak over your situation and circumstance today? Yes, your spoken words really do matter, so speak with conviction and unwavering certainty today.

Speak it, Believe it, Take proper Action and Achieve it! Let's start to speak and jumpstart the creation of our desired outcomes and reality. What say you today? I say we MAKE IT GREAT!!!

Sue W.	Have your word be "not negotiable."
Tonya D.	Set a guard, O lord, over my mouth; keep watch over the door of my lips. Do not incline my heart to any evil thing, to practice wicked works with men who work iniquity. Psalm 141:3-4
Bradford F.	Good stuff Cedric! I agree with you all the way my friend. Keep doing what you're doing.

Feburary 23

Keep your Tools Sharp

"Attitude before aptitude everyday of the week and twice on Sundays."

- Cedric R. Crawford -

Attitude before aptitude and altitude everyday of the week and twice on Sundays. We'd have to be two different types of *"crazy"* to think our aptitude smarts will compensate for a poor attitude. Our attitude is a tool. Day-to-day that tool is either working for us or against us. Our attitude will make or break us in any business or endeavor, so we must always, always, always pay special attention to this tool and keep it positively sharpened.

I was recently pulled over by a motorcycle cop for driving a little faster than the posted speed limit. Initially I was upset when I saw the lights and heard the siren, but quickly I composed myself and pulled out my secret weapon, my positive attitude and blindsided him. He never saw it coming. I started by immediately admitting my error with a big smile and offered up no excuse for my wrong doing.

A short conversation ensued after being asked by the officer, *"Where are you headed?"* I told him I was on my way to change the lives of a bunch of teenage boys at a local high school and I was going to use the incident of being stopped by an officer in my presentation today. I then gave him a choice of the story I would share. I said, *"You could give me a ticket to teach them that if you break the law, you suffer the consequences. Or, you could let me off with a warning to show that even if you screw up in life sometimes, if you manage to maintain a positive attitude, you just might get a warning."* The officer laughed and then gave me his answer.

I'll reveal his surprising answer a few months later on down the road in another section of this book. So stick around and read on with a positive attitude. Make it GREAT.

Feburary 24

Fun-Snack Fridays

"Don't forget to do your part in making someone else's day great."

- Cedric R. Crawford -

Meet Christian in the bottom left picture. He always gives us our ice-cream scoops at Rite-Aid on *"Fun Snack Fridays."* Little Chance and Chayse always look forward to this day. We usually drag one of their friends with us too. Little Emily Rose Fick was the lucky one to join us today. She loves chocolate and she rarely finishes her small cup, so we call her an amateur ice cream eater. But for me, Chance and Chayse, we consider ourselves professionals. Chance likes strawberry and Chayse keeps me guessing. For me, my flavor is black cherry because I love cherries and I'm black.☺

Some *Fun Snack Fridays* we decide to change it up a bit and get Slurpees from the neighborhood 7-Eleven. When was the last time you gave a Slurpee to a crossing guard and thanked them for all they do? Well, meet Jerry in the picture on the bottom right. Jerry doesn't make much money doing what he does, but he sure takes his job seriously and is always guilty of coming early and staying late. He can also be a bit aggressive when he needs to with speeders and those who don't yield to his handheld stop sign. That's really funny to watch. LOL.

We look forward to making his day too on certain *Fun Snack Fridays* in the Crawford household. My kids absolutely love the opportunity to make other people smile and Jerry the crossing guard is always a slam dunk. My kids even frequently fight over who will be the designated one of the day to hand him his Slurpee. ☺

The way I figure it, our kids have enough stressors in the world of school, so why not have something to look forward to at the end of their school week? Plus this gives me another leverage tool to take away when things aren't going so well in the classroom. I'm happy to report we haven't missed a Friday for bad behavior yet. YEAHHH!!!

Don't miss your chance to do your part in making someone smile regularly. But be warned, it just might make you smile too. ☺ The world needs people like us, so go make somebody else's day GREAT! Feel free to join in and make a friend. You'll be glad you did. Let's Make it GREAT!

Rebecca C. P. *I bet they both look forward to seeing your crew as well....How awesome, not only for you and your kids but you make someone else's day special as well...Not many like you around, your kids are very lucky.*

Feburary 25

BELIEVE

I Call You Overcomer

"Move forward today and everyday hereafter with a renewed vision of who you are, what you're doing and why you're here."
- *Cedric R. Crawford* -

*e*ye's straight ahead will undoubtedly reduce the chances of you having an accident, so strategizing for your future is a welcomed activity in my book. Are you ready to become who you already are? Do you believe you're capable of GREAT things? Never mind. Don't answer those rhetorical questions. I know you're ready. You're welcome to lean on my belief in you until your belief in yourself fully kicks in.

I know something about you even though I may not know you personally. You were built and designed to be an "*Overcomer.*" If that were not true, you wouldn't be here today. You would've acted on the quiet, subtle thoughts of ending it all a looooong time ago. Yes, I know you. I know that your biggest battles in this life are the ones that you fight on the battle field of your own mind due to the countless heartaches and heartbreaks of the distant and not-so-distant past events in your life. But again, I call you "*OVERCOMER!*" because you're still here. I believe in YOU!

Many have missed their opportunity to affirm the strengths in you down through the years, but not me. I will not miss my opportunity to say to you today that you are indeed a rare breed and are destined for GREAT things if you choose to embrace who you have become. Yes, I know your kind very well. I believe in you and to you I say today, congratulations for making it this far in your book of life. Now it's time to turn the page and grab a new ballpoint pen and start writing out the new and dramatically improved "*YOU*" for the entire world to see.

Someone desperately needs to hear your story of how you did it and how you're doing it, so if not for your own sake, do it for them and your actions will not go unrewarded. "*Overcomer,*" you are and I applaud your efforts thus far, but your standing ovation awaits you in the days ahead.

So move forward today and everyday hereafter with a renewed vision of who you are, what you're doing and why you're here. Let there be no question in your mind that you were custom-designed for a task such as this. I say again, I believe in you and I encourage you to believe in "*you,*" for if you truly believe in your heart all things then become possible for you.

Congratulations in advance for those lives that will be forever changed because you did not pass on your unique opportunity to share your story like "*Most People*" would've. Let's continue to make it GREAT together!!!!!

You're AWESOME just for being here. Don't take that awesomeness to the grave with you. Not you… Let's share it. Believe in your heart that you can.

To Be Continued...

www.CedricCrawford.com

GIVING

Give and Be Given Unto

"The law of reciprocity is so strong and unwavering that even non-believers can take advantage of it."

- Cedric R. Crawford -

Setting a goal to positively impact someone's life daily will result in us being positively rewarded ourselves because the law of reciprocity states that if we give with a grateful heart we will receive. So, let's make a point to give without want and this will open up the opportunity to have our own needs met.

This may come as a surprise to most, but I believe our Creator placed this law of reciprocity in the universe and it's so strong and unwavering that even non-believers can take advantage of it. Be advised that this giving does not have to be monetary in nature only. It can also be of your time and talents to those who are in need. I must caution you to not make the vital mistake in waiting to give out of your abundance and excess, but make a point to give out of your scarcity, for this type of giving unequivocally carries more sacrificial significance.

Bless someone with that smile of yours or a nice compliment or a kind gesture today. It won't cost you a thing and you just might make their day, and yours too. We only get one time through this "life" thing so let's make our best efforts to give to others who are in need as we attempt to make it GREAT!

LIFE LESSONS

Know the Story?

"Be careful not to pass judgment on others before you know their whole story."

- Cedric R. Crawford -

I was working out at the gym today and I ran into an older, gray-haired gentlemen in the locker room. This gentleman was the one who would never speak back when I pass him in the gym and he would never acknowledge my eye contact and kind head and hand gestures when I'd see him from across the room. Being the persistent guy I am, I thought, *"Now I have him cornered."* His locker was right next to mine and he would have to speak to me. So, I made eye contact with him from about three feet away and raised my voice and said, "Hi, how's it going?" He then said, "Well, *for an old man that can't hear or see worth a darn, I guess I'm doing OK."* We both laughed and proceeded to carry on a nice, casual conversation. Then it suddenly hit me that he never acknowledged me before because he couldn't see or hear me. I must admit that I felt like an idiot.

Well, I guess I have to take back all those bad thoughts of how rude I thought he was. His name is Dennis and he's a very nice guy. I guess the lesson is we can be nice to everyone and resist the urge to pass judgment or develop an opinion about them before we know their whole story. I've definitely learned my lesson, so feel free to learn from my mistake at no charge. Let's make it GREAT!

Jabo B.	*...And THAT my friends is food for thought! Thanks Cedric!*
Elizabeth A. C.	*Giving someone the benefit of "I must not know the whole story" and smiling anyway has warmed my heart many times. Just need to remember that 100% of the time.*
Chris S.	*Good delivery and the message is the truth!*
Kiyana S. B.	*I agree 100%... :)*
Mark L.	*Yep.. I say hello to everybody who can hear me!!! At least 3 times before I dismiss them as possible people I wouldn't want to talk to. You're the man bro!*

Feburary 28

ADVERSITY

Overcomation

"Some of the challenges, changes and adversity that we're currently running from, we need to consider turning around and running toward."

- Cedric R. Crawford –

I've discovered that some of the challenges, changes and adversity that we're currently running from, we need to consider turning around and running toward. I'm convinced we'll appreciate the person we'll become after going through the process of what I call *"overcomation."* Don't bother looking this word up in your dictionary, it won't be there because it doesn't exist. I just created it today to serve my purpose. I define this word as the act or process of one overcoming a challenge or adverse situation.

Take heart and comfort in knowing that a better version of *"You"* awaits on the other side of your overcomation. So, let's stop running from *"it"* and turn around and run to *"it"* so we can get through *"it"* and embrace the new person we become on the other side. Let's make this good day a GREAT DAY!

March 1

Plan A and Plan B

"If Plan A is to Accomplish the goal, then Plan B should be to Believe that it's possible."

- Cedric R. Crawford –

I invite you to consider the following thought as you continue on your journey today:

If our Plan A is to *Accomplish* the goal, then our Plan B should be to raise our level of *Belief* that it's possible. I've found our level of belief serves as the catalyst for ultimately accomplishing our biggest goals in life. Lose this Plan B and we can kiss Plan A goodbye.

Are you absolutely certain that *"it's"* possible for you? Is your level of belief where it needs to be for this stage of your life's journey? Hmmmm… Chew on this food for thought for a while and ponder your honest answer.

I encourage you today to continue to believe *"it's"* possible for you whatever your *"it"* is, and be sure to keep the main thing the *"main thing"* and don't lose your focus. Keep moving forward and remember that as long as we're heading in the right direction, the size of our steps don't matter. Let's commit to take yet another positive step or two or five forward today as we attempt to make this good day a GREAT day on our journey.

NOTES

- There's nothing that can cost us more in life than a closed mind or clinched fist. If our minds are closed to new thoughts, ideas + ways of doing things, the cost of not changing can be astronotical!

- Those who are waiting w/out taking action are doomed to have a fight over those things that are left behind by the people who are taking action now!

- Faithfullness, honesty stubborness to stay = long marriage

- After going through the mental process of becoming an attractive person, success will automatically follow.

- 2 wrongs can get you 2 steps closer to a "right"

- The spoken word brings into existence that which did not exist before; speak it, believe it, take proper action + Achieve it!

March 2

Priceless Moments

"The most meaningful moments are the ones that don't have a price."

- Cedric R. Crawford -

New Shoes = **$26.80**
Red-Rose Corsage Wristlet = **$15.00**
Dinner at the famous Rosemary's Creamery = **$33.15**
Ticket to our first Daddy-Daughter Dance = **$20.00**
A night out on the town making a memory with my youngest daughter that won't be soon forgotten
= **PRICELESS**

My littlest princess couldn't stop smiling all night as she was wined and dined and taught what to require and expect from a *"gentleman"* on her first date. The food was good, the conversation was great and the dancing was *"to die for."*

These opportunities don't come often in our lifetime. So, let's make every effort to take full advantage of them and make them GREAT!

March 3

Living a "Good Life"

"Turn off CNN 'Constant Negative News,' NBC 'Nothing But Chaos,' ABC 'All Bad Catastrophes' and CBS 'Continuous Blood Shed.'

- Cedric R. Crawford -

*e*ver heard of the *"self-fulfilling prophecy"*? It's when you're constantly being told something over and over and eventually you start to believe it and it then starts to manifest in your life. I figure if this philosophy is true, then why not use it to our benefit and advantage?

We could start by constantly affirming ourselves and speaking words of encouragement to the man or woman in the mirror on a daily basis. My favorite book states that we should call those things that are not as though they were in our day-to-day lives. Then with persistence and proper consistent action, watch the magical transformation happen.

I invite you to consider turning off the CNN *'Constant Negative News,'* NBC *'Nothing But Chaos,'* ABC *'All Bad Catastrophes'* and CBS *'Continuous Blood Shed'* and turning on the good stuff. I guarantee if you tune into the good news, good people and good books, you will find yourself living a *"good life."* It won't hurt to try this one out for a while if a change is needed. Just a thought for you to ponder today as we all attempt to make this good life, GREAT! "Time for Change?" Hmmmm…

March 4

SERVICE

Do *"Good"* for *"Nothing"* today

"Be a 'Good-for-Nothing' in your community and make a difference starting today in some way."

- Cedric R. Crawford -

I spent all morning with two big *"good-for-nothings."* Both Chad Hymas and Kevin Hall are world-class authors and speakers. They flew all the way from the great state of Utah to do *"Good"* for *"Nothing"* in the Bakersfield Community. It's people like these guys that make the world a better place. What they did today for the sake of the KATC in Bakersfield will never be forgotten by many.

The KATC (*Kern Assistive Technology Center*) is a non-profit organization that helps people with disabilities be more self-sufficient in their own homes and out in public. I salute these two great men for their commitment to regularly serve the world community by giving of their time, talent and treasures without want. We are definitely kindred spirits and we have a lot of work to do.

I invite you to join us on our worldwide quest to sow *"good"* into our communities and the world at large. May we all take notice of their great example and follow suit. Be a *"good-for-nothing"* in your community and make a difference starting today in some way. Oh, be sure to take this breadcrumb and make it GREAT.

March 5

FOCUS

Momentum

*"We must make the decision to boldly take action and attack
life or life will eventually boldly take action and attack us."*
- Cedric R. Crawford -

I've learned the hard lesson that we must choose to embrace change or eventually we will be embraced by change. We must make the decision to boldly take action and attack life, or life will soon boldly take action and attack us. I've also discovered that just standing on the right path is not enough, we must move forward or be prepared to be moved out of the way or just be flat-out run over by those who are moving forward. Be advised that when you're on the right path, baby steps at times are okay as long as you're headed in the right direction.

Also a feeling of fear is totally acceptable periodically along our journey. Remember that FEAR is just an acronym for *"False Evidence Appearing Real"* and not *"Forget Everything And RUN!"* Be not dismayed or distracted by this *false evidence* and don't let it bring you to a standstill for I've come to know and understand that an object in motion tends to stay in motion. Momentum can be an awesome and powerful thing when you're headed in the right direction and the goal is clear, so be sure to take full advantage of it whenever possible.

My two words for you today are, *"You're There!"* and now is the time to put all doubt aside and embrace your unfolding future and boldly move forward. You have separated yourself from the masses of *"most people"* just by making a definitive decision to act now in your own best interest.

I say to you, don't be afraid to make a mistake or fail, for that is just part of the process. Learn your lessons quickly, get up and move on knowing that the greatest among us all had to walk this path at one time or another. The clearer and more defined your goal is, the more people will fall into place along your path. Yes it's true, the right people will show up as we continue to move forward with clarity of the goal. Stay *focused* for one more day and let's make it GREAT!

March 6

CHILDREN

An Unexpected Source of Wisdom

"Are you listening to the voices of those little people around you?"

- Cedric R. Crawford –

Anytime I want some material to write about, all I have to do is strike up a conversation with one of my kids. They have an incredible ability to see life in a totally different way than we adults, and I've found the younger the better. My kids have truly become an amazing, unexpected source of content for living a good life. We just have to listen and recognize the parallels and adopt some of their behaviors and philosophies.

I believe the answers to life's most complicated questions lie in the simplicity of a child. So, my question today is, *"Are you listening to the voices of those little people around you?"* Whether it's our own kids or the children of someone else, I encourage you to just strike up a casual conversation with a child from time-to-time. Ask some questions, listen intently with an open heart and mind and take note of what you hear and see. I think you'll be pleasantly surprised at what you observe and you may even get a good laugh or two.

The biggest surprise for me in this *"life"* thing is when I discovered that a childlike faith is one of the biggest keys to making it great. Don't make the common mistake of walking through this life too seriously with a dill-pickle face. Smile, play, laugh, pray and make a point to have a conversation with someone under forty inches tall every now and then. Then follow through with a childlike faith. Yes, I'm convinced this is yet another awesome key to living a "*good*" life. So, let's continue to Make it GREAT!

Susan O. J.	*I ♥ talking to my kids!!! and they are more fun if they are young....I had a conversation last night with my 3 yr old friend Kate and it was amazing!!! (and so comical)*
Elizabeth A. C.	*Grandkids are fabulous to discuss life with too!! Brings big smiles to your heart!!*
Sandra K.	*My granddaughter recently reminded her grandfather that her birthday was coming. He asked her how old she would be, and she answered, five. He replied, " 5, that's old." To that she said, " yep, I'll be over the hill." You are right, if you sit and listen, and talk "with them" they will say amazing things. "out of the mouth of babes"*
Corilee M.	*Absolutely my friend!!!! I have been blessed to watch my children grow from my eyes as a child when I was 14 to my eyes as a woman now at 32.. I often hear from others that I grew up too fast having babies when I was a baby but I disagree, my children have by far been my greatest teacher in life thus far and I too have a love for all children and appreciate every spoken word. The love, the innocence, willingness to forgive and acceptance of us all for what we are rather than what others think we should be is amazing to me... I was taught by my children and many others as well that Love, Forgiveness and acceptance is a beautiful way to live your life... Thanks for the reminder Cedric.. Life is grand my friend.. :)*

March 7

LIFE TIP

Deep Breath, Exhale and Smile

"My sure-fire way to deal with stressful situations is to just take a deep breath and exhale as I smile and remind myself that this too shall pass."

- Cedric R. Crawford –

*D*o you ever notice that time appears to speed up just when you need it to slow down or people appear to be moving slower when you're in a hurry? Or the grocery store clerk in your line asks for a "*price-check*" or "*manager assistance*" when you're running late? I'm sure that I'm not the only one this happens to.

This used to bother me in the worst way but I reached a point of being able to keep my sanity amidst the fire of frustration, discomfort and inconvenience. If we take the time to stop and step out of the frame we can see a better picture of life and small, petty things in any form aren't worthy of stressing over. Refuse to give yourself over to the stress-mongers in your life, this is one war you can't afford to lose. Most people are choosing to major on the "*minor*" things in life when we really should make a point to major on the "*major*" things in this life.

The following is my unsolicited remedy if pettiness should ever attempt to rear its ugly head in your near future. Just take a deep breath, exhale and smile and remind yourself that "*this too shall pass.*" Life is still too short to sweat the small stuff. Let others around you lead such a life majoring on the minor, petty stuff, but not you.

Feel free to utilize my technique anytime you like and pay no royalties. Works for me. Make it GREAT.

March 8

STORY OF OVERCOMING

Enough was Enough

"You would be surprised at the kind of stories you would hear
if you just say "Hi" and lend an ear."

- Cedric R. Crawford -

I was talking to my delivery woman not long ago and she shared the most interesting story of her life with me. She met her husband at the tender, young age of 14. He was five years older, but the age thing didn't really seem to be that big of a deal back then. They were in love and married young and didn't waste any time at producing 8 kids over the span of 16 years. "*I always wanted to have a BIG family,*" she said with an even bigger smile on her face.

She said, "*My husband was a San Francisco police officer and he always managed to bring his job home with him. I put up with severe abuse for years because I was deathly afraid of what he would do to me and the kids. He would always tell me that he could kill me and get away with it because he knew how to cover his tracks. I believed him, so I stayed.*" She also stated that several attempts at counseling failed miserably because he thought he was *God* and could do no wrong, so the abuse continued.

She further explained how over the years he managed to squeeze every bit of her vibrant, energetic, outgoing traits out of her like a dirty dishrag. "*I felt like I was just 'doing time.' My kids became my hope and my reason for living, so I poured myself into raising them and being as active as possible with them.*" Over time she also became cut off from all her friends and her only sister. "*I developed a 'fake smile' for the general public, but if they only knew what I was going through behind closed doors.*"

This was her story, but this was only part of her story, not the whole story. After 34 years of enduring the hardships and severe abuse, one day he left the house after a heated argument. She made up her mind at that point that "*enough was enough*" and she was done. This was her opportunity to seize the moment and take some action steps toward creating a better life, so she quickly changed the locks and got a restraining order against him. She said, "*He kept trying to come back but I stood my ground.*" She was quietly willing to accept death before conceding to let him back into her life.

"*It was over,*" she said. "*I finally had the strength to make a change. Mentally I ran as far away from this man as I could... He died a few years ago, yet the mental scar he left on me and my kids still lingers today, but I'm proud to say that I'm much happier now than I've ever been. People who knew me years ago say the vibrant, energetic, outgoing girl they once knew is now back, and that makes me smile.*"

When asked if she had any advice for others, she said, *"If you're severely suffering at the hands of another as I did and he's not willing to go to counseling and honestly wants to change, you're fighting a losing battle. Your life is worth so much more… He thought he was God and eventually he had to answer to Him."*

I've come to know and understand that sometimes the hardest thing and the right thing are the same thing. Life's too short to spend it in misery and fear enduring a constant barrage of physical and mental abuse. We only get one time through this thing with no *"do-over's."* So I encourage you, whoever *"you"* are to make those difficult right choices over the easy wrong ones before it's too late.

This was her story and she took control of how it would end. The faces may change, but if the story and facts are the same, it may be time for a change. How do you want your story to end? Hmmmm… Be encouraged today and be blessed with the necessary strength to make your life GREAT!

You would be amazed at the stories you'll hear if you say *"Hi"* and lend an ear.

March 9

PERSONAL DEVELOPMENT

A Sure-Fire Investment Tip

"Knowledge gives us the power to create whatever we believe is possible for ourselves."

- Cedric R. Crawford –

After over sixteen years in the real estate investing industry, I can honestly say without reservation that the most lucrative and important amount of square footage of development I've had the privilege of working on in my entire career is not square footage at all, it's square inches. The development of the small, six inches of space between my ears. Yes my friends, we should invest more time developing and working on ourselves then working on any job, and the results will make all that we do even better.

Warren Buffet, one of the richest men in the world, has been quoted as saying the best investment a person can make in this world is in himself. I concur. Knowledge gives us the power to create whatever we believe is possible for ourselves. So let's seek to be better and we will inevitably find that we will become better. Stay in a constant state of growing and learning so that your knowledge will increase along with your power to create. An investment in ones self is definitely money well spent. So invest wisely as you attempt to make it GREAT!

March 10

MARRIAGE AND RELATIONSHIPS

MYTH BUSTED!!!

"What happens in Vegas doesn't always stay in Vegas."

- Cedric R. Crawford -

I took this picture last night with my bride. What's the special occasion you may ask? Well, today is *NOT* our 15th wedding anniversary, that's not until June, and no it's *NOT* Karen's 45th birthday, that's not until July. But today is just as special. In fact, everyday is special because I have a special bride who accepts me in spite of all my faults, fallacies, habits and hang-ups.

I'm not one that uses the word *"lucky"* often, but I have to honestly say that I definitely got lucky when our paths crossed and our worlds collided on that 28th day in the month of May. It was the year of 1994 and days before O.J. Simpson would have his infamous slow-speed chase down the notorious 405 Freeway in Los Angeles. He was running away from the law and we were running away together. I'm not sure if he did it or not, but I know I did it. I sure did do it alright. I got "LUCKY"! I got lucky and found a diamond that was not in the rough. I won't bore you with the details, but talk about right place at the right time.

A good-ole Texas boy and an old-fashioned "P.K." (*preachers kid*), California girl meeting in the entertainment capital of the world. It had all the distinct makings of a happenstance, chance meeting at a dimly-lit night club called "*The Metz*" on the Las Vegas Strip sandwiched in between the Great MGM Grand Hotel and a Fat Burger joint. She was brought to my attention by my good friend Daren Castain, I took the plunge and rolled the dice and it came up Lucky #7. I was probably the 7th guy that asked her to dance, but for some unknown reason she chose me and we've been dancing ever since.

We became the exceptions to the rule of "*What happens in Vegas stays in Vegas.*" We happened in Vegas, but we didn't stay in Vegas. I may have lost in the game of check-mate at the casino but I won big in the game of life-mate at the club. We started as good friends and grew into a great family and I find myself smiling big and often because of my Lucky take-home winnings from Vegas. Yes, today and everyday is indeed a special day because of my special gal, Karen Ice.

I invite you to reflect back on the story of your encounter with that special someone that's in your life and revisit those feelings of excitement and romance regularly. My good word today for you couples out there is to abandon not those things that brought you together in the beginning. Always remember that the perfect relationship is not without its imperfections. The best of relationships require routine maintenance check-ups to make sure they continue to function at their optimum level.

So keep your fingers on the pulse of that relationship and be sure to stay close to that mate as you both attempt to make it GREAT!

After all these years I can honestly say that I'm still feeling Lucky. LOL.

March 11

STRUGGLE

Struggle 101

"For the course of 'Struggle 101', Bs and As, number grades and GPAs don't matter, it's just Pass or Fail."

- Cedric R. Crawford -

In our noble quest to graduate to the level of accomplishing our biggest goals and dreams in this life, we must clearly understand that *"Struggle 101"* is not an elective course. It's an unavoidable prerequisite and without it, obtaining our biggest goals and dreams is nothing but a pipe-dream.

As a self-proclaimed, valedictorian, honored graduate student of the elite Ivy-League *"School of Hard Knocks,"* I declare that you must commit to stay the course on your way to graduation. You're guaranteed to never graduate high school if you drop out in kindergarten. It's also expected for you to demonstrate noticeable improvement over a reasonable amount of time. We must also understand that our education does not stop with our graduation at any level, in fact it should intensify.

Finally, be advised that Bs and As and number grades and GPAs don't matter for this one, it's just pass or fail. On our way on this journey through this institution called *"life,"* we must all commit to persist until we pass and then share our story of how we made it over. Let's all recommit to pass with flying colors as we attempt to make it GREAT! I wish you continued blessings on your journey…

Diane B.	*So true, I tell this to my children and students everyday. Thanks for the encouragement....again:))*
Karen B.	*Struggle 101 , hahhaaa.....Sometime's it's actually not that funny until you look back later though, eh?*
Scott B.	*Well said, CRC! In fact, I heard a long time ago that the worst thing we could do in bringing up our children was to produce "grad-uates." That indicates you are done learning. We must see life as a journey and a process and develop ourselves as "lifetime learners" instead. May we never feel like we have arrived, and always have a hunger to learn more.*

March 12

Avoid the "OMG" Reaction

"I wonder if the animals of this great planet of ours think we're silly because most of us choose to neglect our body in our youth and struggle to repair it in our later years?"

- Cedric R. Crawford -

I realized an interesting dichotomy recently. It appears that the large majority of us spend the best years of our lives neglecting our body and health in the relentless pursuit of what I call the "M & Ms" (*Money and Material things*) of life. Then when we get older we end up spending our accumulated "M & Ms" in an effort to take care of our neglected body and poor health. Hmmm… I wonder if the animals of this great planet of ours think we're silly because of this odd behavior.

I've found that when you take a step outside of the picture frame to take a look at the *big picture*, it becomes painfully obvious that our focus resembles the mindset of a rabid squirrel, not realizing the consequences of our actions. It's in our best interest not to wait too late to reverse this trend and start to be more proactive with our body and health instead of "OMG!" (*Oh My Goodness*) reactive.

After all, we only get one time through this "*life*" thing and only one body to do it with, so let's make a point to be proactive in taking care of them as we attempt to make it GREAT!

March 13

Battlefield of the Mind

"Develop a healthy thirst for revenge against the negative self-talk that's gotten the best of you in the not-so-distant past."

- Cedric R. Crawford -

I invite you to join me today in imagining ourselves winning those mental battles we've lost with ourselves in the past. Let's develop a healthy thirst for revenge against the negative self-talk that's gotten the best of us in the not-so-distant past.

Today we solemnly declare that our internal foe won't be given a second chance to knock us up against the ropes of life. Our foe won't have another opportunity to place doubt into our heads about our capabilities and abilities to overcome and become something greater today than we were yesterday.

We understand that the toughest battles we will ever fight are the ones on the battlefields of our own minds. We clearly realize that our "*enemy*" outside is secondary to our "*inner me*" on the inside. We also understand all too well that our inner me knows all of our weaknesses and our strengths, so it is indeed a formidable foe.

Nevertheless, in all of our battles both internal and external, we will ultimately win because we're not afraid to lose. We will *find* because we have dared to seek. And, we choose to live our lives in pursuit of something great and significant for the benefit and service of others today, because we know that tomorrow never comes. Yes my friends, we only have today, this infinite moment in time.

So, we choose today to pursue making our lives matter for much more than just ourselves and our loved ones in our general vicinity. We will pursue making it GREAT for the world! So, "PRESS ON!" I say toward the mark of the high call that has been placed on our lives by our Creator and let's continue to not just make it good but Make it absolutely GREAT!

> Please view the video on:
>
> www.YouTube.com
>
> Search Code: Cedric R. Crawford–(23)

Erika S. D.	I can always count on a quote from you to help when I really need it most!! Thank you.
Stan B.	Strong medicine, Brother, and most welcome! I appreciate, and share many of your views and especially your passion for encouraging others....Excelsior!
Dixie M.	Yes Cedric, you are a voice of blessings in a world that needs to hear you. God blesses you to speak the good news.
Jennifer A. L.	Thanks for the confirmation!!! It's so true God works through his child to help save the ones with their hands out and open.

March 14

Dream Chaser

"Continue to chase that dream like there's no tomorrow,
because one day you'll be right."

- Cedric R. Crawford –

My idea of making it to the pinnacle of success is when the life we're living everyday is better than our night or day dreams. A good sign that we've reached this point in life is when we'd rather stay awake than go to sleep and we frequently find ourselves saying, *"Pinch me, I must be dreaming."*

A few years ago I was at the peak level of success in the area of achieving my financial and material goals. My wife Karen and I had accomplished a goal of designing and building our dream home nestled next to the Kern River in the quiet hills of Bakersfield, California and our real estate investing company was making a pleasing profit. It appeared we could do no wrong. At that time my wife made a comment that I've never forgotten. She said, *"This real estate market is spoiling us."* She was 100% correct in making that statement. We no longer had to work hard for our profits, it was just coming to us based on a successful system of buying and selling that we had in place. I was truly living my *"dream life"* being able to do just about anything I wanted. Sleeping was boring to me, I just wanted to stay awake and enjoy it all.

During this same time I distinctly remember thinking that this level of prosperity couldn't and wouldn't last. Well, I was right. The market started to undergo a HUGE, unprecedented correction and although we thought we were positioned to handle it, we were grossly underprepared for what was to come. In hindsight, that action cleared the way for a new improved *dream* that allowed me to focus more on creating value for the world and leaving a legacy that will continue to inspire, motivate, empower and educate millions, if not billions of people for many, many years to come.

I'll always have a love for real estate and my other businesses, but make no mistake about it, creating content in the space of personal development, personal awareness and self-help is my love. But even more than that, it's my passion and purpose. How about you? What gets you out of bed and fired up in the morning? I invite you to chew on this food for thought today and be honest with where you are, why you're here and where you want to go. Then take the necessary steps it takes to get you there.

We must continue to chase our respective dreams and follow that passion of ours in service to others like there's no tomorrow, because one of these days we'll be right. Let's all make a point to keep making it GREAT!

Please view the video on:

www.YouTube.com

__Search Code:__ **Cedric R. Crawford – (9)**

Bonus DAY 3!!!

BELIEF

Lion or Sheep

A baby lion cub got lost one day when he wandered away from the pack.
He was a few hours old and couldn't see very well so he couldn't find his way back.

A day or two later, the cub ended up amongst a very large herd of sheep.
After traveling all that time while partially blind, he was tired and he needed some sleep.

The lion cub was too young to realize these sheep were not his original pack.
But the sheep took him in and treated him as kin and taught the young lion cub how to act

The first few years he fit in quite well except he didn't think he looked at all the same.
He grazed the ground and meandered around and played a sheepish game.

He spent his days grazing back and forth and even made a sheep sound that was great. Baaaaa!
He was even really good at running fast as he could from predators and would
always manage to escape.

Now that's AWESOME you see, for a sheep that could flee, or so the

young lion cub had been told.

Until that fateful day in the mid-month of May when the lion cub had gotten quite old.
He was wandering around and grazing the ground when he saw a pack of lions far, far away.

He started to gaze and was completely amazed as he watched them all carefree at play.
Then he started to get a little bit upset as he watched the lions all play and laugh.

"Why can't we be footloose and carefree?" Was the question he angrily asked.

"I'm tired of being afraid and running away whenever that pack starts to rumble.
Let's stop this madness and prevent future sadness, who died and made them king of the jungle?"

"Well that's just the way it is…" another sheep said. *"we graze and we sometimes fall prey.*
We never question our fate or start a debate, our Creator just meant it that way."

The lion started to pace with a growl on his face and he thought about making a change.
Then he looked at his friends and new next of kin and thought his actions
might seem a bit strange.

Hmmmm…

Well, the old Lion just accepted that statement as fact, in life, most everybody does
So he lived and he died a scared sheep with no pride, because that's what he believed he was.

So my question today for you my friends as I travel both near and far.
In terms of this lion who believed he was a sheep, just who do you believe you are?

Yes, your thoughts, passions, beliefs and actions do mean a lot, yes it does
Just as the lion who was told he was a sheep and didn't know who he really was.

by **Cedric R.Crawford**

March 15

COMMITMENT

Over My Dead Body

"For what only over your dead body are you willing to settle for?"

- Cedric R. Crawford –

"Over my dead body" is a pretty strong statement, but this type of comment infers that the person behind it is willing to face death before conceding to failure. So this begs the question. For what *"only over your dead body are you willing to settle for?"*

"Over my dead body" will I settle for a life not pursuing significance in the area of service to many. "Over my dead body" will I concede to a *"normal"* life based in mediocrity and *"averagism."* "Over my dead body" will I shoot for a life of comfort and safety because I know that nothing great can ever come from such lackluster ambition and playing small. I now understand that the more I can reach the more I can teach and our service to others should be one of our top priorities for this *"life"* thing.

I invite you to let this comment marinade with you today, then chew on this question for a while and wash it down with a beverage of your choice and get out there and make it GREAT.

"Over your dead body _____."

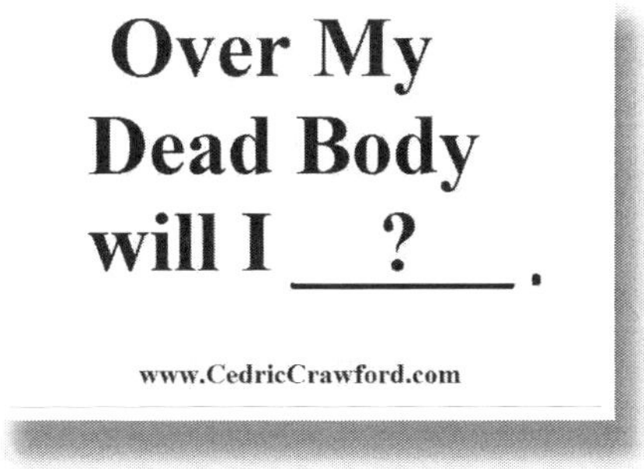

Over My Dead Body will I ? .

www.CedricCrawford.com

NOTES

Now is the time to put all doubt aside + embrace your unfolding future + boldly move forward.

PRAYER

A *"Prayer on Loan"*

"In times of concern help me to learn and discern."

- Cedric R. Crawford -

I'm feeling generous today so I figure I'll lend you my favorite prayer for a short while. I wrote it just for people like us. Please be sure to return it in good condition when you're done:

In times of concern, help me to learn and discern.

In times of dismay, help me to hear and obey.

In times of struggle and strife, help me to get it right.

In times when I feel I'm alone, renew my strength to carry on.

In times of distractions, please refocus my actions.

In times when things seem strange, let me know if I need to change.

In times when it appears others don't care, reassure me that you'll always be there.

In times I can't see my way, give me clarity again for just one more day.

For all that I need to be, thank you in advance for being patient and never giving up on me.

Remember this is a *"Prayer on Loan"* so use it and don't abuse it because I'll surely need it again soon. Let's make it GREAT!

LIFE TIP

The Friend-Making Secret

"He who wants to have a friend must first show himself as being friendly."

- Cedric R. Crawford -

The incomparable Dale Carnegie once made the statement that a person's name is the sweetest and most important sound to them in any language. After giving this statement some careful thought, I agree.

So here's an exercise I invite you to try today. The next time you meet someone, make an honest effort to actually make eye contact and remember their name and repeat it back to them several times during your conversation. This practice will work wonders with the way you're received and perceived. Don't be surprised if you actually make a new friend. Oh, and don't forget to smile as you talk about everyone's favorite subject and topic, which is "*them*."

Master these few things my friends and watch your friends list explode. He who wants to have a friend must first show himself as being friendly. Let's make this day sooooo awesome that yesterday gets insanely jealous.

March 18

DISCIPLINE

21ˢᵗ Century Leverage

"WWMPD, 'What Would My Parents Do.'"

- Cedric R. Crawford -

As a proud "*Generation Xer*" raised by old fashioned "*Baby Boomers*," my most effective form of disciplining my "Generation Y" kids was to threaten them with the action of what I call, WWMPD, "*What Would My Parents Do*." My stories alone of how and what my parents used to do to me and my three brothers when we screwed up was enough to cause a few sleepless nights for my kids.

For years I have relished the opportunity to leverage the stories of my childhood upbringing. Fraught with belts and switches, I methodically used the stories to motivate my kids to take a desired action. This technique I learned at a young age from my mom and her six sisters. We were often times forced to sit and listen to them read the stories from the book of Revelations in the Holy Bible and would be frightened into doing good and maintaining the Christian faith. Those were indeed good ole times.

Yes folks, many of us Generation Xers were raised on the threat of "Bodily Harm" and "Bible-ly Harm," and both methods were affective on me. As a kid, I honestly was more afraid of what my parents would do to me than what the Bible would do to me because I was terrified of what we Texans called, "*Butt Whoopins*." The interesting thing is that my two older brothers and I used to almost always seem to get our "*Butt Whoopins*" at the same time.

I remember one time standing in line in my parent's bedroom mentally and physically preparing to be assaulted by Dad for one of our most recent screw-ups. My two older brothers were actually arguing over who was going to go first because they both wanted to be first to get it over with. Even as an adult today I struggle to understand the logic in that argument. My logic and belief was that if I went last, my Dad would have an increased chance of being tired and remorseful and would probably take a bit more pity on me, so I waited. I also figured while I waited I would cry uncontrollably in advance with snot-bubbles and tears of terror in hopes that this action would evoke an even bigger feeling of remorse and pity, but my efforts were futile. My 5' 9" 330 pound dad had the strength of ten men and the stamina of a gazelle and remorse and pity took a back seat to a "*well-deserved butt-whoopin*."

I must admit that my vivid memory of these past events and storytelling ability have served me well in raising my Generation Yers. But even more than that, I've discovered a piece of leverage that's even more powerful than the threat of bodily harm. This newly discovered leverage appears to be even more powerful than bible-ly harm too. The threat of this one action results in immediate compliance in almost every case, the mire mention of it can make eyes pop open and command attention from Generation Y and even many Generation Xers. Well, what exactly is this new secret piece of leverage?

Hmmmm…

This new secret piece of awesome leverage is simply called "electronic devices." Whether it's a Game Boy or Game Cube or cell phone or iPhone or laptop or desktop, they all have become an extension of the bodies of Generation Yers and many Generation Xers. This has even permeated the lives of many Boomers too. The threat of loosing the privileged use of one of these devices brings immediate and swift compliance in my household.

So ditch the belt and the bible threats and take full advantage of this new form of leverage when the opportunity presents itself. I think you too will find that it's even better than a good old-fashioned "butt woopin." Let's make it GREAT.

March 19

GREATNESS

Seed of GREATNESS

"We must search for our seed of greatness and our "Why" for living as if our lives depend on it because our quality of life depends on it."

- Cedric R. Crawford -

I was visiting the mighty land of the giants in Sequoia National Forest the other day with my family. This is the type of trip that never gets old for me. While walking the *"Trail of the Giants,"* I suddenly had a *"Hallelujah moment of clarity."* Some of those great trees are a few thousand years old and almost 400 feet tall. Although the great Sequoia Redwood trees hold the illustrious title of the tallest trees in the world, the life of each one started by only one single seed. A Redwood seed is only the size of a small oatmeal flake but overtime under the right conditions of soil, sunlight and rain they're able to grow to the massive giants we see today.

Then this thought suddenly hit me. If it is true that we humans are God's greatest creations, then inside of us we should have the potential to do things in this world that would dwarf the massiveness of the world's largest trees. I believe we are all born with a seed of greatness lodged inside of us.

I heard a great speaker, Miles Monroe, once say that the wealthiest place on the planet is the graveyards and cemeteries. This is because most people die without ever realizing the full potential of their seed of greatness. Most people leave this life with all of their potential still locked inside of them only to be claimed by the grave. Only our Creator knows what could've been created or accomplished had they realized their full potential. We must not let this be our fate. We must commit to finding our purpose and *"why"* for living and develop our full potential in this life as if our lives depend on it because our quality of life actually does depend on it.

While on my trip to the Sequoias, I felt inspired to create a reminder of the seeds that created the giant trees of the Sequoia National Forest and use it to remind us of the *"Seed of Greatness"* that exists in all of us. I proudly display this *"dream novelty"* in specific places that I can see and be reminded regularly to continue to fill my day with purpose-filled actions and pursue my goals, gifts and greatness.

These crystal resin crafts all have one single authentic seed from a Sequoia Redwood Tree and are all hand made by me with love. We can all use a little friendly reminder every now and then to keep us on track and on task in this "*life*" thing. And, always remember we only get one time through so let's make our best effort to make it GREAT!

www.CedricCrawford.com/Products

March 20

CHANGE

Got Chocolate?

"If we keep buying the same box of chocolates, eventually we'll know what we're going to get."

- Cedric R. Crawford-

orrest Gump's famous words from his mom were, "*Life is like a box of chocolates, you never know what you're going to get.*" Although this may sound good, the truth is if we continue to buy the same box of chocolates, the chocolates we get inside the box then become predictable.

Such is life, if we continue to do the same things day-in and day-out, we can only expect to continue to get the same old chocolate. Maybe it's time we changed boxes so we can increase the chances of getting some different chocolate. He who has ears let him hear and take proper action if necessary to change those chocolates. ☺ Let's all make it GREAT!

Stephanie B. P.   *Ced, this reminded me of a box of chocolates a parent sent me as a "thank you" for being the one to finally get his son to be able to tie his shoes..... His kids had got in the chocolates and taken bites out of some of them to see what flavor they were..... LOL*

Corilee M.   *You never cease to amaze me my friend... I love this one... Something I have been saying for years... but to be honest, I was always the one who poked a hole in the bottom to see what it was first and if it wasn't one I liked, I put it back with the hole and all and chose something different... surprised!!!!!!!! Wishing you well my USA connection... PS... love the sign I bet Karen had a good laugh... LOL...*

March 21

PERSISTENCE

Black Gold - Texas Tea

"Stay the course because you just might be two feet away from "black gold" and "Texas tea."

- Cedric R. Crawford -

Any worthwhile goal or dream will demand a level of sacrifice. On our journey to the realizations of our goals and dreams we will have several opportunities to quit. We must adopt the philosophy and belief that adjustments are allowed, but quitting is NOT an option. Over time with persistence and consistent effort, those dreams and goals will eventually be realized.

As a child growing up in Texas I heard many stories about people who spent a lifetime digging for what we called *"black gold"* and *"Texas tea,"* which was another name for oil, only to come up dry. But, when others came behind them and started digging where they left off, they immediately struck oil. This means the original diggers were only a few feet away from striking it rich. Hmmmm… If they would've only known how close they were.

The life-parallel here is the difference between those who achieve their goals and dreams in life and the ones who fall short is the achievers hang in there long enough for success to show up.

During the tough times we must ask ourselves the tough question of, "*Do we have the ability to stay the course?*" And for those of us who have already quit, the question we should ask ourselves is, "*Did we quit too soon?*" Remember nothing good and worthwhile comes easy or without reasonable sacrifice.

Be encouraged today and stay the course because you just might be two feet away from "*black gold*" and "*Texas tea.*" Press-on and Make it GREAT!

LEGACY

Challenge

"Find your position in this life and play it like only you can, because only 'you' can."

- Cedric R. Crawford -

We should all challenge ourselves to do something socially significant on this earth before our time is up. For if we travel through this life wondering while we're wandering, when we die it will be as if we never lived. We must commit to take daily steps toward building our positive legacy and doing something significant. We must leave our distinguished mark upon this earth so that future generations will know that we were here and that we cared enough to make a positive contribution that would positively affect their generation.

After living a life of ghetto-broke to millions, then almost losing it all, I committed my life to build a legacy from sourcing and servicing a few to sourcing and servicing billions. My journey and process has led me to adopting this goal as my socially significant legacy to give, Give and GIVE again even after this physical body is no more. I believe this is indeed the true meaning of becoming immortal.

I encourage you too to find your position in this life today and play it like only you can, because only "*you*" can. Let's continue to make it GREAT!

PASSION

Got Passion?

"It's never too early or never too late to make 'it' GREAT."

- Cedric R. Crawford -

I was talking to a group of high school students today about "*Purpose and Passion.*" At this age most high school teenagers are clueless when it comes to knowing exactly what their purpose and passion might be. The shocking truth is that even most adults will live a full life and never discover their purpose or passion. I offered the high schoolers a simple way to find out the difficult answer to this question. I advised them to start by first figuring out what is it they could do seven days a week that makes them show their teeth. Also, find out what is that thing that they can do all day, everyday, without pay, while time just slips away?

Finally, another good question is, what is *"that thing"* that most people compliment them on or *"that something"* that is hard for others to do, but seems to come naturally and easy for them? Then once they've discovered this, they then need to do all they can to put themselves into the position to do *"that thing."* Do this and a positive result is GUARANTEED. So, a good question today is, "What is *that thing* for you?"

Don't be afraid to pursue your purpose and follow your passion in this life. It's never too early and never too late, so *Find it, Follow it* and *Forever Feel FREE*. Make it GREAT!

Jennifer A. C.	*I'm over the top with passion, it's all the people that keep getting in my way!*
Cedric R. Crawford	*Jen, I've discovered that our hands and elbows were created to move people out of our way... LOL :-)*
Wayne L. K.	*Passion? Oh yeah, what you're willing to suffer in order to enjoy. Hmmm...*
Omar R. II	*Cedric, you're the man!! I believe passion is the fuel that makes everything else run. Keep it up!*

March 24

STRUGGLE

The *"Struggle Phase"*

"No matter what we lose or what's taken from us, we still own our smile and our attitude."

- Cedric R. Crawford -

Meet Tommy, better known as "*Smokey*." I had the distinct privilege of meeting him while out on a photo shoot a few days ago. On any given day he would go unnoticed by "*Most People*" in our society because he appears to have lost his status. But as I've said before, I'm anything but "*Most People*."

Smokey just so happened to be hanging out behind a dumpster in the alley behind a building in the downtown commercial district at the location we were conducting our photo shoot at. I noticed him and called him over for a short chat and my photographer April Massirio snapped this photo to capture the moment.

An outcast maybe to most, but he quickly became a friend to me that day. He shared a quick story with me of how he made it to that place and his continuous struggle to get back on his feet. The main thing I noticed about Smokey during our conversation was his smile and his outgoing, energetic personality. His ability to behave in such a manner in spite of his current situation and circumstance made me realize all over again how blessed and fortunate we are for both the little things and the not-so-little things we all have in our lives. No matter what we lose or what's taken from us, we still own our smile and our attitude. The real truth is, the biggest thing we have in life is "*Life*" itself, and that's a great thing indeed.

I invite you to take a short break today and take your focus off of those things you don't have and refocus on those things that you do have. Also realize that what you focus on most will eventually start to develop in your life.

Smokey is in the "*Struggle Phase*" of his life again and how he deals with it will dictate where he ends up and who he becomes in the process. He made my day, so I returned the favor and made his day with a gift that made his smile even bigger. "*Thank You Cedric*" he said. "*No, THANK YOU SMOKEY!*" I said. We exchanged a few more parting words of thanks and encouragement and moved on with our lives.

I don't know what the future holds for Smokey, but I do know who holds our future. Our choices and decisions in these present moments will determine how that future pans out for us. So I say to you today, let's all make a point to do something on a regular basis to make someone else's day GREAT! GO GET 'EM SMOKEY!!!!!!

www.CedricCrawford.com

March 25

DREAM

What's Your "It?"

"If you don't see it in your sleep-dreams, you won't see it on your life-screen."

- Cedric R. Crawford -

I went sky diving for the first time late last night. I enjoyed a free fall for what appeared to be 10 minutes before opening my parachute. I then suddenly lost control of my direction and drifted into the tallest tree in the area. I hung there for a few terrifying seconds before being spotted by friends. I'm glad the sun was shining bright at that time. How is this possible you ask? Well, it's quite simple. I was dreaming last night that I was sky diving during the day.

Sky diving is still on my bucket list. We have to realize *"it"* starts with our dreams. If we don't see *"it"* in our sleep-dreams we may not ever see it on our life-screen.

I've discovered if we really believe *"it's"* possible for us we will harbor thoughts of *"it"* happening in our lives and these continuous thoughts and unwavering belief will eventually manifest itself in our dreams, both day and night. As a result, if we're not dreaming about it, the chances of *"it"* ever happening in our life is not too good.

I've also discovered that most big goals and dreams once accomplished are actually dejavu moments. My prayer for you today is that your dejavu moment will come sooner rather than later. So what's your *"it"* and are you dreaming about *"it"*? Hmmmm... Let's make *"it"* GREAT!

Cindy T.	*Crazy! I believed you for a minute and it scared me!!! Don't do that ha ha .*
Mary C. K.	*Hey...that's my dream too!*
Wayne T.	*Guess we might have to do this together as it is on my list too... My list is not a bucket list though... It is on my live list.... I want to be in my youth living well when I do all these things I want to do... Not when I am about to kick the bucket...too old to enjoy!*

Cedric R. Crawford *Don't mistake the bucket for "old-age" enjoyment. Checking off the bucket list daily...*

Daren C.   *Cedric, when you decide to take the leap let me know I'm in. It is on my forty-4- forty list this year!!!!*

March 26

COACHING

Need to Fire Some Old Coaches?

"You can't learn the best way to build a brick house from a man who's never laid a brick."

- Cedric R. Crawford -

It is my belief that if you can truly convince a man that he is inferior or less than others, you won't have to tell him to seek out an inferior position in life, he'll do so automatically. He will probably tend to speak only when spoken to when in the company of strangers and when he does so he will not make eye contact. There's a good chance that he will typically walk at a slower pace and will speak with questionable conviction. Furthermore, he probably won't really stand for anything but most likely fall for just about everything. He will be easily persuaded by others and very seldom have an opinion about anything that he would care to voice openly in public.

I believe that such a state of any human being is a tragedy, but take heart my friends for if the above is true, then the contrary is also true. If you can truly convince and inspire and motivate a man to believe that he's powerful and capable of great things, you won't have to tell him to seek out and pursue great things, he will do so automatically. He most likely will speak with complete confidence in the presence of others with his head up with a posture of power. Even the pace and speed in which he walks will probably be slightly quicker than the average man. He will stand on his principles and beliefs and values and not be easily jaded and persuaded by others and he's certainly not shy or apprehensive about voicing his opinion.

The difference between the two men is simply what they were convinced to believe about themselves. The reality is that this belief starts in the home at a very young age and our parents, coaches, care-takers and teachers are tasked with what's actually installed into our mental computers. Then after we leave the confines of our childhood, it becomes our sole responsibility to convince ourselves of what's possible. So I invite you to consider the following question today. To whom are you listening? Make sure you're getting your advice and direction from those who have what I call, *"fruit on the tree."* You can't learn the best way to build a brick house from a man who's never laid a brick. It may even become necessary for us to fire some of our old coaches and teachers and remove the outdated mindsets and began some de-programming and serious reprogramming. Hmmmm…

This may be a bit harsh today but it's absolutely necessary if the old software in your mental computer is outdated and is in serious need of updating. Time for an upgrade today? No need to respond, just get it done. Let's continue to make it GREAT!

March 27

Applied Knowledge is Power

"Knowledge is a worthless tool unless it's put into action."
- Cedric R. Crawford -

Throughout my career in the area of real estate investing, I've been to just about every seminar, workshop, presentation, boot camp and backyard barbecue event known to man in this business. One of the biggest things I've noticed about most of the people who participate in these events is that most of them are getting the knowledge, but never change their daily habits and behaviors. So as a result, they never experience any real success.

Knowledge is a worthless tool unless it's put into action. Simply put, knowledge in and of itself is not power, only *"applied"* knowledge is power. To know and not do is the same as not knowing, for it yields the exact same results. Nothing. What difference does it make if I know how to effectively raise money for a worthwhile cause if I never actually raise money for a worthwhile cause?

So if we want to get results and create real change we must adopt an attitude today that we will change our daily disciplines. We must commit today to do what most won't so we can have tomorrow what most don't. If we do the little things daily that most people don't, eventually we will be able to do those BIG things daily that most people won't. No one action can change our lives, it's the accumulation of applied knowledge put into consistent action over time that yields the desired results. We must continue to be aware of what we do or we don't do daily and make it a GREAT day.

March 28

FOCUS

Believe it, Achieve it

"Post your goals and dreams in a visible area so you can visit them often."

- Cedric R. Crawford –

Write your goals and dreams down. Post them in visible areas along side of pictures and things that are associated with your goals and dreams so you can visit them often. This action allows you to remind your mind regularly of what it should be focusing on because our brains were built for incredible speed and not for incredible retention without practice. This also starts the process of seeing things that are not as though they were. Then overtime with persistent effort, those things that were in your mind will become reality.

See it, believe it and with proper action you will achieve it. I've heard it said that any goal or dream not written down is simply day-dreaming. So, let's put that pen to paper and get it done. Maintain your focus for one more day and make it GREAT!

March 29

BELIEF

Limiting Beliefs

"Turn your 'limiting beliefs' into 'unlimited beliefs.'"

- Cedric R. Crawford -

Hands down, one of the most important self-discoveries I made this 21st Century to-date was realizing I have lived with a huge amount of *"limiting beliefs"* for the large majority of my life. It wasn't until I started my quest for more knowledge, self-awareness and surrounding myself with people who were also seeking to grow themselves personally did I awaken to the realization of my own limiting beliefs.

We must all realize that we all have our own set of limiting beliefs. These are the beliefs that we can't do certain things and are less than adequate to accomplish great things. The large majority of these beliefs were installed over the years by people and events in our lives. We must identify our limiting beliefs as soon as possible, then reinstall the belief that anything's possible for us.

I invite you to pull those old, forgotten, neglected dreams off the shelf and re-commit to taking positive steps toward accomplishing them in the days ahead. Let's take our *"limiting beliefs"* and turn them into *"Unlimited Beliefs."* Then, inspire others to do the same. I believe you can make it GREAT!

March 30

The Illusion in Mass Confusion

"Mass hysteria created by greed and fear can also create diffusion, illusion and confusion."

- Cedric R. Crawford -

I believe one of the most important lessons I've learned when it comes to business and investing is mass hysteria created by greed and fear also creates a diffusion of responsibility and false security amongst the masses. Yes, the old saying, *"There's safety in numbers,"* is true however there can be diffusion, illusion and confusion in numbers too. I caution you today to be careful not to fall into this infamous trap. All that glitters isn't gold, sometimes it's fools-gold. Just because a feeling and emotion is popular among a group doesn't necessarily mean the feeling and emotion is correct and the potential risks involved is any less. The promise of quick fortunes in the absence of effort has claimed many victims with stars in their eyes and excitement on their breath.

Simply put, when the masses appear to be all excited and jazzed up, your caution flag should go up. I'm sure many savvy professionals will agree this is the time to step away from the fray of it all and begin your own due diligence. And, don't be afraid to say "No" and let it go and pass on the opportunity if the facts you find aren't accurate and in-line. Yes my friends, the age-old primary emotions that stimulate, motivate and dictate human behavior is still *greed* and *fear* the last time I checked. So be cautious and don't let it manipulate you into doing something you might later regret when the dust settles.

This breadcrumb can save you a lot of money and undue heartache, stress and pain while on your journey through this *"Life"* thing. Trust me I know this breadcrumb extremely well. Proceed with caution as you attempt to make it GREAT!

March 31

Money vs. Memories

"Delay your gratification if you must, but don't delay your memory creation."

- Cedric R. Crawford -

During the seasoned citizen years of our lives, I'm told that one of the most important assets we will possess is not necessarily our retirement nest-egg or free and clear home. And it won't be that retirement bonus or new, jazzy sports-car that gets crappy gas mileage either. All these things will pale in comparison to this one asset that has been declared priceless time and time again by those who have had the good fortune of reaching their golden years. What is this priceless asset you ask? Well, it's simply your *"Memories."*

The memories of the first things you've had in your life,
Like the first time your kid's ever road a bike.

The memories of the picture show,
Or the trips to the local rodeo.

The theme park with the fun rides,
Or when the kids were seekers and they wanted you to hide.

The first time you got that meaningful hug,
Or the unforgettable time you first fell in love.

The time you had more work to do,
But you took the day off to take your kids to the zoo.

No money or material things can ever take the place
Of these memories that will hopefully never be erased.

So if money over memories ever crosses your mind,
Pause for a moment and remember my short little rhyme.

Be ambitious and make as much money as you can,
But forget NOT creating memories with that special child, woman or man.

Memories will keep us warm in those winters of life.
So, Money over Memories? Not for me. Not tonight.

My unsolicited advice today is, please don't be deceived into compromising the best years of your life by chasing the all-mighty dollar at the expense of delaying and deferring the creating of memories. Time can be a lot of things, but it can't ever be regained or recycled.

The last time I checked we still only get one time through this *"life"* thing, no do overs, so go ahead and delay your gratification if you must, but don't delay your memory creation. Let's make it GREAT!

My Viral Quotes
Feel Free to SHARE

"Success and significance in the absence of struggle and adversity does not exist."

"Be sure you and your team are not just on the same page, but also reading from the same books."

"Don't give up on that dream of yours, because someone is unknowingly counting on you to win."

"Your homework for life is to find and pursue your passion until success shows up."

April 1

A Well-Placed Compliment

"A well-placed compliment is priceless yet has absolutely no value unless we give it away."

- Cedric R. Crawford -

I invite you to consider today something that most people overlook or shy away from that really could be of great benefit to their neighbor. This one thing, when properly placed, can make a persons day or week or even their entire month. It can totally boost a person's confidence and almost always positively affect a friend, family-member or even a perfect stranger. I've also found that although you can actually *"pay it"* to someone, it's still priceless while at the same time has absolutely no value unless you give it away.

What is this thing you ask? It's a well-placed COMPLIMENT. I think it's important I emphasize the word, "well-placed" because there are a few weirdos out there that just can't seem to get it right, LOL. Try to make a point to give at least one well-placed compliment away everyday. The results of doing so may even make your day too.

Oh, and for all you pretty women and handsome men, I realize the attention you receive on a regular basis can be a bit daunting and uncomfortable at times, but please realize that every compliment doesn't mean that someone's trying to pick-up on you. Just smile, say *"thank you"* and move on as you absorb the good feeling that comes with a well-placed compliment.

A "Compliment," be sure to give one away today. This is indeed a sweet breadcrumb to making it GREAT. *"By the way, you look fabulous today."*

That smile of yours sure is contagious today.

That shirt is definitely your color.

NOTES

April 2

ACCOUNTABILITY

Your Reflection

"Don't be afraid to look in the mirror and let your own reflection hold you accountable."

- Cedric R. Crawford -

A t times I've found that one of our greatest assets can sometimes be the memory of our last challenge and how we overcame it. Having a good memory definitely comes in handy under certain circumstances and situations where we need to recall how resilient we really can be. In any noble cause, we must resolve to stay the course until success shows up because others are secretly counting on us to win.

Looking in the mirror from time to time, reminding yourself you are capable of great things can be more powerful than you could ever imagine. So, don't be afraid to look in that mirror of yours and let your own reflection hold you accountable, because no matter where you go or how far you run, *"there you are"* and you can never ever get away from *"YOU."* Trust me, I'm a professional and I've tried it on a few different occasions. ☺ Yes, your first and most important accountability partner should be the man or woman in the mirror. He/She may know all of your faults and failures, but he/she also knows all of your strengths and successes.

Life is good especially when you're living it being truthful and honest with yourself. So let's continue to lean forward as we hold ourselves accountable in this life. Make it GREAT!

Nita T.   *Cedric! I've been running from my ALTER EGO but she keeps surfacing!!! That girl wants out! laughing out loud! I love this message!* ♥ ♥ ♥

Jabo B.   *You never cease to amaze us with your 'clarity'.*

"The Silver Hair Club"

"Never underestimate the power of saying 'Hi.'"

- Cedric R. Crawford -

I met Bill, Sam and Willie in the hot tub at In-Shape Fitness Center a few days ago. I said *"Hi"* and struck up a casual conversation with them. They were all in their late 60's and early 70's in age. I've learned that when in the presence of gray hair you should be sure to ask good questions and be careful not to talk too much. It's amazing the amount of wisdom that exists in the *"silver hair club."* So I put my listening ears on and fired away with my questions.

After hearing the stories of these great men, I encouraged them to start the process of writing a book so they could sow into the lives of those that will come after them. The look on their faces after I made that statement was priceless. It was as if they all had a *"Hallelujah moment of clarity."* I further assured them that their life journey of challenges, adversity and triumphs was not just for them, but for them to share the story of their journey and how they overcame and became something different during the process. I told them their story should be written and told from a position of *"You can too."*

As we parted ways, they all stated they would go out and buy a journal and start writing. I know that our lives are filled with great intentions and not-so-great action and the chances are they may never follow through, but it did make for some great conversation. *"To be continued…"* for the books of Bill, Sam and Willie .

It never ceases to amaze me the type of people I meet in that hot tub. Conversations with perfect strangers can change a person's life if you're not careful. I now have three new friends. Never underestimate the power of saying *"Hi"* and striking up a casual conversation. What are you talking about lately. Hmmmm… Let's make it GREAT.

Bill, Sam and Willie…

Just Be Nice

"We should be nice to people who are rude, obnoxious or plain'ole idiots because we may end up being the first and only positive role model they've ever seen in person."

- Cedric R. Crawford -

ever feel like you're one unexpected bad incident away from going "*postal*" on somebody or one idiot away from embracing the infamous act of homicide? Well, when the fire of these moments breech the doorway of your life, I invite you to stop, drop and roll into the following technique. Just close your eyes, take a deep breath and let it out slowly as you remind yourself that these moments happen to all of us at one time or another. And, the moment that you believe these moments can't happen to you is the time that you are most vulnerable. It's in times like these that our ability to maintain our cool-head under fire is most important.

Self-sacrifice to keep the peace should be commonplace in our lives and one of the easiest ways to demonstrate it is by regularly biting our tongue. Sure it may be a bit uncomfortable or even hurt a bit at times, but I've found that the temporary pain can result in a HUGE gain later-on down the road.

Simply put, we should make a point to "*be nice*" to people who are rude or obnoxious or plain'ole idiots because we may end up being the first and only positive role model and example they've ever seen in person. We should refuse to give them a reason and opportunity to pour out more negativity into the world around them. So let's continue to be the exception in this world as we again attempt to subdue the day and use these breadcrumbs to make it GREAT!

April 5

MARRIAGE

Paired for life?

"Crows give great marriage advice."

- Cedric R. Crawford -

I pulled into my driveway not long ago from dropping my kids off at school and I spotted a big black crow eating French fries that had been dropped there the day before. Knowing what I know about crows, my immediate thought was, where is the mate? Seconds later the second one showed up on queue and started helping out. I learned years ago that crows are monogamous and stay paired for life. I'm sure they have arguments and disagreements but apparently they're not aware of any other options but to stay together and work through they're problems.

The most recent American statistic on divorce is one out of every two marriages and increasing fast. I've observed over the years that we tend to be willing to spend so much time and money on the wedding, but so little time and money on maintaining the marriage. Hmmmm... Who would've thought that crows could give good marriage advice? Maybe we can learn a bit from their "*never-say-die*" or "*never-say-divorce*" commitment and way of life in terms of marriage.

I challenge you to leverage your stubbornness and use it to stay in that marriage. Stick around and invest your time and money in an attempt to work it out. "*Can we do it?*" is an easy question to answer "*Yes*" to, but "*Will we do it?*" is much more difficult to answer with a "*Yes*." No need to answer out loud just make me proud and stand out from the crowd.

Marriage advice from a couple of crows. Hmmmm...

Crows like breadcrumbs and I do too, so let's all make it GREAT together.

April 6

Conversation with the General

"To dream is not to sit idly or in reverie gazing upon an unattainable, serene mirage."

- Cedric R. Crawford -

I was having my regular *"Iron-Sharpens-Iron"* lunch today with one of my favorite mentors. His favorite soothing drink is a *"Cadillac"* and he doesn't like chicken-fried steak, shakes or any of my other favorite foods. In spite of the fact that he frequently refers to my gravy as *"liquid sludge,"* we still manage to get along most of the time. As a 78-year-old retired 2-Star General from the Air Force and first African-American to fly U2 spy planes, General James T. Whitehead, or *"JT"* as most call him, is a wealth of knowledge, stories and experience.

Today's great conversation about dreams took place at Bakersfield,, California's famous Rocket Café on South Union Blvd. His view on dreams is one of the main reasons I chose to define *"dreams"* at the beginning of this book. He cautioned me to make sure all the readers know the definition, meaning and intent of the word *"dream"* as used in this book.

For our purposes to dream is not to sit idly or in reverie gazing upon an unattainable, serene mirage. Our intent for dreaming and dreamers is to envision and consider something we believe is feasible and practical and create a plan and set a goal. Then take progressive action steps in the direction of achieving the goal thereby making the dream no longer a dream, but a reality. In a nutshell, stop day-dreaming and put the dream in motion.

It's conversations like these with the General that takes things that could be vague to some and makes them so much more clear. To whom are you listening to regularly? Don't be afraid to upgrade your inner circle if needed, for it just might clear up some things for you too. Another good breadcrumb to making it GREAT!

Doug C.   *What a hero and role model. Incredible!*

SPOKEN WORD

To Ask or Not to Ask

"Be advised today that the power of our own spoken word in
the best interest of our own lives is important too."
                                        - Cedric R. Crawford –

I was walking into the store the other day and a homeless woman was hiding in plain sight out front trying her best not to attract the unwanted attention of those who would have her kicked off of the property. I'm sure you know the type, tattered, dirty clothes, worn-out shoes, disheveled hair, etc.

As I approached the front door of the store, she made eye contact with me and said, *"Hi. Could you help me out with some spare change today sir?"* I immediately straightened up myself a bit and looked her in her eyes as I walked closer to her while reaching for my money clip and said, *"Absolutely! How much do you need?"* She immediately brightened up and smiled a toothless smile and started to laugh as she said, *"Well, I've never been asked that before. I'm afraid if I ask for what I need you won't give it to me."* I returned a smile back to her and said casually, *"If you never ask, you're guaranteed to never receive exactly what you want, and what you get will just be what you get."* She smiled once more and then after a few seconds of awkward silence she said, *"You can just give me whatever amount you'd like."* I conceded and blessed her with a few bills and she immediately beamed me another one of those unique smiles and voiced her sincere appreciation. We exchanged a few more niceties and pleasantries and parted ways extending to each other a Great day.

The short conversation I had with this total stranger was a small example of how so many of us live our lives today in a form of quiet desperation afraid to speak up for what we want out of this life. It appears to me that some of us are so browbeaten and wounded by struggles and adversity of life we dare not ask for what we want for fear that we don't deserve it or are not worthy of it.

I learned years ago the answer to every question you don't ask is always "No." My favorite book states that "we *have not* because we *ask not*," and to "*ask and it will be given unto us*," and to "*knock and the door will be opened unto us."* I invite you to consider today that the power of our spoken words in the best interest of our *own* lives is important too.

This delightful homeless woman with the toothless smile politely rejected the opportunity to speak up and ask for what exactly she wanted. And, as a result, she just got what she got and she was grateful. So my question for you today is, are you asking for what you want in your life, or are you just settling for whatever you get? Are you making bold statements of proclamation daily for what you want or, are you just going through the motions of life hoping for the best? Are you calling those things that are not as though they were and expecting your positive actions to be rewarded or, are you just refusing to call at all? Hmmmm… No need to answer out loud or raise your hand, just hear and understand and make your demand. Let's ask for what we want today and then take massive action as we use our breadcrumbs to make it GREAT!

> **Please view the video on:**
> **www.YouTube.com**
> <u>Search Code:</u> **Cedric R. Crawford – (26)**

> **April 8**

FAMILY

No Place Like Home

"Home is not just were our heart is, it's also where our soul feels free."

- Cedric R. Crawford -

There's no place like home, was the famous words spoken by Judy Garland in her role as Dorothy as she clicked her heels in the 1939 classic "*The Wizard of Oz.*" In hind sight looking back over my life, I must say that although there have been several places that have come close, I agree with Dorothy in that there really is no place quite like home.

As an adult, I still view the home of my parents as "home" and have many fond and not-so-fond memories of the time I invested there becoming a man. Now as a father of four, I can only hope I'm creating the same comfortable and nurturing environment for my kids in our home. My prayer is that years from now my kids will share the same "*there's no place like home*" sentiment.

I've found that home is not just where our heart is, it's also where our soul feels free. Therefore, there's no place like the home I visit from the past and there's no place like the home I'm creating for my kids' present and future. Let's make our homes GREAT.

Elizabeth O.   *The smiles speak for themselves! Beautiful.*

April 9

CONTENT

Content but not Satisfied

*"Push to do more, be more, serve more and see more and you
will soon find that you will have more."*

- Cedric R. Crawford -

My favorite book says that we are to be content with what we have and to keep our lives free from the love of what I call the M&M's of life (*Money & Material*) things. So I invite you to join me today in continuing to be content with what we have but resolve to never be satisfied with what we've done. No matter what hill we've climbed, distance we've run or great thing we've done we can always better our best.

I've learned that satisfaction and comfort are one-way streets that both lead you to a life of mediocrity and we were all intended to be and do so much more. So I encourage you to move forward today content and grateful for what you have but not satisfied with what you've done. Push to do more, be more, serve more and see more and you will soon find that you will have more.

Yes my friends the secret is out. Dissatisfaction is not a disgrace as it relates to service. It's a sign of one who has a servant's heart the size of the planet. So go ahead and be content to never be satisfied with what you've done this side of the universe. Keep pushing, reaching, loving and teaching until your body is void of breath. Then no one can ever deny that you lived a life in hot pursuit of making it GREAT!

April 10

My Letter to Mr. Adversity

"Adversity, a well-known foe that has now become my friend."
- Cedric R. Crawford -

Dear Mr. Adversity,
I'd like to take this time to thank you for being one of the few constants in my life. I've always been able to count on you to show up when I least expect it. The lessons you've taught me over the years have been both pricey and priceless. Honestly, I used to be intimidated by your size and demeanor and disposition but once I realized your true intentions, I started to actually appreciate your purpose.

It's for this reason I write this letter to you to say that it's because of you that I stand here today a better man. It's because of you that my convictions are deeply-rooted. It's because of you that I have a healthy revenge against the mistakes and failures that beat me up and kicked my butt in the past. And, it's because of you that I've adopted *"Overcomer"* as my new middle name.

I'd also like to thank you for being one of the most reliable and dependable beings I've ever known. Even in the times when you walk out on me, I can always trust that you will eventually return even tougher and more intense. Thank you for continuing to challenge me and require me to raise the bar in order to pass your many unexpected test to become a better me.

Finally, our relationship started out rough and rocky and at times I've been guilty of calling you *"Enemy"* and *"Foe,"* but over the years I must admit that I've grown quite fond of you and now I sincerely call you *"Friend."* Thanks for being there for me I couldn't have done it without you. You complete me Mr. Adversity and I'm forever grateful.

Sincerely Yours,

Cedric "Overcomer" **Crawford**

PS.

Tell your nephew *"Negativity"* and your sister *"Set-Back"* that I said *"*WHAZZZUPPPP !!!*"*

I'm still trying to make it GREAT, So see you soon…

April 11

Reach, Grow, Serve and Inspire

"Don't be afraid to take a peek inside yourself and bring out the best in you."
- Cedric R. Crawford -

We all have God-given potential inside of us to succeed and be great at *"something."* We must be careful to avoid letting a humdrum way of life squelch this God-given gift, for our living small is contrary to all that has been placed inside of us by our Creator. We must Reach, Grow, Serve and Inspire others to do the same. In addition to working in our respective careers, let's also commit to a life spent developing our talents to the fullest of our potential. All the tools we need to do so have already been placed inside of us.

My eight-year-old son Chance is a nighttime cuddler and a spontaneous hugger among other things. He also has this amazing ability to stay focused on something if he believes it's not right. As a parent, I've made the conscious decision to affirm his God-given abilities and encourage him to use them for good in this world. He thinks I'm a bit strange, but then a lot of other people do too. It took me a number of years to get this way and it wasn't easy.

I encourage everyone today to not be afraid to take a peek inside yourself and bring out the best in you. Let's honor our Creator by putting the gifts we've been given to good use. What say you? Let's all choose to keep striving to make it GREAT!

April 12

BE YOURSELF

It's Not Your Fault...

"Refuse to let hardships, hang-ups and hard-times bully you into
changing your attitude and the essence of who you really are."
- Cedric R. Crawford -

Ok, I'm not sure who this post is for today, but I feel led to encourage someone to cheer up and realize that it's not your fault that you were born with a heart that's capable of trusting to the point of exposing yourself to emotional heartbreak and harm. It's not your fault that many have taken for granted your ability to be loving and forgiving to the point of being taken advantage of again-and-again. It's not your fault for being born with a spirit that desires to please and bring joy to others. So erase any thoughts that you're less than adequate when it comes to attracting and keeping a good mate. They were all just incapable of realizing and recognizing their *"good thing"* in you and that's not your fault.

These characteristics are rare and admirable and something to be proud of and soon the day will come when you're given your hearty approbation and affirmation of appreciation. The day will come when you'll breathe a sigh of relief as your faithfulness and trustworthiness is reciprocated. The day will come when you'll truly smile and say, *"I am enough and a worthy companion is just a plus."*

I encourage you today to hang in there and refuse to let hardships, hang-ups, heartbreaks and hard-times bully you into changing your attitude and the essence of who you really are. Your true *"You"* will indeed get you through without major compromise. So, don't give up on trusting yourself and continue to be yourself, *"B-U."*

Know and understand today that none of us are without flaws and imperfections and it's our flaws and imperfections that make us perfect for that perfectly, imperfect person. So continue to patiently *"B–U"* and it'll see you through, after all, everybody else is already taken. A vital breadcrumb to making it GREAT!

SEED OR GREATNESS

The Seed of GREATNESS

A great speaker once asked the question, *"Where's the richest place on earth?"*
So, I immediately started thinking of all the places I'd heard of since birth
Like the oil-rich fields of Kuwait or the South African diamond mines.

And Palm Beach, Florida or Beverly Hills, California had even came to mind

Or the massively wealthy Desert Sheiks of a country called Dubai.
Or a small country called Monaco where the cost of living is sky high

But no the real answer caught me off guard and was even a little bit scary.
He said the richest place on earth, my friends, is the Graveyards and Cemeteries.

The reason was quite simple and I was even a bit surprised.
The graveyard and cemeteries are full of gifts and potential that's never been realized.

That book never written. That song never sang
That dream put on the shelf with the other positive things.

That building never built. That invention or cutting-edge idea.

That unspoken word of encouragement someone desperately needed to hear.

That meaningful conversation with that person dealing with strife.
That email or timely phone call that would've saved that young boy's life.

Yes, the graveyard is full of them all, far too many for me to count.
The people who died with their seed and gift locked inside and they never figured it out.

I'll never forget that day for me. A defining moment in my life you see.
I realized my gift was not about me. But to help others discover what THEY could be.

The tallest tree in the world starts with one tiny little bitty seed.
So if we're God's greatest creation, then inside we have everything we could ever need.

Yes, we all have a seed of greatness he said and yes you have a great seed too.

But, it can only reach its FULL potential by the things that you choose to do.

So, choose today that when you die, your gift will have been used.
Don't be like most that never looked for that seed and never paid their dues.

"No, Graveyard you will get NOTHING from me!"
"When I die, this body will be void you see."

I challenge you to find your passion and gift and that's the key.
Then grow it to its greatest potential for the whole world to see.

It took quite sometime, but now it's happening for me.
Don't wait for him, or her, or he, or she.
Today let's make this decree, *"Grave! You'll get nothing from ME!!!"*

by **Cedric R. Crawford**

Please view the video on:

www.YouTube.com

Search Code: **Cedric R. Crawford – (15)**

April 13

FAITH

Act as if...

"The ultimate act of faith lies in the process of 'Acting as if...'"
- Cedric R. Crawford –

While talking to a friend this morning about coming expectations of the future, it suddenly occurred to me that it may be a good time to remind others this week that the ultimate act of faith lies in the process of *"Acting as if..."*

When parents are expecting a baby to be born, they usually can be found preparing their home and life for the eventual arrival. So too it is when we're casting our vision and goals and dreams, it's in our best interest to make the proper preparation mentally, physically and spiritually to accommodate the desired outcome. I am convinced that this is the ultimate sign of faith and belief that an event will occur.

Simply put, the rain will always most benefit the fields of those who are prepared to receive it. Another way to look at it is when trying to survive on the island, the best show of faith and belief and commitment is to burn the boat. This leaves no other options and room for doubt in succeeding. Your actions or inactions today will no doubt determine and dictate your results tomorrow.

So, my good word for you today and everyday here forward is to demonstrate the strength of your faith and belief by *"Acting as if..."* and if you commit to do this regularly, eventually you won't have to *"Act as if..."*

Let's wrap our hands around the throat of this life and choke it until it gives us what we want. Let's make it GREAT!

April 14

PSA(Public Service Announcement)

Swim, Swim, Swim!

"The ships of our goals and dreams never come in, we have to swim out to them."

- Cedric R. Crawford -

As a kid and young adult I would always hear people making the comment that they were waiting for their ship to come in. Once I reached adulthood and started my own family, I started to realize a few things that made this common statement grossly inaccurate. Over-time as I began to look around and communicate with others who had achieved levels of great success and significance in their lives I eventually realized an interesting fact.

I hate to be the bearer of bad news but don't kill the messenger. For those of you who are waiting for your ship to come in, the ships of our life's goals and dreams never come in, we have to swim out to them. We can't buy into the lie of being idle. We have to put feet to our faith and the proper behavior to our belief. The accomplishment of anything worthwhile or significant in life will take proper work and consistent effort, and this work and consistent effort over time will produce results. We must make the mental shift and believe our most sincere goals and dreams in life are in deed worthy of our best efforts.

So, let's take our kids by the hand, put on that wetsuit of wisdom and jump into the frigid waters of fear and swim, Swim, SWIM out to that ship until we WIN! I believe there's no better example for our kids and loved ones than the one we are willing to set by our actions. So, keep on swimming I say as we all continue in our tireless efforts to make it GREAT!

Gilbert G.   *That's one photo that your child will forever be inspired by......*

Dixie M.   *Cedric...This comment is priceless with much truth. It's like jump out of the boat.....or comfort zone... Thanks Cedric!*

April 15

Stay the Course

"It's OK to step out of the kitchen for a short break from the heat, but don't you dare quit.."

- Cedric R. Crawford -

Ever heard the phrase, *"If you can't stand the heat, get out of the kitchen."* This is an enduring phrase that has been repeated by many. I'd like to add just a bit to it today for those who are pursuing something Great and significant. It's OK to step out of the kitchen for a short break from the heat, but don't you dare quit. You have my permission to get back in that kitchen of life and finish what you started.

We must be willing to endure a little heat and discomfort in order for us to achieve our ultimate ambitions in this life. What better life can be lived than one following an unwavering passion, belief and purpose. A life lived driving, striving and fighting for a cause that is noble and just. It seems to me that such a life and deeds cannot go un-noticed by our Creator who designed and created us for such a life as this.

So, I emphatically say to all who are in hot pursuit of a noble and just cause today, STAY THE COURSE! Stay the course, even if your cause has become unpopular. Stay the course, even if you're tired of being tired. Stay the course, even if your own self-doubt and fears are starting to crowd out your faith and belief. Remember to never forget who you're doing this for and that you were meant, built and designed to endure. So be encouraged today and stay the course and make if GREAT!

!!! Stay the Course !!!

NOTES

April 16

LIVE LIFE

Memories and Moments

*"In life all we really have to remind us of how we lived it is the
memories we've created and captured in the many moments."*

- Cedric R. Crawford -

The family and I were invited to a BBQ and Easter-egg hunt a short while ago. We knew the Easter-egg hunt was a bit premature and technically not suppose to happen for another few days, but sometimes you have to break the rules to create the memories. After some great food and wonderful conversation, the kids were turned loose to begin their frantic search for the several hundred eggs that we hid. All the parents rushed to take their pictures with their iPhones and cameras. Amidst the kid's frantic search for eggs and the adults frantically trying to catch the memories, I had one of my *"hallelujah moments of clarity."* In life all we really have to remind us of how we lived it is the memories we've created and captured in the many moments.

So go ahead and pull out those cameras and recorders and capture your life's memories and moments because years from now our minds will need a reminder of how we lived. Don't waste the precious moments. Create those memories and let's make it GREAT!

| Dawn S. | *Living Loved in Abundance!!* |
| Dixie M. | *Love it...Cedric...everyday is a celebration...* |

April 17

KINDNESS

Creative Kindness

"Kindness can turn your terror into a treat."

- Cedric R. Crawford -

My 76-year-old neighbor, Iko, does her walk every morning without fail. She used to be greeted at my fence by my angry, barking dogs Sophie and Cody and had to endure 15 to 20 seconds of terror everyday during her morning stroll. Wisely, she started to bring treats for them with her everyday and leveraged the opportunity to show my dogs a little love and positive attention. Now at approximately 8:05 a.m. every morning, both Sophie and Cody sit quietly with their ears perked up anxiously awaiting their morning treat and positive attention. Now, with or without treats, she's greeted with sure excitement instead of sure terror. I guess you could say she turned her terror into a treat.

What a great example of how our kindness can make a friend or two. Let's challenge ourselves to use our creativity and ingenuity to come up with a clever way that we can show that loved one or co-worker in our lives that causes us terror and stress a bit of consistent kindness to win them over. This will even make our own lives a little better too, guaranteed. Let those creative juices flow as you attempt to make it GREAT!

Chris P.   So Cool! LoL. My neighbors spoil my dogs too. Treats, playing Frisbee, little kids stopping by. Kindness, its good stuff!

Joan M. D.   This is such a great example of kindness... :)

April 18

LISTENING

"Listening Therapy"

"Sometimes the single most encouraging and uplifting thing we can do in the moment for a friend is absolutely nothing at all."
- Cedric R. Crawford -

I was talking to a great friend this morning and she was looking for some encouraging words that she could offer one of her family members in their time of need.

After a brief moment of thought, I advised her we as human beings in crisis often times expect the answers to our biggest problems to come in a profound and complicated package of words or actions.

But, this life has taught me sometimes the best words or actions are actually *no* words or actions at all.

I've found sometimes our mere presence and availability alone in the moment is the single most encouraging and uplifting thing we can do. Sometimes the silence can truly speak volumes and the words we *don't* say actually may help the most. Allowing the other person to talk-it-out and work through their own feelings may ultimately deliver the desired results they were looking for. Yes, sometimes *"listening therapy"* may be the best therapy in the moment. Hmmmm…

So I invite you to consider the following today. Don't be afraid to shut up and just be there for that special someone and let your presence say what no words could ever articulate.

Just a little food for thought for you today. Let's continue to lean forward in this life as we attempt to Make it GREAT for ourselves and those around us. GREAT DAY!

Corilee M.	*You are such a Great kindred soul Cedric, truly admirable in every meaning of the word... I have also learned that often saying nothing and just being is more beneficial to those expecting something. I often think that as I grow (and I don't mean grow up either hahaha) some people fade away but I have noticed that the old and the new that linger are the ones that I have chosen to be a part of my blessings. In return I find that life just keeps getting better and better along with all of those who have continued to be in it. Much love and laughter to you and yours my friend. Stay real and keep spreading the love!!!!!*
Heather I.	*Cedric you always know the right words to say. I thank you for everything.*

April 19

LIFE LESSONS

Follow Instructions

"It's not always what you say or how you say it. It's sometimes about who you're saying it to."

- Cedric R. Crawford -

As a kid growing up in the *"hood,"* I remember walking through the heart of the west Dallas Housing Projects to grandma's house with strict instructions from Mom to avoid speaking to, or making eye contact with anyone. The west Dallas housing project area was approximately eight square miles and grandma lived in the center where all of the senior citizens lived. The entire housing project area was made up of two-story apartment units that were designed for low income families to live and have their rents subsidized by the federal government.

The vast majority of these apartments were occupied by single moms with several kids living on the welfare system. Most of the parents in this area didn't spend much time supervising their kids either. Needless to say, without the proper supervision, the housing project area was infested with unsavory characters that in a lot of cases were looking for trouble to satisfy their twisted definition of fun.

I remember having this feeling of fear hovering over me while walking through the housing project, so me and my two older brothers were walking at a fast pace. We eventually got to a clearing area where there were two large basketball courts. There was a lot of activity in that particular area and I remember us approaching the basketball courts to watch. As we stood there I began looking around and thinking that this wasn't as bad as I thought it would be. I then made eye contact with a menacing looking guy that was looking like he was having a pretty bad day. He then said, "What?" as he gestured simultaneously with an up-nod of his head. I then beamed one of my signature smiles at him and responded back with the same question but with a friendlier tone, "What?" Suddenly, he started to approach me saying, "What? What you looking at homeboy? You want some?" as he clinched his fist. I quickly said, "No, I didn't do anything." He then angrily said, "You looking at me like you got a problem." I again said, "No. I don't have a problem." Just then I got the saving-signal from my big brother Bennie saying it's time to go. "Woooosh, that was close," I said to myself.

As we walked away, the guy began following us with a few of his friends. At this time all I was thinking of was to keep walking and not to speak to, or make eye contact with anyone else just like Mom said. After what seemed like a few minutes, which was actually a few seconds, the guys stopped following us and went back to the courts.

In hindsight, I learned two valuable lessons that day. The first lesson is the importance of following the instructions of someone who knows what they're talking about, especially Moms. If you don't, you're opening yourself up to the possibility of something bad happening to you. The second lesson I learned was to be careful about what you say because what you mean may not be received in the same way. It's not always what you say or how you say it, it's sometime about to whom you're saying it.

So, listen to your Mom and watch what you say to others as you attempt to make it a GREAT life!

April 20

ACTIONS

Do Something

"You can't complain if you can make a change."

- Cedric R. Crawford -

I was in my truck stopped at a red light not long ago when I suddenly noticed this man with no legs in a wheelchair sweeping the parking lot of a corner convenience store. I thought to myself, "Now this is definitely something you don't see every day." I quickly grabbed my camera to capture the event on film.

I can only speculate about what type of hardships he has had to deal with in his life and I typically would expect to see someone like him on a corner somewhere holding a sign looking for assistance, but not this gentleman. He evidently decided that he may not be able to do much, but he could "do something."

I know that everyone with a severe disability or handicap is not in dire straits and I don't know his story, but just watching him "do something" fired me up. He's decided to be an active participant in his on life. He's made a conscious decision not to leverage his disability for a sympathetic gesture or handout. He's decided to not just sit and complain about what he can't do and focus on what he can do. He decided to not make excuses but to make a contribution and simply "Do Something" productive in the direction of his own best interest.

So, I guess a good question for you today is, "*What's Your Excuse?*" Are you complaining about something that you can actually take a part in changing today? There's a lot to be learned from something as simple as this photo. I like to say it this way, "*You can't Complain if you can make a Change.*"

I encourage you today to make a point to "*Do Something*" everyday in the direction of bettering your situation and circumstance because I've heard that "*Nothing from Nothing leaves Nothing.*" So, "*Do Something*" and make that "*something*" GREAT! GREAT DAY!!!

THANK YOU

Write that book!

"Out of all the books you'll ever read for inspiration in life, the one that may end up inspiring you the most is the one you write."

- Cedric R. Crawford -

Three years ago today (2009) I reluctantly decided to take the plunge and open a Facebook account. I must admit that all of the limited information I had about social media at that time was primarily negative. In spite of this fact, I figured I could leverage the Facebook medium to create a platform to deliver hope, motivation, encouragement, education and inspiration to a world that has been poorly underserved in these areas. The pleasant surprise for me over the last three years was the transformation that I personally have gone through. I didn't expect that my own writings would be so cathartic, therapeutic and uplifting for me too.

You see, contrary to popular opinion, I too have had to deal with adversity and struggle regularly like the rest of the world. During this process I've now acquired the belief that out of all the books we'll ever read for inspiration in our life, the one that may end up inspiring us the most is the one *we* write. So if you haven't started your book yet, it's not too late to make it happen. Somebody needs to hear your story including you. Grab that pen and paper and start writing out your life as you attempt to share your own breadcrumbs to making it GREAT!

| Sherrea J. | *Without your love, thoughtfulness, wisdom, knowledge and under-standing sharing what God has placed in you causes a great blessing in me and I'm sure the lives of others. Just want to say thank you. BLESSINGS...* |

April 22

MARRIAGE

That Special One

"May you find that "special" someone that frequently makes you show your teeth."

- Cedric R. Crawford -

While sitting in my home office last night I suddenly heard the familiar sound of spontaneous laughter coming from my wife, Karen, as she was lying in bed with all the kids watching a movie. There aren't many other sounds that actually can bring a spontaneous smile to my face. I absolutely love to hear her laugh and play with our kids. It doesn't matter what's going on around me, her genuine display of joy brightens my day.

My prayer is that those who are searching will find that "*special*" someone that frequently makes them show their teeth and makes this life a little bit more worth living and Mondays more meaningful. Yes friends, that special someone can actually help you to make it GREAT!

Paul L. V.	*Cedric this is beautiful and I know exactly what you're saying. Love is powerful to infinity.*
Deanna L.	*Cedric you two are a beautiful couple.. Oh I can't wait to meet that right person ..who I can share the same mindset with and travel with. Watch out amazing race here we come.. lol... I know he's out there .*
Deanna H. E.	*Yes my friend is pretty special and can always put a smile on your face and warm your heart, I am blessed to have her as my special friend!! :-)*

April 23

Your Destiny = Your Choice

"Let's lift our family and friends up while we're climbing to our own new heights."

- Cedric R. Crawford -

I learned years ago that our destiny is not by chance, it's by our choices. When we make the decision to change the way we think for the better, we have to attempt to get our friends to change too. Then, if we can't change our friends, we have to then be willing to *"change"* our friends. Our new way of thinking has to be protected and the best way to do this is to create relationships with others who understand and affirm it. Failure to do this will eventually result in us slowly sliding back into the pattern of thinking as we once did.

Now let me be clear, I'm not suggesting that we leave our family and friends but we have to safeguard the time that we choose to spend with them. Some have referred to this time allotment as an 80/20 rule. We must make a conscious, intentional decision to invest 80% of our time with those who are encouraging, inspiring, motivating and uplifting and the remaining 20% of our time with those who we have what I call a *"default"* relationship with. *"Default,"* meaning that they may not display all of the affirming qualities described above, but they're family or long-time close friends.

Our destiny has, and always will be our choice. Let's lift our family and friends up while we're climbing to our own new heights if they want to embrace the journey with us as we attempt to make it GREAT!

Corilee M.   *I must say that this is a favorite.... I am a firm believer in choice my friend... and although I don't think we can change anyone, I do believe we have the choice to change who we want to be, where we want to be, and who we want to surround ourselves with... I have had to disassociate myself from many over the years because I wanted more for myself and my children. When people put you down enough you start to believe it (again another choice). Much love to you and yours.. Keep'em coming big guy... Enjoy the journey every moment!!!!!!!*

April 24

EASTER HOLIDAY

He Has Risen!

"Are those Christ-followers just a bunch of weirdo's? Check for yourself."

- Cedric R. Crawford -

"He has Risen!" seems to be the catch-phrase of the day and the overwhelming response has been, "He has Risen Indeed!!!" Those Christ followers sure are weird with their belief that on this day in history over 2000 years ago the ultimate, impossible act became reality. That's just plain Weirrrrd..... Can their basis for this weird belief be substantiated?

Well, an extremely intelligent Atheist spent two years researching, probing and asking the tough questions to expose the truth about the strange and unusual happenings so many years ago. His findings on his journey led him to becoming a weirdo too. Lee Strobel is his name and "The Case for Christ" is his bestselling book. The facts have led Lee to becoming one of the biggest converted members and advocates for the Christian Club of faith. Can it be true? Well, those Christian weirdo's all seem to believe it is. What say you? Do you believe or is it just a case of mass hysteria? Hmmmm... Chew on this one for a while as you continue in your efforts to make it GREAT!

Oh, I'm one of those weirdo club members too. Happy Easter from the Crawford's. Let's continue spreading the good news as we attempt to make it GREAT!!!

Renee T.	*I read that book it was great !!, so I guess I'm one of those weirdo's also ...LOL...*
Harold F.	*You are in GREAT company! Thought I share something I came across-"For those who believe, no proof is necessary. For those who don't believe, no proof is possible." - unk.*
Chris P.	*Good Stuff! Christ is risen indeed... Honestly, I believe it takes more faith to believe in nothing than to believe in God. I've known very intelligent people who will do mental contortions to believe that there is no God. The cool thing about Jesus is we get free will. So if anyone doesn't believe what I believe, I respect that, because my God gave them that right. But in my experience, I have learned that I can count on my God..... Blessed Be The Name of The Lord. Christ is risen indeed!*

April 25

Don't Waste Time with Time Wasters

"Some people are going nowhere fast and want us to go with them. Don't go!"

- Cedric R. Crawford -

One of the worst things we can do on our life's journey is to hang around people who are lazy and going nowhere fast and want us to go with them on their journey to nowhere. If this applies to you, I invite you to consider the following instructions. DON'T GO!!! Refuse to go sliding down that slippery slope to nowhere.

I believe time can be utilized in only three different ways. It can be *"Spent," "Wasted,"* or *"Invested."* I've found that some people are so caught up in the drudgery of a mundane, humdrum life that the words of a truly positive message no longer inspires them. It appears that they have become content with *"wasting"* time and *"spending"* countless hours watching others live-out their dreams on the drama-filled TV or playing meaningless video games and other mind-numbing activities. These activities are fine in moderation, but overuse appears to be the case with most.

We must not let this be our fate in life and make a conscious decision to limit our time with those *"time-wasters"* and people who have no positive drive and have become immune to the positive messages spoken around them. Simply put, don't *"waste"* time with time wasters that are more content with *wasting* and *spending* their time primarily on things that just entertain them. I invite you to choose to primarily *"invest"* your time in things that feed and nourish you and are designed to ultimately make you better today than you were yesterday in every way.

Finally, we must resist the tendency to adopt the *"I've heard that before"* mentality and continue to make an intentional effort to be inspired and never grow weary of those who speak and deliver a positive message. Let's continue to lean forward as we attempt to Make it GREAT!

Laura K. *Love that message Cedric. When people come to 'this' realization and remove themselves from 'negative' people and situations, and ask that 'only kind, caring, loving and genuine people come into their existence'...all of a sudden, life will become very 'POSITIVE' for them!*

Cam R.   *This is the year to have more people who 'add value' to our lives rather than taking away from it! Its not that you aren't there for people who 'need' more but you make sure the balance is right in your life! :0)*

Tiare F.   *This one can sure cause a person to have an 'aha' moment!!! Thanks Cedric!!!*

April 26

WRITE

Why do I write?

"Our biggest fear should be of one day dying after having lived a life that was average and mediocre and didn't matter much for the world."

- Cedric R. Crawford -

I'm often asked the question *"why do you write?"* Well, here's the short answer. It's because I'm afraid. One of my biggest fears is of one day dying after having lived a life that was average and mediocre and didn't really matter much for the world. For *"most people"* this thought may never cross their mind but it appears for me this thought crosses my mind on a regular basis. So, I write to breathe inspiration, motivation and life into others. I speak to uplift and encourage others to take action with their passions and push through struggle and adversity. I aspire to write books, CDs, DVDs and more with content that will continue to get countless others to think twice and make good choices long after I'm gone.

I've realized the only way to become immortal is to leave bits and pieces of ones self in others in the form of the written and spoken word so that the best parts of us can live-on in others. I also want nothing more than to create a platform for others to tell their respective stories and create positive content that will continue to inspire others.

Let's take our collective passions to inspire and create an inspirational movement and change the world one person at a time. Dare to join me today and let's take this *"good"* world and make it a GREAT world!

Lisa M. F. *WOW!! Thank you for showing your vulnerability Ced. You are so honest to express, that, even YOU have fears!! Fears of not living up to your potential. That is a GREAT FEAR to have!!! Xo*

April 27

HELP

To Help or NOT to Help

"A sad and unfortunate reality is that we can't help those who do not want to participate in their own extraction and rescue."

- Cedric R. Crawford -

For those of us who are on a journey toward something bigger than ourselves, we must beware of the competing affections of things or people that are not worthy of our time or best efforts. The sad and unfortunate reality is that we can't help those who do not want to participate in their own extraction and rescue. We can't help those who don't want to be helped or doesn't know they need help. The person who's walking in darkness yet does not realize it will never seek out the light, just as a person who does not know they're wrong will never seek to be right.

Nevertheless, we're charged with continuing to love them but be sure to maintain control and safe-guard the time you invest with them or giving them too much of your time may cause you to stumble and struggle. It may even be necessary to love them from a safe distance for a while. Simply put, we must first get our selves together and focus more on the major things that can help us become better and less on the minor things and toxic/negative people who are designed to distract us and bring us off the course that has been chosen for our life. Some people just aren't ready or willing to change or do something different in their own best interest. Yes, this is a harsh reality but truth is not always rosy.

Let's maintain our focus while creating a better life and lift up the *"willing"* while ascending to higher heights. Let's make it GREAT!

April 28

TEXTING

The "Technology Conundrum"

"Don't let technology deprive your loved ones from seeing your lovely face and hearing your pretty voice."

- Cedric R. Crawford -

I was hanging out with some buddies yesterday doing the *"lunch"* thing at one of my favorite spots called RJ's in Bakersfield, CA. I had an awesome time talking about future goals and ideas and ways to create value and help others on this journey called *"life."* While driving home after our lunch my body began to digest the patty-melt and fries and my mind began to digest the conversation we had and I stumbled upon another one of my *"Hallelujah moments of clarity"* that prompted the following PSA–FYI *(Public Service Announcement – For Your Information)*:

I thoroughly enjoyed our conversation and realize that the experience couldn't have happened in cyberspace. This affirms the point that we must beware of what I call the *"technology conundrum"* as it relates to our communication and social skills today. What is this you may ask? Well, it's the action of accepting words on a page and a text or electronic message as a default that's used to communicate to friends and family. Technology is meant to help us do things better and more effectively and efficiently, but I believe that overuse and abuse of it can hurt us in the long run. I'm even finding that attempting to actually call someone on their cell phone now a days rather than text or message them is becoming almost offensive to some people. Hmmmm… I think we can all agree that technology overall is a *"good"* thing, but even too much of a *"good"* thing can yield *"not-so-good"* results.

May I be so bold as to offer a bit of unsolicited advice to you today? While this *"technology"* thing may be convenient and more efficient at times, let's be careful not to make the huge mistake of depriving our loved ones of what they like most about us, which is our pretty face and lovely voice. We must make a point to go see that relative or take that friend to lunch or call that brother or sister that you haven't made time to speak to lately.

Engaging in the actual *"physical"* act of socializing and communicating and being in community with others is an absolute must to preserve all those precious characteristics and traits that make us who we are as human beings in this world. Let's be careful not to let technology damage and retard the social skills of our generation and the generations to come.

Simply put, you can't eat a patty-melt and fries over the internet, at least not yet. ☺ So, get off the *internet* more often and get on over to your *"inner-network"* of family and friends and be more intentional about staying physically connected. This is just another PSA-FYI for you today reminding you to make it GREAT!

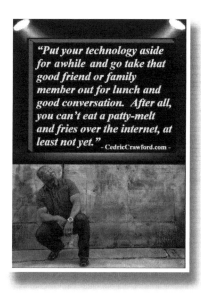

"Put your technology aside for awhile and go take that good friend or family member out for lunch and good conversation. After all, you can't eat a patty-melt and fries over the internet, at least not yet." - CedricCrawford.com -

Laurel D. H.   *Please allow me to use my technology to say how much I LOVE your message today!*

David B.   *I was thinking the same thing, I have to admit, texting has damp-*
ened my spelling. On occasion while writing a report I catch myself
wanting to shorten or abbreviate vs. spelling the word, Webster
style (dictionary)..lol

April 29

COMMUNICATION

The #1 Most Over-Looked Skill

"Communication is the doorway through which all must
pass to achieve their loftiest goals and dreams this side of the
universe."

- Cedric R. Crawford -

It never ceases to amaze me how little attention most people pay to the #1 most important skill this side of the galaxy. This one skill is a *"must have"* to excel in any endeavor in life that has to do with people. What is this skill you ask? Communication.

Just a couple of years ago my wife and I had successfully entered into a contract to sell one of our most expensive, high-priced properties ever. The time came to close escrow and to our surprise we received a report that there was an issue with the two-year-old septic tank. I quickly requested two different bids to replace and repair the septic tank. Since this new finding happened two days before the scheduled close of escrow, the buyer felt uncomfortable with closing escrow without the necessary work being completed. As a result, the buyer agreed we could close escrow and insisted we the sellers would have to keep all the funds from the sale in escrow until the septic tank issue was resolved. This amount was a significant amount to us and we had subcontractors waiting for payment from the sale.

I personally spoke with the buyer to explain to him the extent of his request and offered to leave ten times the amount that it would cost to replace the entire septic tank in escrow until the issue was fully resolved to his satisfaction. To my dismay, he insisted and dug his heels in on his original request. I then distinctly remember taking a deep breath and resisting the urge to lash out at him for not understanding how unreasonable his request was.

All of a sudden, I got an idea. I decided to use an analogy from a business industry that he was very familiar with to help him to see the depth of his unreasonable request. As a result, he voiced his understanding and agreed to my terms. This was definitely a use of the communication skill at its best in my life. A far cry from the old Cedric if I might add.

Without a doubt, communication is not only the key to massive success, but it's the doorway through which all must pass to achieve their loftiest goals and dreams this side of the universe. The ability to effectively communicate with others, and to speak their language is a skill that transcends all space and time. Master this skill and watch your wildest dreams come true. Let's continue to communicate our way to making it GREAT!

April 30

FIGHT

FIGHT ON !!!

"If we never rise above the fog of life, we will never be able to see what's possible for us just above the clouds."

- Cedric R. Crawford -

Throughout life I've discovered that *"finding"* is reserved only for those who dare to seek. I've also learned that opening doors are only possible for those who are bold enough to knock. And, seeing what's really important in this life has absolutely nothing to do with our physical eyes.

If we don't seek we will never find. If we don't knock the door will never be opened unto us and if we never rise above the fog of this life, we will never be able to see what's possible for us just above the clouds.

Life can be very stubborn at times and we have to be willing to whip it into submission until it gives us what we want. Contrary to popular opinion, there's no room for meek and mild passivity in this fight. We have to be willing to take off our gloves and start swinging bare knuckles and physically engage in the confrontation of life's problems, adversity and challenges to get the desired results we want.

So, put on your *"fighting-face"* today and start swinging jabs, uppercuts and right-hooks and don't stop until you WIN! Congratulations in advance for your inevitable victory.

After the fight, *"Life"* had these words to say, *"No matter how hard I hit him, he just wouldn't stay down."* FIGHT ON and Make it GREAT!

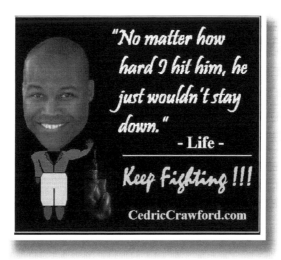

Sarah M.   *Just what the Doctor ordered! THANKS!*

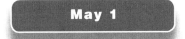

May 1

Doing Bad by Yourself?

"Going through bad times with someone you love sure beats
going at it alone any day of the week and twice on Sunday's."
- Cedric R. Crawford -

Ever heard the phrase, "*I can do Bad all by myself?*" Well, that's definitely true, but I think going through bad times with someone you love sure beats going at it alone any day of the week and twice on Sunday's.

I believe that the average person would be two kinds of crazy and three kinds of foolish to ignore the possibilities of forming a positive, strategic alliance of support with that special someone in their life and busting up these so-called "*Bad times.*" After all, they say there's safety in numbers. OH, and don't be surprised if this alliance process actually brings you closer together with that special someone. Stranger things have happened so I've heard and experienced first hand.

Be sure to keep in mind that at the end of the day, trials and challenging times can either bring you closer together or drive you further apart. The unfortunate reality is most people allow it to drive them further apart. So, the million dollar question today is, "*Which direction will you choose to go?*" Make me proud by doing the opposite of the crowd as you continue to make it GREAT!

NOTES

To Bree,

May this book make you
a little bit T.A.L.L.E.R.
as you read it's pages in
the days ahead.

Think
Act
Laugh
Learn
Excel
Reflect

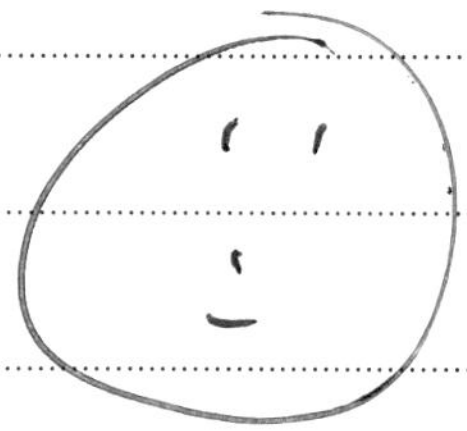

Keep Making it GREAT!!!

May 2

Weeds and Roaches

"For those of you who are pursuing something great, may you
have the resilience of a pesky garden weed and the persistence
of a dirty little cockroach until you WIN!"

- Cedric R. Crawford -

I distinctly remember as a child there were two things we always had a never-ending problem with. No matter how hard we tried to rid ourselves of these two things, they still managed to keep coming back again and again and again. Now as an adult, I'm convinced that man will always have to contend with these same two things until the end of time.

What are these two things you ask? Weeds and Roaches. No matter how hard you fight and wage war against these two unwanted elements of nature, they refuse to give up. They just keep coming back again and again.

A few years ago I learned the reason why most people have a *"Pest Control"* and *"Weed Control"* service. It's because we can never completely eliminate either one of these things forever. Unfortunately, we can only try to control them.

So, this is my prayer today for those of you who are on a journey to do something great or significant in this *"life"* thing in service to others in this world, may you have the resilience of a pesky garden weed and the persistence of a dirty little cockroach until you WIN! Remember it's never too late to start making it GREAT!

Judy M.   *Change your 9 environments!*

CHANGE

Human vs. Elephant

"The desired gain may require temporary pain."

- Cedric R. Crawford -

Did you know Circus Elephants are trained as babies by setting a *"Limiting Belief"* in their mind that change is painful. The trainer ties a tourniquet to the elephant's leg and the harder it pulls away from its position, the tighter the tourniquet gets. This action securely lodges a limiting belief in the elephants mind that trying to escape his chains can cause severe pain. So, ultimately the elephant gives up all hope of breaking free from his captors. The only way to break this belief is if you induce a state of panic in the elephant by threat of death. Unfortunately, the elephant was not given the ability to reason on a level that would allow it to endure the short period of pain in order to free itself from the bonds of its chains.

The great thing about being human is our Creator may not have given us the size and strength of an elephant or the speed of a cheetah, but he did give us a large brain and the ability to process complex thoughts and reason with it. Thank God we understand that we have to be willing to endure temporary pain to achieve our desired gain and aim. There's no need for us to wait for imminent danger or a death threat if change is necessary for us. Just make the decision to start the process today and strive to make it GREAT!

May 4

AVERAGE

Are you thirsty?

"We must have an unquenchable thirst for knowledge and an unsatisfiable hunger to learn more and do more."

- Cedric R. Crawford -

Years ago I discovered a little known secret to obtaining greatness in any area of life. Simply put, it's having an unquenchable thirst for knowledge and an unsatisfiable hunger to learn more and do more. We must resolve that it's no longer OK to settle for being just *"average"* and OK, for there is a seed of greatness inside of all of us and it's itching to get out to unveil and reveal its value to the marketplace and world. The unfortunate reality is that the large majority of people take this seed of greatness to the grave with them, never to have been searched for or discovered.

The great speaker, Miles Monroe, said it best when he stated the richest place on earth is the graveyard and the cemetery. For they are full of those people who died with their dormant seeds still lodged inside. What a tragedy I say.

I vow and proclaim today that this will not be my fate. When I die this body will have been used and void of any further potential. This is one goal I will emphatically obtain or die trying. Care to join me? No need to raise your hand, just hear and understand and make your plans. Let's go pay the price and make it GREAT!

May 5

ACTIONS

Don't Need a Co-signer

"There is no need to wait for someone else to co-sign on your decision and your dreams."

- Cedric R. Crawford -

For those of you who are contemplating taking a positive step in a new direction, realize there is no need to wait for someone else to co-sign on your goals and dreams and decisions. So, don't be afraid to assume full ownership and responsibility for your life actions and outcomes and get started today.

The most important thing is not how you start or where you start. The most important thing is that you just get started. Sometimes it's necessary to just set the date and start the journey alone. Others will eventually join you when your level of commitment exceeds their level of expectation.

Remember the greatest among us all had to blaze the trail and at times walk in seclusion. So what are you willing to go over the hill and through the woods for? Are you willing to be tarred and feathered for your faith? Are you willing to take an arrow in the abdomen or a bullet in the back for your belief? Hmmm… No need to answer out loud, just make me proud and stand out from the crowd with a smile. Make it GREAT!

May 6

PERSEVERANCE

Watch for the Signs

"Evil will not stand by and let the good go unchallenged, guaranteed."

- Cedric R. Crawford -

I've found that one of the single most accurate signs that we're on the right track and on our way to doing something that's significant and making a difference in this world, is when we feel like we're being attacked by challenges, obstacles and distractions. If this is true, then the opposite is also a good sign that we may not be on the right track.

If we're not encountering turbulence on our flight of life's journey, then we may want to re-check our destination point because evil will never just stand by quietly and let the good go unchallenged in this world, guaranteed. So, for those of you who are having some problems and struggles, I say to you today, "*Keep up the good work because you're on the right track and it won't be long now.*" Embrace the struggle as your affirmative sign and Make it GREAT!

Mike B. R.	*Good one Cedric! One of my favorite quotes we share with our kids is, "For every good thing you want to do there will be an obstacle."*
LuTrina S. W.	*I'm on the right track now! Before I was just riding! Now I'm in TOTAL control! I'm driving yall! And it's Magnificent!*
Jabo B.	*It's NOT about surviving the storm as much as it is DANCING in the rain!*

May 7

LIFE LESSONS

I Miss My Mom…

"You never know what's going on in the life of the person sitting behind you, so be nice to everyone."

- Cedric R. Crawford -

I had the awesome opportunity to hang out with my favorite 10-year-old Chance Crawford and his best friend Kielyr not long ago (*pictured below*). We took a field trip to the Planetarium to learn about telescopes and planets and space and stuff. While on the trip a little guy behind us kept peeking over our seat attempting to include himself in our conversations and activities during the exciting bus ride. I'll just call him Little John to keep him anonymous. Blonde hair, blue eyed, freckled face and just as skinny as a rail, he would laugh the cutest laugh at my "*G-rated*" jokes. A bright smile with bright colored clothing to match he was a delightful unexpected addition to our trio. Caught up in the fun and action of it all, I was suddenly blindsided when Little John leaned forward on the back of my seat with his arms folded and head down and spontaneously made the following comment to me, *"I miss my mom."*

Caught off guard, I quickly asked, *"Is she at work?"* He said, *"No."* I then asked, *"Is she at home?"* He said, *"No."* Finally I asked, *"Well, where is she?"* He then said, *"I don't know, my dad won't let me talk to her."* I asked, *"When did you last talk to her?"* He said, *"Four years ago."* Whoa...

I wish you could have been there to experience that moment of reality check for me. I was so dumbfounded and stunned you could've knocked me over with a feather. To think that I was having so much fun with the kids as I was sharing my stories of what it was like when I was riding the bus to school as a kid their age 30+ years ago. I must admit I wasn't prepared to hear that statement coming from the seat behind me.

But the story doesn't end there. That was just the beginning of our day. In usual fashion, I saw this as a unique opportunity to make sure he felt a little bit more special and accepted in our group. So yes, our trio of me, Chance and Kielyr became four with Little John and the fun began.

No, we couldn't change the reality of the absence of his mom from his life, but we could change the outcome of his life experience in those few moments and I'm happy to say we did not disappoint. I made a mental note to myself that from that day forward whenever I see him I will make a special effort to make him feel just a little bit more special.

This little life lesson has taught me you never know what's going on in the life of the person sitting behind you, so it's imperative for us to assume the worst and just be nice to everyone as we hope for the best. Especially nice to those who we know are in need of something special.

The unfortunate reality is there are a countless number of Little Johns out there in someway, somewhere. Don't miss your opportunity to take the time to brighten someone else's day as you attempt to make this good life a GREAT life!

Cam R.	*Wow Cedric.... totally profound and a wake up call... a sad wake up call.... ☺)*
Cameron Y.	*Good for you. things like that will change the world. one person at a time.*
Steph P.	*That is so true, there is always someone worse off than ourselves. Thanks for the reminder. Heartbreaking.*
Ann I. W.	*So many of our little ones are carrying heavy burdens that they have no control over. You were such a wonderful blessing for that child.*

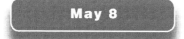
May 8

FAILURE

The "Shock-collar" of Past Failures

*"Has your fear of failure, discomfort and pain conditioned you
to play small and focus on helping and inspiring only those
who share your last name?"*

- Cedric R. Crawford -

I dropped by my buddy Brent's house the other day unannounced and I was greeted at the front gate of his yard by two of his barking dogs. One was a huge Labrador and the other was a small size mystery mutt. Brent's wife Kim, opened the front door and yelled, *"Go ahead and open the gate and walk up to the house, but make sure you stay on the cement walk way!"* The thought of following her instructions made me a bit uneasy, so I yelled back, *"Are you sure this is okay?"* And she said, "Yeah! You'll be alright, just stay on the cement!" I hesitated a bit more, but eventually I slowly got the courage to open the gate.

As I was walking on the cement walk way, the dogs kept barking and looking at me with a menacing look but it was if there was some sort of invisible barrier that was holding them back. I must admit I was a bit bewildered and perplexed by what I was seeing but I kept moving forward.

I eventually reached the front door and safely entered the house without a scratch. Naturally I was curious to understand what had just happened, so I asked Kim. She said the dogs used to wear a shock-collar and it would shock them anytime they reached a certain point. I suddenly realized that even now that they don't have shock-collars on, they've made a mental note that crossing the imaginary line means discomfort. WOW!!!

Needless to say, this got me to thinking of the direct parallel that exists with us humans. We often times allow our past failures, loss and pain to stop us from pursuing things that are worthy of our best efforts. Just as the dog is conditioned by shock-collars we can be conditioned by our past failures. I truly believe that one of the biggest sacrifices a person can make in this life is to settle into a life of average, mediocrity and comfort to avoid the risk of failure, loss or pain. We were designed and created for sooooo much more.

So a good question for today is, Are your spoken words and actions worthy of plagiarism? Are your current goals and dreams suitable to be envied? Are your true intentions in all that you do deserving and befitting a noble and just man or woman of honor? Or, has your fear of failure, discomfort and pain conditioned you to play small and focus on helping and inspiring only those who share your last name? Hmmmm...

These questions can serve as a litmus test for a life that's destined to do something special. If the masses aren't being inspired by your actions, then dare I say you're leaving sooooo much more on the table of life than you were designed and created to do and be. Chew on this thought for a bit and decide what the next action-step is for you if needed. Don't let the *"Shock-collar"* of failure and pain bully you into the corner of comfort and complacency. Not today.

Don't plot to kill the messenger on this one today. I'm just looking to inspire others to take these breadcrumbs and make it GREAT!

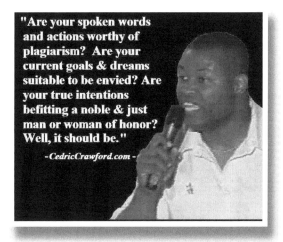

"Are your spoken words and actions worthy of plagiarism? Are your current goals & dreams suitable to be envied? Are your true intentions befitting a noble & just man or woman of honor? Well, it should be."

-CedricCrawford.com -

May 9

Parent Responsibilities

"Be sure to make it a good life and leave behind only the best of you in those who remain."

- Cedric R. Crawford -

Meet the Crawfords. I'm the third born of four boys. Yes, most people think we look alike and unlike most, we're actually a lot alike. These guys are definitely my best friends and when we're together, excitement is an understatement. I remember the many days catching Mom on her knees praying for our Creator's protection over us and our lives and as an adult I've picked up the same habit. No, we cannot watch our kids 24/7, but I believe that our Creator can and will if we're humble enough to ask for assistance.

On this day in 2008 at the tender age of 59 my mother took her last breath as she left this world and entered another. Because of her, I no longer fear dying, for I know just as she was the first to greet me in this world, she'll definitely be the first to greet me in the next. Her life was definitely filled with *"good"* and she took full advantage of her responsibility as a parent and left behind the best of her and her faith inside of us.

I often reflect back to that day of May 9th of 2008 when my brothers and I were all scheduled to meet in west Dallas, Texas to spend what we thought would be our last Mother's Day with my Mom. My airplane flight was scheduled to land in Dallas at approximately 6pm that evening. It was that Friday morning at exactly 4:06am (Pacific Time) when I got the phone call from my dad that altered a part of me forever. Even though I knew that we wouldn't have her with us much longer, I still was shaken by the enormity of the actual reality of her departure. I can only speculate to the reason why God didn't allow me to be there when she drew her last breath, but nevertheless, I've accepted it.

A giver in life and also a giver in her death as I now have become considerably much more in-touch with my emotions and find it much easier to cry and feel compassion for others. For this I say, *"Thank you Mom for making this possible."*

May these written words today serve as a reminder for us to make our lives GREAT and leave behind only the best of us in those who remain. Let's choose to make it GREAT!

Demetria S.	*Wow cedric you've done it again...she speaks right through you daily. ..such a blessing, I do the same for my teen boys and baby girl...the things mom don't think we listen to is just mended into our spirits anyway...*
Karen B.	*You are an Awesome testimony of her legacy Ced !*

May 10

BELIEVE

Do you Believe it's YOU?

"Thousands if not millions of people are waiting for you to step up and into your passion and area of greatness so you can inspire them to overcome their challenges."

- Cedric R. Crawford -

As I look around today, I realize that absolutely everything we see was birthed by someone's imagination and idea. The dreamer envisioned it and then used their belief as fuel and as a result they were able to make their idea become no longer just an idea, but a reality.

What do you *"believe"* is possible for you? Do you believe you're capable of doing something that is significant for the world? Do you believe that you were created for something Great? Do you believe that thousands, if not, millions of people are waiting for someone to step up and into their passion and area of purpose so they can be inspired to overcome and win too? Those people just don't know that that person of inspiration is *"You."* Do you believe it? Well, I do. There's no need to answer this question out loud just take the necessary action steps and make me proud.

Conceive it, Believe it, and Achieve it. Then go tell someone all about it. We're waiting for *you* to make it GREAT! So, let's get going.

To be continued based on your *belief* level while on your journey....

May 11

CRITICISM

Never-ending Criticism

"Let the criticizing critics do their job, because it's their job."
- Cedric R. Crawford -

The Great Philosopher Aristotle is well known for one of his quotes stating, *"To avoid criticism, say nothing, do nothing and be nothing."* After really considering this timeless quote, I must respectfully disagree with the great philosopher. The simple truth is that even if we say nothing, do nothing and be nothing, the critics will still have their way with criticizing our laziness.

I remember as a young teenager in high school at L.G. Pinkston High School in Dallas, Texas, I played just about every sport offered at the school and tried to participate in just about every school activity that was organized. Additionally, I held just about every title a student could. I was aware and very careful not to be conceited, boastful or cocky and tried to treat everyone around me with respect and dignity.

In spite of my efforts, one day I overheard a couple of girls talking about who they were going to vote for at the *"Mr. Pinkston High"* election. One girl said that she was going to vote for me, but the other said she was going to vote for my friend Daren because she thought that I was too cocky and *"full of myself."* They weren't aware that I had heard every word they said. Needless to say, I was shocked and I struggled to make sense out of why she would make such a statement about me when she really didn't even know me. In all honesty, I couldn't even remember ever carrying on a conversation with her before. It was then that I realized that the old timeless phrase of pleasing people was true, *"You can please some of the people some of the time, but you can never please all the people all of the time."*

I've come to realize that it is just in some people's nature to criticize others and they can't help but to look at others with an eye of condemnation and criticism. The unfortunate thing about this fact is that no matter how hard we try, we can do nothing to help these people. They have to want to change before any real change will happen for them.

Simply put, we can't afford to waste our time trying to please everyone. This will only lead to frustration and repeated disappointment. The unfortunate truth is there really is no way to avoid criticism in life. So we might as well live a life striving to "*Make 'it' GREAT*" and let the criticizing critics do their job, because, "*it's their job.*" So, let's go make '*it*' GREAT!

Diane K.   *Cedric, I look for your thoughts everyday as well. Thank you. This is an interesting one, though. I think Aristotle might have been speaking about the people who just skip under the radar, never drawing attention because they don't want criticism or negative attacks. They may avoid the critics, but they also avoid the glory. To me it means: Go forth boldly.*

Cedric R. Crawford *I agree Diane, we both can agree that Aristotle was not an advocate for doing nothing, but I'm attempting to motivate by showing how ridiculous it would be to do nothing just to avoid criticism. I think after further thought, even he would agree that ultimately "criticism" can't be avoided. Makes you think though, huh? Mission Accomplished... So much more to say about this subject so, stay.*

May 12

OPPORTUNITY

Don't be P.O.O.R.

"Many people give up right before they were going to be rewarded for their efforts for hanging in there."

- Cedric R. Crawford -

I was recently talking with my friend, Eugenie who lives in Gambia, Africa. She was sharing with me a little snapshot of her daily life and future expectations. She works six days a week doing 12-hour days and doesn't complain, because she's one of the few people who are fortunate enough to have a job in her poverty-stricken community. She makes a whopping $150 a month (*US dollars*) which translates to approximately .48 cents per hour. In addition to that, she also makes time to do house-cleaning and other odd jobs on the side for extra pay.

When asked to what she attributes her drive and mental toughness, she responded, "*My kids need me to make money to provide for them. I have to make money to keep them in school to get their education because in my country, the only way you can make something of yourself is if you have an education.*" Eugenie has never been married and has one child of her own. She also adopted her uncle's daughter as a baby several years ago. So, for the past several years she's had much more than just herself to be concerned about. Honestly, I have to leave out some of the details of Eugenie's life situation at her request for fear of some dire consequences if some others knew some specifics. So suffice to say her struggle is a special one indeed.

Her dream is to one day be able to come to America and start her own hair salon because she loves to do hair. She is very enthralled and fascinated with the stories about the opportunities that we have in America to work hard and make a living or build your own business by the sweat of your brow and work of your hands. She's surprised at the number of people in America who aren't willing to work and choose to spend a lifetime being content with just being supported by the government. She states that no such thing exists in her country and any person who would accept such a position in society would be subjected to scorn and ridicule and would be rejected by their family, friends and community.

The saga of her life continues everyday and her faith, belief and determination remains unshaken. I told Eugenie that we could learn a lot from her work ethic, drive and mental toughness. She laughed and said, "*People in your country are so blessed and fortunate to have such opportunities, but they don't know what they have.*" I agreed.

Eugenie's words served as a reminder for me. It is my humble opinion that we must refuse to be P.O.O.R. (*Passing Over Opportunities Repeatedly*). We can't let ourselves become immune to all the different types of opportunities that surround us in this wonderful country. We must avoid the ever-present temptation to dismiss the idea of seizing the opportunity to better our lot in life simply because of what our neighbor will think about us or any other convenient excuse for complacency and inaction. Truly, America, in spite of its many short-comings, is indeed still the "*Land of Opportunity.*"

Are you still following your passion and chasing your dream or did you put that dream on the shelf a long time ago? Did you give up? If your answer is "*Yes*" then ask yourself, did you give up too soon? I've come to realize that many people give up right before they were going to be rewarded for their efforts for hanging in there. Don't let that be you. Eugenie promised to never give up on her dream and only time will tell. To be continued…

Dust off that dream and throw gasoline on that fire inside of you and get excited again about the possibilities. Opportunity is all around us so don't miss it. Hang in there for one more day because someone's secretly counting on you to WIN! So, make it GREAT!

May 13

OPPORTUNITY

An "Open Mind" is an Asset

"The most valuable asset that anyone could ever have is an 'Open Mind.'"

- Cedric R. Crawford -

Over the many years that I've been in business as an entrepreneur, I've realized that one of the most valuable assets that anyone could ever have is an "*Open Mind*." I can't tell you how many countless opportunities I probably missed out on down through the years simply because I didn't know what I didn't know but I thought I knew. So, it's safe to say that a "*Closed Mind*" can cost you so much more than just money.

At this stage of my life I'm finding the more I learn, the more I'm realizing I didn't know and need to know. Please don't make the same mistake I did over the years. Keeping our mind open increases the chances of something positive falling in. So I guess it's fair to coin the phrase, "*Open Mind Asset, Closed Mind Liability*." Let's all keep our minds open and continue to use these breadcrumbs in our attempt to make it GREAT!

Paul L. V.	*Cedric well stated and here I go. If I knew then what I know now, I would have had more opportunities leading to more success." Life is GREAT:)*
Michael M.	*Somebody told me once that a mind is like a parachute. It doesn't work if it won't open. ;)*

May 14

CONVERSATIONS

Are you a 'Goal Getter'?

"Goal Getters have to be comfortable with being uncomfortable until it's no longer uncomfortable."

- Cedric R. Crawford -

Spent some time with a few cousin-in-laws last night. As we talked over dinner, I discovered that one of them had emigrated from Mexico to America over 55 years ago at the tender age of 13. She spoke absolutely no English at the time and was told that she had to attend public school. As a Spanish speaking seventh grader, she had to invest half of her days in the kindergarten classroom learning the basics of English. Needless to say it was extremely uncomfortable being the giant in the land of five-year-olds. I asked how she managed to deal with the ridicule from the other students. She said, *"It didn't bother me at all because I couldn't understand what they were saying."* She contributes this early childhood experience to teaching her that in life we sometimes have to do things that are uncomfortable for a while to achieve a desired result. But it was certainly worth every minute of the experience she says.

This is truth at its best. We have to be comfortable with being uncomfortable until it's no longer uncomfortable. Surprisingly enough, she also credits her bilingual skills with having years of job security with her employer. She's now long since retired and enjoying her life in the Palm Springs area of California with the handsome American man she's loved over the last 30 years. Her name is Alice and she is every bit of the meaning of her name, which is "*noble and truth*." She's definitely a "*Goal Getter*" in my book and that's why I had to include her in my book. ☺

To all you other Alice's out there I say to you today, hang in there and continue to do those positive things which may be uncomfortable for you until it becomes comfortable for you as you attempt to make it GREAT!

Trisha B.	*Reading this gave me chills! I Love hearing awesome testimonies.*
Rabecca E.	*Thank you so very much for sharing that story. My dad's family is from Mexico and your story really touched home for me and really helps put those little things we have to get over to succeed in life in perspective! Thank you again... Have an awesome day.*

May 15

ATTITUDE

ATTITUDE CHECK!!!

"Check yourself before you wreck yourself. How's your Attitude today?"

- Cedric R. Crawford -

B ack on February 8th I shared the story of how important it is to keep our attitude tool sharpened. After blindsiding that police officer with my positive attitude, he casually took my license and registration back to his buddy and seconds later came back and made this statement. *"I've been on the force for over 15 years and I must admit that I've never had anyone put me in a pickle quite like you just did."* He then showed me his teeth, chuckled a bit and sent me on my way with a, *"Slow it down and stay out of trouble." "Sure thing Mr. Officer, thank you very much,"* was my response as I slowly resumed my travels. Just another classic case of how a positive attitude can save the day and your pocket book.

For those of you who are wandering if I shared this story later that day with the high school kids at the assembly I was speaking at, the answer is *"Yes."* They loved it and now have a new strategy to apply in their lives to help them make it GREAT.

An old-school rapper by the name of Ice Cube used to have a lyric in one of his songs that said, *"Check yourself before you wreck yourself..."* For my purposes today, this statement can be used as a reminder to keep our attitudes in check before we end up in a *"wreck."* So, do you need an attitude check today? Hmmmm... Make it GREAT!

NOTES

CHOICES

The Butterfly and the Bee

The Butterfly and the Bee.

One's a slave and one is free.

The Bee works hard the whole day through
Cause that's what Bees are programmed to do.

They toil and labor day in and day out
Flying here, flying there and all about.

A Bee is known for being very busy,
So busy it would make most of us dizzy.

The Butterfly's existence may seem kind of odd.
To date I can't explain what's the Butterfly's job.

Maybe his job is to rival the Bee.
Are just flying around up and down from tree to tree.

Or maybe it's something else that most fail to see.
It's the metamorphic change that makes the Butterfly free.

Could this really be, the change we see?
Could we change a Bee and make it free?

Well, maybe not a Bee, but we can change you and me.
Yes, we can change you and me if we want to be free.

The master key is inside of you and me,
And I can be free if I really want to be.

The problem you see, is most think they can't be free.
They've given up their dreams and now they're a Bee.

The way we think makes us a Butterfly or Bee.
The choice belongs to only you and me you see.

Choose to follow the Butterfly's and reject the Bee.
Ignore this directive and you'll never be free.

I'm no Bee, you see, I was meant to be free.
I'll step out of the box and pursue what's right for me.

Now I can truly be free with my dreams in front of me.
I'll set goals and work smart and be free soon you'll see.

No, I'm no Bee, I too can be free.
Thanks for these kind words that rescued me.

A Butterfly I'll be for all to see,
I'll spread the word that all can be free.

IT'S TRUE! IT'S TRUE! We all can be free!

Just look inside and there you'll find the key!

SO, SPREAD YOUR WINGS AND FLY WITH ME !!!

Jump out of the box of everyday living in comfort. Find your passion and purpose and create value for others and make a difference in this world. Your playing small will not serve to inspire others to greater heights. See your dreams clearly. Set some lofty goals. Make some commitments. Hang out with other dreamer-driven-dragons. Go out and do the work and don't give up on that dream of yours. Inspire others to do the same. Be that Butterfly that you already are. To be continued...

by **Cedric R. Crawford**

ACTIONS

Need a kick in the butt?

"Procrastination is the mother of mediocrity and the father of failure."

- Cedric R. Crawford -

Ok, I'm having a *"Kick-butt"* day so I really feel the need to kick somebody in the butt today. Please allow me to issue an unsolicited friendly reminder to everyone. As I always say, procrastination is the mother of mediocrity and the father of failure.

If we want *"it"* we have to get off of our butts and go get it. Remember, ships of success don't come in, we have to swim out to them. So put on your favorite swimsuit and GET TO SWIMMING and make it GREAT!

Cam R.   *I needed my butt kicked today. I've been trying to overcome something that I feel is like a losing battle... I feel like giving up on it but I can't! Thanks a bunch.*

Fred W.   *Ouch, that hurt, Cedric. :)*

LEGACY

The Canvas of Life

"On what canvas will you choose to paint your legacy?"

- Cedric R. Crawford -

s I look at my life today, I have to say that there are several things that I'm very grateful for. But the thing that tops the list is the opportunity to be an *"active"* father with my two boys Cedric Jr. and Chance. They're definitely two characters with totally different personalities but they manage to get along well most of the time in spite of their four year age difference. They just can't seem to get enough of the stories of my past troubles and triumphs. But the ironic thing is I'm learning as much from them as they're learning from me.

This is definitely the canvas on which I choose to paint my legacy. What's yours? What canvas will you choose to install and deliver the paint brush strokes of the best parts of you and your life? Like it or not, the chances are somebody's watching you and are taking good mental notes. So what are you going to do? No need to answer out loud, just make those kids proud. Let's choose to do those things that are legacy driven as we continue in our efforts to make it GREAT!

May 18

FALLIBILITY

A Pocket Full of Rocks

"Don't crank up that bus and throw him under it just yet, and please keep the stones in your pocket because all human beings are fallible, including you."

- Cedric R. Crawford -

n the news a few days ago our beloved seven time Mr. Olympia, Block Buster Movie Star, Former Governor of the beautiful state of California admitted to fathering a love child with one of his twenty-year house employees. Arnold Schwarzenegger managed to keep this information a secret for over thirteen years. The news stations all over the country quickly mobilized and jockeyed for position to catch any piece of newsworthy info that can be used to report to the public in an overall attempt to say, *"We got the scoop first."*

As fate would have it I just so happens to live approximately 300 yards away from the home of Schwarzenegger's mistress and son. There appeared to be over fifty news and radio stations and magazine reporters camped out all down the block waiting for a glimpse of the mother and son which never came. I took the liberty and opportunity to capture the following picture below for your viewing confirmation.

All this hubbub of activity gave me pause to think and reflect a bit. I'm reminded of a verse I read before in my favorite book, "*He who is without sin, cast the first stone.*" Hmmmm... As such, my words for today are, "*SURPRISE! Mr. Schwarzenegger is a fallible human being.*" This is definitely a case of a bad choice that has been magnified in the public's eye. Yes, even the greatest among us all was tempted.

I feel compelled to write a few words in the sand today and suggest you don't crank up that bus and throw him under it just yet, and please keep the stones in your pocket because all human beings are fallible including you, last I checked.

I humbly submit the following: It's okay to beat him up a bit, but then let's lift him back up. Fallible human beings we all are, that's just what makes us human. Let's all continue in our efforts to make it GREAT!

Anthony McC.   *Cedric, it would sure be nice if the World put all that energy into childhood obesity or even finding cures for all diseases. It's a shame that we live in a world of drama. What a mess. Let's move on people. I enjoy your words. See you at the top!*

Michelle N.   *As always the child will be the one who will suffer the most for the adult indiscretions. It is a shame there are not laws in place to prevent this intrusion into their lives.*

May 19

MARRIAGE AND RELATIONSHIPS

Date today?

"Don't let the business of life and kids take you away from what brought you and that special someone together in the first place."

- Cedric R. Crawford -

Ahhhh… A weekday lunch with my beautiful bride is always a welcomed event. Great conversation coupled with an endless bowl of Pasta Fiogole and breadsticks was our choice at the famous Olive Garden today. There are a lot of things I miss out on in life but weekly lunch with Karen and a regular date night is not one of them. It seems to me that one of the biggest mistakes we can make in our relationship, in my humble opinion, is to let the business of life and kids take us away from what brought us together in the first place.

Yes my friends, this is a very important piece of the marriage and relationship puzzle. I honestly believe we have to continue to be intentional about paying attention to that significant other, for this too is definitely worthy of our best efforts.

So make an intentional point to take that special someone out on a regular scheduled, predictable basis and constantly work on making that marriage and relationship GREAT. I think we can all agree that great marriages don't grow on trees are happen by accident.

Trisha B.	*Love it Love it Love it!!!!!*
Dawn G. G.	*Great advice, Cedric! Possibly your best so far!*
Cameron Y.	*I agree!!!*

May 20

CREATIVITY

"*In-the-box*" Indoctrination

"We're all born to be creative and adventurous and then somewhere along in life the process of in-the-box, inhibiting indoctrination begins."

- Cedric R. Crawford -

As I gazed at this recent photo of my kids today, I couldn't help but to start thinking about our kids and the future of our world. Over the years it has become more apparent to me that our kids unfortunately live in a world where they're told more about what they *"can't do"*

than what they "*can do.*" They tend to be reminded more of their *inabilities* and *limitations* than their *abilities* and *limitlessness.*

As I think about our God-given abilities I realize that we're all born to be creative and adventurous and then somewhere along in life the process of *in-the-box, inhibiting indoctrination* begins. Strangely enough, this limiting indoctrination appears to start in our own household, then it progresses out to the schools and the community and even some churches. The interesting thing is that this indoctrination is pervasive and widespread yet so subtle, benign and non-threatening that it has become widely accepted in our day-to-day life as the "*norm.*" It is for this reason I believe we should be ever so cautious of what we say and don't say to our kids.

It is my humble opinion that the fundamental principles that govern the overwhelming majority of our current educational institutions are actually designed to strip our minds of our natural creativity and imagination and place us in a "*box*" way of thinking about the world and what's expected of us in society. Experience and history has taught me that no one can achieve anything great, cutting edge or original with normal "*in-the-box*" thinking. Our human minds are capable of so much more than we give them credit for if we just continue to stimulate and advocate for creativity in our day-to-day activities.

The good news is that we as parents will always have control over what we encourage our kids to do and how we encourage them to think. Our kids are more distracted and overly-medicated than ever before. Diagnosis and misdiagnosis are becoming more commonplace and we're attempting to bridal the high-functioning creative minds of our kids with a pill or two in an attempt to keep them "*in the box.*"

I'm fully aware that when I write such things it doesn't always sit well with all the readers and may come across as what some would call "*preachy*" and opinionated but I feel that I would be doing the world a huge disservice if I didn't attempt to shed light on this overlooked issue. Yes, in this life there are many things that we have no control over, but this is not one of them. Our kids need us now more than ever before to step up and embrace and encourage the creative process and not skirt our responsibility as parents, teachers and mentors in this area. We should allow them to flex their adventurous muscles from time-to-time. We should continue to encourage them to use their God-given, independent thinking abilities and let those creative juices flow for those creative juices can sure be sweet sometimes.

We must make a point to point out their strengths and encourage them to tap into their dreams and to set goals and be willing to fail as they boldly move forward with inner confidence in their own capabilities. Let's not be so quick to talk them out of the things they want to do, but to talk them into that which they were gifted to perform and passionate about. I'm absolutely certain and convinced that these actions and efforts will be rewarded with the production of positive fruit for many, many years to come.

Let's be sure to encourage our kids and give them the best chance to win and achieve a life being innovative, productive and creative while pursuing their passion and making it GREAT!

May 21

DON'T QUIT

WE FIGHT!!!

"The battle is not reserved for the quick, the strong or the fast,
it's reserved exclusively for the resilient and the unyielding that
are committed to win and overcome or die trying."
- Cedric R. Crawford -

We Fight! When times are tough and the battle is rough, We Fight! When the chips are down and no one else is around, We Fight! When life comes at us hard and we're caught off guard, We Fight! When we're doing all we can and things aren't going as planned, still We Fight! In dark of night or broad daylight, We Fight! When we're taking abuse and considering an excuse, yes, We Fight! When times are bad and we're tempted to wave the white flag, still We Fight! When we're taking a hit and we're ready to quit, yet We Fight! When we're losing our clout and others count us out, We Will Fight!

Yes, we are a bold, resilient few that never say die under any circumstance. In times of adversity we're prepared to come out yelling, kicking, screaming and swinging, for we know that the battle is not reserved for the quick, the strong or the fast. It's reserved exclusively for the resilient and the unyielding that are committed to overcome and give it their BEST down to the last second or die trying. Yes, this is a tall challenge but we accept.

Others may cower away from such duty and responsibility, but not us. Not today. Anyone can captain a ship in calm waters, but we understand that true leaders and captains know that they must step up to perform when the wind blows and the wave's crash and the crackle of the thunder and lightening flash makes you second guess why you're here. Young, old, big, small, short, tall, hair or bald, we all boldly stand and echo this message down through the generations, "We may rest but we won't stop. We may bend but we won't break. We don't quit, we fight, We Fight, WE FIGHT!!!"

May you too join the creed of our crew today and proudly proclaim the same in pursuit of your goals and dreams. WE FIGHT! Let's wrap our hands around the throat of this life and choke it until it gives us what we want, and what we want is to make it GREAT! WE FIGHT!!!

May 22

PERSONAL DEVELOPMENT

Work-in-Progress?

"Entertaining our minds can change us for a day, but Educating our minds can change us for a lifetime."

- Cedric R. Crawford -

As I pause for a moment to look and listen for a profound message to deliver to you on this delightful day, I feel a slight tug on my heart to offer the following words of education and encouragement.

I recently read somewhere that the average person invests less than $10 a year in their own personal development. Normally a statistic like this would be pretty shocking to me, but not in this case. Why? Well, it's because I used to be one of those people. Years ago I used to be so caught up with the day-to-day grind of life that I didn't have time to invest in my own personal development. But that was not the end of my story. That was just the beginning. I eventually ran into some new friends who were able to express to me the importance of continuing to develop oneself personally. That's when things started to change for the better for me but of course this sentiment and philosophy is not shared with the masses.

Now as I look around I've noticed that tickets to see our favorite singer or entertainer at the largest venue in the area quickly sell out, but events that are designed to educate us or equip us and make us better people will struggle to fill the seats even in the smallest of venues in any given area. This sad reality is disheartening and does not paint a pretty picture for the future of our world because our younger generation is watching us and taking copious mental notes.

So I say today, we must make the personal commitment to continue to keep our minds sharp and never cease in developing ourselves personally, physically, emotionally and spiritually. We must refuse to adopt the widely accepted belief that education stops with graduation, for this type of thinking shall surely guide our individual lives straight toward mediocrity and *"average"* at best.

We can never learn and see what we don't allow our eyes and mind to learn and see. We can never know what we don't know unless we make an effort to know it. We can never become better people unless we make an investment in ourselves to become better in every aspect of life.

On our respective journeys and quest for knowledge and experience I've learned that we can never *"arrive."* Our appetite for more wisdom should be unsatisfiable. Our thirst to know more must be unquenchable. In fact, I've found that the more I know, the more I want to know. On your journey you may notice that just like the strongest drug, the quest for knowledge and wisdom can also be addicting, but no rehab is necessary for this one.

Out of all the projects I've worked on and completed over the years the only one that I'm proud to say I've never completed is the project called, *"Me, Myself and I."* Hence, my personal motto is, *"I'm a work in progress that's never to be completed."* Feel free to adopt the same if you'd like and pay it forward.

The harsh truth is *"most people"* won't even make time to read a small entry such as this on a regular basis to help them grow. They'll quietly complain and say things like, "*It's too long*" or "*I just don't have the time.*" Most people are waiting for "*spare time*" to work on themselves. News Bulletin: "*SPARE TIME*" DOES NOT EXIST! We must "*make time*" to better ourselves.

So my final, rhetorical question today is, "*Where are your priorities focused? Are you a 'Work in Progress?' Have you 'arrived?'*" No need to answer out loud, just make your Creator proud and stand out from the crowd. Continuing to *entertain* our brains can change us for a day, but continuing to *educate* our brains can change us for a lifetime. Let's be proud to be a "*Work in Progress*" as we continue to collect these breadcrumbs to making it GREAT!

May 23

AVERAGE

Not Average

"We pray not for an easier life but for an increase in our ability to endure."

- Cedric R. Crawford -

After so-called friends stab us in the back and life punches us square in the face for what seems like the 20th time and we ask ourselves the question, "*Am I supposed to just get back up again?*" The answer is an emphatic, "*YES!*" We've already read the book about how to handle life's adversity and know the stories of the ones who overcame and became something GREAT. So, we pray *not* for an easier life and one without struggle and adversity but for an increase in our ability to endure, the knowledge to make wiser choices and for the strength to OVERCOME.

The average person would throw in the towel and waive the white flag of surrender during repeated tough times of adversity, but we're anything but "*average.*" We're striving for something good, we're striving for something GREAT. Let's make this day so awesome that yesterday files a lawsuit for discrimination.

| Ivan V. O. | *It was once said that so many people come within inches of their success, only to quit after having come so far. Perseverance is one of the hallmarks of a successful person!* |
| Karen B. | *Ahh....The Power of our CHOICE to act in our own best interest and let it overflow to others... Best to you Ced!!* |

FEAR

Afraid of Heights?

"In the battle against fear, winning sure feels good."

- Cedric R. Crawford -

I'm not really afraid of heights, I'm just afraid of falling from them. I spent all day at Knott's Berry Farm Theme Park in Buena Park, California a few days ago with my family. I have a huge fear of the sudden drop of the *"Supreme Scream"* which is about 200 ft. high. This ride brings you up slowly and drops you into a free-fall for what seems like a minute. Out of all the 40-plus rides at the theme park, this ride is always at the top of my list because I feel I always have to keep overcoming my fear.

In my eyes FEAR means False Evidence Appearing Real and not Forget Everything And RUN!!! In the battle against fear, it sure feels good when I win even if it's just on an amusement park ride.

What's your Fear? We all have at least one. Are you taking steps to overcome it on a regular basis? Hmmm... I encourage you today to face it head-on and get used to being a Conqueror. Victory over a bitter fear sure taste sweet. Another great breadcrumb for you today so let's make it GREAT!

May 25

EMPOWERMENT

Beware of the Snakes of Well-Intention

"Choose to be empowered by cynicism and encouraged by the nasty "N" words. The Nevers, Nos, Nots" and the "No shows."

- Cedric R. Crawford -

On your journey through this "life" thing some people around you may attempt to squash your goals and dreams with a sharp comment or two. I call these people *"Snakes of well-intention."* Have you been bitten and victimized by the vicious bite and fast-acting venom of one of these vipers lately? If so, I say to you today, don't lose your focus. Let this venom be the fuel for your vision. Choose to be empowered by cynicism and encouraged by the "N" words. The "Nevers, the "Nos," the "Nots" and the "No shows." Shake off the nasty non-sense of the naughty naysayers.

Make a commitment today, while the weather is good so when the storms roll in, you will not fold up your umbrella of armor and run for cover. You will stand your ground and not retreat into that foxhole of fear in the face of adversity for you know that all great men and women have realized their greatness or significance on the other side of such adversity and hardships.

Then when the day comes that you stand face-to-face with your achievement, may you then be so bold to tell the story of how you overcame and became. I encourage you today to hang in there and continue to fight the good fight because someone is secretly and unknowingly counting on you not just to win, but to win BIG. So carpe diem (*seize the day*) and make it GREAT!

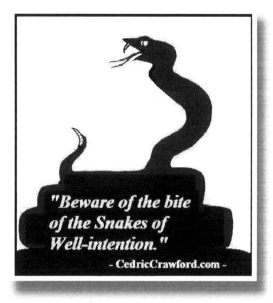

"Beware of the bite of the Snakes of Well-intention."

- CedricCrawford.com -

May 26

You're Not Alone

"Fight for your right to a better life until hell freezes over, then put on some warm clothes and ice-skates and keep going."

- Cedric R. Crawford -

Over the years I've learned that our challenges in life exist to give us an opportunity to overcome and become stronger. No matter what our struggle or situation is, I'm here to declare the bold statement of, "*You have not been singled out!*"

Please allow me to give you some unsolicited words of encouragement today. Your challenges, obstacles and struggles have been allowed in your life to give you an opportunity to show you can overcome. Our Creator designed you for a task such as the one that's before you now, and if not you, then who would be more suited to overcome and complete it.

So, why not you? I encourage you today to fight for your right to a better life until hell freezes over, then put on some warm clothes and ice-skates and get back out there and fight, Fight, FIGHT some more until you win! Make it GREAT!

May 27

CONVERSATIONS

Important Journey

"The most important journey in life is the one from your head to your heart."

- Corilee Mann -

My good friend made a statement to me recently that threw me for a loop, and that's pretty hard to do these days especially since I weigh over 220 pounds. J I must admit that I had mixed feelings about the statement when she made it. On the one hand, I loved the statement but on the other hand, I hated the fact that I didn't come up with it first. She said, *"The most important journey in life is the one from your head to your heart."* Dang that's good!

Corilee Mann is her name from Kamloops, British Columbia in the great country of Canada. What a life story she has of overcoming and becoming something beautiful. Be on the lookout for her book that will be coming out soon. Glad to see yet another member in the fight against the unacceptable status quo. Yes indeed the most important journey we will ever take in this life is the one from our heads to our heart. So, be sure to travel lightly. Oh, and continue to use your breadcrumbs to make it GREAT!

May 28

PARENTING

An Oscar Performance, BRAVO!

"Our kids are quietly counting on us and really do need us to step into our parent roles and play them to Oscar caliber."

- Cedric R. Crawford -

I was just thinking about my four little contributions to this world and thought I'd share the thought. I believe one of the biggest mistakes we can ever make as it relates to our kids is leaving the complete education of our kids in the hands of school teachers. It always has been and always will be our responsibility to educate, motivate and inspire our kids in concert with their teachers. This process should be looked upon as a *"team"* effort.

We must continue to capitalize on those teachable moments and stress the value of honesty and integrity. Let's help them to set goals and finish what they start. Our kids are quietly counting on us and really do need us to step into our parent roles and play them to Oscar caliber. So let's all keep strive to make it GREAT!

May 29

The Wise Owl

"Beware of those who look wise but have bared no positive fruit."

- Cedric R. Crawford -

I was hanging out at the Fresno Zoo yesterday with my little first grader Chayse Marie and her friend Stevie when we came across the biggest owl I've ever seen. It's a Eurasian Eagle Owl which is the largest owl species in the world.

After doing a bit of research, I discovered an interesting fact. Although we consider owls as *"wise,"* compared to other birds, they're at the bottom half of the species in the intelligence category. People throughout history have readily accepted and regarded owls as wise because of their look alone. Know any humans like this? Hmmmm.

My PSA (*public service announcement*) for you today is, beware and don't be easily fooled by those who look wise but have bared no positive fruit from their actions. FYI. Let's continue to make it GREAT.

May 30

Memorial Day Appreciation

"Mere words in any language are inadequate to express
the level of appreciation for those who have willingly placed
themselves in harms way and paid the ultimate sacrifice to
safeguard the freedoms we enjoy everyday."

- **Cedric R. Crawford** -

I was at the gas station yesterday teaching my 7-year-old Chayse-Marie how to pump gas. She really gets a big kick out of doing *"grown-up"* things. We were at pump #12 and an elderly gentleman who looked to be about 70 or 80-years-old pulled up to the pump directly across from us. He got out of his vehicle and started the process of pumping his gas. While pumping his gas he started to take notice of me and little Chayse going through the instruction process. He commented, *"Looks like you're putting her through training a little early."* I then said, *"Well, you never know what a kid is capable of doing until you give'em a shot."* We both laughed then a casual conversation followed.

He told me he had come to Bakersfield, California back in 1942, but his many years of service in the military has taken him all over the world and he chose to retire here in Bakersfield. I beamed one of my trademark, signature smiles at him and said, *"Do you mind if I shake the hand of a man that has done so much for our great country?"* By the look on his face I could tell this doesn't happen to him often. He smiled and said, *"Absolutely not."* I grabbed his right hand firmly, looked him in the eyes and thanked him for his service to our country with a smile. He then said, *"Well that just made my day."*

I glanced over at his wife sitting in the passenger seat of the car with the windows rolled up. She had been turned around in her seat watching our interaction the whole time. She probably couldn't hear what we were saying, but the big smile on her face showed that she new it was good. We followed with a few more niceties and pleasantries and then went on our merry way. I truly believe the feeling that I got from knowing he was positively affected that day from something I said was priceless for me this Memorial Day weekend.

I'd like to further take this opportunity to say to those of you who have served in harms way dealing with the bullets, the bombs and the bloodshed of battle, *"Thank You."* To those who are actively serving stateside and abroad, I too say to you today, *"Thank You."* And, to those who've paid the ultimate price so that we may enjoy the freedoms we have in this great country of ours, no words in any language are adequate for me to express the level of my sincere appreciation for all that was gained by your loss. So, here's a heartfelt smile for your sacrifice. ☺ Indeed this book would have not been possible if it wasn't for the sacrifice of so many.

As we all pull out the old flags, fishing poles and grills this Memorial Day weekend, be sure to recognize and realize the significance of the day. Make a point today to grab a veteran or active duty soldier and make them a celebrity as you express your sincere appreciation for their service.

It would also be nice if it wasn't only this day that we felt this way. So what say we make this a habit? Most people would pass up this opportunity, but the question is, *"Are you 'Most People?'"* No need to answer out loud, just let them know you're proud as we continue to spread these bread-crumbs around and make it GREAT!

May 31

Don't Toss out the Baby

"Not everyone will agree with you and vise versa, for it's our differences that make us as unique as a fingerprint."

- Cedric R. Crawford -

I had this interesting thought this morning while writing poolside at the local fitness club. Ever heard the phrase, *"Don't throw the baby out with the bath water?"* Well, I personally believe this enduring phrase suggest that just because a system may have a few problems or glitches doesn't necessarily mean you have to scrap the whole thing. FYI, this applies to people and organizations too.

Just because we may not agree with all the views of a person or organization doesn't necessarily mean we should disassociate and disconnect ourselves. News Flash: THE PERFECT PERSON OR ORGANIZATION DOES NOT EXIST! Not everyone will agree with you and vise versa and disagreeing on some things is perfectly normal. It's our differences that make us as unique as a fingerprint.

So go ahead and throw the dirty water out but for goodness sake, please seriously consider keeping the good baby. That just makes good sense. Let's make it GREAT!

**My Viral Quotes
Feel Free to SHARE**

"The minefield of Adversity has claimed the goals and dreams of many who lack Passion, Persistence and Perseverance. Don't let it be you. Not Today."

"Great leaders understand they have to do what they have to do when they have to do it so they can get through it, but never do they compromise their integrity to get it done."

"Victory and Success has many suitors but only the committed and persistent will eventually have their date."

"Anger and frustration doesn't perform well boxed in and bottled up under pressure. So find a healthy way to let it out."

"I'd rather be happy living in a hovel in a hamlet than living miserly miserable in a mansion."

"A suitable mate has to be much more than a thin waist and pretty face."

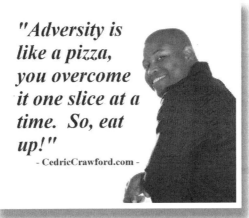

June 1

BELIEVE

Don't Be Out-believed'

*"**Adversity** is looking for every opportunity to put you into a choke-hold and strangle the belief out of you, so don't let it win. Not today."*

- Cedric R. Crawford -

After playing football for 16 years of my life, one of the many things I remember is that whenever we were preparing to play a team that had a losing record our coaches would encourage us to start the game with a ferocity that would crush the other team's belief and will to win. We figured if we could score a few touchdowns early on our opponent, we could crush their belief and remind them that they "*suck*" and weren't prepared to do what it takes to win. Failing to do this effectively could result in an increase in the opposing team's belief and will to win.

As an adult, I now see the same parallel exists in life. Victory and success belong to the person or team who believes in it the longest. Needless-to-say, this truth actually works both ways. A good footnote for us this week is for us to remember that when adversity comes out swinging hard at us, we have to buck up and start swinging back just as hard. We can't let anyone "*out-believe*" us, not this time around.

So I say on this glorious day, be encouraged and know that we can be victorious over our current situations and circumstances. Adversity is looking for every opportunity to put you into a choke-hold and strangle the belief out of you. So, don't let it win! Like it or not, our kids will learn the lesson of how to deal with adversity by watching us, so we must pay careful attention to what our actions are telling them.

Strap on your gear for life and ramp up your belief and commit today to overcome and then watch who and what you become in the process. Let's all continue to lean forward one more day as we attempt to make it GREAT! "Got Belief?"

NOTES

June 2

Time?

*"Investing in the commodity called <u>time</u> wisely in life will
definitely give you a chance to smile from the grave."*

- Cedric R. Crawford -

I had the opportunity to hang out in the waiting room of my doctor's office a few days ago and I managed to move a few steps closer to my goals while I was there by writing a few fresh pages of content in my trusty old journal.

Years ago I discovered time can be utilized in only three different ways. It can be wasted, spent or invested, but never recycled or regained. I believe time is the most precious commodity one could ever possess this side of the universe. The blessing or even perhaps the curse is that we all have it to utilize as we see fit. That's right, we all have this thing called *free will* and the way we utilize our time can become either a blessing or curse to us. Hmmmm...

So, don't miss those opportunities to invest your idle time while others are wasting and spending theirs. Investing in this precious commodity wisely in life will definitely give us a chance to smile from the grave. More breadcrumbs for your day. Be sure to keep making it GREAT!

Please view the video on:
www.YouTube.com
<u>Search Code:</u> Cedric R. Crawford – (16)

June 3

AVERAGE

Dare to Fail

"Be the exception to the unwritten rule of mediocrity."

- Cedric R. Crawford -

I've been gaining clarity in understanding the reason why we eventually succeed is because we're not afraid to fail. We eventually grow stronger because we're not afraid to acknowledge our weaknesses. We ultimately hit our homeruns because we dare to keep swinging the bat. We eventually score touchdowns because we're not afraid to say, *"Give me the ball and let me run!"* We continue to make major steps forward because of our ability to plow through the minor setbacks.

We must continue to refuse to let those cynical voices around us succeed in talking us back into the "Box" of life and pursuing a goal of comfort and *"averagism"* after every challenge or failure. We can't expect the average person to understand our journey and process of positive change if they have yet to start their own journey.

Be advised that in this life we may be a lot of things but *"Average"* is not one of them. We continue to strive to be the exception to the unwritten rule of mediocrity. Words like normal, typical and usual do not describe us. We are indeed persistent, vigilant overcomer's and understand that we eventually win because we are not afraid to lose. The difference for us is we understand that we must fail our way to success in this life. We understand that there's no special potions or lotions or special elixirs or silver bullet that makes the magic happen. So let's fail forward fast and furiously today.

I say with emphatic passion on this day, when you give it your best the score board becomes obsolete and can never, ever make you a loser. So let's all push to make our best better today and leverage our breadcrumbs to make it GREAT!

Anything but *"Average."*

Mark L.	*Daring to be different comes with a price and a HUGE payout! People remember those who have made a difference simply by being different! ☺)*
Rick G.	*So True!!*

June 4

GIVING

No-Brainer

"The best form of giving is giving out of scarcity and sacrifice rather than waiting for future abundance."

- Cedric R. Crawford -

*e*ver heard the term, "No-Brainer?" This refers to knowing or doing something without having to think about it. Would it surprise you to know most of us live the majority of our lives in what I call "No-Brainer" mode. Most people are stuck in a pattern of comfort and find themselves simply Ok with just being Ok and getting by. Using their time, talents and treasures to serve others has become a distant future thought based on a contingency of "when" things get better for themselves.

If this applies to you, I invite you to please allow me to give you some unsolicited advice today. Don't make this mistake, for I've found the best form of giving is giving out of scarcity and sacrifice rather than waiting and hoping for future abundance.

Dare to turn that brain back on and kick that comfort to the curb and get back into the hunt to create a life of substance and significance through your service to your fellowman or woman. I sincerely believe scarcity presents an awesome opportunity for us to "give" our way out of a rut or slump in life.

So, go ahead and give of your time, talents and limited treasures to bust up these challenging times. Now that should be a "No-Brainer." Let's continue to make it GREAT!

June 5

DREAM

Dreams Aren't Microwaveable

"Our goals and dreams aren't microwaveable, so pull out that crock-pot and start the marinating process."

- Cedric R. Crawford -

I've got a little food for thought for you today that's sure to be a breakfast of champions on your menu for life if you dare to indulge. I've recently started to notice the fast food, immediate gratification world we live in is slowly eating away at our respect for the "Creative Process." As I look back over my own life I must shamefully admit that I grew up with what I call a "Win the Lottery" or "Hit the Jackpot" mentality. I was foolishly looking for a way that would allow wealth and significance to come quick and easy. For years I thought that I was in the "know," but I later figured out that I was actually in the "Don't Know."

Winning the lottery or hitting a quick monetary jackpot or windfall may bring instant wealth, but there will be no inspiring story or significance tied to it because there will be no lessons learned or character earned during the process. It's no surprise that the overwhelming majority of people who "get rich quick" end up right back where they started, or even worse less than five short years later. Simply put, obtaining may be by *chance* but maintaining and sustaining must be by *change* only. A significant *change* in you. It's not about the money you gained, it's about who you became.

We must not forget the things that truly carry lifelong significance take time to create and our goals and dreams are not microwaveable. Success and significance don't come in a bag at a drive-thru window. So put away the popcorn dreams and pull out that old crock pot and be prepared to let those goals and dreams marinade as you work through your necessary process to become better today than you were yesterday in every way.

We must be willing to pay a reasonable price with our time, treasures, talents and tears in order to triumph. Yes, success will show up when you commit to the journey and the creative process. So, I guess a good question today is, "*Are you committed to stay the course through the process?*" Hmmmm... This is definitely a vital breadcrumb to making it GREAT!

"*Our goals and dreams are not microwaveable. So pull out that crock pot and start the marinading process.*"

www.CedricCrawford.com

June 6

GIFTS

Use your Gifts for Good

"*I would rather know there's a slim chance of success than a fabricated belief of never failing.*"

- Cedric R. Crawford -

I would rather be told the hurtful truth out of love and respect than an encouraging lie out of pity. I would rather know there's a slim chance of success than a fabricated belief of never failing. And, I would rather go to battle with three trusted, courageous comrades with conviction than with 300 cowardly convicts with no conscious or commitment to the cause.

Our fight is noble and just and the war has already been fixed for us to win and WIN BIG because of our unwavering faith and belief. Let's continue to use our Gifts to serve others and make this world a better place. Let's just make today GREAT, tomorrow will take care of itself.

June 7

Did you save room for Dinner?

"In life don't be afraid to break the rules sometimes. Dessert first can be a marvelous thing."

- Cedric R. Crawford -

I spent some time hanging out with my favorite ten-year-old, Chance, yesterday at his favorite gourmet restaurant, the world famous Denny's. He really looks forward to his *"He and Me Time."* To start, we usually split a strawberry shake and I always let him choose between the glass or the mixer cup. He always chooses the glass. (*FYI, when sharing a shake, the mixer cup usually has more.*)

An older couple in the booth behind us saw us drinking our shakes and the lady said, *"Are you guys just having dessert today?"* I replied back saying, *"We think life is too short and unpredictable. Anything could happen at any given time, so we like to eat our dessert first sometimes."* We all laughed together then she said, *"Well then we need to start doing that too because you're right. You never know when it's your time to go."*

We sure manage to meet some of the nicest people at Denny's on our dates. Ralph and Esther were definitely no exception.

In life don't be afraid to break the rules sometimes as long as nobody gets hurt. Dessert first can be a marvelous thing. Chance and I are definitely two strange birds that don't always fly straight. The funniest thing is, our server usually ask us, *"Did you save room for dinner?"* Maybe not, but we did save room for our breadcrumbs and we intend to keep making it GREAT! Dare to join us.

June 8

IDIOTS

Who's the Biggest Idiot?

"Sometimes you just have to let idiots be idiots. Please don't join them."

- Cedric R. Crawford -

Today I'm a bit ashamed to admit that I find myself asking the question of *"Who's the bigger idiot?"*

I was driving down the street heading to an appointment and suddenly a Mini-Van came whizzing by me at a high rate of speed followed by a small, 4-Door Sedan only to be stopped by other cars up ahead at a stop light. I said to myself, *"What are these two idiots up to?"* The light turned green and off they went again. The Sedan eventually sped up and passed the Van and then abruptly changed lanes in front of the Van and slammed on the brakes. The Van responded by quickly changing lanes and passing the Sedan and cutting the Sedan off and slamming on the brakes.

It didn't take me long to figure out that I was witnessing a textbook case of *"Road-Rage."* So, being the curious and concerned person that I am, I thought I'd be a good citizen and follow them to make sure they were safe. Yeah Right! But they were heading my direction. So, I sped up and followed behind them and watched them repeatedly try to assault each other with their vehicles.

This continued until we got on the freeway and then my curiosity got the best of me. I just had to see what these people looked like, so I sped up to catch them. At this time they started to really pick up speed, so I did the same because I was determined to see if these were two male idiots or female idiots or both. So, I floored it and started to get closer and closer, suddenly I looked down at my speedometer and realized that I was going over 95 mph trying to get a peek at two idiots.

Then it hit me. Now I'm an IDIOT! I'm an idiot for even trying to see what the idiots look like. Ughhhh! So, I quickly came to my senses and slowed back down to the flow of traffic and conceded to let them remain anonymous.

So, today I ask myself *"Who was the bigger idiot?"* The Van, the Sedan or the Black Man? ☺ Well, surprise! I'm not perfect. I get caught-up in the craziness of life too. But I promise this is one mistake I'm not soon to repeat. Let's stay on track in the right lane and let the idiots be idiots while we attempt to make it GREAT!

Shannon R. M.	*Thanks for sharing. Sometimes we all get off track and follow "losers" and before we know it, we find ourselves in the wrong place at the wrong time! Glad you were safe and it turned out well for you!*
Patricia H.	*A great reminder to not adopt a herd mentality.*

June 9

ACTIONS

Blind Leap of Faith

"Success has no feet, so it can't meet you half way. You've got to get up on your feet and go get it!"

- Cedric R. Crawford -

I was sharing with a large group of entrepreneurs the other day that I've discovered in life there comes a time or two when you have to take a *blind leap of faith* based only on how you feel about something. The great motivational speaker, Les Brown, once said that we must have the courage to leap and then grow our wings on the way down. What a classic statement.

I believe that if we take the time to become more aware of ourselves and who we are and what our purpose is in this world, the *"blind leap of faith"* then becomes not so blind. In fact, it should then become painfully obvious that we were created for such a task or venture that is before us. Lions know no fear and their heart is wired to overcome and conquer or die trying. So too should we be when it comes to seizing opportunities.

So I say to you today in this moment, no more second-guessing. Don't be afraid to be wrong. Fear of failure is not your ally today. You've prayed enough and now it's time to trust your God-given gut and intuition and follow your heart as you JUMP!!!

Success belongs only to those who are able to recognize their opportunity and carpe diem (*seize the day*). So, remember success has no feet, so it can't meet you half way. We have to get up and go get it! Leap into action with the fearless heart of a lion and SIEZE THE DAY and make it GREAT!!!

June 10

BATTLE

Good vs. Evil

"Evil will never sit idly by and let the good go unchallenged."
- **Cedric R. Crawford** -

Over the years I've realized life's struggles, challenges and disappointments don't just all of a sudden come to a screeching halt just because we find religion or get a huge dose of positivity. We must be even more vigilant and prepare to fight some major physical and psychological battles because as I've said before, evil will never sit idly by and let the *good* go unchallenged.

But take heart my friends and be encouraged today for I'm told that the referee in our good fight has already been bribed and paid off by a HUGE silent partner with deep pockets. So, in any cause that's noble and just, we simply cannot lose because in every book I've ever read, "*good*" triumphs over "*evil*" everyday of the week and twice on Sundays.

So let's commit to fight everyday in pursuit of our respective noble goals and ambitious dreams as if it's our last day on Earth, and one day we'll be right. Until then let's continue to make it GREAT!

"Feel like you can't win? Just stop, raise your hands, look up and smile. The referee in your good fight against evil has been bribed and paid-off by a HUGE silent partner with deep pockets. So don't worry, you can't lose. Just keep on fighting."

- CedricCrawford.com -

Edward S.	*Well said my friend....*
Sandra K.	*Your words of wisdom are always appreciated, have a Blessed Day...*
Jabo B.	*I love my daily dose of C.R.C.!*

June 11

Time for Change?

"Positive Change is Good. Just any old change is not a good thing."

- Cedric R. Crawford -

I remember years ago when I was working in corporate America for one of the largest insurance companys in the US, my boss was relocated to another city. He was then quickly replaced by a much younger guy that had little experience on how to manage an already productive team of adults. The new boss started to take advantage of the watchdog system that was already in place via the phone, computers and door monitors. He immediately began to micro-manage and nitpick in an attempt to affect change and justify his job. *"Big Brother"* had just descended upon us all in a very real way.

As a result, the production of our team started to slide right along with the morale. My co-workers went from loving their job to taking regular sick days and vacation time just to avoid coming in. Whoever coined the phrase *"Change is good"* definitely didn't consult with our team.

My experience has led me to believe that one vitally important word was left out of this enduring phrase. So today, I feel the need to add this one word to the phrase so future generations won't get confused. That word is *"Positive."* Yes, *"Positive Change is Good."* Just any old change is not a good thing.

So the question today is, *"Is there a need for positive change in your future?"* No need to raise your hand, just hear and understand and make your plan. Let's all continue to make it GREAT!

Stan B.   *I perceive that "change" is inevitable, only what we change into is the question. Thank God, we get to choose...Choose well and change is AWESOME. Great message Ced, thanks..☺)*

June 12

Patrick's Day

"Are your words building up or tearing down those around you?"

- Cedric R. Crawford -

After being the baby boy of three brothers for almost 10 years, all of a sudden Mom and Dad came to us telling stories about having a bun in the oven. Since I was the baby and was inevitably about to lose my rights and baby-boy privileges, they thought the least they could do was give me the opportunity to name the new-comer. So after careful thought, I came up with the name, Patrick Jermaine.

As a 10-year-old, I actually thought it was pretty special that I got to assign the name of another human being. But when reality set in and my privileges and hang-out time with Mom started to erode away, I was forced to accept my new role as the "*third born*" of four and not three. Whenever Mom was headed to the store or anywhere, she would always yell, "*CEDRIC!!! COME ON!!!*" So, I would immediately stop whatever I was doing and run to get into the car with her eagerly anticipating our journey to wherever. But this quickly eroded away and became a thing of the past. Reluctantly, I settled into my new role and became comfortable playing my new designated position as third born of four.

I'll never forget my senior year in high school, it was just me and little eight-year-old Patrick. Needless-to-say, I didn't think it was cool to be seen hanging out with my little brother. He was definitely a major cramp in my style and nuisance at best. In spite of not being welcomed around my friends, he would still manage to slide in whenever we were around. Honestly, I didn't like it one bit and I found myself putting him down and making him the butt of most of my jokes. My friends thought this was extremely funny and we would all laugh at him, but none would laugh as loud as me. I was callous, cold and just down-right cruel. What's worse is I didn't even know or understand what I was doing and at the time it just seemed funny. Surprisingly, little Patrick would laugh with us as we were laughing at him. He would do this freely with no problem if it meant that he could hang around his big brother and his friends.

If I live to be 100 years old, I'll never forget the day I was *put on notice* of how powerful our words and actions can be in the lives of not just ourselves, but others around us. My little brother was lying in bed with my dad having a typical father-son spontaneous conversation. My dad asked him how he felt about each one of his brothers. He had nothing but good things to say about first born (Bennie) and second born (Zimbalis), but when asked about his feelings about me, he paused, took a deep breath, and then started to cry. He spent the next few agonizing minutes explaining to Dad how he looked up to me, but how I constantly put him down and made him feel like he was stupid, ugly and unwanted.

Well, after this conversation, my dad dismissed little Patrick and casually called me into his room. I remember standing at my dad's bedside as he explained to me in detail what had just happened. He reminded me of the power of my words and actions and that my little brother looked up to me. He challenged me to use my words and actions toward my little brother for "*good*" and to build him up, not tear him down. I was dumbfounded and in a state of shock from hearing this.

It has been 20 plus years since and I still struggle to fight back the tears as I recall this story. I can't believe how stupid and self-centered I was and I wouldn't wish this type of treatment on anyone, let alone an eight-year-old kid. But my story doesn't end there. I immediately changed my ways. I started to take him with me on several of my sports outings and other events, or just to the corner store. I never again uttered any negative words or jokes about him and defended him to the point of a physical fight with anyone who would dare talk to him in such a way. Yes, my life changed for the better from that defining moment forward.

As a result, I have carried this same sentiment and actions into my adult life and I make the conscious decision everyday to speak words to build people up and not to tear them down. I encourage you to also lift others up with your words because you never know whose looking up to you or looking to you to affirm them. Let's all continue in our efforts to make it GREAT!

June 13

Are you Pretty?

"Be sure to hang out with the right Pretty Club in life. Those
who are pretty positive, pretty ambitious and pretty successful."
- Cedric R. Crawford -

As a kid in elementary school I used to always think of myself as the ugly brother, so I didn't have a lot of confidence in my looks. My best friend Clayton was always the one who seemed to get the pretty girls and I had to just settle for the leftover friend who usually didn't look so hot. As a result, I never really felt like I belonged in the *"pretty"* club.

By the time I reached high school, I started to get a bit of positive attention so naturally my confidence in my looks got a decent boost too. I must admit that although I didn't feel like I was in a *"pretty"* club, I'm sure others thought I was. The funny thing is I didn't do anything different, I just grew up.

The interesting twist to this is as an adult I've noticed that *"pretty"* people still tend to always hangout together. Those who are *pretty* lazy, *pretty* complacent and even those who are *pretty* ugly sometimes. But, no matter how flat you make a pancake, there is always two sides. So, you also have those who are *pretty* positive, *pretty* ambitious and *pretty* successful

The law of association states that you will become the common denominator of the group that you invest the most time with. So, be sure to choose your *pretty* club wisely while you attempt to make it GREAT.

June 14

'Til Death Do You Part

"Remember to never forget that the grass isn't always greener 'over
there,' it's just an illusion created by the desert heat of marriage."
- Cedric R. Crawford -

My beautiful cheerleader bride and I have been together for over 18 years and we just celebrated our 15th Wedding Anniversary today. Although we're both slightly north of forty years old, I honestly still feel like I'm in my mid-20's. I found myself recently reflecting back over the years gone by and felt inspired to once again put pen to paper.

I learned early on in marriage that a pretty face and a hot body only gets you so far. Ultimately, there has to be something more that keeps you around and engaged after the 24/7 excitement dissipates and life starts happening. I realize there are several strategies to increasing your chances of winning at the game of marriage, but I believe I stumbled onto the most effective strategy years ago just by paying attention to what worked for my mom and dad and what also works for us.

It seems to me that there's no room for dependence or independence in marriage. The healthiest marriage appears to be the one that contains an element of *"interdependence."* Those who work the hardest at maintaining this delicate balance will dramatically increase their chances of achieving the elusive *"until-death-do-you-part"* goal. I've discovered that life's challenges and adversity will either drive you together or drive you apart, there's no third driving direction. Additionally, a commitment to love each other *"in spite of"* and not *"because of"* appears to be key. A great rule of thumb I've also discovered is, before you speak, ask yourself if the comment you make is going to help the situation or make the situation worse. Will the comment lift your spouse up or put them on edge and bring them down.

Finally, we must keep in mind on our marriage journey that love is not finding the *"perfect"* person, it's being able to see an imperfect person and still love, respect and honor them in spite of their imperfections. Remember to never forget that the grass isn't always greener *"over there,"* it's just an illusion created by the desert heat of marriage sometimes. Yes it's true, the grass is always greener where you water it.

Ignore these basic rules at your own peril. This too is worthy of our best efforts so let's all continue to make it GREAT!

Yolanda S. P.   *Congrats.. I know it took much prayer, love and respect for one another..May you have continued success.*

Saundra B.-W.   *Happy Anniversary!!! Love is in the air.*

June 15

PERSEVERANCE

This Too Shall Pass

"You can borrow my favorite phrase in times of trouble, 'This too shall pass', but be sure to return it for eventually I'm sure I'll soon need it again."

- Cedric R. Crawford -

Pssst, let me let you in on one of my little secrets. Whenever I'm faced with adversity or suffering of any kind, I've always found comfort in telling myself this four word phrase, *"This too shall pass."* These four words have served me greatly over the years and on the other side of the phrase always stands a better man. No the phrase doesn't make the pain go away, but it does paint a picture of a brighter day.

We must remember that while going through trying times, the very words "*going through*" infers that we will eventually reach the other side. So keep moving and be encouraged today and hang in there. I'll lend this phrase to you if needed only if you'll promise to give it back to me later, for I'm sure I'll eventually need it again sooner or later.

Keep going through and see it through as you attempt to make it GREAT!

NOTES

June 16

Put on Notice

*"We can and will be held personally liable for any and all
damages that are caused to other people's lives as a result of us
NOT finding and using our gifts to help others."*

- Cedric R. Crawford -

In the many years that I've been in the area of real estate investing I've learned many things. One of the most important things I've learned is when a landlord is *put on notice* of a hazardous issue that exist at their rental property, it is their responsibility to abate the issue. A failure to do so can be construed as an act of negligence if the unaddressed issue causes harm to the occupants.

Surprisingly enough, I've discovered that herein lies a direct parallel to life. We're all hereby *"Put on Notice"* that there exist a seed inside each and every one of us that is destined for greatness. It should be our life's goal to seek out and find this seed of greatness and grow it to its full potential to positively affect those around us and to make this world a better place. We could be held personally liable for any and all damages that are caused as a result of us NOT finding and using our gifts to help others in the world. Someone needs you to step into your role and area of greatness and play it well for their sake. So don't delay, act now and make it GREAT!

June 17

Opt-in on Opportunities

*"Crisis creates a plethora of opportunities so choose to opt in on
the opportunities that abound around you in times of crisis."*

- Cedric R. Crawford –

I've discovered in life that opportunities knock all the time. Most people just either can't recognize the sound or they have so much mental wax buildup in their ears that they can't hear it.

The good news is these issues can be corrected very easily by committing to have an open-mind where prejudgment does not exist. Crisis creates a plethora of opportunities so look around and choose to opt-in on the opportunities that abound around you in these challenging times. Adopting this philosophy and behavior is sure to help you make it GREAT in the coming days.

James B. Jr. *ABSOLUTELY!!!! The mind is like a parachute, it works best when open.*

Bonus DAY 6!!!

<u>Maybe Later, Not Today,</u>
<u>I Just Don't Have the Time</u>

I had this thought some days ago and created a short nursery rhyme.

I called it, "*Maybe Later, Not Today, I Just Don't Have the Time*.
The name was created based on the excuses that some choose to favor,
And the many things we miss out on for stuff put off 'til later.

Like when your daughter or son comes to you and say "*Daddy, let's go out and play*,"
And you're watching your favorite show or football game and you casually push 'em away.

Or when you had another appointment and they wanted you to stay.
A phrase you know all too well, "*Maybe later, Not today.*"

Or that dream or special something that you always wanted to do.
But "*I just don't have the time*" is the phrase that came from you.

Excusitis is a disease that we all will have to fight.
It takes us away from what we can do today and we struggle later to make it right.

These convenient phrases or used by those with more important things to do.
"*Maybe later, Not today, I just don't have the time,*" don't let this short rhyme be you.

by Cedric R. Crawford

June 18

Raise Your Expectations

"One of these days you're going to totally catch me off guard by
taking full responsibility for your actions."

- Cedric R. Crawford -

"One of these days you're going to surprise me by maintaining control of your anger. One of these days you're going to totally catch me off guard by taking full responsibility for your actions."
These were the words I used when speaking to one of my "group-home" boys yesterday when he flew off the handle about something that was petty and inconsequential. I'll just call him, Anthony, for now. Anthony stopped and looked at me with a mean look on his face, but he didn't say a word. At that very moment I could see that he heard me and the wheels were turning. You see, Anthony didn't know what I was doing, but I did. I was setting a positive expectation for him

and with the proper reinforcement and consistency, he will eventually "*get it.*" I understand that it's really not his fault he was raised in a household where being "*out-of-control*" was the norm. I also understand the pattern and cycle of violence can be broken and the age of 12 is just as good a time as any.

This week is the first year anniversary of when I first made myself available 17 hours a week to be a positive, male role-model in the lives of several young boys ages 10-15, whose fathers are absent from their lives. These boys are living out their childhood in a group-home setting struggling to get along with other boys who are not related to them. To-date the experience has been extremely challenging at times, but small victories, minor rewards and subtle splashes of brilliance keep me coming back again and again to see what happens next. I'm not soon to leave this group for I feel I need them just as much as they need me.

Later that night when I was tucking Anthony into bed, he said, "*How did I do today?*" I told him he may have lost a few battles, but the war wages on and tomorrow he will have another crack at getting it right. He repaid me with a smile. To be continued...

In this "*life*" I've found that our kids can easily rise to low expectations, so it's up to us to set the expectations high and to make them clear and instill the confidence in our youth that "*it's possible.*" "*It's possible*" to achieve that which you desire most if you're willing to take the necessary steps to make them become a reality in your life. By the way, this works for adults too.

So don't miss your opportunity to play your part as an affirmer and encourager in those lives around you. Let's continue to Make it GREAT!

Deanna Lazarus. *Not only are you doing great work with those kids, but a little of what you said hit home for me... I had to be a little hard on my son today, but at the same time be encouraging too..;)))))*

June 19

FATHERS DAY

Happy Fathers Day!!!

"May your daily mantra be, 'No need for flowers at my funeral for I receive them daily from my kids while I live.'"

- Cedric R. Crawford -

Ahhhh, what an awesome day. I must admit that I always look forward to this special day. A day that I awaken in the morning with the words, "*Happy Fathers Day!*" followed by a big hug and kiss from all that occupy the household. As a self-proclaimed dedicated father, nothing makes me happier than knowing I'm truly loved by my four little munchkins.

I was hugging my oldest daughter Monique a few days ago and I told her that I was so proud of her. She said, "*For what?*" I replied. "*I'm proud of you for just breathing and knowing you're my daughter.*" She smiled and then we both laughed together as we shared a moment. I know that I'm not the only one that feels this way about my little contributions to this world. I'm sure there are millions of others out there that would give their right arm just to be able to hold their kids with their left arm. I do not take my good fortune for granted.

So, I say to you fathers, and *mothers who serve in the role as fathers,* may you be so fortunate to experience and receive the same love back to you that you give out to your little ones. May your days ahead be filled with smiles of pride and joy when you see their actions affirming in you that all you've taught them was good enough. And, may your daily mantra be, "*No need for flowers at my funeral for I receive them daily from my kids while I live.*"

Happy "*Fathers Day*" and "*Mothers who serve as Fathers Day*" to all that apply. Let's keep making it GREAT!

Dixie M.   *Great pictures...No words needed...the picture speaks Love.....and looks like you all have fun together too!*

June 20

Today's Your Day !!!

"May my words give you hope and encouragement to keep you steadfast and unmovable for just one more day."

- Cedric R. Crawford -

For that person who's struggling with adversity and feel like you're about to say "*uncle*" and throw in the towel and wave the white flag of surrender, may my words give you hope and encouragement to keep you steadfast and unmovable for just one more day.

For that person sitting on the fence of indecision about something that could possibly change your life, may my words give you that slight nudge of affirmation that says, "*no risk, no reward.*" And finally, for that person who is battling with the "*you*" of the past and feel like past temptations are quietly calling your name. Be encouraged today and know that you can endure and move closer to a better you because the new word that defines you is "*overcomer.*"

May these words empower all of you and remind you that indeed today is your day to be a conqueror and boldly move forward into your rapidly unfolding, positive future. So march on with confidence and make it GREAT!!!

Chris P.   *Just one more round. Just one more round.*☺

June 21

DISCIPLINE

D8

*"It's pretty tough to get out of trouble and become prosperous
with the same mind that got you in trouble."*

- Cedric R. Crawford -

Over the years I've come to realize that it's become increasingly harder to eat right when all the bad food taste so stinking good. It's also hard to buy healthy food when all the bad food is constantly on sale. And, it's even harder to get out of trouble and become prosperous with the same mindset that got you into trouble. The solution to all these issues have one thing in common, *"Discipline."* It took me a few times of repeating this lesson over the years before I learned it, hence I am reminded of the phrase, *"Lesson continued until lesson learned."*

We can't win without that *"discipline"* thing in our lives, so here's a friendly reminder today of my *"D8-Formula"* that states, *"Doing Daily Disciplines Daily Develops Dominance and Determines Destiny"* in life, without exception.

Simply put, if we want to continue to grow and experience real, positive change in our lives, we will have to upgrade our mental mindset and download some new software that will improve the way we think and the results we're getting in this *"Life"* thing. The way I see it is we all have only 24 hours in any given day and our daily disciplines will definitely determine whether or not we become better today than we were yesterday.

So, let's be found guilty of doing the difficult right disciplines over the easy wrong disciplines as we continue in our quest and attempt to make it GREAT!

Laurie A.   *Upon listening to my son's interpretation of Siddhartha...I read your quote and thought bingo....*

June 22

TRUST

Can you be Trusted?

"Kindness can turn your terror into a treat."

- Cedric R. Crawford -

As a 6-year-old kid, I distinctly remember being introduced to the water of a swimming pool by being tossed into the deep end by one of my dad's friends. This created in me a terror of deep water and as a result my heart would always start pounding harder and harder anytime I was attempting to approach the deep end of a pool. It took me several years, but after teaching myself to tread water and effectively hold my breath, eventually I overcame my first major fear. I now look back and applaud that little boy for not giving up and letting his fear win.

As an adult, I certainly didn't want my kids to have to deal with this kind of terror and fear of deep water. So, I chose to introduce my kids to the water by me first diving in and showing them that I could be trusted to be there for them when they did the same. The true feeling of knowing that someone trusts you with their life is priceless. I've found in life that if we establish trust first, everything else becomes so much easier. Conversely, if there's no trust in any situation or relationship, the door of tension, frustration and fear will be swung wide open.

All of my kids absolutely love the water now and it makes me smile knowing that I had something to do with that. So my question for you today is, *"Can you be Trusted?"* Hmmm… Make your plans and make it GREAT!

Mary C. K.   *As children we always knew we could trust Daddy's open arms.... what a wonderful feeling!*

DREAM

Unrealistic Dream

"Don't let others lack of vision cause a lack in your vision."
- Cedric R. Crawford –

As we approach yet another delight-filled day I would like to give you unbridled permission to have an *"Unrealistic Dream."* I believe if our goal is noble and of great significance we have to be comfortable with it being *"unrealistic"* in the eyes of most of those around us.

The thought that we could light up a room by the flip of a switch was definitely unrealistic for it's time, but Thomas Edison and his assistant, Tesla, dreamed it was possible. The idea that a human could achieve sustained flight in a cigar-shaped vehicle with wings was inconceivable to many, but the Wright brothers not only were conceived and believed it, they ACHIEVED it. The very notion that a person could communicate voice-to-voice with another person hundreds of miles away was nothing short of ludicrous and humorous, but Alexander Graham Bell and his trusted assistant Watkins weren't laughing. Despite the laughter and ridicule of the naysayers they worked to make it happen.

So, I say to you today, don't be discouraged if others don't believe in your goals and dreams or can't see your vision. To some they may seem esoteric and unrealistic for you to obtain, but don't let their lack of vision cause a lack in your vision.

Be sure to stay focused on your goals and dreams and keep your vision clear because cloudy vision can result in a rain on your parade. Believe it's possible and it then becomes possible for you. Got Goals? Got Dreams? Got Milk? Go get it and make it GREAT!

Jeff C.   *Great analogy!*

Please view the video on:

www.YouTube.com

<u>Search Code:</u> **Cedric R. Crawford – (2)**

June 24

Fathers Who Stay

*"Some fathers would give their right arm just for the chance to
be able to hold their kids with their left."*

- Cedric R. Crawford -

S tephanie R. *"Hello, I know I don't know you well but I am hoping you have a few words for some-one I care for deeply. You are always about "make life great!" (amazing by the way). I have an issue that I am asking you to just read and maybe help me give a few words. I am a proud mom of five and I love my man more than words can describe. He is an amazing father and friend. He has a history with the mother of his children involving drugs, he has gone through the medical and mental steps to get through but she hasn't. He needs some words as I think all single dads do. Can you please talk about being a dad even though you have an amazing wife! Maybe what you would do if you didn't have her. He is in envy of you. I just want him to know he is doing amazing!!! Thank you."*

Hi Steph. I'm fortunate to receive blessings from many sources in my life, but few are more special than the blessing of someone's request for my words of encouragement for another. Thank you for considering me, Steph. While reading your message a few minutes ago my mind immediately started to race through the archives of the many experiences I've been exposed to throughout my life. Here it goes…

To whom it may concern:

I've discovered in life that we men have many "rights" but very few "privileges." I've observed that one of the biggest privileges that most men take for granted is the privilege of being a father. I believe this privilege is given to us by our Creator and should not be skirted or taken lightly. For all those men, married or single, who have chosen to stay and be the man in that child's life, I say to you "Bravo!"

One of the secrets to being the perfect father is knowing and accepting the fact that we're anything but perfect. We refuse to let the world define the standards of what constitutes a great father because we know and understand that attempting to live up to the standards and approval of man will always disappoint. For that married or single father who's not sure if they're doing enough, don't fall into the trap of judging your adequacy or inadequacy by what your neighbor is doing. If you're there playing your active role and you're striving to do better and be better, you are definitely enough. Be encouraged today and know that in this life as a father you may be called many things, but inadequate you are not.

I have but one regret in life and that is I don't have the privilege to play a major active role in the life of my oldest daughter because she lives outside of the country at this time. It is for this reason I say, take advantage of your opportunities to have them close, because many fathers would give their *right* arm to just be able to hold them close daily with their *left* arm. Eyes straight ahead and keep leaning forward as you attempt to make it GREAT !!!

Stephanie R.   *"Thank you so much. I know he enjoyed reading this. We both had tears in our eyes. It is so very true that many people do take parent-hood for granted not just the father's out there. We are taking the* *necessary steps to try and make their mother see how extremely lucky she is just to have these beautiful little girls. I only hope that one day she will accept that just because they aren't together that it doesn't make him any less of a dad or man. I love the saying any man can be a father but it takes a real man to be a dad. I hold that true everyday and continually tell him he is amazing. I truly appreciate you taking the time and giving some words to him. He gets stronger and more certain of himself as the days go by. We are going to print this out so when he feels frustration or inadequacy he can get his little reminder. Again I Thank You. Stay amazing!!!"*

Just sharing my breadcrumbs trying to make if GREAT Stephanie.

To be continued…

DREAM

Our Dreams are NOT for SALE

"Take the barcode off of your goals and dreams and place them in the "priceless" glass case behind the counter."

- Cedric R. Crawford -

Over the past few years I've received several offers to partner with a few different companies or organizations. Some of the offers have been pretty significant however I've found that the company or product or service provided has nothing to do with my passions, goals and dreams. In fact, I've often realized that the activity would be more of a distraction than a help to me. I have the feeling that I'm not alone in this belief.

For those of you who can identify with me, I invite you to consider the following today. There are many of us who become easily distracted by "*good*" money at the expense of putting our goals and dreams on the shelf. Maturity in business and life has taught me that our dreams should not be for sale. "*More focused than ever*" should be our statement of the day and every day here forward.

So let's take the barcode off of our goals and dreams and place them in the "*priceless*" glass case behind the counter and stay focused on why we're really here. Found your "*Why*" yet? No need to answer out loud, just make me proud. One more day of focus and yet another step closer to that goal or dream as we all attempt to make this good day a GREAT DAY! NOT FOR SALE !!!

Dawn S.   *I love this Ced... I too have seen so many people sell out for a biz deal or money and they end up empty in the end anyway. Good word!! ;)*

Tony R.   *was told I should be living better by a friend...they couldn't understand my sacrifice for my goals n vision....Thanks Ced..*

Keep the Family Together

"Our 'thoughts' and 'ideas' are a happily married couple, and
their union gives birth to offspring called 'words.'"

- Cedric R. Crawford -

I took a glance at my wedding picture today and had this sudden *"hallelujah"* metaphorical moment of clarity. See if you can follow this:

Our *"thoughts"* and *"ideas"* are a happily married couple, and their union gives birth to offspring called *"words."* But these words are absolutely worthless without the brothers of consistent *"action"* and the actions have to be supported by the unwavering sisters of *"belief."* These sisters of belief are charged with the task of offering encouragement that accomplishing the goal of the original thoughts and ideas is possible.

Finally, ultimate success would not be possible without the Grandfather's watchful eye of *"commitment."* This commitment is the ability to keep the family together to see it through and to categorically refuse to settle for anything less than the goal of the original thoughts and ideas.

Failure can only exist in the absence of one of these vitally important family members. Keep this family unit together and watch your wildest dreams become reality. This may sound a little deep, but it makes perfect sense to me. I hope it helps you to make it GREAT!

June 27

Inner Confidence

*"Outward appearance can affect our level of confidence, but
our inner confidence level is even more important than anything we could possibly dress ourselves in."*

- Cedric R. Crawford -

I distinctly remember as a kid in elementary school I had two pair of pants I considered decent enough to where to school. During this time in Texas we were not allowed to wear shorts to school, so I would wear one pair of pants on Mondays, Wednesdays and Friday's and another pair on Tuesdays and Thursdays, hoping no one would notice. My favorite pair was the doo-doo brown colored dress slacks with the pleats in the front. I remember the extremely confident feeling I had when I was wearing them.

As a family always struggling to make ends meet, we couldn't afford much more than what we had. A few years later I moved up in grade level and I also wised-up. I had a buddy named Gene who lived a block away from me who was equally as underprivileged. We came up with a great idea to start sharing clothes, only there was one minor issue. Gene's parents were smokers which created a slight problem for my clothes.

Gene also had what we called a *"Jerry-Curl"* which also caused a problem for my clothes. A Jerry-Curl is the result of a process where African-American, wooly hair is made to be curly and it required a liquid solution product called, *"Curl Activator"* daily to keep the hair moist and curly. The problem with this was the curl activator managed to get onto everything including my clothes he borrowed. I remember spending a decent amount of time regularly trying to remove the curl activator and smoky smell from both of our clothing.   Gene also had a Michael Jackson *"Thriller"* and *"Beat-it"* jacket that I thought was the best thing since sliced bread, so I didn't want to pass up the opportunity to in-clude this in my wardrobe. All-in-all, I figured that being able to wear the type of clothing that made me feel more confident was an acceptable change-off.

Interestingly enough, as an adult I still find that what we think about our outward appearance's can really affect our level of confidence for the better or worse. In addition, I've also discovered that our inner confidence level is even more important than anything we could possibly dress ourselves in. Work on getting this one figured out and everything else is just icing on the cake. Look good, feel good and be good today and make it GREAT!

Lisa F.   *Cedric, I think I may remember those brown slacks---If they are the ones I am thinking of---you wore them to church too--LOL! Keep up the good work.*

June 28

TALK

Talk is CHEAP!

"Most say that 'Talk is Cheap', but I declare that this 'Talking' is absolutely necessary to start the process of change."
- Cedric R. Crawford -

I was working out at the gym today and I saw a guy on the treadmill doing what most people do on a treadmill, which is run a long time without ever getting anywhere. I must admit I think that a treadmill is a perfect metaphor. *"Most people"* spend their best years spinning their wheels day-in and day-out on the treadmill of life doing mundane, humdrum things that ultimately don't get them any further in life than the week before. Thank God that's not an *assigned* fate but it's a *resigned* fate.

This particular guy at the health club had on a shirt that had the words, *"Talk is CHEAP!"* on it. I cracked a smile as I read it, then I had a sudden thought that popped into my head. It's true that most people say *"talk is cheap"* but I declare *"talking"* is absolutely necessary to start the process of change. Yes my friends, our words are indeed powerful and it's the spoken words that initiate the process of change.

What words are you speaking today and everyday? Are you building a legacy with your *"life works"* or are you just spending your *"life working?"* Hmmmm…

Remember we only get one time through this *"Life"* thing, so if you haven't started the process of making it GREAT, it's time to get started. It's never too late to use these breadcrumbs to make it GREAT!

June 29

PAST AND FUTURE

Leave the Past in the Past

"The sooner you can rid yourself of the transgressions of yester-

day, the sooner you can embrace the triumphs of tomorrow."

- Cedric R. Crawford -

With every precious heartbeat we move further and further away from our past and into the open arms of our unfolding future. If you're feeling like your life is moving too slow or maybe not even moving at all, dare I say it may be because you're attempting to drag that past of yours with you. If this shoe fits you, I have three words of unsolicited advice for you today, *"LET IT GO!"*

The sooner you can let go of the past, the sooner you can start moving faster towards what is meant for you in your future. The sooner you can rid yourself of the transgressions of yesterday, the sooner you can embrace the triumphs of tomorrow. We've passed the test and challenges of our past and as a result, we have been made stronger and are better equipped to face the challenges of our unfolding future.

I've come to realize that our Creator is much more interested in what we do in the days ahead of us than what we've done in the days behind us. It's okay for us to give up on the hope or belief that the negative things that have happened to us or we've done in the past could have been different. Simply put, we can't un-spill the milk or unscramble the eggs of our past. So, just drink it up and eat it up so you can move on up to higher heights in your life. Giving up on this unrealistic hope of your past being different will definitely free you up to pursue the maximization of your full potential in the days ahead.

That which we endured and overcame in the past has made us what and who we are today and to undo the past would take it all away. We overcame and became something new as a result.

So, be encouraged today and know indeed our best days are still ahead of us. Let's continue to strive to better our best in the days ahead and leave the past in the past as we attempt to make the future GREAT!

June 30

MARRIAGE

Respect the Creative Process

"Your Dreams are not microwaveable, they require your time, treasures, talents and tears."

- Cedric R. Crawford -

Not log ago my beautiful bride Karen and I had the special opportunity to share a panel with two other couples at a MOPs Event (*Mothers Of Preschoolers*). I must say after 15 years of playing this marriage sport we're getting closer and closer to getting it right. We both believe that when it comes to the marriage preservation approach and style, one size doesn't necessarily fit all. One size may not even fit most. But one size fits us. As a panelist we made no claims to be so-called marriage experts or know-it-alls. However, we did extend an invitation for the attendees to take a peek at some of our tips, techniques and takeaways.

During our journey through this forest called *"marriage"* we've experienced our fair share of highs and lows, ups and downs and fights and rough nights. But through it all we've discovered a style that works for us and we understand all to well that the perfect marriage is not without its flaws, faults and fallacies.

We've found that the best marriages are built around positive intentional acts and a willingness to play fair and ultimately managing to have fun and not be too serious. Being stubborn enough to stick it out and stay when most others may walk away can be key too, and simply knowing when to shut up and say nothing can be magical.

A ton of fun it was to be a part of such an awesome event and great, down-to-earth panelist. As a self-proclaimed work-in-progress, I managed to take some good notes myself. I encourage you today in your marriages and relationships to be proactive instead of reactive and understand that a better marriage or better relationship starts with a better *"YOU."* I know these few breadcrumbs can be extremely beneficial in helping you to make your marriage and relationships GREAT!

Middle of the YEAR Bonus Words!!!

CHOICES

If a bird can be FREE, Why not me?

One day while sitting at my desk I looked out the window and noticed a bird flying by. This day was no different then any other day and this bird was no different then many others I've seen. But what was different was a sudden thought popped into my head that had never happened before. With all the different forms of life that inhabit earth, we as humans are the only species that have made a mental choice to give up our true freedom. No other species has to toil through a day with stressors that were created by their own hands. Now don't be so quick to checkout on me just yet. This thought may be one of the biggest *Breadcrumbs to Making it GREAT* yet. So hang in there with me on this one.

Thinking back since the beginning of time as we know it, we were created and endowed with many freedoms and over time we've chose to bridal those freedoms. We've swapped freedom for limiting structure that over time has evolved into a slave-like way of life. Our thoughts have, time after time, been captured and subdued and now conforms to a slave-like existence. The large majority of people in developed countries of this world will spend overwhelming portion of their lives going to a workplace where they often don't like the people or the work. They will compromise this dislike and discomfort in exchange for some form of currency. They will then budget their life and lifestyle around this currency and continue to live at the level that their respective currency affords while always seeking more. This action will usually continue until their senior years of life. Some will die before their work years are complete. Some will retire between age 65 and 72 and spend their last few years hoping they don't die before their money runs out.

What's wrong with this picture? Most people are so caught up in this matrix of *"in the box thinking"* that any suggestion that does not conform to this *"swapping hours for dollars"* way of thinking will be met with ferocious opposition. One thing is clear though, we definitely have been trained well. This slave way of thinking has been entrenched so far into the human psyche that nothing short of an all out revolution will change our world.

Everything in nature is free except our species. Again, this is to our own doing or undoing. Are we victims of progress or digress? We've become experts in the area of stress creation and confusion transfusion and nothing is more securely lodged then the ignorance of most of the so-called experts. If we believe we know it all, we don't see a need to learn anymore.

If that bird can be free, then why not me? This question starts the journey of knowledge of how true freedom is obtained. Was I making an impact or huge difference in this world on my job? Absolutely not. My job was filling a niche need creating profits for a money-hungry boss that could care less about positively impacting lives. So my search began.

What is true freedom? Well, true freedom as defined by me became the ability to choose when, what, where and how without fear of retribution. This is a very tall order, but that bird had it figured out. There's many possible courses to take to try to get to this level of freedom but most won't even start the journey. Don't be surprised because after all, its human nature. Or is it?

I believe human nature is for us to be free, but as we traverse through this *"life"* thing, we often-times become indoctrinated to believe otherwise. I humbly submit that we were born to be free, and we were programmed to be enslaved. Now is this anyone persons fault? To that I answer, *"Absolutely not."* It's a collective effort that has been perpetuated over time. The task of all task has now become, how do we extricate the affected people from their enslaved way of thinking. Stay with me here as I invite you to consider a few of my unsolicited suggestions.

After searching and researching, I found one common theme that exist in the lives of those who have achieved what I believe to be a true level of freedom. This quality transcends all other misdefined versions of true freedom. This element, if left out, true freedom will never be obtained. This component not only affords physical freedom, but it also nails the ever illusive target of freeing your mind. Is this possible you ask? Yes my friend it is.

This true freedom quality is woven into the very fabric of our being and will motivate us even when gold and silver loses its luster. This gem-of-a-find should be spelled out in gold lettering to emphasize its undying significance. What is this majestic nugget you ask? I'll preface the answer with a question; If time and money were no issue for you, what would you be doing with your time and your money? If all of your current financial obligations were no more and your wealth pit was deep as the day is long, what would make you smile daily? Human nature suggest that every answer to this question would include some level of helping someone else. Our deepest desire that's universally shared is we would want to, in some way shape or form, help other people on there journey. Yes, the most profound findings can be so simple.

The great news is we all have this *"helper-nugget"* buried deep inside of us. The problem lies in us not knowing how to get the time and money issue out of the way. A suggestion I might add is to find a community or organization to partner with that allows you to truly help others around you who share your passions and values about life. Then use your gifts to benefit and encourage them and as result, you will soon find yourself also being encouraged. Yes, building a community that advocates and perpetuates helping others is truly a gift that will keep on giving.

Are the fouls of the air special? Are the beast of the fields chosen? No. We have the same endowments. We have choices in spite of what the world around us suggest. Please don't kill the messenger today, but please do consider killing-off the old way of thinking if needed. You can choose to be free and pursue true freedom by following that passion of yours. I'm trying to change the world one person at a time and I'm one person behind. Are you interested? I think we need a freedom revolution. Let's role!!!

by Cedric R. Crawford

July 1

Embrace Technology for "*Good*"

*"A tool is neither good nor bad, it's what we choose to do with
the tool that determines what it is."*

- Cedric R. Crawford -

I was hanging out in one of my favorite spots for relaxation yesterday, the hot tube at In-Shape Fitness Health Club, and I met a guy named Steve. Steve is a "*do-everything*" type of guy at one of the local churches in the area. He was sharing with me how happy he was with having the opportunity to positively affect the lives of the youth at his church. I then asked Steve if he had a "*Facebook*" presence and the look on his face was priceless. He emphatically said, "*Noooo, I don't believe in that stuff.*" I said, "*You mean you don't believe in social media?*" and he again said, "*Noooo, that stuff is nothing but trouble.*" This was not the first time I've heard this from someone who had been either misinformed or inadequately informed about social media.

Steve went on and on about how much damage Facebook, MySpace, Craigslist and others are causing in the world community. After letting him express himself for a few minutes, I then asked him what he thought about money and whether he thought it was good or bad. He then said, "*Money can be used to do good things or bad things.*" I agreed with him and then further stated that money is neither good nor bad, it's just a tool and some choose to use it for good and others choose to use it for not-so-good. He nodded his head and voiced his agreement.

I then told him to use the same scenario and replace money with "*Social Media.*" Social media is just a tool of the latest technology and we can choose to use it for good or not-so-good. I cautioned him further to not make the mistake of turning a blind eye to how this medium can be leveraged for good. At this point I could see that a light went on in Steve's head and he immediately changed his opinion and said, "*You know what, your absolutely right.*" I must admit it feels good to be right sometimes.

I told Steve briefly about what I was doing in the area of social media and encouraged him to create a presence in social media too and how he could use it to sow *good* into the congregation at his church. He was visibly pleased with the suggestion and stated he would definitely look into it further. We both agreed that our meeting was no accident.

You'd be surprised what you can learn or discover in a hot tube at an In-Shape Fitness Center if you just say "*Hi*" to a stranger and lend an ear. I'm eagerly waiting for Steve to "*friend*" me on Facebook. ☺ Make it GREAT!

Karen B.   *...encounters with You do that to People.*

NOTES

July 2

FOOD FOR THOUGHT

Your Special Day

"You're only as old as your mind thinks."

- Cedric R. Crawford -

Over the years I've noticed an interesting dichotomy in terms of the process of aging. Most of us as kids feel the need to look older and act older and we will often times adjust our age up a year or two or six. I remember I used to use my mom's black eyeliner to lightly color my peach-fuzz mustache in hopes it would make me look a bit older. I used to harbor a bit of jealousy for the boys in my school who were blessed to have facial hair early. But as an adult I realized that growing up and maturing mentally has absolutely nothing to do with body and facial hair and we usually will reach a point where we no longer want to look older. In fact, most will often times start to reduce their age or even refuse to talk about it at all.

After giving it some thought, I'm of the opinion that the age-comfortable-years seem to be somewhere between 21 and 29. Hmmm… I haven't yet been able to quite figure this behavior and phenomenon out yet to articulate an explanation in words, but I'm working on it. However, I do know our minds appear to be incapable of recognizing age and are only capable of recognizing levels and degrees of knowledge and wisdom. So, this appears to lend a bit of credence to my newly created saying, "*Your only as old as your mind thinks.*" Just a little food for thought for that mind of yours today.

Oh, Happy Birthday to my bride Karen! Of course this comment doesn't apply to you sweetheart. May you make this day as special as you are, twenty-one for the twenty-fourth time.

Be sure to make your special day special too as you grow-up while growing old. Make it GREAT!

July 3

MONEY

For the Love of Money

"Money as a primary motivator will ultimately disappoint over time, guaranteed."

- Cedric R. Crawford -

I was talking to this friend of mine a few weeks ago I hadn't seen in over twelve years. During our conversation she shared with me she had just recently changed jobs and her sole reason for the change was she would be making $1 more per hour. She stated that she absolutely loved her previous job and the people there but she was a struggling single parent of a one-year-old, which made the $1 temptation too good to pass-up. Well, after her first few days on the new job, she knew she had made a big mistake. Her days went from being busy with productivity to doing almost nothing at all for eight hours. She went from a boss who loved what she was doing to a boss who was sexually harassing her and degrading her almost daily. Yes the pay was more, but the cost was too great. She expressed that she felt trapped because she couldn't get another job right away and she couldn't go back to her old one.

After hearing her heart, "*What did you learn from this?*" was my question to her. She said that she felt she had compromised the quality of her daily life for an extra $160 a month and that she would never again let money be the primary reason for any future decisions. I told her most lessons about money usually come after people have lost money, but in her case at least she didn't lose money. I further assured her she would recover from this lesson and to use her idle time at work to put together a plan to change her situation and circumstance.

I'm happy to report she formulated an awesome plan and left her job after receiving a multiple-month severance package and was later hired by an employer that she loves and appreciates again.

Life indeed comes at you fast and hard and the lure of money can jade us all sometimes. I believe money as a primary motivator will ultimately disappoint over time, guaranteed. But take heart that if we commit to not let money be the primary factor in our decision making process, we have a much better chance of being happier in this "*life*" thing. Another great breadcrumb to making it GREAT.

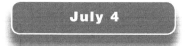

July 4

HOLIDAY INDEPENDENCE DAY

Happy Independence Day

"The only freedoms we lose are the ones we give away to others in power."

- Cedric R. Crawford -

Be sure to celebrate this 4th of July as if our natural freedoms are under attack, because they are. Be advised that the only freedoms we lose are the ones we give away to others in power. You don't have to look very far to see other countries that have stripped their citizens of their inalienable rights and God-given freedoms in the name of some distorted version of unity, safety and stability. A great man once said, "*He who is willing to give up his freedoms for safety deserves neither freedom nor safety.*" I couldn't agree more.

We must safeguard our freedoms as this is one of the most precious commodities one can possess. Thank you Lord for the freedoms we enjoy as you have bestowed upon us and please restore those who have had the misfortune of having them stripped away.

Be safe today as you rise and fall under the freedoms made possible by the sacrifice of an unknown number who paid the ultimate price so we American's may continue to celebrate on this day. Let's continue to make it GREAT!

Chris P.   *Amen! "To sin by silence when they should protest makes cowards of men." ~ Abraham Lincoln 16th US President. Happy 4th!*

July 5

HONESTY

Call Their Bluff

"Honesty truly is the best policy because if they call your bluff,
the jig is up."

- Cedric R. Crawford -

I remember driving home to Dallas, Texas from my college at the University of Utah in Salt Lake City to pay my parents a surprise visit during my summer break in the year of 1992. I did the 1,292 mile drive in just under 20 hours straight. My little charcoal grey Hyundai GLS 4-door Sedan didn't have an air-conditioner, but dollar-for-dollar it was one of the most reliable vehicles I've ever owned.

I remember I would always carry my fake toy gun underneath my seat just in case I ended up in a bad situation. The original color of the gun was bright orange when I bought it at Smith's Grocery store in Utah, but I later spray-painted it a flat-black color. It really did look convincing from at least three feet away.

After making the long trip home without incident, I arrived at about 4:30 am jazzed up on caffeine. I snuck into the house and just sat there on the couch staring at the ceiling waiting for Mom and Dad to wake up to find me in the living room. My little brother found me first and I was still able to preserve the element of surprise for my parents. I always got a kick out of seeing their faces when I just walked into the room and jumped into the bed with them. Ahhhh, those were great times…

I hung out with my little eleven-year-old brother, Patrick, all day and at the end of the late night we found ourselves at a Burger King drive-thru located on the corner of Singleton and Industrial Blvd near the west edge of downtown Dallas. After ordering our usual cheese Whoppers with fries and strawberry milk shakes, we noticed a strange man approaching my car. He appeared to be a homeless man with the usual tattered clothing and long scraggly beard and afro with a raggedy ball cap.

He stumbled over to the passenger side of the car, leaned over and asked the usual question, *"Can you spare some change for me to get a bus ticket to Oak Cliff?"* He was about three feet away from the car but even that distance couldn't mask the odor of booze and BO. I immediately said, *"Hey, we're headed that way so why don't you just hop on in the back seat and we'll take you on over there with us."* After hearing this, the look on Patrick's face was priceless. Knowing that we live in west Dallas and this homeless guy was trying to get to Oak Cliff which would be across town from us, Patrick looked over at me and abruptly exclaimed in a whisper, *"What!? Noooo man… Are you serious!?"* I cracked a casual smile and quietly reassured Patrick that everything would be alright, after all, I had a gun just in case I needed it. The guy then said, *"No, no, I don't want you to go through that trouble, I can just take the bus."* I said, *"There's no trouble, we're going that way anyway, so just hop on in."*

The guy kept insisting that I just give him the money, but I continued to offer him the ride. Finally the guy just walked away mumbling to himself. Patrick looked at me with this puzzled look on his face, as if to say, *"You're crazy."* I then told him that if the guy's intent was really to go to Oak Cliff, he would have attempted to get into the car to ride with us, then I would've told him that I would give him the money for the bus ride. "*It's best to just be honest because if people call your bluff, the jig is up. Calling his bluff allowed me to see his true intentions,*" I said.

"*Ohhhhh…*" said Patrick, "*I get it now. Man you sure are smart!*" We laughed together and drove on home eating our Whopper and fries and sucking down our shakes. I didn't miss my opportunity to show Patrick that day that honesty is indeed the best policy and calling somebody's bluff can expose their real intentions. I wonder if Patrick still remembers this incident. Hmmmm.

Don't miss your opportunities to reach one and teach one as we all pay our lessons learned forward to our fellowman and woman. Just another small breadcrumb to make it GREAT!

July 6

DON'T QUIT

Hang In There

> "*If you commit to hang-in-there through the tough times and uncomfortable moments, eventually success will show up for you.*"
>
> *- Cedric R. Crawford -*

I was having a conversation with one of my neighbor's high school age kids today about football. He was telling me that he spent his entire freshman season as a backup player and didn't get much playing time at all. As a result, he advised me that he was not planning on returning to the field the next season. After hearing this, I felt that I had to say something about his decision. Here's a sneak peek at what I said to him: "*What would've happened if you would've quit school in kindergarten? Well, you definitely wouldn't have reached the 10th grade. I guess it's fair to say that you kinda hung-in-there until it all started to make sense and work out for you. Well little guy, it's the same for football. In the beginning it may not seem like fun at times, but if you hang-in-there, you'll eventually start to like it, then eventually you may even start to love it.*"

"*I played football for 16 years of my life, but few people know that I quit football my 2nd year because I didn't like it. At the end of the season my mom and dad made me go to the awards banquet and I had to watch my brothers and friends all get their awards. It was then that the enormity of my decision hit me right square between the eyes. I'll never forget sitting there in a pool of regret while I watched them get their awards with a smile. It was then that I made a pact with myself and vowed to never quit again. After months of practicing and working on my game, I eventually became pretty good at the sport and started to like it. Then I started to love it. Then it ended up changing my life. So today you have to ask yourself did you quit too soon.*"

Well unfortunately, not every story has a happy desired outcome, but he did say that he will give it some more thought. To be continued… I'll keep you posted.

Be advised that in life we can't always start off being the best at something, but if we commit to hang-in-there through those tough and rough times and uncomfortable moments, eventually success will show up. So keep hanging-in-there and make it GREAT!

Please view the video on:

www.YouTube.com

Search Code: Cedric R. Crawford – (5)

July 7

PERSISTENCE

A Game of Dog and Bird

"Never let your vigilant-guard down and never ever give up on your worthwhile goal."

- Cedric R. Crawford -

everyone's heard of playing a game of *"Cat and Mouse,"* but how about a game of *"Dog and Bird?"* I captured this special photo a few days ago and just had to share it with you. Everyday without fail the birds from around the area take advantage of a free meal courtesy of my two Blue-Queensland Healers, Sophie and Cody's dog food bowls. These birds are usually extremely cautious and quick and day after day they're vigilance has scored them the spoils of success.

In spite of this fact, Sophie and Cody continue to try to defend their food, but the birds are just too quick and always manage to get away. But not this time! After failing hundreds of times before, Sophie's persistent effort finally paid off. One of the birds made the grave mistake of letting its vigilant guard down and Sophie pounced scoring a dramatic kill. Sophie was so excited that you would've thought that she had won the Eukanuba Doggy-Olympics. She barked and rolled and barked and rolled some more over her prey as if to bathe herself in the glory of victory.

After watching through the window witnessing this event, I couldn't help but to see the direct parallel to life. Today the comfort of complacency caused a harmless bird its life and the unrelenting persistence of a dog resulted in massive success. I know this is not a *"G-Rated"* scenario, but this double life lesson is a good one.

Never let your vigilant-guard down and never ever give up on your worthwhile goal. Don't miss the message here today. Let's stay the course and be persistent until we WIN! Make it GREAT!

Rene L.   *What a great story! (Tear jerker)*

July 8

Those Dang Trees

"Tune-out so you can tune-in."

- Cedric R. Crawford -

I was trying to see the forest but those dang trees kept getting in my way. It wasn't until I rose above it all that the view became clear and free of noise and obstructions. I've found that when we turn down or tune out the noise in our life, it is then we can hear the sound of the quiet whispers of wisdom and the little lessons of life hidden in plain sight in the simplest of things around us.

There are gentle messages of genius on the breath of the wind and ripples of the smallest signs and signals riding on the rays of the sun. I know this sounds a bit deep, but you'd be surprised what you'd hear and discover if you just make the slightest of efforts to just be still and listen.

We must always find some time to tune-out so we can tune-in. Failing to do so will in most cases result in a life that is chaotic, frustrating and full of unfulfilled goals and dreams. This is just one of the many keys and breadcrumbs to making 'it' GREAT. Let's continue to honor our commitment to making this life GREAT!!!

Jabo B.   *Life hidden in plain sight.....that was one of my revelations last year! I like the way you think! In fact it was that revelation that has inspired me to begin writing.*

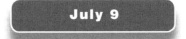

July 9

FOCUS

A Task Such as This

"There are none of this world greater than he who is masterful at bringing out the greatness in others."

- Cedric R. Crawford -

When adversity strikes are you able to *"put up your dukes,"* stand your ground and mount a fierce defense? The greatest among us are those who when adversity strikes, they are able to rise to the occasion because they operate under an unwavering belief they were built and designed for a *task such as this.* The greatest among us are able to still see clearly the goal even when the fog of fear and frustration roles in because of their exceptional ability to remain focused.

Those who are greatest among us understand their role is to inspire, motivate, encourage and stimulate others to be great in times of adversity and uncertainty. There are none of this world greater than he or she who is masterful at bringing out the greatness in others. So the question today is, *"Are you a Great one?"* Chew on this food for thought for a while and be honest with the man or woman in the mirror.

Let's continue to stay focused as we wrap our hands around the throat of this life and choke it until it gives us what we want. Let's continue to make it GREAT!

July 10

SERVICE

Hands to Serve

"You're never too young or never too old to use your gifts to serve and help a few souls."

- Cedric R. Crawford -

I had the awesome opportunity to deliver a message to a group of over 300 yesterday and had a great time doing it as usual. This is truly my area of passion and purpose and I do not take it for granted. The message of the day was *"Using your Gifts to Serve others"* and highlighting the fact that *"Most People"* don't. A great man once said that our *"service"* is the rent we pay to occupy a space on this earth. It took me a number of years to understand this principle fact, but I finally got it and I absolutely love sharing it with others.

The audience was one of the best and I wish I could take them on the road with me. The interesting thing is I always find it quite easy to get people in the audience to raise their hands or clap their hands, but I realize that getting them to *"use"* their hands to serve others is a whole different story.

The thought of the day was, "*You're never too young or never too old to use your gifts to serve and help a few souls.*" I think they got the message. Don't you miss it. At least not today. Find that gift and leverage it in service to the masses and then stand back and watch what happens in return. I don't believe in magic, but this will definitely be a magical moment when it all starts to fall in place for you.

Let's continue to use our hands the best way we can "*to serve*" our fellowman. Yet another small breadcrumb to making it GREAT!

Joyce W. V.	*I got it!*
Jabo Baldwin	*Love it!*
David C.:	*Prayers answered.*

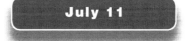

July 11

GREATNESS

Let Their Light Shine

"Become masterful at letting others light shine around you and its then you will experience the increased intensity of your own light."

- Cedric R. Crawford -

I was hanging out with a great group of friends not long ago sharing and swapping some great conversation over an awesome platter of Mexican food. We managed to do a lot of laughing and smiling as we swapped stories and ideas of different interest and desires. I honestly can never get enough of this type of adult interaction. To watch the fire and passion in the eyes of others as they share their thoughts, successes, goals and dreams never gets old for me.

Over time, I've discovered in life there's nothing more rewarding and gratifying than surrounding yourself with great people who have great hearts and are great at what they do. Then topping it off with a fostering environment where you encourage each other to be great, for as we all should know by now, there's no one greater than he/she who makes and allows others to be great.

I'm reminded of an old Southern Baptist church hymn I used to sing as a kid, *This little light of Mine*. The lyrics are as follows: "*This little light of mine. I'm gonna let it shine…*" For these purposes as an adult, I've found we must become masterful at helping other's light to shine around us and it is then we will experience the increased intensity of our own light. This truth falls under the "*Give and Receive*" category, so don't miss the message today as you attempt to light the path for others who sometimes see no light at the end of their tunnel. Yes, this is yet another breadcrumb to making it GREAT!

July 12

MONEY

Can money make you happy?

"It's not the money that makes you happy, it's what you choose to do with the money that determines your happiness."

- Cedric R. Crawford -

All my life I've heard the comment, "*Money doesn't make you happy*." The interesting thing was that most of the people who were repeating this statement never really had much of it in their lives and they spent most of their waking hours chasing more of it. To the untrained eye this behavior could definitely cause a bit of confusion and definitely I had an untrained eye at that time. So, I was eager to find out for myself.

During the height of the real estate boom during the years 2002-2007 the city of Bakersfield, CA was in the top one and two spots for property value appreciation in the country. It just so happens my wife and I had made our part-time business in the area of real estate and had several dozen properties before and during this time. Almost over night we saw our small six-figure a year business increase to a six-figure a month business. Our *smart* work had finally paid off and people thought we were geniuses, but the only thing we had done was position ourselves to benefit from the enormous real estate growth.

At this time money became overwhelmingly plentiful. The more we made, the more we'd give to our church, family, schools, our tenants and even perfect strangers in need. My wife and I then accomplished the goal of designing and building our own multi-million dollar luxury dream home. We started to take more family trips to see my family in Texas and fun trips to exotic places and theme parks for fun and taking people along with us. During this process the things that made me the happiest was watching others experience happiness and knowing that I had a little something to do with making it possible.

Finally, I had found out for myself first hand that it's not the money that makes you happy, it's what you choose to do with the money that matters most. Money will come and go but true happiness is what I know. We don't have anywhere near as much money as we once did, but happiness has not eluded me.

Simply put, money is just a tool and can be used for good or not-so-good means. Having money just gives you the option to do more of the things that make you happy, like giving and creating for those who are less fortunate. Money also has a knack for uncovering the true you that's underneath, either good or not-so-good. So if you're a mean, hateful, nasty person, money will make you more of the same. Conversely, if you're a sweet, loving, giving person money will intensify the sweet flavor of the loving and giving of you too.

Don't abuse your money tool. I invite you to choose to put it to good use today. It really is your choice so choose wisely. Let's choose to leverage that money tool of ours for "good" as we continue in our efforts to make it GREAT!

July 13

AVERAGE

Anything but "Average"

"The world needs 'non-average' people like us sprinkled around
to insert flowers where weeds are trying to grow."

- Cedric R. Crawford -

Ever heard the phrase, "*Misery loves company?*" Well, I ran into one of misery's cousins named "*Complainy*" a few days ago and found out that complainy loves company too. As I was standing in line at the local grocery store the woman in front of me started complaining to me about how slow the store clerk was moving. She was visibly surprised when I made an uplifting comment with a smile. I gently stated how hard the clerk's job must be when so many people arrive at the same time and they're all in a hurry to get to their next destination. She definitely didn't expect that statement to come from me.

In life, I've found these types of incidents to be common and I don't think I'm alone. I've also discovered the easiest conversations to engage in with strangers are the ones where they're complaining about something and for some odd reason politics seem to top the list as the most popular. It's easy for the "*average*" person to add to the fray by complaining too, but much tougher for the "*average*" person to be creative and insert a positive, uplifting comment while smiling.

It appears to me that shared conflict has a knack for bringing people together for a journey down a road of complaining. May I humbly suggest that we not go down that road? The world needs *"non-average"* people like us sprinkled around in many areas to capitalize on the many opportunities to insert flowers of positivity where weeds of negativity are trying to grow.

So, I invite you to join me today and everyday hereafter in being anything but *"Average."* Before partnering up with the cousins, Misery and Complainy, ask yourself, *"What would the average person do?"* and then do just the opposite. Don't miss the message today. Let's continue to lean forward and be the example as we attempt to make it GREAT.

"AVERAGE?" I think not.

Claudia A. S.	*Great message! Thanks for sharing it!*
Henjathang T. S.	*"Go ye!" :)*
Teresa M. C.	*Awesome reminder.... Thanks!*

Bonus DAY 7!!!

PERSEVERANCE

Do it Anyway…

When you feel like doing the right thing will make others think that you're strange, do it anyway.

When no one else will speak up and say what needs to be said, speak up anyway.

When what's right isn't popular and what's popular isn't right, do the right thing anyway.

When there's not much to smile about, smile anyway.

When crying may show others that you're weak and vulnerable, cry anyway.

When it's easy to do the wrong thing when no one is looking, do the difficult right thing anyway.

When obstacles seem insurmountable, press on anyway.

When it becomes unpopular to stand up for your beliefs and values, stand up anyway.

When people you share the same last name with say you're crazy for pursuing your passion and dreams, pursue them anyway.

When it becomes difficult financially and emotionally to stay the course, stay the course anyway.

When the fight seems futile and unwinnable, fight on anyway.

When others say it can't be done, may that quiet, still voice inside of you scream out, "SHUT UP!" and do it ANYWAY!

by Cedric R. Crawford

July 14

PAIN AND SUFFERING

Enduring Chronic Pain

"We are indeed capable of accomplishing and enduring great things, even in the area of suffering."

- Cedric R. Crawford -

Meet the lovely Esther Flores. This picture captures the essence of her bright eyes and smile to match. Her hair is always flawless and she's always nicely dressed when I see her. A great friend she has been to me and my family and all those she has come into contact with over her almost sixty years on this earth. As calm, cool and collected as all appears to be on her surface, you would never know that she's been dealing with chronic pain over the last 17 years.

The last two years have been chronic, never-ceasing, excruciating pain that frequently causes her to lose focus. Normal things that most people take for granted like balancing a checkbook would take her hours to do and sometimes a couple of days. Her nights are spent trying to negotiate a temporary truce with her pain just long enough for her to experience a small amount of natural sleep without the assistance of medication. Yet, in spite of all she endures and suffers through she still manages to cling to her independence as best she can.

From countless doctor visits, to acupuncture, massages, pills, powders, liquids, shots, etc., she has invested a small fortune in her quest for relief but all to no avail. To date she describes the migraines as the worst toothache, earache or headache you've ever had and it never goes away. She does not want to burden those around her with her constant grimace or complaining, so she struggles daily to stay positive. Thoughts of suicide have been visited on numerous occasions but she figures there must be a better plan for her life if she's still here. When asked how she manages to get through the day, she credits her ability to endure with her unshakeable faith and spiritual relationship with God. She understands that God never promised us we would live life without the pain and sorrows and struggles of tomorrow, but he did promise that he would be with us. She clings daily to God's promises and although she may not understand the meaning of it all, she finds comfort in the hope that tomorrow will be just a little bit better than today. She says, *"My daily prayer to God is, if it's not your will to remove the pain, then continue to give me the strength to endure and the ability to experience joy in the moments in spite of the pain."*

Esther says with tears in her eyes, *"For those people who are out there suffering as I do, I want them to know that they're not alone. God continues to help me and he can help them too if they trust that he knows what he's doing and lean not to their own understanding. We can do all things through Christ who strengthens us."*

Esther's example in my life has been without parallel to date and I can't begin to imagine her chronic pain. Her story of tolerance, endurance and undying faith should be a lesson to us all that we are indeed capable of accomplishing and enduring great things, even in the area of suffering. To you, Esther, I offer the most sincere thanks for your example and may we all be inspired by your continuous struggle.

Let's all continue to count our hidden blessings as we attempt to make it GREAT!

July 15

FAIRNESS

Life's Not Fair

"The biggest disservice we could ever exact upon our kids is to shelter and shield them from failure, loss and adversity in life."
- Cedric R. Crawford -

Being a devoted father of four I've discovered over the years that one of the worst things we can do to our kids as parents is to paint them a rose-colored picture of life. I feel that one of the biggest disservices we could ever exact upon our kids is to lead them to believe life is fair. We must not make the classic mistake of attempting to shelter, shield and safeguard them against failure, loss and adversity. There are huge, invaluable lessons and messages in those challenges, and avoiding them places our kids at a significant disadvantage out the starting gate of life.

Our daily prayer for our kids should be, "*Lord, please protect our little ones 'through' all hurt, harm, danger and adversity and when they fall, please give them the strength to rise, recover and realize the lesson in it all.*" This type of prayer acknowledges that we understand that challenges are a way of life and without them we can not grow. Nope, life isn't always fair and some people's struggles are more intense than others, but we all have our individual cross to bare and lessons to learn. So my good word today is to learn those lessons fast and understand the struggle is necessary to succeed at anything in this "*life*" thing. No doubt this is a good breadcrumb to making it GREAT! So, let's make it GREAT!

NOTES

July 16

We Pray NOT

"Lord, we're not asking for much. Just give us the ability to use the ability you've given us to the best or our ability and we'll settle for the results."

- Cedric R. Crawford -

on't forget today that we pray not for our mountains to be moved, but for the strength to climb them. We ask not for our stumbling blocks to be taken away, but for the wisdom to recognize them and go around. And, we make no such request for our life to be *"Easy,"* but for the resilience and focus and tenacity to hang in there and overcome when it's *"Hard."*

Lord, we're not asking for much. Just give us the ability to use the ability you've given us to the best or our ability and we'll settle for the results. Don't wait to make it GREAT!

July 17

Bearing Positive Fruit?

"Like fruit, our lives too will be of no real consequence unless someone is able to taste and experience our knowledge and wisdom."

- Cedric R. Crawford -

I was hanging out with my other set of boys at the group-home a couple of days ago investing a little time with what I call my *"extended family."* I was sitting outside under a peach tree watching the boys play dodgeball and a peach suddenly fell right into my lap. I thought it was a bit strange that of all the places that peach could've fell, it just so happened to land on me. Any normal person would've probably just tossed it aside and moved on with life, but as you should know by now, I'm anything but *"normal."*

This actually got me to thinking. In many ways our lives are just like a piece of fruit hanging on a tree. We are suppose to receive all of our nutrients from the tree itself, which is like our parents, mentors or role-models and then we're dropped and released out into the world to hopefully make a positive difference and bear more fruit. The sad and unfortunate reality is as I looked on the ground that day, there was tons of fruit that were just going to waste and rotting into the earth.

Like the fruit, our lives too will be of no real consequence unless someone is able to taste and experience our knowledge and wisdom. We must refuse to let the best parts of us be absorbed back into the dirt of the earth. We must be intentional about enriching the lives of others. We must make an honest effort to let others taste and see what we have to offer and sow positivity into our fellow-man and woman and encourage them to do the same.

It breaks my heart to know that the overwhelming majority of the kids in group-home settings like my boys will probably fall short of making any real positive contribution to our society because of a shortage of others who would genuinely show an interest in enriching their lives. I employ you today to not let your life be that peach that never left the shade and comfort of the shadows of the tree from which it was birthed. Don't let the soil of the earth claim your seed of greatness and gifts and internal treasures. Go forth today and bear positive fruit for the ages by sharing your time, talent, treasures and stories with others around you both young and not-so-young.

In a world full of distractions and noise, our kids need us now more than ever before to help them to focus on what really matters in this "life" thing. It's up to us to show them the true meaning of "No child left behind." Let's not let 'em down. Not today. Let's bear positive fruit and make it GREAT!

James B. Jr.   *That's a strong message brother and kudos to you for giving back and reaching back to help someone else's child aside from doing a wonderful job of raising your own. Keep being a blessing to others. That's why GOD continually has his hand on you and has ordered your steps thus far. Make it a blessed week!!!!!*

July 18

STRUGGLE

Ups and Downs

"Celebrate the feeling of triumph in the ups and passionately embrace the lessons in the downs."

- Cedric R. Crawford -

I've learned over the years that if there were no downs in life, we wouldn't have anything to look up to. Winning would feel empty and void of any real significance if we didn't know how it felt to lose. And without experiencing the failures in life, success would have half its value and just "suc" (suck). These types of contrast are absolutely necessary in life and without them life would fall short in the "make sense" category.

It may be of some comfort to know that even the best among us have their fair share of ups and downs occasionally. I've found that the very definition of life has to incorporate the reality of ups and downs, if not, it's fair to say you're probably dead. So as a result, I invite you to consider the following thought today and understand that your current position in life, up or down, is simply just part of the process of life. The down days can build character and resilience, and the up days can build confidence and self-esteem.

So, I invite you today to join me as we choose to celebrate the feeling of triumph in the ups and passionately embrace the lessons in the downs on our way to living a life that matters. Let's continue in our quest to Make it GREAT!

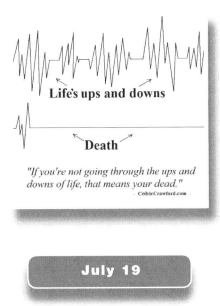

July 19

The Marriage Menu

*"Be sure that special someone will love you for the good, the
bad, the happy, the sad, the calm and the mad."*

- Cedric R. Crawford -

I was thinking a little about marriage and family today while viewing this picture and the following thought came to mind.

Before taking the plunge or jumping the broom into that blissful institution of "*Marriage*," be sure that special someone will love you for the good, the bad, the happy, the sad, the calm and the mad.

They'll stick around through the broke, the rich, the mansion or ditch and healthy or sick they won't through a fit.

During the times you can't have your way be stubborn enough to stay and trust that it'll all be Ok if you just make it through the day.

The old, the new and the times when you don't have a clue, they'll still love you and commit to work it through.

Yep, I know that's a tall order on the marriage menu and the bill may be a little bit steep, but this is just a small tip for those who are dining out and shopping for that special someone.

And for those of you who already have that special someone and are maybe feeling like that special someone isn't so special anymore, I've found that this "*Marriage*" thing works best when you play it like a sport. So, play fair as you play to win as a two-person team. This is a very important breadcrumb to making your marriage and relationship GREAT!

Lorette L.   *We can't ask for anything more out of life, than a good family that sticks together, and loves together. That's why we are here, that's what we all want....unconditional Love. :)*

July 20

Focus

In Due Time

"'In due time' is the reward for those who embody and possess the rare ability to stay focused and disciplined through the various processes of life's changes and challenges."

- Cedric R. Crawford -

"In due time" is the reward for those who embody and possess the rare ability to stay focused and disciplined through the various processes of life's changes and challenges. Those who are capable of continuing to see clearly their goal and staying the course in spite of the occasional fog of finances, fear and frustration will fair well in their favorable future.

The fearless few who are able to function consistently at a high level in the absence of a task master will eventually reap the rewards and experiences shared only by a distinguished minority. So the question today is, "*Do you see yourself as part of this distinguished minority group?*" Do you feel you can be counted on when others are being counted out? Do you feel you have what it takes to stay the course and make it GREAT in spite of what your physical eyes may see all around you? Hmmm...

Being exceptional is simple but it's not easy. The steps to subduing this life in the days ahead and bending it to your will and making it GREAT is simple but the process is not easy. Are you willing to travel where few are willing to tread? Are you willing to do at least one thing different today that will set you on the course to positively changing your tomorrow? Are you willing to take one focused, daily discipline, action-step today and everyday that will move you one step closer to that goal or dream of yours? Hmmm...

There's a toolbox that is designed to help you uncover and discover the keys to shift your career, your business and your life into high gear-overdrive toward becoming better and keep it there indefinitely even while you're sleeping. That toolbox is called, "*Bread Crumbs to Making it GREAT.*"

CONGRATULATIONS!!! If you've made it this far in the book you have just separated yourself from the overwhelming majority of those who purchased the book then put it on the shelf with the others after reading only the first few pages. The business of life has a way of bullying us all at times and forcing us into a life of survival instead of *thrival*. Don't let it happen to you. Not this time.

So continue to defy the laws of the "*Most People*" Syndrome and recommit today to keep this book and others like it close by you for quick reference. For only the proper application of this information, motivation, inspiration and education can result in a transformation and lead you to your desired destination. So keep going, your half way there. Yes, these bread crumbs can lead you to making it GREAT if you let them. Keep making it GREAT!

> *(If you made it this far in the book, I'd like to add you to a special, personal list of mine that will be given access to exclusive slight-edge information or other valuable tips, tools and takeaways at low to NO cost to you. This is just my small reward to you for being exceptional. So, email me at TheBook@CedricCrawford.com to be added to my list and continue to make it GREAT! You'll be glad you did.)*

July 21

CRISIS

What will they say about you?

"Our gratitude and service to others opens the door for us to attract what we desire most in life."

- Cedric R. Crawford -

Five years from now will others look back and say that you were a great source of encouragement and hope, or will others say you needed a great source of encouragement and hope? Will you be remembered for what you did to help others to survive and thrive in these turbulent times or will you be remembered for the things you chose not to do to help others through their struggle. Are you building people up, or thinking only about numero uno lately?

I've learned that our gratitude and service to others opens the door for us to attract what we desire most in life. We're the only ones who have control over how people will view us a few years from now. Lets make the choice today to make sure that others will have only positive memories of what we did when times of crisis and uncertainty reared its ugly head and became widespread. Keep making those great choices as you continue in your efforts to make this life GREAT!

July 22

RECOGNITION AND
RELATIONSHIPS

The Secret PR Juggernaut

"CHOCOLATE! The best kept secret PR juggernaut this side
of the universe. So spread the word and the chocolate."

- Cedric R. Crawford -

I was having a candid conversation with an old business colleague not long ago and I had the opportunity to share a few thoughts with him. He was looking for a little advice on how to get some of his service providers motivated so I let him in on my little-known secret that has served me extremely well in the past. Almost every service provider I know find it hard NOT to have a positive response to my secret WMD (*Weapon of Mass Development*).

Out of all my investments in advertising, marketing and business tools, I've found this one thing to be pound-for-pound and dollar-for-dollar the single most economical, efficient, effective PR tool this side of the universe. What is this public relations juggernaut you ask? Well, it's plain ole, everyday ordinary Chocolate. Yes, my friends the best things in life aren't really as complicated and complex as we may expect them to be.

I can't tell you the countless times that I've invested good money in purchasing chocolate that was specifically designed to be hand delivered personally, *with a smile and short conversation*, to my service providers in the field of operations. The results are nothing short of phenomenal.

At least once or twice a month appears to be the optimum and most effective frequency. A little recognition and chocolate to brighten someone's day can go a long way in raising your value in the eyes of others. When done properly, this action allows others to associate you with the sweet flavor and good feeling chocolate can bring and as a result, others will won't to satisfy you and your agenda more than those who don't use the chocolate WMD. Master this little known technique my friends and watch how fast you get attention to your problems and concerns. It works for me. You should try it sometime.

Let's take this life and choke it into submission with kindness and make it GREAT!

"CHOCOLATE! The best kept secret PR juggernaut this side of the Universe. So, be sure to spread the word and the chocolate."

- CedricCrawford.com -

Encouragement and Affirmation

"We shouldn't have to look very far for someone in need of our kind words of affirmation and encouragement today, so open your eyes and look around."

- Cedric R. Crawford -

I've been gaining more clarity and now realize that in terms of *affirmation*, we may very well be someone's last chance to hear that they can get through the day. The opportunity to be affirmed and encouraged by someone else may never come for them, so it's in our best interest and theirs that we act now to uplift and motivate that person around us that needs it most while we still have the chance.

We shouldn't have to look very far for someone in need of our kind words of affirmation and encouragement today, so perk up those ears and open your eyes and look around. Let them know today that we all were built to overcome all of those things that are allowed to pass our way. The person that they'll become on the other side of their challenges and struggles is so worth it. Let them know that they can choose to hang in there and do more than survive, they can THRIVE! So don't wait to help someone else make it GREAT! It won't cost you a thing but the return can be HUGE!

Jabo B.   *I am challenged.....Thanks for the word!*

Diane B.   *That is a tremendous message.*

July 24

Make Your Mark (Tattoo)

"A benign decision made in a few wild and crazy moments of insanity can resign us to a lifetime of residual affect and consequences."

- Cedric R. Crawford -

Not long ago I was at my son Chance's school preparing to go on one of his field trips. There were many parents present at this time and as usual I was one of a few dads that was there. The third graders were all excited for the trip. While standing behind one of the parents of one of the kids, I noticed that she had several tattoos on her body including several around her neck. During the chaos of the group I took advantage of the distractions and was able to read some of the words on her neck and to my shock and amazement, she had the profanity four letter word "F**K" on the back side of her neck in plain sight. I let out a spontaneous, audible gasp, "Ohhhh!" and couldn't believe what I was seeing. I then quickly tried to wipe the dumbfounded look of surprise off of my face before anyone noticed. I then took another closer look to make sure that I wasn't wrong, and yep, unfortunately I was right.

After seeing this, my first thought was, I wonder what state of mind she was in when she had this particular tattoo done. My second thought was, I wonder if she regrets the choice she made to have it done and my third thought was, what kind of job does she have that allows her to display her tattoos?

I'm always interested in talking to people and finding out their story but on this occasion I couldn't seem to get her to chat much. So needless to say, I never got the answer to my questions but it did make me think. It's interesting to me how a benign decision made in a few wild and crazy moments of insanity can resign us to a lifetime of residual affect and consequences.

I must admit that although I don't have any tattoos on my body, I actually generally like them and find them to be visibly attractive on the body when done tastefully. I would never consign myself to a thought of developing an opinion about someone's character strictly based on their choice in tattoos because I understand that the tattoo is permanent but the mind-frame and mindset the tattoo was conceived in may no longer be the same.

My thoughts are in terms of choosing to adorn and mark one's body for the world to see doesn't really require any considerable effort or talent. It seems to me that the choice to do so is simple and the process is relatively easy. But to make a visible, positive mark on the world or even just one's community would be much more difficult, but so much more rewarding and beneficial for our fellowman and woman.

As a result of the aforementioned, my unsolicited advise would be not to make any radical, permanent decisions before the age of 25 because your mindset and mind-frame just might change when the real world comes-a-knocking. Just a little food for thought for you today. Let's go make our mark and make it GREAT!

July 25

"Why"

"Your homework for life is to find your "why" for living and make it GREAT!"

- Cedric R. Crawford -

I truly believe that one of the greatest tragedies in life is not someone living their life and not knowing why they had to die, but someone living a life and not knowing why they were living. We were not designed and created to just occupy space on this planet and live out our existence with no significant purpose for the world.

The great kings and queens of the aristocracy society got it all wrong because being great has absolutely nothing to do with our bloodline. We were all uniquely designed to be great at something. Knowing "why" we were created is the most important piece of the puzzle of life. The unfortunate reality is that "most people" don't even look for the answer to the question "why," let alone find it. But we're NOT "most people."

Some of us are committed to help "most people" understand this truth and encourage them to search and find their true "why" for living. For those of you who haven't found it yet, your homework for life is to find that "why" and make it GREAT! Here's a helpful tip for discovery: Take a peek inside and you might find the answer is a lot closer than you think.

Bobbie N.   *You are so right Cedric ...Thank you...I am going to share your wisdom with "Most People."* ♥

Shawn G.   *"Whatever you are, be a good one."* Abraham Lincoln

July 26

Time

Love is spelled "T-I-M-E"

"Money will come and go and Work will always be there in one form or another, but we can never ever get the Time back once it's passed."

- Cedric R. Crawford -

Was at the park hanging out with my little kiddos the other day and I had this thought. I felt like I should issue a reminder and refresher about this "time" thing as it relates to our spouse and kids. So, I grabbed my trusted journal and started writing the following. I'm constantly being reminded that our kids and spouse still choose to spell Love "T-I-M-E" and not "M-O-N-E-Y" or "W-O-R-K." I know that I've mentioned this "time" concept and philosophy before but I feel it's soooo vitally important that it bares repeating.

Now I'm not unmindful that our respective means of income is important and absolutely necessary, however, I do submit that the time we invest in our spouse and little people should be just as important. We must make sure our calendars include scheduled T-I-M-E for creating memories and just plain old, unadulterated F-U-N with our spouse and little munchkins too.

I've also come to realize that M-O-N-E-Y will come and go and W-O-R-K will always be there in one form or another, but we can never ever get the T-I-M-E back once it's passed. It's not recyclable.

Simply put, LOVE = TIME, so don't miss the message here. This is just a little friendly reminder today. Another vital breadcrumb to making it GREAT! Enjoy.

Karen B.   *It's essential. You can always get more money.... You can never get more time.*

July 27

TRUTH

The Honest to God TRUTH

"Beware of schemers, scammers and false prophets with gold and silver tongues exacting abuse on the truth rendering it almost unrecognizable."

- Cedric R. Crawford -

One of the most valuable lessons I've come to understand over the course of my life is just because well placed, articulate words are flowing from the mouth and lips of a well-dressed, good looking individual on a stage, platform or behind a podium or lectern doesn't necessarily mean that what's being said is accurate, right or true. We've been endowed with an inalienable right to check for ourselves and arrive at our own reasonable conclusion of what has the *"Ring of Truth."* I readily admit that this message may seem a bit radical to many but underneath it all here lies the truth.

Over the years many have attempted to flip, turn, twist, manipulate, compromise and distort the truth to fit their agenda or justify their actions. After so many years of abuse, the real truth is becoming more and more indistinguishable.

We should in deed beware of schemers, scammers, snake-oil salesmen, politicians, preachers, professors and false prophets with gold and silver tongues exacting abuse on the truth rendering it almost unrecognizable. I've heard it better said before that truth is incontrovertible. Malice may attack it, ignorance may deride it but in the end it remains unchanged, TRUTH!

I will not attempt to add any comment to what I believe the truth is, I will just say that discovering the truth for yourself will take consistent due diligence in any situation or circumstance, and over time your educated, informed mind, body, heart and soul will not disappoint in letting you know what's real and what falls short of the mark. So don't be afraid to dig deep and there you are sure to find your answer, and that's the truth. Another step in the right direction today and make it GREAT!

July 28

The "*Least of These*" in Disguise

"The 'least of these' as referred to in the Bible comes in many different disguises."

- Cedric R. Crawford -

"The *Least of These*" as referred to in the "*Good Book*" (*Bible*) strolled into my life a few days ago as I sat in the lobby of a local Christian school chatting with my friend, Donna. He was brilliantly disguised as a homeless man and outcast of society with a black duffle-bag draped over his shoulder and a cane in his hand as he walked with a limp over to us with a look of desperation on his face. I'd seen his type many times before tattered, torn and dirty clothes, ratty and matted hair and a toothless grin, so we greeted him with a smile and kind words.

Most people would probably have been turned-off by his appearance and demeanor, but I was actually turned-on and eager to hear his story, but there was just one small problem this time. He couldn't speak or write. Ughhhh!!! Definitely a challenge on our hands I thought. I've been here many times before but never with an individual that couldn't speak or write.

He put his bag down, handed me his California Identification card and began in his attempt to communicate his desires to us. Forrest was his name and it was clear that he was going through some significant struggles in his life. "*How can we help you?*" was the question we asked and after several minutes of grunts and different hand gestures in a futile attempt to communicate, we all started to become a bit frustrated.

We offered him some cold, bottled water, some cookies and a short prayer for his safety but I wasn't content to just send him on his way. So I grabbed his bag and walked with him to a local park. 100 degree, summer Bakersfield, California weather with no clouds in the sky, yes it would've been easier for me to drive him in my air-conditioned, luxury vehicle but I wanted to walk a mile in his shoes with him (*so to speak*). As we walked on the hot pavement in the sweltering heat no words were exchanged, but I felt some type of strange connection and bond being established between us. I can't really explain it or put it in words but I felt as if though a quiet voice was whispering, "*This is good,*" and we were being smiled upon in the moment. Hmmm…

Once we reached the park we shared a table-bench with four strangers, Destiny, Daniel and Elder Wilson and Elder Furlough from a local Mormon Church. I introduced my new friend Forrest to them and we all engaged in a casual conversation while Forrest listened in. Several minutes later the others left and it was just me and Forrest again. I lightly pounded my fist on the table and voiced my frustration of not being able to communicate with him adequately. Then it hit me. "*Charades!!!*" I said to myself. "*I can find out more about him with charades.*" So the game began.

I spent the next several delightful minutes with Forrest uncovering some interesting facts of his life. A seventy-year-old, homeless, 10-year military veteran just passing through Bakersfield looking for a cool place to lay his head for a couple of hours before he moves on. I gave him a few words of encouragement followed by some sincere words of appreciation for his service to our country. I then took the opportunity to bless him with a few dollars and some bus fare and sent him on his way with a smile.

I shared this story with you today in hopes that it will spark something in you that will drive you to seize the opportunity to be kind to the *"least of these"* in the world around you when the opportunity presents itself. I hope you can see yourself modeling similar behavior that brightens someone else's day in an awesome way. You never know, we may be the only face of the faith they see.

I can't pretend to know what the future holds for Forrest, but I do know who holds the future for all of us and He wants to partner with us on our journey through this thing called *"life"* to make it great.

So, I encourage you today to keep the faith or join the faith and let's continue in our best efforts to make it GREAT while helping others to do the same.

July 29

ENCOURAGEMENT

Lift People Up While Climbing

"Toxic environments breed toxic people."

- Cedric R. Crawford -

We should never use our feet to walk over people but to walk over to them and offer our assistance. We should never use our stern voice to spew hatred and discouragement to our neighbor but be found guilty over and over again of uttering kind words of affirmation and encouragement. Finally, we should never use an accusatory, pointed finger to put people down or to assign blame, but use an opened, helping hand to lift them up, dust them off and push them in the right direction.

It's impossible for people to rise to the highest of heights if we set the lowest expectations. Contrary to popular opinion, there are redeeming qualities in every individual if we choose to look past what our physical eyes may see and look inside for those qualities. Everyday we are in many ways granted several opportunities both big and not-so-big to contribute to positivity in the world by building people up. Or we can choose to make a contribution to the negativity in the world by tearing people down. We must remember to never forget that whichever one we choose to do most will eventually come back to our own doorsteps to pay us an unannounced visit. So, choose wisely because as they say, *"What goes around, comes around."*

My prayer today is that this message will reach the eyes and ears of that boss, manager, supervisor or spouse that mistakenly believes that productivity or compliance only comes by the rule of an iron fist of violence, a verbal threat or a harsh tone. What a compromise to make for something that will not last or count for eternity or sow *good* into this world.

So the question today is quite simple. Are you creating an environment of toxicity, or a haven and refuge for nourishment and mutual respect? For those of you in positions of authority over others please be advised that the destruction you can cause by toxic words and actions of negativity in the many lives around you can run deeper than you'll ever know. Here's a tip: Toxic environments breed toxic people.

My sincere prayer today is may we all make the right choices to *"lift people up while climbing."* May we all experience the warm, fuzzy feeling of walking into a room bringing life and being celebrated with smiles and cheers, rather than just tolerated and segregated with frowns and jeers as you suck the life out of the room. Make your respective environments GREAT before it's too late.

July 30

FUN

"*Fun*" Defined

"To kids, 'fun' is just fun no matter where it's done."

- Cedric R. Crawford –

I learned a very important lesson a few years ago that has actually saved me a lot of money. This truth had always been there in plain sight, I just hadn't slowed down enough to pay attention to it. This exciting, welcomed discovery was a realization that my kids seem to have just as much fun down the street at the local Chuck-E-Cheese and Camelot Theme Park as they do two hours away and $75 per ticket later at a theme park with a catchy name and over-priced "*everything*." They're laughs and smiles are exactly the same. Hmmmm… They also appear to experience the exact amount of excitement at the Dollar Movie Theatres as they do at the Ten Dollar Movie Theatres and simple walks to the local park ranks pretty high on the "*fun*" list too.

For years I have foolishly tried to define "*fun*" for my kids and completely ignored their definition. I implore you to please learn from my mistake and it will definitely save you some much needed money in the long run. An occasional visit to a pricey, popular theme park or movie theatre is great but don't forget that for our kids, "*fun*" is just "*fun*" no matter where it's done.

Don't miss out on your opportunities because they're kids only once. No "*do-overs*." Just a little "*food for thought*" for you today as you attempt to make it GREAT!

Leth J.	*I have four kids and I have learned my lesson too. Its true! It's not about the Name or the Money its about having a great time with family and friends. Thanks for sharing.*
Vicki R.	*I REALLY like this. Bottom line is, what kids want is your TIME.*
Rubi F.	*Definitely. Me and my wife learned that too. All they want is for you (the parents) to spend time with them. The FUN seems to be the same whether it is the pricey places or just your local parks.*

July 31

RESPECT

Hard Lessons from Little Ole Granny

"Lesson repeated until lesson heeded."

- Cedric R. Crawford -

This hot summer has reminded me of an important lesson I learned about respect and not abusing and confusing kindness with weakness from a little old five foot nothing, 115 pound lady that had a special way of using a *"switch"* to get her point across. Just plain ole *"Granny"* is what we called her, but she was anything but just a *plain ole Granny* in my eyes.

It was one of the hottest days in the summer that July in the late 70's when my Mom's Mom, *Myrtle Marie Allen* (aka: *"Granny"*) sent me out to the back yard to get a switch off of the horse-apple tree. A *"switch"* is the southern name for a small branch from a tree and it's used to administer disciplinary action in the form of swats. The swats were usually applied to the buttocks area, but Granny's eyesight wasn't so good which often times resulted in me getting hit everywhere but the buttocks.

I remember I was about seven or eight years old at the time with a nappy Afro-puff hair-do, gapped front teeth and energy to burn for days. Mom and Dad were at work this day and Granny was on duty. She was always very quiet and reserved accept when me and my brothers would do something to screw up. My small, unassuming Granny didn't demand much in her life, but one thing she refused to compromise on was demanding her respect. Menacing looking she was not, but she could definitely hold her own when that switch was in her hand.

I don't really remember what I did this particular day to bring down the wrath but I do remember the lesson taught by the swats. After being told several times to do something and me not responding, she'd finally had enough. I was then instructed to go out into the back yard to the horse-apple tree with the following words, *"Boy! Go get me a switch off of that horse-apple tree so I can whip your butt, and it better not be no small switch or I'm gonna double up your whipping."* After begging and pleading for mercy with no luck, I finally found myself at the infamous tree looking to pick out the best branch I could find. Even as a kid I remember thinking this was cruel and unusual punishment. But I had repeatedly made a conscious decision and choice to disrespect my Granny by not following her specific instructions. Her mercy and kindness has its limits too and now I had to suffer the consequences for my actions.

I cried all the way on my walk to and from the tree and I really cried during the process of getting my admonishment, but I definitely got the message. I'm reminded of my phrase, *"Lesson repeated until lesson heeded."* I learned the hard way that day that abusing someone's kindness and mistaking it for weakness can eventually have dire consequences. Simply put, just because someone is nice and patient with you doesn't give you cause and pause to take advantage and run over them.

Well, you'll be happy to know that I didn't have to repeat that lesson. Thanks Granny for catching me young. I'll be sure to pass your message on so others can make it GREAT.

Chris S.   *I heard about them, switches. I've even witness them (switches) applied to other family members so that was enough to make me clean up my act or get in behind the others with hopes that the giver's arm would be tired of swinging them small branches. LOL. Great story, Cedric!*

My Viral Quotes
Feel Free to SHARE

"There's less pain in small change."

"Lesson repeated until lesson heeded."

"To be copied is the best of compliments."

"A follower-less leader walks alone."

"Great friends don't let great friends go without knowing they're great friends."

"When we're all alone, temptations are most strong."

"Amidst our struggles, stress, strain and strife, our silent partner whispers, 'This is for my glory.'"

"Many people unknowingly give up right before they were going to be rewarded for their efforts of hanging in there. Don't let it be you. Not today."

August 1

Attitude Appointment

"When scheduling your activities for the day, be sure to schedule your attitude and mindset in advance also."

- Cedric R. Crawford -

I started my day looking at my desk-calendar to determine today's activities; 9:30am swimming lessons for Chance and Chayse, 1pm eye doctor's appointment for me, 6:30pm football practice for Little "C" and the most important thing written on the schedule today has a highlighted circle around it, *"Maintain Positive Attitude."*

When scheduling your activities for the day I've found that it is just as important to also schedule your attitude in advance to remind you of the correct state-of-mind to stay in during your day. I've also read somewhere that writing a goal down dramatically increases your chances of accomplishing it. So what better place to do it than your daily calendar when it comes to your *"state-of-mind goal"* for the day? Works for me, try it sometime and you might agree. Yes, this too is a great breadcrumb to making your day GREAT!

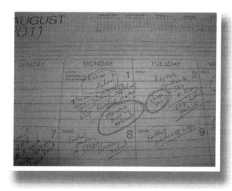

NOTES

August 2

SMILE AND LAUGH

Got Jokes?

"Laughter can boost your immune system so your best joke just may save somebody's life today."

- Cedric R. Crawford -

In life I've discovered that it's hard to be sad when both the sun and a big smile are on your face. ☺ In fact, I'm convinced that one of the main reasons the sun was created was to cheer up the downtrodden and to thaw-out a cold heart. Also I read somewhere that recent studies show a daily dose of one minute laughter can boost our immune system for up to 24 hours. Hmmm. So if this is true, then your best joke just might save somebody's life for a day.

So, keep those jokes close, loaded and ready to fire today at a friend, family member or even a perfect stranger. *"Most People"* may pass on this opportunity, but as I've said before, we're anything but, *"most people."* Let's keep making it GREAT.

August 3

FOOD FOR THOUGHT

Don't Swat that Fly

"What would you do differently if you had the life expectancy of a common house fly?"

- Cedric R. Crawford -

The strangest thing happened to me this morning. A fly landed on my shirt and for the first time I didn't attempt to swat it. I had this sudden thought that the average house fly only lives for two weeks and I wondered how many days this particular one had left.

I thought it would be down-right cruel and insensitive for me to shorten its already short life span by swatting it. I know this sounds weird, but it made me think of the following question. What would we do if we knew we only had a few days to live? Is there anything we would consider changing about our lives. Is there anything we would want to tell someone close to us or not-so-close to us? What would we do differently if anything?

These are some key questions to ask ourselves and we have to be honest with the answer. The simple truth is, we just don't know when it's our time to go so I guess we should prepare for the worst and hope for the best. So, I guess we'd better get to work on making the necessary changes in our lives before we get swatted. This is just a little food for thought in the form of the usual breadcrumbs for you today. Make it GREAT!

| **Kevin C.** | *Cedric, love your posts. Gotta run, suddenly, I have lots to do.* |
| **LuTrina S. W.** | *Uniquely used to clarify we're not going to be here forever! So, get a better relationship with Him!* |

FIGHT

Fight or Flight

"In the midst of chaos and uncertainty our natural "fight-or-flight" instinct is prepared to kick-in, but we choose not to flee, but stand and fight."

- Cedric R. Crawford -

Times are tough but our will to overcome is tougher. Some complain of inflation but we continue to strive for a higher elevation. There's talk of depression but we choose not to participate as we maintain our aggression. We continue to reach for the top because we know it's the bottom that's overcrowded. The words *normal, typical* and *usual* do not describe us. We are indeed a strange breed and a little bit different than the "*Average Joe*" in the way we think and act.

In the midst of chaos and uncertainty our natural "*fight or flight*" instincts are prepared to kick-in, and while most people would be ready to flee, we boldly affirm that we are anything but "*most people*." Our unwavering belief remains strong and we unanimously choose not to flee but to stand and fight our good fight of faith everyday of the week and twice on Sundays. We have a complete understanding that our faith is the substance of things hoped for and the evidence of things not seen. Therefore, in spite of what we may see with our physical eyes, our resolve remains strong because our minds eye reflects a clear picture of total and complete victory. Our imagination has securely lodged a favorable vision of unquestionable triumph on our internal movie screen.

In pursuit of that which we seek, we will categorically refuse to retreat or back down. Instead, we will stand firm and demand the unconditional surrender of anything or anyone who dare to stand in the way of us and our ultimate goal. We know our fight is in deed noble and just and absolutely worthy of much more than just our best efforts.

Today we make this solemn decree that until we draw upon our last breath in these fallible vessels, we will choose to stay the course until success shows up. We smile and rejoice in advance for we know we have unfair favor and our respective battle is fixed for us not just to win, but to WIN BIG! We continue to achieve because we continue to believe it's possible for us.

So I say to you today, be encouraged and use these small breadcrumbs to boldly move forward with the highest degree of certainty and make this "*good*" day a GREAT DAY!!!

August 5

AVERAGE

Can't Take it With You

"Money and Material things collected on this side of life are
not transferrable so the Egyptians and Great Pharaohs had it
all wrong. You can't take it with you."

- Cedric R. Crawford -

I've discovered life is really a journey. So, on our trip we must be sure to enjoy all the seasons including the occasional *Fall*. We must be sure to leave the emotional baggage behind for this trip because it will just slow us down. Besides, when we reach our destination, that baggage definitely won't fit into the overhead bin for our final flight over to the other side. I've read in my favorite book that this world as we know it is not our home. This is just a dress rehearsal for the real show on the other side of our consciousness.

I've come to understand that M & Ms (*Money and Material things*) collected on this side of life are not transferrable, so the Egyptians and the Great Pharaoh's of Egypt had it all wrong. You can't take the M & Ms with you. But all that we do by using our Time, Talents and Treasures to help build up others and make this world a better place will live-on in spite of the absence of our physical body in this life.

Don't miss this breadcrumb message today and be sure to make an intentional point to leave the best of yourself in others as you traverse this *"life"* thing. The average person won't take the time to make this action a priority, but we're anything but *"average."* Let's continue to refresh and affirm our neighbor and make it GREAT!

August 6

PSA(PUBLIC SERVICE ANNOUNCEMENT)

Pigs Love Mud

"There's nothing we can say or do to convince the inconvincible."

- Cedric R. Crawford -

I feel the need today to issue one of my Public Service Announcements (*PSA*). We must be careful about arguing with competitors and friends or engaging in useless debates. I've found this activity is much like mud-wrestling with a pig, you both get nasty and dirty and the pig loves it.

I've also found that this can be a source of undue stress, frustration and tension and it almost never ends in anything positive. In most cases it's just better to agree to disagree and move on to the next topic. A difference in opinion makes our wonderful world go round, so if we all agreed on everything the world just might stop spinning, and we definitely don't want that to happen.

I've also discovered that strangely enough, some people live and breathe for the opportunity to debate an issue. Even offering irrefutable evidence will fall short of convincing a debater to change his or her mind because their intent is not to learn or be informed and educated, their intent is to "win." I now understand that we can't say the right thing to the wrong person and we can't say the wrong thing to a person that's hungry for change and prepared to gorge them self on the knowledge and wisdom of those who can help bring about change. Simply put, there's nothing we can say or do to convince the inconvincible. The human need to save face will trump the need to concede almost every time.

Please be advised that ropes are designed to be pulled not pushed, so don't go trying to teach a student that's not ready for a teacher. I must admit that it took me some time to learn this lesson, but I'm happy I can pass it on to you today. Don't be shy about learning from my mistakes. You can't possibly make all the mistakes you need to make in this life anyway, so allow me to help you with a few of mine. Leave the debating for the debaters and let's invest our time in making this life GREAT!

August 7

PARTICIPATE

"Greatness Leaves Clues"

"I don't believe in magic, but I do believe in magical moments."

- Cedric R. Crawford -

I just got back from the MonStars of Motivation Event in Sacramento, California put on by my buddy and fellow motivational speaker, Kevin Bracy. As I always say, *reading, listening, participating* and *congratulating are* vitally important along your life's journey. *"If you're not living on the edge, you're taking up too much space,"* was my favorite quote of the weekend. We must become comfortable with taking some risk then rewards become possible for us. I don't believe in magic, but I do believe in magical moments and I made sure that the last several hours were indeed memorable. My and Kevin's goal is to continue in our attempt to change the world one person at a time. We desire nothing more than to encourage people to tap into their own greatness and bring it to the surface for all to see and benefit from. As Kevin says in his book so appropriately titled, *"Greatness Leaves Clues,"* I concur that greatness leaves clues indeed. You can find Kevin at his website, ***www.KevinBracy.com***.

No question about it, we have a lot of work to do, but I'm definitely up for the task. We're both having the time of our lives, living our dream and want you to embark upon a journey that allows you to do the same.

Live with intention and not by default. Take the opportunity to be proactive instead of reactive in your life. What events are you participating in regularly that are pushing you closer to your goals and dreams? Don't be afraid to stand out from the crowd in your area of *greatness*. Keep making it GREAT!

August 8

Feeling Lucky?

"Luck is nothing more than a lazy man's definition of positive results achieved by people who take proper, consistent action long enough for success to show up."

- Cedric R. Crawford -

My prayer for you today is that in your quest to achieve your goals and dreams you will have the long-range vision of the great Hubble Telescope. May you have bulldog tenacity and persistence to be steadfast and unshakeable in the face of adversity. In the midst of chaos and uncertainty, may you have laser focus through the fog and render all distractions moot and obsolete.

If you're starting to feel like your cause is no longer popular and you're walking alone, may you find comfort in knowing that if your cause is to make a positive impact on the world and the people in it, then your cause is in deed noble and just and has not ceased of being worthy of your best efforts. If that still, quite voice inside is whispering to you, *"Give up,"* may I be so bold to add a few words to that statement with an exclamation from my megaphone of affirmation and emphatically say, *"DON'T Give Up Until You Win!"*

Be encouraged today and know that you're not alone in your struggles. All the *Great* ones of the past had to blaze this trail to procure the title of being *"Great."* I do not wish you luck on your journey today, for I believe that luck is nothing more than a lazy man's definition of positive results achieved by people who take proper, consistent action long enough for success to show up. However, I do wish you the best of what your efforts and actions deserve on this day and everyday here forward. Let's not wait for *"it"* to come to us, let's go out there and get it and make it GREAT!

August 9

Got a Solid Plan-B?

"Don't wait 'til it starts raining before you buy your umbrella."
- Cedric R. Crawford -

on't wait 'til it starts raining before you buy your umbrella, don't wait for it to snow before you buy a shovel and please don't wait for the floods to come before you build your house on higher ground. If you're worried about the security of your job in these turbulent times of uncertainty, start preparing for the possibilities before your worst fears become reality. I've found that one of the worst things we can do in our careers is assume that our current employment will be there for us indefinitely. This belief will put you in what I call an *"out-of-control predicament."*

I'm reminded of when I was just 12 years old and my mom had been working for a famous retail store for over 11 years faithfully showing up on time and never taking a sick day. She went out of state on a church retreat one summer. Their vehicle broke down causing a delay in her return, so unexpectedly she had to call in to advise her boss that she wouldn't be able to come in until a day later. As a result, she was abruptly fired.

I've never forgot how that event turned our lives upside down. My mom struggled to find employment at that point. Her boss will never know the depth of what she did that day when she fired my mom. In hindsight, this was actually a good thing because it forced my mom to renovate, innovate, rejuvenate and recreate herself. She eventually went back to school to get her Associate's Degree so she could start teaching at the pre-school level. Having no control definitely affected our family and left a mark on me that I'll never forget. But as they say, *"once bit, twice shy."* This event also showed me at an early age that it is very risky to place your life and the stability of your family's well-being into the hands of an employer.

As fate would have it, I suffered the same fate almost 20 years later under slightly different circumstances while employed by one of the largest insurance companies in the world. But this time I had a well-placed, Plan B that I had been working on part-time that made the untimely termination a non-issue.

I caution you today that the biggest oxymoron I know of is the phrase, *"Job-Security."* Don't wait until it starts raining to buy your umbrella. Make sure your Plan B is solidly in place or just roll the dice and hope everything works out. This breadcrumb-food-for-thought can save you more than you'll ever know. So, eat up as you attempt to make it GREAT...

August 10

What's the Weather Like Today?

"The weather on your inside is directly determined by the way you deal with the weather on your outside."
- Cedric R. Crawford -

What's the forecast for your life today? Is it clear, sunny skies with a slight favorable breeze from the north, or is it partly cloudy with a chance of showers and thunder storms?

I have good news, you are the weatherman or woman for your life and whatever you say goes. The days of faulty inaccurate weather predictions are a thing of the past. I invite you today to take a look at this "life" thing from a different perspective. In your world, you're in complete control and can make a conscious decision of what type of weather you would like today and refuse to let your external environment dictate your attitude.

The catch is it's not what's happening with the weather outside that matters most, it's how you deal with what's happening with the weather outside that makes the difference. Simply put, what's happening on your inside is directly determined by the way you deal with what's happening on your outside. If we choose to stay in control of our attitude, emotions and mindset, joy and happiness will be a common occurrence no matter what's going on around us.

So what's your weather like these days? Hmmm... Don't miss this message here today and make your weather prediction as you wish. I hope you choose to make it GREAT!

August 11

INTEGRITY

Make My Day

"True honesty and integrity shines even in the absence of earthly eyes."

- Cedric R. Crawford -

Our honesty and integrity in the eyes of others is important, but it's our honesty and integrity in the eyes of the one who never blinks that matters most. We can all be expected to do what's right when others are looking, but true honesty and integrity shines even in the absence of earthly eyes.

I was at our local Winco Grocery Store today purchasing a few necessary items. My cashier appeared to have had a long day and was visibly not in the best of moods. I took this as a great opportunity to say "Hi" and strike up a casual conversation. She had her name tag on so it was easy for me to continue to refer to her by name. As our casual conversation continued I could see her face start to show signs of life.

She eventually finished ringing up my items and I handed her some cash. In her haste to get to the next customer in line I noticed that she had given me one large bill too many. I quickly pointed out the error and she corrected it and gave me the correct change. She was full of thanks and commented that *most people* would've just walked out because no one would've known. I then told her that I wasn't "*most people*" and "*I*" would've known. We both exchanged smiles and more pleasantries and wished each other a great day and went on our way.

This was definitely integrity at its best in my book. This action in her words, made her day and little did she know, it made my day too. If given this same set of circumstance what would you have done? Hmmmm... Give it a bit of thought today and be honest with the man or woman in the mirror.

We must make a point to let our honesty and integrity shine always for we're never completely out of view of the eye's that really count.

Another simple breadcrumb to making it GREAT! Enjoy.

August 12

BETRAYAL OF TRUST

Smoke in the Hall

"Pray for peace but keep a gun in your sock."

- Cedric R. Crawford -

If I close my eyes and tilt my head to the left side just a bit and concentrate real hard, I can remember the distinct smell of the dry powder chemical in a fire extinguisher that reminds me that human beings are capable of some major disappointments and betrayals of trust.

It was many years ago but it seems like just yesterday, I was working as the lead staff in the high security unit at a Juvenile Detention Center. I personally referred to the center as a Juvenile Prison because it was a lockup facility with a lot of the same attributes as the adult prison system. After being on staff for a few years at the facility, I learned quickly that juveniles can be just as violent and destructive as adults. My high security unit was referred to as "2-A" and I was responsible for housing the most serious level 3 and level 4 offenders with charges ranging from armed robbery to first-degree murder.

It was a normal evening in the summer of 1998. I had one of my star inmates out in the unit on a work detail sweeping and mopping the floors. So that he will remain anonymous, I'll refer to him as Carlos. Carlos was not only respectful, but also mild-mannered and likeable. He was really a textbook example of what we would call "*institutionalized.*" He had managed to build up a pretty awesome rapport with all the staff in our unit over a period of several months, including me. This particular night we had just finished processing a few new inmates and I was preparing to have them escorted to their respective, newly assigned units. I had been working in the units all day as usual and this night I figured I would take the opportunity to get out by giving my support staff a break and I agreed to escort the inmates to their units. I instructed my support staff to stay behind and I had complete confidence that the unit was under control. All the other inmates were locked up, except for our one star inmate, Carlos, who was out detailing the floors.

I successfully transported the new inmates to their units and was having a short conversation with the unit staff in the other unit while he was processing the inmates. Suddenly, I heard the institution alarm go off. This alarm automatically shoots a large dose of adrenalin through my veins as my body quickly prepares to go to battle. There's a monitor mounted on the wall in the staff-counter section of every unit and it highlights the unit were the action is taking place. I quickly glanced up at the monitor wondering where the action could be, and to my surprise, it was my unit. I took pride in having the cleanest shift with no incidents for many consecutive months but it all suddenly came to an end. "*NOT MY UNIT!*" I yelled as I rushed to the door and opened it. It led me to what we call the "*ramp.*" The ramp was the equivalent of an open-air, outdoor, fenced-in hallway that is approximately the length of two football fields. My unit was almost half that distance away.

I started to run and as I was running I noticed there was a huge cloud of smoke down at the door of the entrance to my unit and the entrance of the front intake processing/booking area. The intake processing area is the area where all the juveniles are booked once they enter the facility and the door to it was directly across the ramp from the door to my unit. This area is also the closest thing to freedom for the inmates. I continued to run while at the same time trying to visually process what I was seeing, but it just wasn't making sense to me, at least not until I got there.

Upon my arrival to the entrance to my unit, I discovered that two windows on the doors leading into my unit had been broken out and smoke was everywhere. I quickly figured out that no one would be trying to break into my unit, they would only want to break out. So, I turned to look at the booking area and I saw that the window had been broken out in the entrance door for their area too. At this time, I still hadn't figured out where the smoke had come from. It didn't smell like fire induced smoke, but it was just as thick and choking.

I quickly entered the booking area and heard the secretaries at the intake desk up front yelling, "*HE'S UP HERE, HE'S UP HERE!*" The main entrance has two "*sally-port*" doors that lead to the outside world and one can't be opened unless the other is closed. I quickly ran toward the sound of the voices of the secretaries in the front and was absolutely shocked and amazed to see that my "*star inmate,*" Carlos, had managed to bust through a grand total of four security door windows and was working on the fifth and final one to freedom when I arrived. To my surprise he had managed to use a fire extinguisher to smash the glass and keep the other staff at bay, which explained all the smoke.

Fortunately, he was trapped inside the sally-port doors at this time and we were able to take an alternate door around to the outside of the main door where he was trying to get out. After a short struggle, we eventually were able to regain control and remand him back into secure custody. Yes folks there were five windows to freedom but he came up just a bit short.

After the incident I asked Carlos why he took such drastic actions. He said, "*Sir, I was just stressing about some stuff that's happening with my girlfriend and family and I just felt like I had to get out of here.*" It was obvious to me that his rational mind had been altered so much by the stress he was feeling that he evidently wasn't able to successfully reason with himself to avoid such an action.   This whole incident served as a reminder to me that we humans are capable of some really crazy things in our moments of desperation or temporary insanity. I learned never to take for granted and assume that a smiling face and mild demeanor is not capable of betraying your trust and taking advantage of you. Unbeknownst to Carlos, he was due to be released a few days from the day the incident took place.

In this life we should always pray for peace but you may want to keep a pepper-spray gun in your sock and stay ready for war, for all that looks good and righteous is not always good and righteous. Let's make it GREAT!

August 13

DREAMS AND INSPIRATION

From Obscurity to Ovation

"Inspiration begets and inspires Inspiration."

- Cedric R. Crawford -

From obscurity to ovation. From not many knowing who you are to not many NOT knowing who you are. From leaving her household with a little-known name to becoming a household name. From "*I have a dream*" to "*I think I'm dreaming.*"

Gabrielle Christina Victoria Douglas is her name and she's also affectionately known as the

"Flying Squirrel," but those who know her best prefer to call her *"Gabby."* A few days ago she secured herself firmly in the record books as becoming the first African American woman to win gold in the Olympic Artistic Gymnast Individual All-Around Competition. Yes, her story is an inspiring one because it embodies the three absolutely necessary components and elements that make any story inspiring, which are the Dream/Goal, Struggle/Adversity and the Triumphant Victory.

To the untrained eyes of the cheering audience her performance at times may have appeared to be one that was executed with ease and little effort, but make no mistake about it, this was made possible only by the countless hours invested in advance when no audience was watching and no voices where cheering.

I truly believe her podium composure exhibited the night of August 2, 2012 in London, England undoubtedly came from the realization of a déjà vu moment of her life long dream. I'm sure she would say that she's been there before hundreds of times in her night and day dreams and to finally see it in live view makes all the hard work worth it. A dream that was ignited and given promise not-so-long ago by the inspiration of her childhood Olympic Hero Dominique Dawes. This serves as a definitive example that Inspiration begets and inspires Inspiration so I had to include her story in this book.

Don't let the absence of tears during her national anthem ceremony and medal presentation lessen your belief in her patriotism and level of genuine joy for her accomplishment and being honored in that moment. For I'm sure she can passionately tell you about the countless hours spent weeping and shedding tears of stress and strain behind closed doors wondering if her moment in the bright lights and flickering flashes of gold reflection would ever come. Yes I know you Gabby. I know your battle all too well. It's one that's shared, fought and lost by many who give up for one reason or another, but not you. Not this time.

The struggle for the gold must have been tough but the realization of finally achieving it must have been a bit anticlimactic in the wake of your many victories along the way. You hung in there during those quiet nights when all was gone and you were left alone to wrestle with your biggest enemy which turned out to be your *"inner-me."* You stayed the course even when the woman in the mirror doubted whether it was all possible and worth it. You even fought through that quiet voice that attempted to make it seem okay to quit, and for your sacrifice to make it great I say to you today, CONGRATULATIONS!!!

KUDOS for being the exception to the unwritten rule that states when things appear to be insurmountably hard it's okay to shut it down and go home. No, you're not the first to traverse this road of *Dream, Struggle* and *Triumphant Victory* and after your outstanding exhibition and performance demonstrated days ago I'm quite sure you definitely won't be the last. There's no doubt that you surely will be an inspiration for many more to embrace their struggle and adversity as they attempt to accomplish great things. You're proof-positive that reasonable sacrifice over time coupled with focus, discipline, perseverance and persistence will not disappoint.

Thanks for seeing it through and being an inspiration because sooooo many others struggle as you do. Thanks for your message of *"You can too"* delivered by your undying efforts and consistent actions. More AWESOMENESS to come from you no doubt. And, the time will eventually come when the lights, cameras and accommodations fade away in the darkness of time, but still hold to your memory of the moment you shined because of your ability to endure and overcome. Congrats again I say Gabby and keep making it GREAT!

For all of you who dare to dream and are willing to work to win I say to you today. Never tire of being inspired by others story of accomplishment as you continue leaning forward in your noble efforts to make it GREAT!

August 14

MARRIAGE

H2O

*"There's nothing more magical than a husband and wife team
with a common dream working together like H2O with the
right balance and flow."*

- Cedric R. Crawford -

I was lying in bed this morning listening to the sound of the early morning rain hitting the pavement outside my windowpane and a thought suddenly came to my mind. Water can't flow without the marriage of the elements, H2O. Both elements must work together in order to create water. On the surface there appears to be only two elements (*hydrogen-oxygen*), but it's the unseen element that makes the union sustainable. Yes it's true, a three-strand cord is not easily broken. I believe our Creator has placed the secrets to protecting the institution of marriage in plain sight all around us. We just have to slow down, be still and listen.

Another interesting thing with water is that too little of it can cause a catastrophic drought and too much of it can cause a devastating flood. But the right balance of it can yield a crop that can feed the multitudes. As I've said before, I don't believe in magic, but I do believe in magical moments, and there's nothing more magical than a husband and wife team with a common dream working together like H2O with the right balance and flow.

To that end, I must say that we all have an opportunity daily to become masterful at this skill in our relationships. We must be sure to support each other and factor the third, unseen element into all of our major decisions and watch the magical moments happen.

Feel free to read between the lines on this one and don't miss the message and definitely use this breadcrumb to make those marriages and relationships GREAT!

Bonus DAY 8!!!

INDIVIDUALITY

DON'T FOLLOW THE HERD!!!

There once was a sheep that lived in a herd.
They followed each other around which seemed absurd.

Their common lives lived day in and day out.
Wandering while wondering what life was about.

Eat a little grass here, drink a little water there,
Aimlessly living life without a real care.

Till that one fateful day when a big lion passed by,
With a big smile on his face and his head held high.

The sheep thought to himself, *"What's up with that guy,"*
"Smiling all the time without a care in the sky."

"It must be nice being the king of this land,"
"Descending from upon high to grab as many of us as he can."

"I wonder which one of us he will choose today,
We're poor defenseless sheep and to him we fall prey."

A sheep is totally reliant upon the movements of the group.
One thought that doesn't match the rest, you'll end up sheep soup.

But this lion was different from other lions you see.
He would pluck out a few sheep, and later set them all free.

How dare he upset the flow of all things.
The sheep must conform like the water in the spring.

But as strange as this sounds there was one shocking fact,
The sheep he set free chose not to come back.

The cycle of comfort was very hard to break,
But after the awakening, the sheep all felt great.

This lion had taught them to think on their own,
To make the wise choice and sometimes travel alone.

For conforming to the group is not always so wise,
As most sheep end up sheared and herded for the rest of their lives.

by Cedric R. Crawford

August 15

WAR

Don't Answer the Door

"When anger and rage creeps up on the doorstep of our mind
and rings the doorbell demanding entry into those critical mo-
ments of our life, don't open the door."

- Cedric R. Crawford -

The history of this great world records many great men who were capable of leading others into battle and procuring a victory in magnificent fashion while at the same time sending thousands of souls to their maker. But I humbly submit to you today that the truly *"great man"* or woman is the one who can prevent the battle and the wars from happening. I've come to understand that the ability to be violent is easy and when we're angry, this ability comes naturally to most of us. But the ability to be peaceful and non-combative when our adrenaline is pumping and blood is coursing through our veins during a fit of rage and anger is something that may take a lifetime for some of us to develop.

The phrase, "*Cooler heads prevail*" comes to my mind here. I submit that we should decide in advance that when anger and rage creeps up on the doorstep of our mind and rings the doorbell demanding entry into those critical moments of our life, we may peep through the peep-hole but we should categorically refuse to open the door. We must be okay and comfortable with placing war and the loss of life on the "*Not an Option*" shelf hereby forcing us to seek other non-combative solutions.

I know this is a tall order and some exceptions are necessary, but I sincerely believe if we choose to adopt this overall sentiment and attitude, I'm confident this world of ours will be a much better place today than it was yesterday. More people will still be here to share it with us too.

Is it time for a change in thought for you today? Chew on this breadcrumb for a while as you continue in your efforts to make it GREAT!

NOTES

August 16

Your TV cost you WHAT?

"Choose to 'invest' your time rather than 'waste' your time."
- Cedric R. Crawford -

How much does your TV cost you? A few hundred dollars you may say. But wait, have you taken into account the countless hours spent watching it which prevents you from working toward your goals and dreams? Now, how much does your TV really cost you? Hmmmm…
    I used to be part of the very popular club of people that choose to spend an overwhelming amount of time peeking in on the lives of other fictional and non-fictional characters as they live out their dreams. 'Til one day I had an epiphany and decided that every minute I spend reading, listening, watching or participating in anything that doesn't feed me mentally, physically or spiritually is a minute wasted. I now choose to *"invest"* my time rather than *"waste"* my time. Now don't get me wrong, I do manage to have my fill of entertainment from time-to-time, but I'm careful to maintain an *"everything in moderation"* perspective.
    Heard this before from me? Well, I believe this *"time"* usage thing is so important that it definitely warrants reiteration. So how much did my TV actually cost me you ask? I got it on-sale and it still has cost me too much, and I'll just leave it at that. Let's get used to turning that *"TV"* thing off more so we can invest more of our time into those things that will help us make it GREAT.

August 17

May…

"May our conviction be the yeast that empowers us to rise
from every fall."
- Cedric R. Crawford -

My hope and prayer today is that passion and purpose will be the vehicle that drives us through our life. May conviction be the yeast that empowers us to rise from every fall. May there be countless moments in our life where we genuinely love the activity of actually *"living."* May our God-given ingenuity motivate us to go against the grain of a humdrum-mediocre life. May we develop an unquenchable thirst for knowledge and wisdom. May we strive to leave only the best of ourselves in those who we come into contact with daily.
    May we rise from our beds daily with renewed vision and the strength to overcome whatever

challenge or adversity the day holds for us. May such words as these continue to motivate, inspire and empower us to boldly move forward into our days ahead with complete confidence, solid belief, unwavering certainty and unfailing faith. Finally, may we all choose to take captive and subdue this day and bend it to our will, and our will is to make it GREAT!

August 18

Forgive and be Forgiven

"It's in the times when a person has done us the most wrong
that the power to forgive is the most strong."

- Cedric R. Crawford -

I've learned over the years to never underestimate the power of sincere forgiveness. It's in the times when a person has done us the most wrong that the power to forgive is intensified and is then most strong. The average person may find it easy to forgive for the little things, but the big stuff is reserved for those who are anything but *"average."*

I've found that having the ability to exercise the power of forgiveness during the most challenging times can actually alter the perpetrator's life for the better. For when someone has truly wronged you and they know they've wronged you and they're expecting your worst, it's then we have the opportunity to show them our best by offering them complete forgiveness

Leveraging forgiveness in this manner not only speaks to others, but it serves as the best relief for ourselves in the process too, for forgiveness is really primarily designed for the forgiver.

So, let's choose NOT to be the *"average"* person and to forgive so that if the time comes for us down the road, we will also be worthy of being forgiven. Don't miss this breadcrumb today as you attempt to make it GREAT!

Gilbert G.	*Here goes sum more Cedricism...! I love it man, thanks for sharing that. I think more than ever that needed to be told now so your timing couldn't have been more precise. Thanks for bringing that value Mr. Crawford.*
Angela A. F.	*Beautifully stated! I'm very forgiving. Wish I was more forgetful, lol! Make it great!*
Chris P.	*Good Stuff! Spot on! It's also a commandment for Disciples of Jesus Christ. A friend of mine recently told me, we are called to be fruit inspectors, but that is different than being a Judge. A part of me forgiving is simply acknowledging that I am not the other person's Judge. It also gets me out of the way of whatever judgment is upon them. To coin a phrase, "Make It Great!"* ☺

FRIENDS

Let a Friend be a Friend

"When heartache sets in, one of the worst things we can do is NOT let our friends be a friend to us."

- Cedric R. Crawford -

I've noticed that when some of our friends are going through the fire of life, that's usually when we may often times find it tough to get into contact with them. This is when they may stop answering the phone and ignoring messages and other attempts to reach out to them. May I caution you today not to take this action personally. This is when a true friend needs to go over and kick in the door and offer the following statement, *"I'm here for you even in the bad times, so please let me be your friend."* Also be aware that during these trying times, sometimes there's no need for words. This might be difficult for some of us but sometimes we have to just shut up and listen and be there in the moment for them.

I found that when heartache sets in, one of the worst things we can do is NOT let our friends be a friend to us. Negative self-talk increases in times of suffering and it causes most people to hunker down and hide from those who can help them most to recover. We must not allow ourselves to fall into this trap. We must choose to make the tough choice and let that friend be a friend, then be willing to return the favor when and if the opportunity presents itself in the future. After all, that's what friends are for. Another valuable breadcrumb. BAMMM! Let's make it GREAT!

FEAR

Speed Out of Your Comfort Zone

"FEAR is a well disguised motorcycle cop hiding in the bushes of life waiting to arrest unsuspecting individuals attempting to speed outside their comfort zone."

- Cedric R. Crawford -

I was driving my kids to school not long ago and I noticed a couple of motorcycle cops hiding behind some bushes and I suddenly had one of my *"hallelujah moments of clarity."* As a result, I now have a new metaphorical definition of Fear: *Fear* is a well disguised motorcycle cop hiding in the bushes of life waiting to pull-over and arrest unsuspecting individuals attempting to speed outside their comfort zone. Most people may believe that FEAR stands for *"Forget Everything And RUN!"*

But we're not *"Most People."* We know that FEAR is just *"False Evidence Appearing Real."* Our radar detection of awareness gives us a form of diplomatic immunity.

I've recently started to see more and more of the popular *"No Fear"* brand on t-shirts and bill-boards around town, but I choose an alternate statement. My statement is, *"Got Fear, but doing it anyway."* I've learned that fear can actually be a good thing in that it promotes preparedness and sparks adrenaline. So we must choose to embrace this *"Fear"* thing.

We understand that we succeed not because we have no fear, we succeed because we continue to act in spite of our fear. So, speed-on out of that comfort zone quickly and continue to conquer that ominous four letter word with the comfort in knowing that all the best things in this life exist on the other side of FEAR. Let's continue to be bold as we attempt to make it GREAT!

Ryan S.   *It's crazy how GOD uses off-the-wall situations to spark those moments of clarity.*

August 21

Interstate of LIFE

> *"On the 405 freeway of life, you're destined to get a lot further faster if you're in the carpool lane, so be sure to take a few people along with you for the ride."*
>
> *- Cedric R. Crawford -*

On the freeway of life we have the fast lane, the slow lane, the carpool lane and the shoulder. Me and a couple of my friends were driving on the infamous, *"parking lot"* 405 Freeway in Los Angeles, California the other day in the carpool lane just whizzing by all the other stopped vehicles. I couldn't believe how many cars only had one person in them. Having my friends in the vehicle with me made it possible for me to keep moving while others were at a standstill. Then, as usual, I had another one of my sudden *"hallelujah moments of clarity."*

This phenomenon is not unlike our life's journey. So many people are trying to achieve certain goals but they appear to be content with going it alone and looking out for only the interest of themselves. Most of them are afraid to let others come along for the ride for fear of one bad thing or another or just plain-old stubbornness.

It seems to me that if we want to achieve significant things in this life, we have to be okay with letting others with similar interest or a common goal get in the car with us and share their knowledge and talents. In a lot of the cases, going-it-alone can retard our progress and lead to a standstill or even complete breakdown and failure.

The simple message today is, on the 405 Freeway of life, you're destined to get a lot further faster if you're in the carpool lane, so be sure to take a few qualified people along with you for the ride. Buckle up and drive safely and don't forget to make it GREAT!

August 22

Affirmative Words in Action

"You can do great things in this world with your gifts, if you
choose to do great things in this world with your gifts."

- Cedric R. Crawford -

I was with the group that day when we walked away but I *wasn't with* the group that day when we walked away. Those sincere words of affirmation that day resonated deep into my core. The power of affirmative words is immeasurable, especially in a kid's life.

It was years ago in the winter of 1985. It was a regular school day and I was in my 8th Grade, third period English class. My teachers name was Ms. Mills. She was the tall, blonde hair, blue eyes type with a pretty face and figure to match. She always dressed nice, smelled good and always had control of her class while she wore a big smile on her face, but not this day. I was seated at the middle of the classroom in my desk. I was actually leaning back in my desk with the back two feet only touching the ground. Suddenly, I reached what I call the *point of no return*. This is the point where you've gone passed the center-balance line and you're chair is destined to make a connection with the ground. I fell over and made a loud crashing noise and the entire class burst into laughter except for two people, me and Ms. Mills. She quickly stood up and regained control of the class with these words, "*Ok class, settle down!*" and then she looked over at me with those piercing blue eyes and said, "*Come see me after class Mr. Crawford.*" The whole class responded with an ominous, "Ooooooo…"

At this point, I wasn't really shaken up about what she said, but I was shaken up by the name she used when she said it. She called me "*Mr. Crawford.*" At this stage of my life the only person that called me that name was my dad and it was almost always right before he gave me a good-old-fashioned butt whooping. So needless to say, I was immediately terrified. This was during the time when Texas schools had the "*corporal punishment*" rules allowing teachers and administrators to administer paddlings to disruptive kids in the classroom. As a result, I was expecting one of three things to happen. Either I was going to get a paddling by Ms. Mills after class, or she was going to call my dad and he would do the honors when I got home, or both she and he would get me. From that moment on I don't remember what we studied in class that day, but I do remember the second hand on the wall clock suddenly becoming audible.

I used to associate the ringing of the class bell with the sound of freedom, but not this day. The ringing of the bell suddenly started and the beating of my heart suddenly stopped. I remember my so-called friends walking by my desk whispering, "*Ooooo, she's gonna tear your booty up.*" along with other snide comments. I took my sweet little time gathering my books so-as to delay the moment of the inevitable paddling.

I then approached Ms. Mill's desk and immediately started to make my pathetic plea for leniency and if you would've been there, you would've heard her abruptly cut me off and say something that, even if I live to be 100 years old I will never forget. She said, "*Shut up and just listen. There's a time and place for everything we do in life and today wasn't the time or the place for what you did. Cedric, you're a very smart boy and you can do great things in this world with your gifts, if you choose to do great things in this world with your gifts.*" She continued tell me a few things about what I could expect from the "real world" and the next levels of education. Then she told me that my gifts would take me places in life if I learned how to turn them on and turn them off when needed. Then she said, "*You're dismissed.*"

I must admit that I was so dumbfounded in that moment that you could've knocked me over with a feather. That day she gave me much more than any paddling or harsh word could have ever done for me. She gave me something that I had never really received before from someone who didn't share my same last name. She gave me the gift of *Affirmation*. She affirmed something in me that I didn't see in myself at the time. When I was expecting her worst, she in turn chose to leverage the moment for "good" and gave me her best, and it changed me.

As I said, "*Thank You*" and hurried out of her classroom, my friends were waiting outside the door, listening for the ominous sound of a butt being swatted by a paddle. I flung the door open and they immediately said, "*What happened?*" I simple replied, "*Nothing. She let me go.*" My friends where upset that I got away with something they felt they would've paid for dearly. Yes in deed, I may have walked away with the group that day, but I was no longer mentally with the group that day. Those sincere words of affirmation resonated deep into my core. The power of affirmative words became real for me and I've never forgotten it.

Our words can be used to build people up, or tear people down. We must be ever-careful about what we say, when we say it and how we say it, for if done correctly, it can quite possibly alter someone's life for the better. It did for me. Who do you need to affirm today? NO need to answer out loud, just make me proud. Let's make it GREAT!

Please view the video on:

www.YouTube.com

Search Code: Cedric R. Crawford – (17)

August 23

Silence is a Gift

"One of the most overlooked skills in the area of communica-
tions is the ability to know when to just shut-up and listen."
- Cedric R. Crawford -

Over the course of my life I've found there's something mystical and magical about silence. Some say its *"golden."* I say it's a *"gift."* I truly believe that one of the most overlooked skills in the area of communications is the ability to know when to just shut-up and listen. A one-sided conversation of one talker and one listener is necessary from time-to-time and I've discovered that so much more can be learned from listening than talking. Maybe that's why our Creator gave us two ears and one mouth. Hmmmm...

So let's make a special point to use our *"gift of silence"* and shut-up and listen twice as much on a regular basis. I know for me and a bunch of others this may be a HUGE challenge, but let's give it our best shot. We just might hear something that we've been missing.

Here's a fun fact for you, the word S-I-L-E-N-T and L-I-S-T-E-N both have the same letters. So which one of these are you doing most of these days? Hmmmm... Please don't answer out loud, just make me proud. Be sure to put on those listening ears and make it GREAT!

Donna M. V. *Good point! I never thought of it like that and I guess in this case two is better (ears vs. mouth), also I think my husband would appreciate this lesson, so if you don't mind I would like to pass this along! Thanks!*

Jabo B.   *This is something I am really trying to take hold of this year. I'm find-*
                    ing that by doing more listening and less talking, I'm making changes
                    in relationships and I am seen as more trustworthy and wise.

August 24

Stay Thirsty

"Keep your learning churning and you're sure to increase your earning."

- Cedric R. Crawford -

What a great day to be above ground, alive and breathing. If you don't believe me, try being below ground holding your breath.

Once again, the sun didn't disappoint this morning, it was just as reliable as usual in its rising. A nice cool breeze is blowing in from the North East and not a cloud in the sky for as far as the eye can see from where I'm standing. No, it's not just a *"good"* day, it's a *"GREAT"* day to walking among the living having yet another crack at this thing called *"Life."*

My good word today is, we must be careful not to make the big mistake in thinking that after graduating from school we're done with learning. In fact, our quest for knowledge should be ongoing and even intensified after graduation. I've observed that most people fall into a life of average and mediocrity because they don't know what they don't know, and they don't realize they don't know and they need to know more. We can't let this be our fate.

I invite you to consider letting your appetite for knowledge be unsatisfiable and your thirst for wisdom unquenchable. I encourage you to press on today with a new understanding and a new or renewed belief that knowledge alone is not power. It is the knowledge in *"action"* that creates the power.

So, keep your learning churning and you're sure to increase your earning in the days ahead as you attempt to make it GREAT.

August 25

MARRIAGE

It's a MIRAGE!!!

"The desert heat of marriage has been known to cause mirages,
illusions and visions of greener grass on the other side."
- Cedric R. Crawford –

In marriage, I've found there are a lot of "*ings*" you have to deal with. First there's the engagement ring, then the wedding ring, then the sharing and bonding. But then eventually comes the arguing and the struggling and it all can become frustrating and disappointing. Mix all this madness together and before you know it, you're grow-ing together.

It has become painfully obvious to me that in any relationship, you're either moving forward or moving backwards, there's no third direction. Marriage and any relationship is a team sport, and as we all have heard before, "There's no 'I' in TEAM." This may come as a surprise to some, but conflict is a totally natural phenomenon in relationships. So don't feel like your issues and quarrels in your relationship aren't normal. We have to work together in this marriage thing to make it work or frustration and disappointment will slowly dismantle and compromise the union.

Let's commit to be intentional about what we do to preserve our relationships. Most people would be content to shut it down and pack their bags for the road, but we're not "*most people*." My favorite book gives us written permission to play the marriage sport as hard as we've ever played any other sport in life because it's definitely worth our best efforts to win. Don't be easily duped and fooled by the mirage of the greener grass on the other side and a better life flying solo. The desert heat of marriage has been known to cause illusions, visions of grandeur and hallucinations, especially when you're focusing on the negative things that you don't like about that spouse of yours. Never forget that the greener grass on the other side will also need balanced exposure to the elements of sun, soil, wind and rain in order to survive and thrive too.

Focus more on the positives in that partner and hang in there and play nice today. Things can and will get better if you commit to work on the single most important element in the relationship first, "*YOU*." Continue to be encouraged and make it GREAT!

Amanda D K.   *Excellent words of encouragement and truthfulness that there is*
no "I" in TEAM. Wow, to look at a relationship as a sport is the

way to work it out and want to make the best out of any situation. Thanks for all your words they really mean something once you take time to think about it. Thanks Ced.

August 26

Thanks "Soccer Mom"

"Need something done? Get a Soccer Mom."
- Cedric R. Crawford –

I've had the distinct privilege over the last nine years to work from home, which has afforded me the ability to invest a lot of time actively participating in my kid's lives. Needless to say, this has also resulted in me being around a lot of what most people call, "*Stay-at-home Moms*" or "*Soccer Moms*," but I prefer to call them, "*Home Engineers*."

Over these activity-filled years I've learned to never underestimate the power of a group of dedicated Soccer Moms. Watching these Mom's in action rallying around a worthy cause or mutual goal is nothing short of phenomenal. They have a "*Never-say-die*" attitude and a "*Just-get-it-done*" mentality. Getting them to agree may be a challenge at times, but once you've got them all nodding their heads in the "*Yes*" direction for the cause, watch out world, because they will not be denied. There aren't many things stronger than the heart of a volunteer and Soccer Moms are the crème-dele-crème. As a result, I now have a new saying, "*Need something done? Get a Soccer Mom.*"

So, if you're a *Work-from-home Mom* or *Soccer Mom* or *Stay-at-Home Engineer*, please allow me to give you a big, fat "*High-Five*" for all that you do to make this world go round. Your tireless efforts have not gone unnoticed. Your coming early and staying late is not in vein. Those bright eyes all around you are taking notice and are quietly thanking you for your unyielding service to them and this world.

Please take the time to breathe in this acknowledgement, affirmation and congratulations today and know that you play the most important role of anyone in this world of ours because you are in direct contact with shaping and molding the future of this world. That future is sitting in that car seat behind you everyday. Keep doing that thing that you do so well and make it GREAT!

Thank You! Soccer Moms! www.CedricCrawford.com

Laurie A. *Well said....and yes.....the future generations need love and guidance...proud to be a stay at home mom....difficult for others to remember that we have degrees, have held court in the corporate world, can cook, drive, take care of our children and still have a smile on our face when hubby get's home even though we aren't raking in fist full of cash.....money cannot buy you happiness--it just affords more choices...an applause for all those dads who give of their time for their children.....awesome job friends....which includes you Cedric. Muah! Mr. C....*

Jennifer Anderson-Campbell *Amen! Just remember sometimes those "soccer moms" become "hockey moms" or "baseball moms" too. It goes for all select/travel sports we are all the same. We get'er done. Our kids sometimes just choose to change sports. ☺ So true Laurie! I always ask where is my degree for motherhood. Cedric, it was very well said and it is so nice to hear a man say it!*

August 27

CHOICES

Choice, Chance and Fate

"The choices we make and the chances we take will determine our fate."

- Cedric R. Crawford –

We don't have to wish upon a shooting star to make our wildest dreams come true. We don't have to carry around a rabbit's foot or four-leaf clover to bring luck and success into our lives. And a black cat crossing our path or the breaking of a household mirror glass doesn't mean we're destined for luck that's bad. To believe in such things can cause a person to limit their own abilities and short-change themselves from achieving their full potential.

Accomplishing our wildest dreams tomorrow has everything to do with what we choose to do today. Bringing luck and success into ones life is favorable to the ones who have paid the price of discipline and preparation. And, bad luck or bad things happening in our lives is inevitable because bad things happen to both good and bad people. What really matters most is how we respond to those bad things that happen in our lives. I always say, *"Pray for clear skies but also be sure to pack an umbrella."* In other words, expect the good but also be ready for the bad. This type of attitude will definitely separate us from the *"most people"* crowd.

I've learned that our life-course has absolutely nothing to do with fate, it's really just a series of our choices and chances. The choices we make and the chances we take will determine our fate. Let's not just live our lives by chance or default and the luck of the draw, but let's strive to be exceptional and intentional about making this life what we want it to be, and we choose to make it GREAT!

August 28

Service vs. Lip-Service

"The only service that won't be rewarded in this life is 'Lip Service.'"

- Cedric R. Crawford –

I was asked by a friend not long ago to post a comment on the following enduring phrase, "*We must turn to each other and not on each other.*" So, I wrote the following comment and hope that it will add a bit of value to your life also.

I've realized in life that when times get tough and scarcity abounds we have a natural tendency to lash out at those who are closest to us. It also appears we often times allow ourselves to slip into a "*survival mode*" and succumb to our most basic of instincts which is "*selfishness.*" It is for this reason I caution you today to resist this tendency at all cost, for it will only lead to more scarcity and heartache.

I submit that when times are tough, it's in our best interest and the interest of others to look for opportunities to be of more service and to capitalize on giving more of our time and talents to others and not necessarily of our limited treasures (*money*).

Relationships and being in positive community with others is what makes the world go-round and in light of this fact, I've found that you have to GIVE your way out of a "*Scarcity Slump.*" We have to be willing to say YES to NO more procrastination. YES to NO more empty promises. YES to NO more backing down and fleeing in the face of fear and adversity. YES to NO more back-biting and cat-fighting with each other. And, absolutely YES to NO more excuses and "*but*" statements. We must take intentional action steps in the direction that brings us closer together in turbulent times.

Years of experience has convinced me that the only service that won't be rewarded in this life and the next is "*Lip Service.*" So, let's turn to each other and not on each other and see how we can "*Give*" and be of "*Service*" to our fellowman in these challenging times. We only get one time through this "*life*" thing, so let's make it GREAT while we're here.

August 29

GREATNESS

Come Early and Stay Late

"Work hard for a season and our applause will come sooner or later."

- Cedric R. Crawford -

The goals and accomplishments great people have reached were not obtained suddenly without a fight, but while their opponents and companions slept they were working diligently during the night. People don't achieve great things *"all-of-a-sudden,"* it takes time, focus, discipline and persistence. We must be willing to come early and stay late for the sake of accomplishing our biggest goals and dreams.

So I say today we must be prepared to put in those extra minutes and hours of time and focus while others are sleeping or playing. Over time you will gain your edge for greatness and achieving something significant. We must be willing to work hard for a season embracing the thought that our applause will come sooner or later if we don't through in the towel. Yes, this endeavor is worthy of our best efforts indeed. So, hang in there and continue to use these breadcrumbs to make it GREAT!

August 30

FOOD FOR THOUGHT

The Lava Lamp Surprise

"Do we really know how many batteries it takes to make that person tick?"

- Cedric R. Crawford –

I have a little lava lamp that's been sitting on my desk for years. It contains a few hundred small, silver shiny flakes that float in a clear liquid. I use it to serve as a constant reminder of the importance of staying focused and not being easily distracted by shiny objects that are designed to pull us off our course. When the lamp is turned on it emits a light that causes the small, shiny flakes to light up even more, thereby creating even more of an illuminated distraction.

Well, the batteries in my lava lamp have been dead for several months and I haven't bothered to change them until today. I removed the bottom cover and saw one single battery. My immediate thought was, *"WOW, that's GREAT! This thing runs on one little, bitty battery."* I had a little trouble trying to retrieve it but eventually it popped out and to my surprise, another battery rose up into its place. I took that one out too, and then another popped up. Yes, there were a total of three batteries to replace for the one little lava lamp. Those little batteries are expensive, but I really need my *"distraction reminder"* so I figured it's worth the investment.

This little battery changing event wasn't quite what I thought it was on the surface. It reminded me of how easy it is for us to look at something or someone on the surface and make a quick judgment call or opinion, good or bad, without knowing the whole story. I believe that it's in the best interest of all of us to ask ourselves the question, *"Do we really know how many batteries it takes to make that thing or person tick?"* before we formulate an opinion about someone or something.

It's interesting how so many clues and refreshing reminders of how to live a better life exist all around us. We just have to pay a little closer attention. Don't miss this two-fold breadcrumb today of *"being less easily distracted and less quick to judge."* Let's make it GREAT!

Nita T.   *Wow! I watched an episode of Joel Olsteen and he spoke on why we should not criticize and judge, yet be encouraging to your brother. There's always a GOOD message to God's work!*

August 31

ADVERSITY

Adversity Defined

"ADVERSITY is, the Ability to Develop Via Experiencing Real Situations that Involuntarily Train You."

- Cedric R. Crawford -

I was laying in my bed in my most inspirational position this morning, which is flat on my back staring at the ceiling, when I suddenly had another one of my *"Hallelujah moments of inspiration."* So as usual, I reached over to my nightstand and grabbed one of my trusted old journals and started to write out my thoughts.

The idea that came to mind was a new, contemporary, acronymic definition of *"Adversity"* that I think might serve as a great breadcrumb of value for you today. My new definition of *"Adversity"* is, *"the Ability to Develop Via Experiencing Real Situations that Involuntarily Train You."* If you really break this definition down, you'll find that adversity really does give you the ability to develop by experiencing hardships and struggles in situational life events that are designed to make you stronger and help you to grow rather you want to encounter these experiences or not.

So I invite you to think of adversity as a welcomed opportunity to grow and get better. All things that are great and worthwhile were no doubt realized on the other side of "*Adversity*." Be encouraged today if you're experiencing a bit of discomfort amidst a struggle and know that you're in training and a new and better you is coming right around the corner. Continue to lean forward and make it GREAT!

Got ADVERSITY?

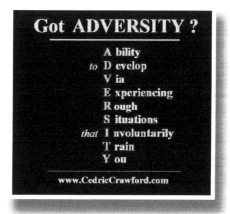

September 1

ATTITUDE

Got a Positive Attitude?

"If you have a crappy attitude in this life, you just might end up with a 'dill-pickle' face in your old age. So be careful."
- Cedric R. Crawford –

One of the most important things I've learned in life is that our *attitude* can be an asset or liability. Our attitude can lead to great success or massive failure in any endeavor we choose to embark upon. I remember when I was a young 10-year-old kid, my two older brothers worked selling candy door-to-door for a company called "The United Youth of Texas." I used to watch the big white windowless van pull up to the front of our house daily during the hot summer days and my two older brothers would wave goodbye as they ran to jump in and head to work. I remember being told that I was too young to participate, so I would always feel left behind as I would stand there, curbside crying as they were leaving.   I'll never forget this one particular day when I was standing curbside crying as usual and the owner, Mr. Jim, yelled from the driver's seat of the van, "*Hey little Cedric, come here!*" I quickly ran over to the passenger side of the van while wiping away my tears and he asked me if I really wanted to come to work for him. Without hesitation I emphatically said, "*YES!*" He then said, "*Okay, when I come to pick up your brothers tomorrow, if you have the door-speech memorized, I'll let you go with us.*" Needless to say, I was so excited that you would've thought that I'd just been given a first class ticket to the moon.

I immediately took that speech into the house and started to devourer it. My mom and dad thought I was crazy with excitement and were quietly happy for me because this could definitely result in bringing more income into the household. I rehearsed, rehearsed and rehearsed some more, and made sure that I knew that speech down to the last letter. I found it extremely hard to sleep that night in anticipation of what was to come the next day.

Well, the next day eventually came and I bound out of bed full of excitement and began to count down the hours to when Mr. Jim was to show up. Mr. Jim pulled up in the white van in usual fashion and finally the time had come and I was definitely ready to deliver. I ran to the passenger side sliding door before the van could stop and flung it open and beamed one of my big trademark smiles at him and said, "*Mr. Jim I'm ready!*" He said, "*Okay, let me hear what you got little man.*" I then immediately broke into song, "*Hi, my name is Cedric Crawford and I work for the United Youth of Texas. The United Youth of Texas is an organization that helps keep young teenagers off the streets and out of trouble. It also gives them a part-time job and a chance to earn some extra money...*"

I completed the entire speech without as much as a hiccup. Mr. Jim was thoroughly impressed with my delivery and he then said, "*You're hired little man. Get on in.*" I immediately said thank you several times as I jumped into the van. I remember being so excited that I was finally being given the chance to show him what a 10-year-old, under-aged salesman could do. My brothers weren't too happy with me being allowed on the team, but I really didn't care, I was just happy to have the opportunity.

Mr. Jim decided he would drop my brother Zimbalis and me off together at the first neighborhood so I could get a little bit of training. My brother told me, "*Let's go to the first house and you just listen to me do it and then I'll let you do the next house.*" I nodded my "afro-puff" head in agreement and briskly began to walk with a bounce in my step, box on my hip and smile on my face as we began our journey. After the second house my brother told me that he would do one side of the street and I could do the other.

I remember being so excited that each time someone opened the door, I would beam one of my big smiles at them and then break into song with my speech. A little cute, black kid with a high-pitched, pre-puberty voice and big positive attitude and even bigger smile to match was practically irresistible to most people. By the end of the block, I had already had my brother beat with sales. I then told Mr. Jim that I was ready for my own route by myself. He was visibly impressed with my attitude and ambition, so he agreed to turn me loose.

I was so excited that it didn't matter if people told me "*no,*" I would still say, "*Thank You*" with a smile and move on to the next house with the same attitude and smile on my face and excitement in my voice. My last house of the day was approached with the same excitement and attitude as my very first.

By the end of the night, I was the top salesman, and as customary, I was allowed to choose the place where we all would go for a late night, fast food dinner and entertainment. At this tender young age, I learned that having a positive attitude no matter what happened previous would always separate you from those who had a crappy attitude. I never skipped houses and I always, always, always maintained my smile and positive attitude. It didn't matter if I was cursed, had a door slammed in my face or was bit by a dog, I would be sure to get my attitude back into check before I ever rang the next doorbell.

As a result of maintaining my positive attitude, less than a year later, I managed to sale 70 boxes in one day beating the previous record of 64. Getting paid $1 per box plus tips put me well over $100, and I was indeed a very happy camper. Prior to that day the only record that I had managed to break was my mom's phonographic record of Aretha Franklins 1970's Christian album with the song, "*Mary, don't you weep*," and that of course wasn't a day of celebration.

Looking back at this time in my life I must say that little 10-year-old boy sure taught me a lot. As an adult I've carried this principle of maintaining a positive attitude into everything I do without exception and have also learned that it helps to live a life of reduced stress. My brother Zimbalis evidently learned this secret too because less than a year later, he beat my record by one box selling a grand total of 71 boxes. I was sure that he had cheated somehow until Mr. Jim confirmed it at the end of the day. I guess there's nothing like good ole sibling rivalry.

Our attitude is 100% our responsibility and no one else's. I've noticed that so many people stubble through this life with a crappy attitude about everything that's not to their liking and as a result, they lead lives that are full of stress, frustration and confrontation. If they're not careful, they may end up with one of those "*Dill-pickle*" faces in their old age.

I've found that we need to wake up everyday and decide in advance that we will choose to have a fresh, new clean slate and positive attitude. If we don't choose our attitude in advance daily, other people or our environment will choose it for us. We can't allow negative people around us, or negative events that happen around us, or to us, dictate our attitude for the day.

If you choose to maintain a smile with a positive attitude regularly, good things will happen to you. Also, be sure to keep that attitude charged and re-charged regularly like you would your laptop or cell phone by plugging it into positive activities and positive people on a regular basis. Be sure to laugh often and don't take yourself or this life too seriously. Do this regularly and you'll be glad you did. This is a definite breadcrumb to making it GREAT!

NOTES

September 2

STRUGGLE

Future Prediction

"I predict in your future that any worthwhile goal, dream or accomplishment in your life will be realized only on the other side of struggle, fear and adversity."

- Cedric R. Crawford –

I'm feeling a little clairvoyant today, so please allow me to attempt to predict your future. I predict you will have several opportunities to win and succeed in the days ahead mixed with some unfortunate experiences of loss and failure. I further predict that any worthwhile goal, dream or accomplishment in your life will be realized only on the other side of struggle, fear and adversity. Finally, I predict you will read a quote from Cedric R. Crawford today that accurately predicts your future and you will say these words to yourself, *"MAN he's good…"*

No need to thank me, this one's on the house today. Just be sure to get out of the house today and use these breadcrumbs to make it GREAT!

Tiare F.	*Good one and thanks for the prediction "on the house" - love it!!*
Karen B.	*Wooot!! Now that's Good Stuff!! ...."man, he's good' !!!!*
Jabo B.	*You were right on the money! LOL*

September 3

CHOICES

Advance Payment Due

"Success and significance tomorrow has to be paid for in advance with every decision you make today."

- Cedric R. Crawford -

Yesterday is gone, tomorrow is not promised and today holds no guarantees. All we really have is this infinite moment in time. It's true that no one really knows what tomorrow will bring until it comes, but the most accurate way to predict and influence what will happen tomorrow is what we choose to do in this infinite moment in time.

The reality is success and significance tomorrow has to be paid for in advance by every decision you choose to make in the present moments of today. Every living being is governed under this same principle. So, set your sights on what you want for your tomorrow and choose your actions wisely today. After all, it really is your choice. So, make it GREAT!

September 4

FRIENDSHIP

True Friend?

"A 'true friend' will answer the phone when a friend's name
pops up on the caller-ID at 1:30 in the morning."

- Cedric R. Crawford -

I've been doing that *"thinking"* thing again lately and have come up with an opinion about what constitutes a *"true friend"* and I would like to share my thought with you today. I sincerely believe a *"true friend"* will let you know if you have a piece of lettuce stuck in your teeth. A *"true friend"* will tell you if your body odor is offensive. A *"true friend"* applauds and encourages your efforts. And, a *"true friend"* will answer the phone when a friends name pops up on the caller-ID at 1:30 in the morning.

So I guess a good question today is, are you a *"true friend?"* Can you be counted on when others are counted out? Can you be trusted to come through when others are just through? Hmmmm… No need to answer here, just let your actions tell the story. Answer that phone. Most people would look for an excuse or reason not to get involved, but we're definitely not *"most people."* Let's be that *"true friend"* and make it GREAT!

Karen B.   *You're One in a million!!*

Cedric R. Crawford *Karen, with there being 7 Billion people on the planet, being One in a Million means that there are 7000 other people in the world like me. Not bad numbers. I actually think we're all unique in our own little way, but being among such an elite group works for me. ;-) Thanks… LOL*

POLITICS

Politics, Presidents and Politicians

"He who has it all figured out with no flaws, let him criticize,
complain and condemn as he casts the first stone."

- Cedric R. Crawford -

Over the years I've noticed a very interesting pattern among the general public when it comes to our nation's presidents. It appears that every president, without exception, has their flaws and is imperfect and *"most people"* are poised to pounce on their problems if given the opportunity.

Many have criticized the current president, complained about the previous presidents and will no doubt continue to condemn the next president after this one. The honest truth is that the presidents may change but flaws and imperfections will remain. So don't be surprised at what happens in the future with the next one.

I've conducted a very thorough investigation into the history of the presidency and I've officially confirmed that every president we've had thus far lacks a 100% approval rating and are frequently the target of retribution, reprisals and ridicule. In fact, it appears in only a few weeks after a president has been in office many people start to remove their placards, banners and bumper stickers for fear that others will attach them to the elected president's actions and views.

As a result, I have personally come to admire every one who has ever had the courage to take on the responsibility the oath of office brings. I truly believe that the nerve and guts it requires to take such an action trumps the struggles, stress and strain that many of us have to deal with in our own lives. I can't imagine the physical and mental pounding one has to endure on a daily basis from those who make it their business to poke, probe and prod in an effort to stir up controversy, contention and dissension directed at the person in office.

So as a member of the general public, our choices are still the same today as they have always been. We can choose to beat'em up, build'em up or just shut up and work on that which we can control. I choose the latter.

My good word to you today is, he who has it all figured out with no flaws, let him criticize, complain and condemn as he casts the first stone.

Let's all choose wisely which group we will be a part of and don't be afraid to share these breadcrumbs with them so they can make it GREAT too.

My name is Cedric R. Crawford and I approve this message. ☺

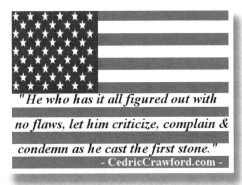

"He who has it all figured out with no flaws, let him criticize, complain & condemn as he cast the first stone."
- CedricCrawford.com -

September 6

EXCUSES

"WHY?"

"When life knocks you down, what's your excuse for getting back up?"

- Cedric R. Crawford -

I've had a few incidents lately where a few different people have totally dropped the ball on some simple task or missed some benign appointments, but managed to come up with some complicated excuses. I must admit that I'm not a big fan of those who make excuses for things. I believe you either do what you say or just shut up and move out of the way. This recent event has caused me to consider the following question, *"Is there a case where making an excuse for something can be considered a positive thing?"*

After careful thought, the first word that comes to my mind that's synonymous with the word *"excuse"* is the word, *"why."* This word implies that there is an excuse-statement that will follow as the answer. In this instance the question I ask is, *"When you fall down in life, "why" will you choose to get back up?"* Ponder this question and figure out your *"excuse"* in advance. This is definitely a case where having a good excuse can be construed as a positive thing. *"FYI,"* doing this will definitely get you through those tough times. Make sure your *"why"* is big enough to keep you pressing forward in an attempt to make it GREAT.

September 7

CHANGE

Adjustment Needed?

"Life lessons are all around us. Don't miss yours."

- Cedric R. Crawford -

I was typing on my computer a few minutes ago and I was distracted and looked away. A few seconds later I looked back at the screen and began typing again but this time I kept getting an undesired result with each key stroke. I looked down at my hands and immediately discovered the problem. I had inadvertently moved my hands a few centimeters to the left onto the wrong keys. I then had a choice to make. I could keep typing in that same position hoping that I would somehow get the right words on the screen, or I could make the necessary changes to achieve the desired result.

Now this may sound simple, but in real life situations you'd be surprised how many people don't make the change. Even after they discover and realize what the problem is and know how to correct it, many still struggle to take the necessary steps toward fixing what's broken. Occasionally we need to take the time to stop and look at the results of our actions and behaviors and be willing to make adjustments if necessary to achieve the desired results.

Life lessons are all around us. They're sort of like "breadcrumbs." Hmmmm... Imagine that. Don't miss this one as you attempt to make it GREAT.

Gilbert G.	*Cedricism at it's best, thanks bro.......*
Sandra S.	*I've stolen Cedricism quotes plenty of times "Make it a great day" LOL... ☺*
Tyron M.	*First I swiped The Law of SUATA, here comes my 2nd act of plagiarism of a Cedricism...*

September 8

POTENTIAL

The Birds

"The signs for what it takes to reach our full potential are all around us in nature, we just have to stop, look, listen and take good notes. Then take ACTION."

- Cedric R. Crawford -

I was flying on a special trip not long ago and I had a spark of brilliance that compelled me to consider birds and their incredible ability to achieve flight. After doing a bit of research, I discovered that the average bird spends the overwhelming majority of its lifetime flying at an average height of 500 feet above ground. However, when it comes time to change to a completely different city or location, birds can maximize their potential and ascend to as high as 29,000 feet. They do this to take advantage of the high winds which allows them to fly further faster and more efficiently. The interesting thing is that the transition from 500 feet to the higher heights is an arduous one and requires a lot of effort.

In spite of this fact, birds have learned over the years that this action is absolutely necessary in order for them to achieve their ultimate goal. It's quite obvious that the birds of nature understand the simple principle that maximizing their potential may require enduring temporary pain to achieve a desired gain.

Would it surprise you to know that we humans are governed by the same simple principles of nature? Changing from one level to the next in our lives to maximize our potential will require work and does not come easy. But just as with nature, we too can experience success in our respective endeavors if we're willing to push through the discomfort and pain of making the transitional-change.

So, I caution you today that on the plane ride to a higher level in your life, be sure to fasten your seat belts and put your seat-backs and tray-tables in their upright and locked positions, for the ascension to those new altitudes will have a bit of turbulence. Nevertheless, if we commit to do today what "*Most People*" won't, we can have tomorrow what "*Most People*" don't because "*Most People*" don't push to maximize their potential. They just fly below 500 feet.

The signs for what it takes to reach our full potential and succeed in this life are all around us in nature, we just have to stop, look, listen and take good notes. Then, take massive ACTION! "*Most People*" wouldn't have made it this far in the book to read this entry today, so congratulations for not being, "*Most People*." If you're one of the few, I'd love to hear from you.

So, drop me an email at Crawford@CedricCrawford.com or send me a message at www.CedricCrawford.com. If I get a message from you, I know you're one of the few that are really serious about your personal development. Keep it going and let's make it GREAT!

Deqoun J.	*You write some INCREDIBLE stuff! Inspiring. Never really gave much consideration to what birds are capable of beyond the amazing ability of flying south for the winter cliche'! Committed to taking life to the NEXT higher elevation!*
Trent B.	*Nice...worthy of plagiarism.*
Jabo B.	*How do you know this stuff! LOL*
Mitzi R.	*Jabo, I doubt he found it flying at 500 feet:)*

Please view the video on:

www.YouTube.com

<u>Search Code:</u> **Cedric R. Crawford – (1)**

September 9

RUDE PEOPLE

Read that book?

"I guess they haven't read 'that book' yet…"

- Cedric R. Crawford -

One of the many things I've noticed as I stumble through this life is some people can be very rude, disrespectful and insensitive to other people that just-so-happen to be sharing the same air and space around them. This may be as a result of the wear and tear of leading a humdrum life where the majority of their time is spent in an area outside of their true gifts or passion or purpose. I catch a glimpse of these negative people when I encounter them at their place of employment, or as a patron at a local store or eatery, or driving through the same parking lot or roadway.

As a result of being a witness to this phenomenon on a regular basis, I've often found myself giving them the benefit of the doubt and quietly saying to myself, *"I guess they haven't read 'that book' yet."* In this instance, *'that book'* refers to any book that states we're not to be engaging in such activities or actions that are rude, disrespectful or insensitive to others. An even better gesture may be to anonymously slip the person a copy of a book that might help them like this book, and bookmark a specific page for them to review. Hmmmm… This definitely couldn't hurt.

So going forward, please feel free to adopt my little phrase, *"I guess they haven't read 'that book' yet"* and/or follow it up with the action of slipping this book or any other appropriate book into the hands of the target. It may end up being the best little investment you'll ever make to positively change someone's attitude, or maybe even their life. Don't be afraid to spread the breadcrumbs around. It just might attract even more birds. Let's make it GREAT!

September 10

LEGACY

Boys Night Out

"Sow the best that you've learned through your ups and downs into your kids."

- Cedric R. Crawford -

We enjoyed a *boys night out* at a local college football game with a great group of guys last night. I discovered that you can really carry on some meaningful conversations when after only 19 minutes into the game your team is already ahead by a score of 42-0. Yes, the beating was that bad. I must say that I'm sure glad that I share the same name as this little guy. He is definitely intellectually miles ahead of other kids his age and it makes me smile to see him practicing behaviors and talking about things that I had no clue about when I was his age. I honestly can't wait to see where he lands as an adult in the coming years.

For all you parents out there, our kids are our opportunity to sow the best we've learned through our ups and downs into them. Yes, little Cedric R. Crawford Jr. is wise beyond his years and it really feels good because I feel I'm a big part of his legacy. Don't miss your opportunities to sow the best parts of you into the next generation and encourage them to do the same. Create those memories and make them GREAT!

September 11

TRAGEDY

9/11

"What was meant or bad actually yielded some good."
- Cedric R. Crawford -

I would be two kinds of crazy and three kinds of foolish to let this day slip away without something to say about its infamous notoriety. This day in 2001 we witnessed an unspeakable atrocity and demonstration of the amount of horror that can be inflicted on innocent beings for the sake of a distorted version of retribution. Out of all the times I've been able to process complex thoughts and make sense of life's challenging twists and turns, I continue to fall short of understanding a reasonable rationale for taking innocent lives for any cause.

Is there a cause that's so great that it would justify such an egregious, callous, barbaric act? I can't imagine there being a "yes" answer coming from the mouth of any sane, rational, compassionate human being. Some may argue one way or another but I will leave the debating up to the debaters while I attempt to advocate peace and understanding.

In spite of it all, what was meant for evil actually yielded some good. This horrific tragedy actually resulted in bringing our great nation together as one. For a few years people managed to put their indifferences aside and come together in a show of solidarity in our great nation. But today, hidden selfish agendas and politics as usual have once again started to divide us.

My sincere hope and prayer is that it will not take another tragedy to bring us back together again. After all, who says that bloodshed is necessary to affect change? I believe there's a better way and it starts with me. I will take the advice of the late Gandhi and actually strive to be the change that I want to see in this world of ours.

I still have great faith in the human spirit and the inherent "Good" that's in us all. Let's recall this day together. Let's all remember where we were and never forget where we're going and remind the next generation from where we've come. Let's all play our respective part in getting us where we need to be, safely. Embracing this breadcrumb of wisdom will definitely help us all make it GREAT.

September 12

PERSEVERANCE

Don't Quit !

"Don't quit on your goals and dreams because someone else is waiting to be inspired by your story of how you overcame and became triumphant in spite of the odds."

- Cedric R. Crawford -

I recently made a little time to *"tune-out"* so I could *"tune-in"* and I've discovered something I'd like to share with you today. I feel that it's necessary for me to say that someone needs for us to follow our dream, our purpose and our passion so we can positively affect there life. So, if we quit on our goals and dreams, we will fail much more than just ourselves.

We must commit to be the exception and persist because someone else is waiting to be inspired by our story of how we overcame our situation and circumstance and became triumphant in spite of the odds. Yes, your story is important and your book needs to be read by someone.

So, pull out that ballpoint pen and lined paper and get to writing and tell that story because *"that someone"* is desperately counting on you to making it happen so they can make it happen too. They can't be inspired by me. It's only your story that can get the job done. So don't let them down. Not today. Hang in there, overcome and make it GREAT! Then tell us all about it.

Jeremy T.   *Never thought of it that way but it's true*

September 13

NOTE TAKERS

Attention Note Takers !

"Leave your pen and pad at home if your intent is not to review the notes you thought were so important to write down in the first place."

- Cedric R. Crawford -

I was at an event recently and almost everyone had a notepad of some sort taking copious notes. I couldn't help but to think of the results of a study I heard that was done a few years ago concerning notetakers. The study showed that the overwhelming majority of people that take notes at seminars, workshops and other events will never review those notes again. They ultimately end up on the shelf of oblivion or lost in hyperspace with the famous missing sock from the dryer. If this is you, I have two words for you today. STOP IT!!! Leave that pen and pad at home if your intent is not to review the notes you thought were so important to write down in the first place.

Our ability to retain information is dismal at best, so it is imperative that notes are not just taken during informative presentations, but those notes should be reviewed several times in order to retain the most important information collected during the presentation. Most people will ignore this principle and continue wasting pen and paper, but as pointed out several times before, we're anything but "*most people*," we will review our notes and save the trees by not wasting paper.

Please don't plot to kill the messenger today, I'm just reporting the facts as I see them. It's ok to share the breadcrumbs and tell a friend to save the trees by not wasting paper taking notes if they don't plan to review them. Let's continue to make it GREAT!

James B. Jr.   *So true, you must study what you wrote, then apply it to real life experiences.*

Doreen M.   *I agree. If I stay an extra day after the event and just review my notes and highlight the areas I need to revisit when I return home this seems to help. I also make a "to do" list that I need to do when I return home as a result of the notes taken.*

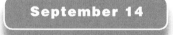

September 14

FYI (For Your Information)

What if?

"I've come to realize that everything around us without exception had to have been created from someone's 'what if' scenario."
- **Cedric R. Crawford** -

Up until a few days ago, one of my biggest pet-peeves was my kids'"*what if*' scenarios. Example: "What if nobody had homework, ever?" "What if all the schools in the country burned down and we had to do school from home?" What if ice cream was mandatory at every meal?"

These silly "*what if*" questions have almost driven me to a state of two kinds of crazy. But I must admit that after much thought, I've come to realize that everything around us, without exception, had to have been created from someone's *"what if"* scenario. The Wright brothers must have said, *"What if we could make this thing fly."* Thomas Edison and his assistant Tesla must have said, *"What if we can make a bulb light up a room."* And, Mr. Bell and his assistant Mr. Watson had to have started by toying with the question of, *"What if I could reproduce my voice to another person over a thin piece of wire."* These are all examples of what I refer to as *"unrealistic 'what if' scenarios,"* because certainly these *"what if"* scenarios were undoubtedly considered unrealistic in the eyes of the general public for their respective times. Nevertheless, these great men were not deterred from taking the proper action to turn their *"what if"* scenarios into reality in spite of the naysayers and non-believers.

So today, I publicly proclaim that no matter how silly or far-fetched the *"what if"* scenario is, I will no longer tell my kids, *"Shut-up with the crazy talk."* I will try to keep a straight face and answer their question or patiently wait for them to work through their own scenario. After all, that's how we sent a man to the moon. Just another little breadcrumb for you today. *"What if"* instead of making the day Great, we made this day AWESOME?

> Please view the video on:
>
> www.YouTube.com
>
> <u>Search Code:</u> Cedric R. Crawford – (2)

Bonus DAY 9!!!

Persistence

Press On!

Press on! Long after the music has faded and the crowd has dissipated.

Press on! Long after the jubilant cheers and people have disappeared.

Press on! After everyone's moved on and your smile is gone.

Press on! After the mission seems no longer popular by those who are popular.

Press on, for you're in rare territory now where only the great ones tread and endure and overcome.

Press on I say today and stay the course for it won't be long now so again I say, PRESS ON!!!

by Cedric R. Crawford

September 15

Conviction!

"There's no submission with high levels of conviction."
- Cedric R. Crawford -

I've discovered something that is amazingly simple, yet it can catapult anyone to success over time. This one thing can make the weakest man or woman bulletproof. It can make a dwarf feel as if he or she is 10 feet tall, and it's the biggest indicator that you will reach your desired goals if you keep this simple thing. This thing is also in plain sight but manages to elude the masses.   What is this thing? CONVICTION! There's no submission with high levels of conviction. If you truly know what you're doing in life is what you're supposed to be doing, then stay the course because you've already won. So, exactly how is your level of conviction today? No need to answer out loud, just make me proud and stand out from the crowd. Develop this one thing and nothing is impossible. Make it GREAT!

NOTES

SERVICE / PURPOSE

Service and Purpose

"Our Creator knew our 'free will' would result in 'free won't' in
most cases, but we were still given the choice."

- Cedric R. Crawford -

As I look around today I realize that everything I see was birthed from someone's idea, then with proper action and adequate time and effort it became a reality. Furthermore, everything we see was created to serve some type of purpose. The keywords here are the words *"serve"* and *"purpose."* That's right, without exception, everything was created to serve a specific purpose in this world. Would it surprise you to know that this includes us too?

Yes, we were indeed created to serve and fulfill a certain purpose, but the unfortunate reality is the *"average"* person never finds out what that purpose is because most are just too busy trying to make it through the day. What's even more shocking is we, as humans, are the only ones that have a choice in whether we serve in our area of purpose or not. Everything else in this world just falls in line with its design by instinct.

I'm sure our Creator knew our *"free will"* would result in *"free won't"* in most cases, but in spite of this fact, we were still given the choice to serve or not to serve in our respective area of purpose and passion. My good word to you today is, we must commit to be the exception and find our purpose and not just settle for being the *"average"* person.

Found your purpose or original design yet? Hmmm… It's never too early and never too late to start making it GREAT!

Michael B.   *I totally agree with this. Everyday is filled with so many responsibilities, but we must still find the time to recognize our true talents and serve them to the world. Or just be the average person. I'm definitely not trying to be that average person though... Good one Cedric!!!*

PERSONAL DEVELOPMENT

What's on your Bookshelf?

"Books and other personal and spiritual development tools in our
homes and vehicles should rank among the most valuable items
in our household because our quality of life depends on them."

- Cedric R. Crawford -

I've recently stumbled onto one of the best kept little secrets that in my opinion is one of the best ways to keep thieves from breaking into your parked vehicle. If implemented properly this anti-theft secret could stop the large majority of car thieves dead in there tracks and send them running down the road to the next potential victim.

The secret is to make sure that you have several personal development books, CDs and other mind-sharpening tools in plain sight in your vehicle when it's parked. The undeniable fact is most thieves have no desire to be associated with such things and widely view these types of items as absolutely worthless. But to the contrary of this thought, I believe the books and personal development tools in our homes and vehicles should rank among the most valuable items in our household because of the knowledge we can gain from them and apply to our everyday lives for the better. Simply put, our quality of life depends on them.

So, I say today, let's continue to upgrade our personal libraries and keep the *"good stuff"* flowing into us on a regular basis. Or at least use it to keep the thieves away. This little breadcrumb can protect you and your vehicle so let's make it GREAT!

September 18

The Underground Railroad

"We're called to be the Harriett Tubman of the 21st Century
in terms of us helping others to gain knowledge and freedom."
- Cedric R. Crawford -

I was lying out under the stars last night with my four kids in the comfort of my own front yard gazing up at the constellations in space. The *"Big Dipper"* was very easy to pick out and I showed them how to use the *"Big Dipper"* constellation to lead them straight to the North Star. I then explained to them one of the significances of the North Star in history and how the so-called, *"Runaway Slaves"* used the North Star as a reference point to make sure they were headed in the right direction to freedom in the Northern states.

I shared with them the story of Harriett Tubman who was a notorious runaway slave who made dozens of trips back down to the South to rescue and escort hundreds of slaves to freedom in the North. She was the lead conductor of the famous *"Underground Railroad."* This *"underground railroad"* didn't have any tracks and certainly no trains. It was a course traveled by foot from the South to the North that included a number of homes of people who were sympathetic to runaway slaves and would provide food, water and hidden shelter for them on their course to finding freedom. I was surprised to find out that I hadn't shared this story with my kids before.

This conversation led me to one of my *"hallelujah moments of clarity."* The nature of what I do in my speaking and personal development business is based on this same premise and concept. I guess I could call myself the Harriett Tubman of the 21st Century. The even bigger reality is, it should be all of our roles to be the chief conductors of the Underground Railroad to Personal

Development and Self-Awareness for ourselves and others. Be mindful today that if you choose to use your gift of greatness to create value for others in this world, the sky alone is the limit for all those involved.

I've learned that true freedom comes from not just knowing this information, but applying it for the good of our neighbors. So a good question for today is, "*Found your area of greatness yet?*" If not, what are you waiting for? Get started today and let's make it GREAT!

> **Please view the video on:**
>
> **www.YouTube.com**
>
> <u>**Search Code:**</u> **Cedric R. Crawford – (3)**

September 19

The Flowers and Weeds of Life

"I trust that you're showing your weeds of doubts and fears the ultimate neglect these days."

- Cedric R. Crawford -

I've heard that in the garden of life there are flowers and weeds. Flowers are your hopes and dreams. Weeds are your doubts and fears. Which one are you watering these days? I trust that you're showing your weeds the ultimate neglect as you shower your flowers with the sunlight of positive daily disciplines and the rain of positive association and affirmation. Do these things and watch your dreams grow like a daisy on steroids.

This simple breadcrumb today can take you a looong way. Keep striving to make if GREAT!

September 20

What's your story?

"We should be ashamed and afraid to meet our maker and Creator with a story of, "I woulda, shoulda, coulda but I didn't use my gifts to serve my fellowman."

- Cedric R. Crawford -

Ｍy life story does not include having been a victim of a tragic, near-fatal accident or having had some type of *"near-death"* experience. I don't have a story of being raised by a single parent or adopted or caught up in the foster care system. I've never been homeless or living out of my car or affiliated with some type of infamous street gang. I haven't had the misfortune of having to live with a severe physical handicap or disability. My story doesn't include having to battle some type of major, life-threatening disease or illness in my lifetime. I didn't grow up in an abusive household or in extreme poverty. I haven't had to battle with any type of alcohol or drug related addiction in the past and I haven't been in trouble with the law or had to spend anytime in jail or prison. My story includes none of the above, but make no mistake about it, I do have a story. In fact, I believe that we all have a story, a story that needs to be shared with others so they too can see that they're not alone in whatever trials, challenges or suffering they have to endure.

My story is one of being rescued from what I call a, *"Most People"* syndrome or mindset. This mindset was taking me down a road of mediocrity. This mindset was pointing me in the direction of an average life at best. A life that was not devoted to serving and creating value for others on a large scale. A life that was centered around just getting by and being okay with just *"being okay."* The late, great Horace Mann from the 1800's said, *"We should be ashamed to die until we've made some major contribution to humankind."* I couldn't agree more with this sentiment. I say that we should be ashamed and afraid to meet our maker and Creator with a story of, *"I woulda, shoulda, coulda but I didn't use my gifts to serve my fellowman."*

I'm happy to say that I am now firmly on a course of building a life that matters in the area of my greatest potential. One of my main objectives in all that I do is to encourage and remind people that we all were uniquely designed to be great at something and we are to use that *"something"* to make this world a better place.

My hope and prayer today is that we will choose not to waste our time, waste our body, or waste our life doing things that won't really matter when we're gone. What will be your story? No need to answer out loud, just make me proud. Let's all choose to make it GREAT!

Diane K.	*Cedric, fantastic story. Reminds us again that good is the enemy of great. Settling for 'good enough' and settling for mediocrity. Not us, my friend.*
Robin B M.	*Thank you Cedric! You AND Karen have been and continue to be part of my story!!! Blessings.*
Vicki R.	*You are such a blessing! Thank you for inspiring me every day!!*
Laura LM.	*Wonderful Sir Cedric :)* ♥

September 21

THOUGHTS

Positive Thought Revolution

"Beware of what we choose to fix our mind and thoughts upon in these challenging times, for our most prevalent thoughts will manifest around us."

- Cedric R. Crawford -

A great verse in one of my favorite, best selling books says, "*As a man thinketh, so is he.*" If this is true, then this means that our daily thoughts are extremely important and powerful. As such, we must beware of what we choose to fix our mind and thoughts upon in these challenging times, for our most prevalent thoughts will manifest around us.

I have a suggestion, how about we start a "*Positive Thought Revolution*" to bust up these turbulent times of uncertainty? I'm sure this "*positive thinking*" stuff could quite possibly change some lives, maybe even yours. Can I count on you to join me today? No need to raise your hand, just get started and do what you can where you stand. I'll go first... Let's all make it GREAT!

September 22

PRAYER

A Contradictory Prayer

"Be careful what you pray for and how you pray for it because
you just might end up confusing the one you're praying to."
- Cedric R. Crawford -

We should be careful what we pray for and how we pray for it because we just might end up confusing the one we're praying to. If we're not careful we may oftentimes find ourselves praying what I call a "*contradictory prayer.*" On the one hand, a prayer for strength and growth while on the other hand, at the same time praying to avoid the rain and strain of adversity can be a bit confusing to say the least.

I invite you to consider the following thoughts if you will. How can we expect to grow without the water and rain and strain of adversity and challenges? The very essence of such elements are designed to make us stronger and wiser. Falling, failing and faltering are absolutely necessary in the success and growth process. So, we pray NOT for a life without loss, adversity, suffering or failure, but we do pray for the ability to utilize those gifts that have been given to us to the fullest of their potential and to the best of our ability. We pray for the stamina to endure through what comes our way and learn quickly from our mistakes so as to not repeat them.

Understand today that no matter how many times you fail you're still miles ahead of those who haven't even tried at all. No matter how small your steps are you're still yards ahead of those who are afraid to move. And, no matter how many times you fall, you're still several feet taller than those who don't even make an effort to get back up again.

A clear prayer definitely clears the air of contradiction. So let's enjoy the rays of the sunshine and embrace the strain of the rain because in it all lie's the hope for growth and strength and a better tomorrow. And never ever forget that life's too short to just make it good, so let's use the breadcrumbs of knowledge and wisdom to make it GREAT!

September 23

TIME

Invest that Time Wisely

"Our time can only be Spent, Wasted or Invested, so choose wisely."

- Cedric R. Crawford -

I was just thinking about when I first started to make myself available on a regular basis to a group of troubled boys at a local group home. My first couple of days spent with them reminded me of how fast things can go from peaceful and tranquil to loud and out-of-control. It may sound crazy to most, but I've actually been craving this type of unique opportunity of interaction and intervention since I left my employment in the Juvenile Hall Institutions years ago. It broke my heart all over again to see how reckless our little people can become in the absence of a positive mentor and role model in their lives regularly.

I know that our time can only be *Spent*, *Wasted* or *Invested*. As a result, I made a conscious decision to *Invest* my time into the lives of those boys with the intention of sowing the best parts of me into them. Today I'm happy to report that over the last year and a half I've learned just as much from them as they've learned from me. I fully expect the material, content and lessons they continue to teach me about life from their prospective will be priceless and I will do my very best to articulate those lessons learned to all of you who choose to continue read my blogs and literature.

How will you choose to utilize your time to affect the future generations? Chew on this one for a while and I hope you will ultimately choose to make it GREAT!

DREAM

Stay Focused on the Dream

*"If you can't see 'it' in your Sleep Dreams, you'll never see 'it'
on the Big Screen of your life.."*

- Cedric R. Crawford -

For those of you who woke up this morning, I'd like to say, "*Welcome back.*" I hope your journey through the dreams of your minds eye has left you with a renewed conviction of what "*could be*" for your life.

I've discovered that if you can't see "*it*" in your sleep dreams, there's a good chance you'll never see "*it*" on the big screen of your life. If you make a point to stay focused on what you're trying to accomplish and engage in the appropriate behaviors on a daily basis, you will eventually start to see your desired outcomes in your sleep-dreams.

I believe this is definitely one of the best litmus test and sign that your time is coming if you just stay on the right track. So, I encourage you today to stay focused on what you want for your life, take proper action daily and then watch the magic moments happen. Let's make it GREAT.

Farah N. A. ⠀⠀⠀ *THE BIG SCREEN... I love that! Dream it and bring it to life!!*

ANGER

Stay In-Control

*"Out-of-control behavior only begets more out-of-control
behavior and yields nothing positive."*

- Cedric R. Crawford -

As I look back over the years in retrospect and hindsight, I realize that I've made numerous trips to the home of "*out-of-control*" anger and rage but I've never felt welcomed there and I've always left feeling remorseful and dejected. As a result, I made the conscious decision to never go back down that dark road to that home again. I've discovered that "*out-of-control*" behavior only begets more "*out-of-control*" behavior from others and ultimately nothing positive or productive can ever come from it.

I've also learned that it's in our own best interest and everyone else's to make the firm decision in advance to never venture down that dark road to pay a visit to that infamous home of "*out-of-control.*"

Simply put, not allowing the actions or inactions of others to negatively affect our mood or attitude puts us in-control and being in-control trumps being out-of-control everyday of the week and twice on Sundays. Not a bad concept, huh?

Let's make a point to stay in-control today and refuse to give our power away as we utilize these breadcrumbs to make it GREAT.

| Karen B. | *Precisely! The Power always resides with Us!* |
| Juanita A. I. | *The peace within...keeps peace within.* |

September 26

MARRIAGE AND RELATIONSHIPS

A Forest Called "Marriage"

"One size doesn't necessarily fit all. One size may not even fit most, but one size definitely fits us."

- Cedric R. Crawford -

Not long ago my beautiful bride, Karen, and I had the special opportunity to share a panel with two other couples at a MOP's Event (*Mothers Of Preschoolers*). After 15 years of playing this marriage sport we're getting closer and closer to getting it right.

We both believe that when it comes to marriage preservation approach and style, one size doesn't necessarily fit all. One size may not even fit most. But one size definitely fits us and as a panelist we are not marriage experts or know-it-alls. We extended an invitation for the attendees to take a peek at some of our tips, techniques and takeaways.

During our respective journeys through this forest called "*marriage*" we've experienced highs and lows, ups and downs and fights and rough nights. But through it all we've discovered a recipe and style that works for us and we understand the perfect marriage is one that is not without its flaws, faults and fallacies.

We've found that the best marriages are built around positive intentional acts and a willingness to play fair and ultimately managing to have fun and not be too serious. Being stubborn enough to stick it out and stay when most others may walk away can be key also, and knowing when to shut up and say nothing can be magical at times.

A ton of fun it was to be a part of such an awesome event and great, down-to-earth group of panelist. As a self-proclaimed work-in-progress, I managed to take some good notes myself.

I encourage you today in your marriages and relationships to be proactive instead of reactive and understand that a better marriage or better relationship starts with a better "*YOU*." Continue to lean forward with positive intention as we all attempt to make our relationships GREAT.

September 27

COMMUNICATION

The Ban Has Been LIFTED !!!

"'Hi' is the two letter word that can get you from point 'A' to where you want to 'B'."

- Cedric R. Crawford -

To all my friends over age 18, I'd like to issue a **PSA-News Flash:** The ban on speaking to strangers that was placed on us as a kid by our parents has just been officially lifted. Speaking to strangers has been vilified for far too many years of our lives. It's time to smile, say "*Hi*" and make a friend. If we all commit to engaging in this action regularly, I have no doubt that the world will be a much more welcoming place.

I've always believed that one of the most common mistakes most people make day-in and day-out is underestimating the power of saying "*Hi.*" This two letter word can get you from point "*A*" to where you want to "*B.*" This word opens up the door to the most important powers in the universe, the power of the spoken word and communication. Simply put, people can only help you accomplish your goals and ambitious dreams if they know what your goals and ambitious dreams are, and saying "*Hi*" starts the process.

So, don't take "*Hi*" for granted by neglecting its usage in the days ahead. Be sure to use it regularly and adding a smile with it makes it even more powerful.

Let's all make a point to smile, say "*Hi*" and make it GREAT!

September 28

LEADERSHIP

A True Leader

"The greatest ship captains are not made in calm waters, so we must not retreat into the bowels of the ship when our friend, family and co-workers need us most."

- Cedric R. Crawford -

Been doing some thinking lately about what constitutes a "*true leader*" and I have a few thoughts to share. It seems to me that if our actions inspire others to be better and do more, then like it or not we're considered leaders. As a leader we should offer H.O.P.E. (*Help Other People Excel*). Also as a leader we should always remember that the greatest ship captains aren't made in calm waters, so we must not retreat into the bowels of the ship when the winds and waves of life are crashing in and our friends, family and co-workers need us most.

Times are indeed tough, but our will to persevere and overcome must always be tougher. "*True leaders*" should always welcome the opportunity to show they are capable of staying the course as they weather the storm.

As a "*true leader*" we are not easily distracted by what we see with our physical eyes for we know that our mind's eye and imagination holds the power to make all things possible for us.

Simply put, we will ultimately achieve because we continue to believe that "*it's*" possible for us. Let's rise to this occasion leaders and seize the opportunity to step into our roles and become that which we already are, "*True Leaders.*" Carpe diem (*Seize the day*), subdue it and bend it to your will as you attempt to make it GREAT!

Beverly L.   *Don't you love it when He whispers?*

September 29

CHOICES

Your Fate Is What You Make It

"Waking up in the morning with the sun shining on this face makes me happy, but waking up in the morning with the sun shining on this face used to make me sad."

- Cedric R. Crawford -

Something that makes me happy: *waking up in the morning with the sun shining on this face.* Something that used to make me sad: *waking up in the morning with the sun shining on this face.*

A few days ago I was having a heart-to-heart conversation with one of my group-home boys at one of the local group homes. He shared with me that he felt like he was born with a disadvantage of not being the *"complexion of connection,"* which is a nice way of saying he was born into a minority ethnic group. He felt that no one would ever understand him and that he was destined to be a negative product of his dysfunctional upbringing and violent surroundings and environment.

I saw this as the perfect opportunity to share with him a small piece of my story that years ago I used to think that I was inferior and destined for little more than leading an average life if I was fortunate enough to make it past my 30th birthday. But I discovered that no matter my skin color or where I came from, I do matter and I have a chance to create a life of significance and possibly even be great at something. So, my journey began making the difficult right choices over the easy wrong ones.

I explained to him that eventually repeating this action over and over again finally led me to accomplishing a lot of my goals and ambitious dreams. I assured him that the same could and would happen for him if he chooses to make the right choices and decisions when the opportunity presents itself. He has a long journey of choices ahead and only time will tell where he ends up. So, *"To be continued…"*

The truth of the matter is we all have a lot of choices to make in the days ahead. Don't delay in starting your journey of making those right choices. Whose life will you touch today with a piece of your story? Are you here to help? I have no doubt you will do your part to make someone else's day GREAT if the opportunity presents itself.

September 30

Average and Mediocrity

Average is the Enemy

"The companion of my companion is my companion and the enemy of my enemy is my friend."

- Cedric R. Crawford -

As I stumble through life I have become more intentional about continuing to increase my network of positive, upward mobile people who are looking to better themselves. My positive association attraction-meter knows no bounds and I like it that way. As a result, the companion of my companion is my companion and the enemy of my enemy is my friend. My Enemy is called "*Average*" and "*Mediocrity*."

If you too are striving to be better today than you were yesterday or working to create or do something significant and bigger than yourself, let me be the first to give you a big high-five and call you "*friend*." We fight for a life that matters in the grand scheme of things and are unwilling to settle for anything less than that which we have been called.

Stay focused and be encouraged today and know that all you do when no ones looking is not in vein. Press-on *friend* for someone needs to be inspired by your story of how you overcame "*average*" and "*mediocrity*" to achieve something great. So make it GREAT!

October 1

Words

My Words Can Be Overrated

"Don't let 'You' talk 'You' out of what you really want to do in your life."

- Cedric R. Crawford -

I was just thinking today what inspiring words could I possibly say that would alert most people to the realization that being comfortable with living an average, humdrum life of mediocrity is contrary to all we were created to be. What phrase could I possibly create today that would keep others moving in the direction of significance? After careful thought, I came up with absolutely nothing. My words may be overrated and useless when it comes to your goals and dreams anyway, but yours aren't. What really counts is what words you're speaking regularly and what conversations you're having with yourself daily.

Be sure not to let "*You*" talk "*You*" out of what you really want to do in your life. "*Can you do it?*" is an easy question to answer. But, the question that makes all the difference today is, "*Will you do it?*" Will you make the necessary commitment today and stay the course when the wind blows and the wave's crash? Will you choose to be the exception and press forward during those times of severe struggle and challenge? Will you be able to embrace the times of adversity knowing and understanding that it's in moments such as these when great men and women are forged and fashioned. Hmmm… Speak your words of inspiration today and continue to make it GREAT!

Lisa M. F.   *Ohhh..that is good! You're making us think of the word. Smart!*

Chris P.   *I think your word is "Humility." And that is a very, very good word my friend.*

NOTES

October 2

Difficult Right Easy Wrong

"We've already <u>Conceived it</u>, *we continue to* <u>Believe it's</u> *possible for us and we fully expect to* <u>Achieve it</u>.*"*

- Cedric R. Crawford -

I was out hiking in the Pine Mountains with family a day ago and I'm always inspired by all the absolute beauty in nature. This type of outing always reminds me that all that we see around us was no accident. With all that prospers and grows in nature, I'm reminded also that our Creator has graced each and every one of us with the talents required for us to succeed in magnificent fashion in the areas of our gifts. It is our job to work to refine our talents and gifts and use them to inspire and encourage others to find and pursue their passion and purpose also.

My prayer for you today is that you will achieve those dreams you hoped for the day you said *"Yes"* to pursuing your passion and purpose in this life. I sincerely hope that we will all choose to make the difficult right choices over the easy wrong choices over and over again in the days ahead.

My wish is that we will also continue to not be easily distracted or enticed by the negative activity of the *"in-crowd"* and hold firm to the belief and understanding that what's right isn't always popular and what's popular isn't always right.

We hereby recommit ourselves today to take yet another bold step in the direction of our goals and dreams and cling ever-so-tightly to our positive daily disciplines for we know that all we do behind the scenes is not in vein. We've already *Conceived it*, we continue to *Believe it's* possible for us and we fully expect to *Achieve it*. Be encouraged today and feel free to use these breadcrumbs to make it GREAT!

Conceive it

Believe it

ACHIEVE IT

www.CedricCrawford.com

DEATH

Got M-i-l-k ?

"When death comes to collect its debt from us, may it find us
in service to yet another person."

- Cedric R. Crawford -

In life some of us may get away with cheating on our taxes and some of us may even file bankruptcy or default on a mortgage or two in our lifetime. Some of us may even be successful in having a debt reduced to almost nothing. But the only debt that can't be avoided by anyone is the debt we all owe to the grave. Yes my friends, no matter what we do in this life, at the end of the day we all have to return these fallible vessels to the grave, no exceptions. But take heart for there is good news. I sincerely believe our souls live-on in *"Phase 2"* in a completely different realm of space with the absence of time.

What we do today determines what happens after we close our eyes and breathe our last breath in *"Phase 1."* Let's not take our countless opportunities to do *"Good"* for granted for there will eventually come a time when the opportunity will be no more.

So I say today when death comes to collect its debt from me, may it find *me Inspiring, Motivating, Empowering, Educating* and *Encouraging* yet another person. Let's make it GREAT.

October 4

TRUTH

Facing the Right Direction?

"The sun is always faithful to shine. The only time that we
experience real darkness is when the earth turns its back to the
sun."

- Cedric R. Crawford -

As the moisture and coolness of the fresh morning dew is slowly burned off by the heat of the early sun rays of the crack of dawn, I can't help but to think how lucky we are to all have yet another crack at making ourselves better today than we were yesterday. We have been graced with a clean slate and another opportunity to get *"it"* right.

I've come to realize that the sun is always faithful to shine. The only time that we experience real darkness is when the earth turns its back to the sun. What a great metaphor for life. I say today that we walk in darkness only because we choose to keep our backs turned to the sunlight of *"truth."*

I'm reminded of when my baby-girl, Chayse-Marie turned three-years-old she started to realize that just because her eyes were covered or her back was turned it didn't mean that the person or problem was gone. The very truth that some of us are choosing to turn our backs and a blind eye to is the truth we need to be facing and having a serious encounter with.

My prayer today is that the days of covering our eyes or turning our back on the truth will become a thing of the past. What's your truth and which direction will you choose to face today? Chayse-Marie figured it out at age three. We can't run from 'it', we have to turn around and embrace 'it'. May the rising sun be a continuous reminder for you to make those "good" choices in the new day. Oh, and let's all choose to make the day GREAT!

October 5

TIME

What time is it?

"If we're still walking among the living we still have a chance to turn our respective situations around."

- Cedric R. Crawford -

We will inevitably get out of the hour whatever we diligently put into the sixty minutes. We will undoubtedly get out of every day what we choose to put into those 24 hours. And, it's safe to say the outcome for our month and year will be a direct result of how we invested those days and weeks. If we don't like where we're at right now, we have to look in the mirror and utter these words, *"What are you going to do differently this minute to start the process of changing your outcome?"* As harsh as this may sound, we have absolutely no one else to blame for where we're at now, good or not-so-good, except for ourselves.

The overwhelmingly good news is no matter what our age, if we're still walking among the living, we still have a chance to turn our respective situations around, or we can just go on and ignore the possibilities and live out the days as we were. The choice is, and always has been ours and ours alone. If change is needed for you today I would hope that you would make the wise choice in this moment and choose to make it GREAT!

October 6

The Quiet Cry for Help

"Be the answer to somebody's prayer, or the solution to some-body's problem, or the miracle that someone has been hoping and waiting for in some way today."

- Cedric R. Crawford -

I just got back from having dinner with my family at one of our favorite local restaurants, approximately 10 minutes after we were seated a man, a woman and small child were seated at the booth next to us. Almost immediately the man began a loud conversation on his Bluetooth cell phone as he started to scarf down the chips and salsa while at the same time occasionally yelling instructions to his daughter who appeared to be about three-years-old.

He appeared to be unaware that he was in a public place surrounded by other parents and kids as he continued to use profane language in a boisterous tone. The look on his wife's face said it all as she would not dare make an attempt to correct his behavior. She continued to look down and around as if to apologize for her husband's actions in public. Even more surprising, he appeared to be perfectly sober while this was all happening. People attempted to continue on with their meal hoping that he would settle down, but he continued on as he practically demanded that the bus boy, not the waiter, bring him a beer.

I must admit my heart goes out to his wife and daughter because I know that they probably feel like they're trapped in what may be an abusive relationship with a sole-provider that rules his house with an iron and uncompassionate fist. I wish I could say I haven't seen this before, but unfortunately this type of dynamic in a relationship is all too common.

I found myself asking the question of, *"What can I do to help her?"* And the answer was, *"Absolutely nothing."* I resolved to myself that any action that I would try to take in that type of setting would most likely result in nothing positive. The unfortunate truth is she would eventually have to dislike her situation and current pain enough to want to endure the pain that it would take to change. I hope and pray that she has a friend or two that knows her plight and will eventually step up to offer her the assistance she needs to change her situation.

For those of you who can identify with this situation I encourage you to make this day the day you say the famous phrase of, *"Enough is Enough!"* and make some changes for the better. And, for those of you who have a friend or family member who is quietly calling out for your help, I pray you will make this day the day you show you can be counted-on and not counted-out.

On this day we should all make a point to be the answer to somebody's prayer, or the solution to somebody's problem, or the miracle that someone has been hoping and waiting for in some way. I invite you to join me this year in helping someone else to make it GREAT as we seek to do the same.

October 7

The Waves of Opportunity

"Our mental surfboards have been waxed, polished and well-maintained to ride the countless waves of the unique opportunities in the days ahead."

- Cedric R. Crawford -

I was hanging out at the beach the other day staring at the waves crashing into the shore and I suddenly felt a small wind of inspiration come over me so I grabbed my trusted old pen and pad and started writing as follows:

For those of us who are seeking to make a positive impact on this world, it's imperative we turn our trials into our triumphs, our mess into our message, our test into our testimony and our problems into our prophecy of a profound winning probability. We must choose NOT to be a victim, but to be victorious, not for our own sakes, but for the sake of those who come after us so that they may see that *"it"* is possible.

In the face of crisis we will not cower away and retreat to that foxhole of fear and trepidation for we know that out of crisis comes *"Opportunity."* So instead, we rise, Rise and RISE again to take full advantage of our moments to shine and show that we were designed for a time such as this. We've already studied in advance so that we can show ourselves approved in times like these. Our   mental surfboards have been waxed, polished and well-maintained to ride the countless waves of the unique opportunities in the days ahead. Yes indeed we are a strange breed better known as *"resilient overcomers."* The words *"no retreat, no surrender"* comes to mind in troubled times for we know unequivocally that anything that's worth-while in this life will always be realized on the other side of fear and adversity. So we press on toward the mark of the high call of our Creator and will not waver in our faith and belief that our goals are possible and our cause is indeed noble and just.

Our victory is inevitable simply because we have made the commitment to not stop until we WIN. So my bold statement to life today is, *"Bring it on,"* for we will stay the course for yet one more day and welcome the challenge of the waves for we know between the crest and the crash of the waves exist the special *"OPPORTUNITY"* to be better today than we were yesterday. So, BRING IT ON I say!!!

What words do you choose to speak today in lieu of the crashing waves around you? I trust you will say the same. BRING IT ON!!! Let's continue in our steadfast efforts to make it GREAT!

Bonita D.   *I totally agree. Thanks for the motivation you have inspired on me today...*

Laura K.   *Yes, indeed...Let's make it GREAT and rise, Rise, RISE to the challenges we all face, with great faith, love and understanding. Thank you Cedric. :))*

Jim and Annette M. *The opportunity is ours to take or waste! Waste not the opportunity, but walk forward and strive to be better than our predecessors. Listen not to those who tried and died. Walk on my friends.*

October 8

FOCUS

My Prayer For Us Today

"May I continue to attack each day with truth because my boys say they want to be like me."

- Cedric R. Crawford –

My prayer for us today as we approach yet another welcomed 24 hours is, may we continue to be honest with the person peering back at us in the mirror. May integrity continue to be the foundation for the way we conduct business. May our mistakes be few and our excuses non-existent. May our passion be our focus fueled by our unwavering beliefs and convictions.

May there be many moments that make us smile with authentic joy. May our hearts deepest desire be to do for others in need. May we have the courage and bravery of a fearless lion in the face of our greatest fears and become unstoppable in our noble and just pursuits. Finally, may I continue to attack each day with these truths because my boys say they want to be like me.

Yes my friends, this life is definitely worthy of even more than just our best efforts. So let's not just make it good, let's subdue it and make it GREAT!

October 9

PERSISTENCE

My Conversation with a Thief

"In your quest to accomplish your wildest goals and dreams, may you be as persistent, focused and determined as a top notch thief."

- Cedric R. Crawford -

I had the most interesting conversation with a reformed thief that was making a last-ditch effort to turn his life around. He prefers to call himself an "*Opportunist*," which I believe is very fitting for his purposes. This "*Opportunist*" has officially retired from his wicked ways and is now looking to cash-in on legitimate opportunities to make a living. For obvious reasons he wishes to remain anonymous. For our purposes today I'll just call him "*Joe*" (*No offense to all the law-abiding Joe's out there.*)

I asked Joe how can the general public better protect themselves from becoming a victim, and he had these words to say, "*There's no fool-proof way to protect yourself from becoming a victim because if an opportunist wants to get what you got, he or she can find a way to get it, but there's a way to become an unattractive target.*" I asked the question of what can I do to make him pass on my house or vehicle and go on to the next one? His response was that a house with an alarm placard has to be assumed that it has an alarm, so next house. A house with a barking dog, lights on or radio on is a huge deterrent too, so, next. An open or half-closed garage door is "*easy pickings*." A neighborhood with "*Neighborhood Watch*" placards and signs is one that he would rather not spend much time casing because of the nosey, well-informed neighbors. An unlocked car makes an easy target too. A blinking LED light on the dashboard of a vehicle usually means that it has an alarm so, next. Leaving valuable items in plain sight in your car can become almost irresistible for a "*smash-and-grab-and-RUN*," which means to smash your car window, grab your items and run to the nearest Pawn Shop.

Joe prefers to burglarize homes during the day between the hours of 10am and 2pm because most people are at work allowing for no surprises. Days when the weather is cool are ideal because most people like to leave their windows open to allow the nice, cool breeze to blow through the house. Joe's worst fear is that someone will actually be home when he enters a house. Most opportunists want absolutely no contact with people. They just want to get in, get some valuables and get out. Joe has several stories of how some of the Big-Job opportunists operate and he stated, "*Some guys can dress up real nice and knock on doors acting like their selling home alarm systems or other stuff to people and they'll ask questions about whether or not they have an alarm or dogs or plans to go on vacation this summer or out of town for the holidays and stuff. After getting this info they can then show up with a U-Haul Moving Truck on a day that they know the resident will be out of town and take their time about cleaning out the house. The neighbors will just think they're moving or something. Those are the Big-Jobs.*"

Needless to say, my conversation with Joe was very informative and he wishes to make it known that he is extremely remorseful for all of those he's victimized. He hopes that something he's shared today will help someone in the future to prevent being victimized by an "*Opportunist*." He attributes his negative actions and crimes committed in the past to his unquenchable thirst for drugs and alcohol, and having a criminal record made it tough for him to get legitimate work. He cautions those who are looking to try to get ahead in life by ripping-off other people. "*God is watching you*," he says with a raised eyebrow and a toothless smile, "*and the outcome is Jail or Hell. I got a lot of making up to do now and I'm doing pretty good.*"

I meet some of the most interesting people just because I'm no longer afraid to say "*Hi*." I'm convinced that my meeting Joe was no coincidence and his story and tips will undoubtedly help somebody out there to become a more unattractive target in the future for some "*Opportunist*" out there.

My prayer and hope for you today is in your quest to accomplish your wildest goals and dreams, may you be as persistent, focused and determined as a top-notch thief or "*Opportunist*." This is definitely a breadcrumb that's worth way more than its weight so let's make it GREAT!

October 10

What's your Bold Statement?

"'Adversity' is a highly trained body-guard of 'Success' and 'Significance.'"

- Cedric R. Crawford -

I've discovered that *"Adversity"* is a highly trained bodyguard of *"Success"* and *"Significance."* It appears to stand about eight feet tall, weighs about 450 pounds and has less than 2% body fat with 32-inch guns. It has a menacing look and can often times be found growling and barking at individuals who attempt to come within striking distance of his employer's *success* and *significance*.

Its primary job is to weed out all those who are not committed to their cause and are not certain of their destination. Adversity is highly paid and has several incentives in its contract to administer unbridled, ferocious beat-downs. It appears to feed off of fear, trepidation and uncertainty and would want nothing more than the opportunity to crush and devour all those who harbor these characteristics.

Its specialty is the unexpected *"sucker-punch"* to the head or gut just when you least expect it. It represents its employer without passion or prejudice and has never relinquished the title of *"Employee of the Month."* It is indeed a formidable foe and is not even above stabbing you in the back if it sees an opportunity to do so.

But take heart today my friends, for I have also discovered that the bark and growl of adversity is far worse than its bite. Its kryptonite appears to be focus, determination, persistence and simply having a *"No Quit"* attitude. It has been defeated and overcome time-and-time again by *"Goal Getters"* and individuals both large and small who are not afraid to stand firm in the face of adversity and demand its unconditional surrender because their motto is, *"I won't give up until I WIN!"* Adversity cannot stand such words of conviction and certainty. It cowers away in the face of such statements of commitment. Bold statements backed by consistent, proper action and focus daily will almost certainly guarantee a victorious battle against this formidable bodyguard of success and significance.

So, what's your *"bold statement"* today in pursuit of your cause and quest to accomplish your goals? What words do you choose to speak over this formidable foe called adversity? No need to answer out loud, just make me proud and stand out from the crowd as you say it loud. Dare to join me today in saying, *"MOUNTAIN MOVE OUT OF MY WAY!"*

Chris P.　　　　*Big smile reading your encouragement! Never give up, no matter what, that's what my 7 year old learned from his Dad...*

> **Please view the video on:**
>
> **www.YouTube.com**
>
> **Search Code: Cedric R. Crawford – (25)**

October 11

SUFFERING

Forged by the Fiery Furnace

"The heart and character of great men and women are forged and fashioned in the crucibles and furnaces of sufferings and hardships."

- Cedric R. Crawford -

Over the years, I've learned that the heart and character of great men and women are forged and fashioned in the crucibles and furnaces of struggle, hardships and suffering.

The reality is there's never a convenient time for adversity, but we must understand that no one can achieve true greatness and significance unless he or she has gone through the *"fire."* Just as gold, silver and other precious metals are forged by extreme heat to remove all impurities and be molded into the desired shape, so too is the process of those who wish to achieve great things among us in this life.

So I say to you this day, be thankful for the good, the bad, the happy and the sad. Count it all joy and view it as an affirmative sign that you're moving in the right direction,. For without the struggles and strains in our lives, great things could never be obtained and sustained.

I invite you to embrace this principle and philosophy in the days ahead and let's continue to overcome and become who we need to be and inspire others to do the same. This is just another breadcrumb to making it GREAT! Enjoy.

October 12

ROLE-MODEL

Our Youth is Our Future

"In life people don't rise to lower expectations and sometimes it's necessary for us to show that we believe in them so that it will increase the chances of them believing in themselves."

- Cedric R. Crawford -

I've had the good fortune to speak to several different kinds of people and audiences over the last several months and I've discovered that there appears to be nothing quite as hard to remove or is as securely lodged then the ignorance of someone whose spent a number of years in a certain field.

Most recently I had a unique opportunity to have a candid discussion with a *boy's group-*home employee and I must admit that I was shocked and amazed at some of the opinions this person had about their job. For the purposes of anonymity we'll just call this person Bill. Bill boasted that he had been in the field of juvenile care providing and children services for several years and had a ton of stories to tell. As one can imagine, I was eager to listen but first I wanted to know what Bill liked best about what he did. Bill simply said, *"I just love working with kids."*

Of course I continued to probe a bit deeper by making a statement that I think he could agree that kids really need a mentor and positive role-model in their lives on a regular basis. He then abruptly stated, *"These kids don't need no mentor. They need a baby-sitter to watch 'em just so they don't hurt themselves or each other."* Well, needless to say I was completely dumbfounded and blindsided by this candid statement, and I was even more shocked when he failed to even make an effort to retract the statement as being a joke.

Bill then proceeded to ask me if in the short amount of time that I'd been coming around, if I saw any positive potential in any one of the 15 boys. I then advised him that based on my extremely limited amount of time invested with most of the boys, I was not in the position to make such a judgment call on specific potential. But, I did caution him that all the boys have the potential to be productive citizens in society with proper intervention. He then looked at me as if to say, *"Well, we'll just see how long you keep thinking that way around here…"*

I've learned in life that people don't rise to lower expectations and sometimes it's necessary for us to show that we believe in them so it will increase the chances of them eventually believing in themselves. Who better to point out their gifts and positive attributes and teach them about choices and consequences than those adults that interact with them on a regular basis? Who better to show them how to treat others with respect and handle responsibility than us? Who else is better positioned to capture those adverse moments in their life and drive-home the vitally important golden rule of treating people the way you want to be treated?

My heart breaks for the millions of kids who have to deal with the absence of an active, positive role-model in their lives that truly understands the plight of the kids and recognizes the importance of their role. I've always counted it as odd that the people in these types of jobs appear to be grossly undereducated, underpaid and receive very little training considering the role they play in the lives of our nation's most precious asset (*children*). It seems to me that this should be considered as one of the most important roles in our world because it's a role that allows us to shape the world starting with our youth.

I'm reminded of the timeless song titled, *"I Believe the Children Are Our Future."* The song also states that we should, *"…teach them well and let them lead the way and show them all the beauty they possess inside and give them a sense of pride."* Yes, this too is absolutely worthy of our best efforts because they're absolutely worth it and they need us to step up now more than ever before to challenge what the TVs, CDs and MP3s are teaching them.

It is my sincere hope and prayer that the Bills and Bettys of the world will read this book and be forever changed in the way they see their role in the lives of our youth. Simply put, to give up on our kids is to give up on our future. Maybe you know a *"Bill"* or a *"Betty"* that could use this book? Hmmmm… It just might be worth the extra investment to place a courtesy copy of this book in their hands.

The Bill in this conversation will definitely receive a courtesy copy from me if our paths cross again. His story is hereby labeled, *"To Be Continued…"* Let's all do our level best to help our youth make their lives GREAT!

CHANGE

The Process

"Blaze your trail then come back and light the path for others."
- Cedric R. Crawford -

I was chatting with my good friend Judy the other day and she was sharing some of the highlights and not-so-highlights of her 25th class reunion. She had the special opportunity to be reunited with old friends, some of which she had not seen in 25 years. Although she was extremely excited about the event, she expressed that she found it increasingly tougher to carry on a positive, uplifting conversation with most of her old classmates. This was very perplexing to her and she couldn't quite put her finger on the reason why. I attempted to give Judy an unsolicited answer to her rhetorical question. I simply stated that, *"You've gone through the positive process of changing and developing yourself personally on purpose and they haven't."*

Over the past few years Judy has been undergoing a major transformation. This transformation is not-so-much physically as it has been mentally. She has become so much more aware of who she is and why she's here. She's now more *"passion-focused"* and *"purpose-driven"* and no longer finds conversations about what's happening to other people and politics as entertaining or as interesting anymore. I cautioned Judy that most of her friends haven't started their process of becoming enlightened or aware of why they're here and what's really important in this life and unfortunately some never will.

The real unfortunate fact is that this phenomenon doesn't just exist as an isolated case in Judy's high school class, but it's unfortunately representative of *"Most People"* on our great planet. But, then again we're not *"Most People."* You see *"Most People"* wouldn't have made it this far in reading a personal development book such as this. But even more than that, *"Most People"* won't even invest time or money in a personal development book period, but you did.

During the process of going through your process understand that some of your friends and family may not understand. Be not dismayed and stay the course anyway because the new and improved you will positively affect all those around you. It will help if you just think of it this way, *"They don't know what they don't know but they think they know."* So, don't be afraid to blaze the trail so you will know then come back and light the path so that they too will know. Congratulations for not being *"Most People!"* Let's make it GREAT.

NETWORK MARKETING

Yes or NO to Network Marketing

"The biggest key to succeeding in any industry is to first realize why many people fail."
- Cedric R. Crawford -

I was recently asked by a good friend of mine to share my thoughts and opinion on how I feel about network marketing. I must admit that I always feel honored when I get such request, for it means that my thoughts and opinions are actually worth something to somebody in this world. Now I don't expect my opinions of this industry to land me in the best of company and social groups but I will take the opportunity to share it anyway

I truly feel that the area of MLM (*multi-level marketing*) and network marketing have long since been vilified by so many across the globe. I'm confident that the reason behind this is simply because bad news travels much faster and more efficiently than good news. It appears a person doesn't have to look very far to find someone who would be more than happy to share a story or two about their negative experience in the area of network marketing. I too used to share the same negative sentiment because of my unsuccessful experience in the industry. But one day when I became more mature in business and the business of life, I took the opportunity to revisit the idea and the possibilities provided by the industry.

In short, my research led me to a new found belief that the business of Network Marketing and Direct Sales at its core when compared to that of traditional business has fundamental principles that far out-weigh any other industry I know of. The principles and disciplines that are encouraged in this industry are tied directly to people not only being successful in business, but also successful and happier in the business of life.

As with any industry, this industry also has its fair share of snakes, schemers and scammers who are willing to compromise their integrity in their pursuit of money, fame and power, but I still believe the true foundational principles that govern the industry are first to many and second to none. So it's for this reason I can't help but to be a huge fan and advocate of the industry.

After thoroughly breaking down the business attributes of direct sales and network marketing, I have come up with the six reasons why this industry is so appealing. I call them the "Six-Ps of Network Marketing." The Six "Ps" stand for *Passion, People, Personal Development, Potential, Product* and *Profit,* respectively. I believe anyone who's seriously considering partnering with a company in this industry should definitely pay close attention to these Six "P's."

First up is "*Passion.*" Passion should be the cornerstone of all we decide to do in this life. If we have no true passion for what we choose to invest our time in daily, it won't last or our lives will be short of authentic joy and true happiness. Passion has to be the number one factor when choosing the right product, service and company. Yes, it definitely has to be something that you can be Passionate about in order for you to be able to win in the long run. If you do what you love, you will love what you do.

Next up is the "*People.*" As a life coach, one of my first recommendations for people seeking to move to a different level in their life is to evaluate their friends and who they're associating with. I then advise them to be sure to get around some positive, *dream-driven, goal-getter, passion-pursuing* people on a regular basis so they can maximize and positively leverage the law of association. The people we choose to associate mostly with in this life will positively or negatively affect our life in the long run. So be sure to choose wisely.

The next one is my personal favorite, which is "*Personal Development.*" Most people believe that education stops with graduation, but I believe this notion couldn't be further from the truth. In fact, after graduation our educational and personal development efforts should intensify. Success in this industry is tied directly to growing one's self personally which spins right into the fourth "*P*" on the list, which is "*Potential.*"

You will have to determine whether or not the mission of the company you decide to partner with is positioned so-as to allow you to reach your maximum potential as a person. Does the company advocate for the unlimited individual growth of its representatives to their fullest of potential spiritually, emotionally, socially and financially? A "*yes*" or "*no*" answer here should lead you directly to your "*yes*" or "*no*" decision to join the cause.

Next is the "*Product*" (*or service*). The product has to matter to people, make sense in business and make a positive difference in the lives of people and/or the planet. This will allow people to experience the feeling of making a positive contribution to the world by helping others.

Finally, the "*Profit*" generated by the sale of said products or services should be designed to reward each person proportionately to their work performed. Also a residual component should exist that allows for one to build an organization that will continue to reward the individual repeatedly for many "*willable*," generational years to come.

I am so passionate about the possibilities and opportunities offered by this industry that I could write a book on the subject of why I believe everyone should have some type of presence in the industry in some way. I think many can agree that more people are starting to realize "*Job Security*" in the traditional business model and corporate America is a myth. Millions of people are starting to receive their rude awakenings to this fact around the country and the world.

I've learned that one of the biggest keys to succeeding in this industry is to first realize why many people fail. Many fail in this industry because they struggle to perform consistently and persistently in the absence of a task master or boss. Without the constant supervision and mandatory requirements of a traditional job and the consistency of a predictable paycheck, most people will become frustrated and run for the hills of comfort. This is a harsh truth indeed but not divulging this grim reality up front to new business prospects would be definitely setting them up for failure. Just like any other business, this too requires *work*. I guess that's why they call it Net-*WORK* Marketing.

Focus and Discipline rules the day and can make much more than just your day in this industry if you commit to adopt the proper principles and follow the Six "*Ps*" to finding your key partnership.

So, if you have a goal of maintaining some type of personal control over your financial future, do not make the mistake of being duped by the belief that a "*good job*" alone is going to do it for you. Yes, some have been fortunate to make a living by giving the best years of there life to an employer in exchange for predictable wages that they can budget there life around and this is definitely not a bad thing. However, it may not be a bad idea to have something developing part-time on the side. So don't quite your day job, but proceed with caution.

This breadcrumb can definitely help you to make it great in not just the network marketing business, but also the business of life. Let's make it GREAT!

October 15

OPTIMISM

Priceless

"Learn to make lemonade out of the lemon-lessons of life."
- Cedric R. Crawford -

Late night grocery shopping with my two boys at Winco Food Store a few days ago, $153.25. Returning to the car to find a dead battery from leaving the lights on, $65. Spending 40 minutes sitting in the car waiting for the tow-truck while talking to my two boys about how to handle adversity and be exceptional men, Priceless.

Over the years I must say that I've become more optimistic about things and I truly have learned to capture every opportunity to make lemonade out of the lemon-lessons of life. I've developed a much better understanding that it's not necessarily about whether we've been dealt a few bad hands in this life, it's about being able to play a bad hand well and exercise what I call our *"bounce-back-ability."* No doubt about it, the glass is half full for me and I not only look for the silver lining in every dark cloud, but I also realize that in every crisis there lies an opportunity in some way, shape or form.

I can only hope that the lessons learned, bridges burned, tables turned and messages earned in my life will be echoed down through the lives of my boys and the generations that follow to better equip others for those twist and turns and curve-balls of life. Be assured they are watching.

The way I see it is, it's up to us to give those little people a bit of a headstart in this *"life"* thing. Don't miss your opportunities to show your *optimism* and cash-in on those priceless moments in your unfolding future and be sure not to just settle for *"Good"* if *"GREAT"* is an option for you.

Gerwyn D.	*Great words of wisdom Cedric, I try to do the same with my two boys as well. Keep smiling and thanks for sharing.*
Bill M.	*It's all about how you look at the world. Your boys will soon be young men with an awesome perspective on the world thanks to a great dad!*

NOTES

Bonus DAY 10!!!

The Skeptical Man

There once was a very skeptical man, who never laughed or played.
He never made friends or took any risk, he never smiled or prayed.

But then one day he passed away and no one shed a tear.
Because he took no risk and made no friends they said he was never really here.

A very strange story some might say, But can this one be true?
That "*Skeptical Man*" who took no risk or made friends, don't let that man be you.

Laugh and play, smile and pray and make a friend or two.
I believe that's exactly what we all were created and designed to do.

by Cedric R. Crawford

Please view the video on:

www.YouTube.com

<u>Search Code:</u> **Cedric R. Crawford – (10)**

October 16

You Will Be Tested

"The question is not 'if' you're commitment will be tested, it's just a question of 'when'"

- Cedric R. Crawford -

Over the course of our life the strength of our resolve and/or love for someone or something will be tested. I'm totally convinced that this is our Creator's way of weeding out the "*non-hackers*" and determining if we're really committed to the person or cause we champion. Letter and number grades are not possible for this type of test it's only pass or fail.

An occasional pop-quiz may occur too from time-to-time. As a result, I've found the best philosophy to have is, "*Don't just Get Ready, but Stay Ready.*" You never know when you'll have to stand up and be counted for your cause and have your commitment card stamped and validated. A great man once said that it is far better to be ready for an opportunity and not have one, than to have an opportunity and not be ready for it. I've also read somewhere that "*Luck favors the prepared.*"

All of these statements and proclamations are right on target in my eyes. So, the question is not "*if*" you're commitment will be tested, it's just a question of "*when*." Will you be ready? Will you be counted among the ones who were able to persist and overcome? Hmmmm... No need to raise your hand or answer out loud, just make me proud and stand out from the crowd as you continue in your efforts to make it GREAT!

October 17

ENCOURAGEMENT

Unique One of a Kind

"We're not one in a million or billion. We're a 'Unique,' original ONE of a KIND."

- Cedric R. Crawford -

Today I had the unique opportunity to deliver a unique message to an audience of a couple hundred unique individuals about what it really means to be "*unique*." We're not one in a million or billion. We're a "*unique*," original ONE of a KIND. Each and every one of us was designed with a unique job to do that only we can do and no one else can do it quite like us. The challenge is for all of us to find that unique gift and purpose of ours and expose it to the world for *good*.

We emphatically refuse to settle for anything less than what our original design was meant for, Greatness. I think they got the message. Let's all commit to find our gift of greatness and make it GREAT!

Kimberly Price.   *You did a great job.*

Nicholas Carpenter *Cedric my man, just wanted to let you know that what you said today during Splash Zone was pretty powerful and awesome stuff. I know it was all meant for kids, but some of what you said really got to me this morning. Thanks for bringing us God's Word in that way.*

October 18

GOALS AND DREAM

Fight for Goals and Dreams

"Our goals and dreams won't fight for us, we have to put forth an effort and fight for them."

- Cedric R. Crawford -

It just dawned on me that in real life cows don't actually give us milk, we have to take it from them. Sure they don't put up much of a fight but we still have to make an effort to take it from them. So too are our goals and dreams. Our goals and dreams won't fight for us, we have to put forth an effort and fight for them and be willing to go get what is right for us.

If we know that we can do better and be better and don't strive to do so, we don't have to answer to anyone but ourselves and our Creator. Make no mistake about it, a better job, a better income, a better marriage, a better life and a better anything starts with a better "You." Yes, a better "You" makes all goals and dreams that much more attainable.

I learned a secret some time ago which had really been in plain sight all along and no real secret at all. If we strive to make ourselves the best we can possibly be in any given area, all that we seek will rise to the surface and find us. This is real, practical stuff and not just lip-service. I live a life with this type of thinking and mindset every day and I'm blessed to say that life is good because I choose to make it so. I insist on it.

Simply put, we can always better our best, so be encouraged today and continue to strive to be better today than you were yesterday in every way and then let the chips fall where they may. Fight for those goals and dreams for one more day. Take another swing today and make it GREAT!

October 19

GREATNESS

Beware of the Dill-Pickles

"Don't make the big mistake of taking life too seriously and end up stuck with a dill-pickle-face in your old age."

- Cedric R. Crawford -

Just a friendly reminder today that life is short and unpredictable and we only get one time through with no do-over. With every breath we breathe we move one breath closer to our last breath, so let's live and love like we're a breath away from our last because one day we'll be right.

The greatest men and women of our past had to pass this way too. They breathed the same air, walked under the same sun and slept under the same moonlight, but what made the truly great ones so great was their ability to endure hardships and not settle for anything less than the desired result.

It is for this reason I say to you today, if you believe that greatness and significance is truly an option for you in life, then how dare you settle for good. Pursue greatness and don't make the big mistake of taking life too seriously and end up stuck with a dill-pickle face in your old age. Laugh, smile and say "Hi" often. Make a point to enjoy this life. After all, you only get one body and one time through, so make it GREAT!

October 20

WEAKNESS

Weakness to STRENGTH

"Real confidence can be built by working on the six inches of space between your ears."

- Cedric R. Crawford -

It's interesting how some things that may have been considered as a weakness can drastically change for the better for us over time and become a strength after a little work. I remember as a little kid I used to hate my smile because I had a large gap between my two front teeth. This resulted in me having slightly lower self-esteem. Smiling was a bit hard for me at times so I avoided it as much as possible.

Over the years, as I got older I slowly started to build confidence in my smile one tooth at a time. This confidence was not built by traditional surgery, but by what I passionately refer to as a surgery of the mind. As a result, I now believe that one of my most redeeming attributes has actually become my smile. I now love my signature, trademark, toothy, cool-aid smile and wouldn't trade it for the world.

I often times hear from others that my smile is inviting and contagious. Needless to say, this really reinforces my confidence and, believe it or not, I now actually find it hard NOT to smile. It took some work over the years to achieve this level of confidence and now something that I used to consider as a *weakness* has now become a *strength*.

Is there something that's negatively affecting your confidence today? Hmmmm... I invite you consider taking that perceived weakness and turning it into a strength. It all starts with working on the six inches of space between your ears. It worked for me so I know it can work for you. Special I am not, but the process of change is incredibly powerful. Let's take that weakness and make it GREAT!

Karen B.	*This is Great Ced !!! 'Surgery of the mind'. I LOVE it!!*
Lisa M. F.	*Moments ago! I was scared to paint decorations on my furniture because I'm not "as good" as the professionals. But I went for it in my own style and I'm so happy I did! I love it!*
Diane K.	*I have exactly the same thing with my teeth.... just makes it easier to floss. Often what we think are weaknesses are really gifts.*
Stephanie B. P.	*Awesome advice, and by the way, an awesome smile!*

PERSONAL DEVELOPMENT

Weirdism

"Weirdism: *The process of being considered weird by others when you start to talk and act differently as a result of engaging in positive personal development activity.*"

- Cedric R. Crawford -

I created a new term a while ago called, "*Weirdism*." I define this term as the process of being considered weird by others when you start to talk and act differently as a result of engaging in positive personal development activity regularly.

If you're going through a changing process whereas you're reading, listening and participating in positive stuff designed to improve you personally, spiritually, mentally and physically, you may start to say and do things that others may consider as "*weird.*" Please take this as a good sign that you are indeed on the right track and headed in the right direction to becoming something special, so keep going.

Be encouraged today and know the greatest men and women this side of the universe were no-doubt considered "*weird*" at one time or another because of the words they used and their thought patterns and daily activities. So, welcome the "*weirdism*" and know that you're on your way to making it GREAT!

KINDNESS

Celebrated or Tolerated

"*Be sure to pepper your environment with treats-of-kindness so you will be celebrated rather than just tolerated.*"

- Cedric R. Crawford -

I was talking to my 76-year-old, 84 pound, four foot 10 inch tall Japanese Master Tailor Iko (*pronounced "eeko"*) not long ago. She lives alone by choice and she says that she lives a simple life full of routine. Her best friend is a small, Apple-Face Chihuahua named Plum who was the last gift given to her by her husband a few years ago before he passed away.

Part of Iko's daily routine is getting up bright and early every morning, seven days a week and walking the neighborhood streets. She loves and lives for the daily opportunity to walk her usual route with a bag of treats in hand so she can feed the eight dogs and one cat on her route.

It just so happens, my two Blue-Queensland Healer dogs, Sophie and Cody, are part of her route too. It makes me smile oftentimes as I watch from the window as my dogs sit patiently watching and waiting for Iko to appear. Their ears perk up as they hear her footsteps from over 100 yards away and just like clockwork, she shows up at exactly 8:05am. They greet her every morning with excitement as if it's their first time all over again. Iko absolutely loves the reaction she gets from all the pets on her route and she looks forward to it daily. I think that it's safe to say that my friend Iko is definitely celebrated everywhere she goes and not just tolerated.

As you think about how you're going to make this new day better than yesterday, I invite you to consider the following. Are you "*Celebrated*" everywhere you go or just "*Tolerated?*" Hmmmm… Don't be afraid to pepper your environment with a few treats-of-kindness like a few hearty, genuine compliments, a listening, compassionate ear and a big smile with a hand full of sweet candy from time-to-time. This can definitely move you into the position of being celebrated rather than just tolerated in your daily space. People love to be around other people who are positive, encouraging, nourishing and uplifting.

Be encouraged in the days ahead and be sure to lift others up while you're climbing. Iko would definitely say choose to do those things that result in others "*Celebrating*" your presence and not just "*Tolerating*" your presence. It's amazing how I've learned so much from a woman so little.

One step closer today than yesterday. Let's take this breadcrumb and make it GREAT!

October 23

OPINION

Flat Tea-Cakes

"It doesn't matter how flat you make a tea-cake, it still always has two sides."

- Cedric R. Crawford -

I remember as a kid my mom used to make southern tea-cakes in the oven and they always tasted sooooo good to me. Some would be thick and some would be flat, but the taste was always the same. This memory of this gave me one of my, "*hallelujah moments of inspiration*" I'd like to share with you today.

It doesn't matter how flat my mom would make those tea-cakes, it still always had two sides. One side might be a little softer or crispier than the other, but they still had two sides. This same parallel exists in our everyday lives. We must remember not to be so quick to formulate a negative opinion or thought about someone else based on one side or version of another person's story. Because no matter how good and reasonable it may sound, there's always another side.

A common courtesy would be to reserve our opinion or thoughts about another person until after the important facts are observed from both sides, for I've found that one story can sometimes be completely different than another at times. Yes, those "*tea-cakes*" always have two sides.

Just a little small breadcrumb morsel for your day. Keep your wallets in your pocket, this one's on the house. Thanks Mom. I promise to keep trying to make it GREAT!

Courtney H.   *Cousin, my grandmother used to make the same tea cakes and I miss them so much.* ☺

Cedric R. Crawford *Those two sisters are both probably making those tea cakes together sharing an oven in heaven cousin... J*

October 24

No Limits

"You'd be astonished at the things we could accomplish if no one was around to say it can't be done."

- Cedric R. Crawford -

Over time I've discovered that we'd be surprised at how far we can run without a mile-marker. We'd be amazed at how long we could last if we weren't paying attention to time. And, we'd be astonished at the things we can accomplish if no one was around to say it can't be done.

As I look back over my life I realize that some of my greatest accomplishments have come in the absence of those who would say it couldn't be done. I realize that I might have questioned some of my greatest successes had someone been there to question my ability to succeed. If we take the Limits off of life, we just might find that almost anything is possible.

For those of you who are surrounded by naysayers and dream-stealers, be sure to make a point to act as if they're not there and succeed anyway. Let's live without limits and make this Life GREAT.

October 25

"True Wealth"

"True wealth is self-sustaining, selfless and builds on itself, for the more you give away, the more you gain."

- Cedric R. Crawford -

s I opened my eyes from my slumber this morning I was immediately reminded of the many people who need to do the same. Many people need to *"open their eyes and wake up today"* to see what really matters most in this thing called *"life."* Over the years this life has taught me that it's not the money, power or material things that determine our *true wealth*. *"True wealth"* is only determined by our knowledge gained and what we do for our fellowman.

Money, power and material things are just tools and they should be used to make this world a better place for all that inhabit it. My favorite book states that *"to whom much is given, much is expected."* It seems to me that *"most people"* overlook or can't see this important responsibility because of the fog created by a hectic life. *"Most People"* appear to be disillusioned by the haze or confusion caused by unbridled, selfish ambition. So a good question today is, *"Are you 'Most People'?"*

I've come to know first hand that money, power and material things can all eventually be lost or taken away, but *"true wealth"* is sovereign, indestructible and incapable of being lost, and once gained it can never be stripped from the grasp of those who possess it. I've also discovered that *"true wealth"* is self-sustaining, *selfless* and builds on itself, for it appears that the more you give away, the more you gain.

So the ultimate goal should be for us to inculcate and feed our minds with more knowledge and wisdom so we can share more with others for the purpose of enriching their lives too. We should leverage more of our tools of money, power and material things to affect positive change in the lives of our fellowman. I am thoroughly convinced that these positive actions and good deeds are in fact noble and just and will not go unrewarded by the one who will judge us all at the end of our days.

So I say to you today, go ahead and build that *true wealth* with a heart of gratitude and always be willing to share and share alike. NO we're not *"Most People,"* *"Most People"* wouldn't have made time to read this entry today. But you did, so congratulations because you're definitely NOT *"Most People."* Stay the course and continue to keep devouring these breadcrumbs daily to increase your *"true wealth."* Let's continue in our noble efforts to keep making this life GREAT!

October 26

SUICIDE

"Thoughts" of Suicide

"You can't play the game of life to its fullest potential if you throw in the towel before the clock runs out."

- Cedric R. Crawford -

I was driving my two youngest kids to school this morning when we suddenly heard on the radio that the famous Creator of the 35-year long hit show titled *"The Soul Train"* was found dead in his home this morning. Officials said the preliminary indication was that his death appeared to have been caused by a self-inflicted gunshot wound to the head.

After hearing this, my 10-year-old son, Chance and my 8-year-old daughter Chayse had the following conversation:

Chance: *"Well, he's definitely not going to heaven."*

Chayse: *"Why."*

Chance: *"Because he murdered somebody."*

Chayse: *"Who?"*

Chance: *"Himself."*

Chayse: *"Ohhhh…"*

This is definitely one of those many statements that I hear from my kids that make me say, *"Hmmmm..."* The radio host went on to say that he had been battling with some challenging health issues off and on and this may have opened the door for him resolving to end his life on his own terms. Hmmmm.

I must admit that this is a tough one. Many have debated the act of suicide down through the years as it relates to religion and spirituality and the debates are sure not end anytime soon. However, I believe Chance raises a pretty valid point in saying death by ones own hand is self-inflicted murder. And, surely one of the most popular of the notorious Ten Commandments is *"Thou shall not Murder."* Hmmmm… This definitely can make you think. I invite you chew on this one for a bit and to give it some thought today about what you believe and why. Just consider this one as a little breadcrumb as food for thought today.

My thoughts are, you can't play the game of life to its fullest potential if you throw in the towel before the clock runs out. If you're still breathing, I'm convinced that you still have some job to do. Hmmmm… Who would've thought a seemingly benign conversation between two elementary students could spark an adult *"thought tank."* Let's all continue to make it GREAT.

October 27

PASSION

High Five

> *"Your decision to leverage your passion for the good of others will undoubtedly have a positive affect on many who come in contact with you this side of the universe."*
>
> *- Cedric R. Crawford -*

I have two simple questions today. Question One: *Found your passion?* Question Two: *Using your passion to enrich the lives of others?* If you answered *"Yes"* to both of these questions, please allow me to give you a BIG *"High Five"* today for you have done what *"Most People"* will never do in their lifetime.

The unfortunate reality is the graveyards and cemeteries are claiming thousands and thousands of body's everyday that still contain an unused seed of *passion* in them, but not you. You have made a choice that will surely rob the grave of yet another victim and silent victory. Your decision to leverage your *passion* for the good of others will undoubtedly have a positive affect on many who come in contact with you this side of the universe. But even more than that, you are in an awesome position to encourage others to not only find their *passion*, but to serve it up to the world for *good* also.

Yes the grave is winning, but with your help we will eventually tip the odds in our favor. So, here's a big "*High Five*" today and everyday hereafter in advance for your efforts to make this world a little bit better today than it was yesterday friend. I may not know who you are, but I definitely know who you are if you share this same sentiment. So, "*High Fives*" today and everyday as you go on your way to make it GREAT!

Sandi L.	*I've found it ~ High Five!*
Kimberly S.	*High five!! :)*
Cathy N.	*High five...lol*
Nita T.	*High Five Cedric! ;~)*
Jacqueline H.	*High Five!!*

October 28

AVOIDANCE

Running?

*"Our choices today will undoubtedly make us who we are
tomorrow and our decisions in every moment will shape our
future destiny in every way."*

- Cedric R. Crawford -

A great thought just hit me today after being prompted by an old friend to come up with something to say about "*running*."

I am not unmindful of the fact that there are many people both young and not-so-young that have spent a lifetime running from their past or current problems, struggles and challenges of today. I learned something several years ago that has changed my life for the better. The very problems, struggles and challenges that we're running from, we need to stop, turn around and then "*run to*" because of the person we will eventually become on the other side of the problems and struggles.

I'm absolutely convinced that our Creator allows such things in our lives in order to make us stronger and more determined. Our choices today will undoubtedly make us who we are tomorrow and our decisions in every moment will shape our future destiny in every way.

So I say today, be sure to choose wisely and make the bold choice to stand your ground and face that which you have been avoiding all these years. Please allow me to congratulate you in advance for who you will become in the process. Keep running in the right direction and make it GREAT!

Erika S. D.	*Oh my goodness Cedric I did exactly that this week!! Something that I had allowed to be so painful to me for the last 20 yrs. Something I felt controlled my anxieties and fears and even my trust in God sometimes! I laid it down this week like a heavy backpack I insisted on carrying on my journey!! When I made the CHOICE to face it head on and lay it at the feet of Jesus I was surprised at how easy it was! Yes it hurt to face it and I cried and maybe even mourned but then I truly felt the weight lift and felt relieved! Now it is just something that happened to me not something that I will allow to define me anymore!! I am new in Christ and know that he has set me FREE!!*

October 29

PARENTING

The Road of Life

"We should always seize the opportunity to prepare our kids for the 'road of life' instead of attempting to prepare the 'road of life' for our kids."

- Cedric R. Crawford -

In life I've found that one of the biggest disservices we can ever exact on our kids is attempting to shelter them from all failure, struggle, disappointment and consequences in this world. The loving parent in us all has the tendency to automatically want to safeguard our kids from such things, but an overuse of this tendency can severally retard their societal adjustment/growth and have catastrophic results on our kids' lives down the road.

I've found that in most cases, we should seize the opportunity to prepare our kids for the "road of life" instead of attempting to prepare the "road of life" for our kids. This action will set our kids up to win in the game of life and not have unrealistic expectations of what life is all about. The honest truth is life isn't always "fair," life is just "life" and it comes at you in all directions and it's almost never convenient or comfortable. Some are born rich, some are born poor. Some are born "with" and some are born "without." Unfortunately we can never choose the "hand" we're dealt, but we can choose how we play the "hand" that's dealt to us.

We must not miss the countless opportunities to capitalize on the situations and circumstances where struggle and disappointment exists in our kids' lives and leverage them for "good." They need us to be those parents that care enough to allow the life lessons so that it will shape them into who they need to become so they will not just win at the game of life, but WIN BIG! Unrealistic expectations of life can hurt for a lifetime. Let's set our kids up to make it GREAT!

October 30

ENRICHMENT

On the Right Track?

"Ambition should never be self-centered but calculated with the intent to enrich the lives of others."

- Cedric R. Crawford -

As I look back over the years at what I thought was living the "good" life and being ambitious, I'm amazed at some of the things I saw and heard people do to get ahead. I myself can't honestly say that I wasn't tempted to cross the line in many areas, but fortunately I refused to adopt the pervasive and widely accepted "dog-eat-dog" mentality of the business world.

Reckless ambition was demonstrated all around me and at times my own ambition was poorly focused but the life lessons taught to me by my parents afforded me the ability to maintain a level of integrity that separated me from the masses in business.

The common phrase, "Nice guys finish last" has been repeated by many but I've found it to be grossly inaccurate because our main accountability is not to man. Aside from this fact I still shutter to think of the number of years I wasted strolling through this life with poorly focused ambition ignoring what really matters simply because I didn't take the time to slow down long enough to listen to the messages in plain sight around me everyday.

Thank God my story doesn't end there. My favorite book teaches me it is because of the grace of my Creator that I can stand before all today and profess that I'm not who I once was or used to be. Strangely enough I have become a new creature and no longer walk, talk, think or act the same way. My ambition is no longer poorly focused and self-centered but it's now calculated with the intent to enrich the lives of others and to store up treasures in the hereafter. My sight and vision is no longer short but is now long-range and sustainable. It is truly my heart and soul's desire to rescue as many others as possible from the mindset I once had and set them on a new course that will ultimately afford them "true fulfillment, self-worth and happiness" in this life.

For those of you who are already "on the right track," to you I say, "Bravo." Be encouraged today and know all you do to enrich the lives of others behind the scenes is not in vein and your efforts will not go unrewarded. Yes, your applause will come sooner or later for your undying commitment and noble deeds. Again I say, "be encouraged" and stay the course for one more day because someone is secretly counting on you to save them with your story of how you made it over and how they can too. Let's stay on track and continue to make it GREAT!

October 31

Looking for a Change of Venue?

"We may consider a change of venue, but nothing will really change until there's a significant change within you."

- Cedric R. Crawford -

I've been gaining more and more clarity as the days go by and it seems clear to me that nothing great or significant can ever come from living a life of comfort, mediocrity and predictability. As I continue to Read, Participate, Listen and Associate, I'm finding more and more evidence that great things rarely come out of the usual routine or trails that have already been blazed.

For those of you who are not content with just *"getting by"* and living an average life, but are striving to leave a huge, positive dent in this world for the better, I say to you today. Be encouraged as you continue your noble quest to make it GREAT as you attempt to create your positive legacy for the ages and generations that come after you.

And for those who want to change course and direction and start to build a better career or life that really matters in a different area, space or location, let me remind you that a better anything first starts with a better *"you."*

So it doesn't matter how far or how fast you run or where you run to, you can never get away from you.

It doesn't matter where you go or what company or business organization you change to, what matters most is if a change is made in you.

Positive results in what you say or do will never come true unless there's a real positive transformation that happens in you.

We may consider a change of venue, but nothing will really change until there's a significant change within you.

A better family, better friends, better finances and better fringe benefits start with a better "*You.*"

The most important factor in the equation of life and business is "*You.*"

So don't waste time assigning blame or pointing the finger at your crew. Point that thumb back at "*You*" and commit to do what you need to do to make a better you.

Commit today to make "*You*" your daily project for the better, OR don't be surprised when you get more of the same results down the road.

Don't forget we still only get one time through this "*life*" thing, so let's not spend it spinning our wheels without paying attention to the main thing, "*You.*" Let's make it GREAT!

My Viral Quotes
Feel Free to SHARE

"Anger and frustration doesn't perform well boxed in and bottled up under pressure. So find a healthy way to let it out."

"I'd rather be happy living in a hovel in a hamlet than living miserly miserable in a mansion."

"A suitable mate has to be much more than a thin waist and pretty face."

"Having regular conversations with others about their goals and dreams helps you to focus more clearly on yours."

"What does accomplishing the BIG GOAL mean? Well, just ask the one who's one step away."

"The unexpected is never convenient, guaranteed."

"Don't wait 'til it starts raining before you buy your umbrella."

"The most effective master teacher/guru this side of the universe is 'life' itself."

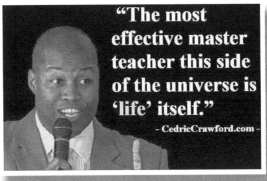

November 1

FEAR

A Life That Matters

"Creating a life that matters chases away the fear of death."
- Cedric R. Crawford -

A few years ago my wife and I realized one of our dreams of designing and building our riverfront dream-home in the hills of Bakersfield, California. A short time after accomplishing that goal I remember being in the master bedroom suite lying on my back on our black leather sleigh bed staring up at the 18 foot, coved ceiling taking it all in while breathing a silent sigh of relief. Suddenly out of nowhere a random thought came to my mind that resulted in me developing a fear that took precedence over all others. This fear gripped me the very moment I awakened to the possibility of what could happen. This fear became as real to me as the very air I breathe. What is this fear? It's the fear of dying after living a life that didn't really matter for making the world better and enriching the lives of others.

Looking back over my life after building a successful business with my wife and all the other accomplishments and goals I had achieved up to that point, I honestly couldn't say that I had created anything that would be able to withstand the wind, the rain and the other elements of this world and live-on indefinitely creating value for others in my absence. So, it was that day I began my first steps toward my journey to creating a life of meaning, memories, significance and legacy.

That day I began to focus on what was most important in this life and began to, in the words of the song written by the group Point of Grace, *"Turn Up The Music."* I made a promise to myself and my Creator that I would be a willing conduit to deliver a message of Hope, Inspiration, Motivation, Encouragement, Empowerment and Education to others world wide. I vowed that I would give this mission my best efforts and the highest and utmost priority in my life and create positive written and spoken content that will outlive my grandkids', grandkids', grandkids'. I committed to make the M & Ms (*Money and Material things*) of life no longer my main priority.

I'm now happy to say that I am no longer afraid of dying, for I know my life does matter. I'm on my pursuit and path of purpose now and many of you have shared your hearts with me of how something you've heard or read from me that has inspired, motivated, encouraged or educated you in some positive way and this definitely makes me smile. Nope, no more fear of death here my friends, for I now know that all the content I created yesterday, today and tomorrow will never die.

Can you say the same today? Are you creating *"positive-passion-fruit"* that will endure through the ages or are you primarily driven by the M & Ms of life? Are you living a life that will truly matter for making this world a better place even in your absence? Hmmmm… Give it some real thought today and remember it's never too late to start making it GREAT. So, turn up the music and make it matter.

NOTES

November 2

Living Under the Influence

*"Driving under a negative influence can get you a ticket to
jail, but living under a negative influence can get you a ticket
to hell."*

- Cedric R. Crawford -

Driving under a negative influence can get you a ticket to jail, but living under a negative influence can get you a ticket to hell. Living under the negative influence of what you may ask. Well, it's living under the negative influences of those who are around you daily. Yes my friends, the negative influences of those whom you choose to associate with on a regular basis can make your life a living hell.

To whom are you listening to and with whom are you associating with daily? Are you choosing to invest most of your time with those who are positive, encouraging, uplifting and supportive, or have you become comfortable with sharing company and space with those who are discouraging, disgruntled, argumentative and pessimistic? Your honest answer to this question will dictate whether or not you end up living a life fraught with stress, strain, heartache and pain or a life of joy, happiness, fulfillment and progress.

I invite you today to seriously consider being caught living under *"positive influence"* in this life. Upgrade your circle of friends if needed. Protect your positive mental mindset from the would-be negative influences that surround us all. We only get one time through this "life" thing so let's keep leaning forward in a positive motion as we attempt to make it GREAT.

November 3

Ladders and Rental Cars

*"Be sure to perform regular maintenance on your goals and
dreams and make sure your ladder of success is not leaning
against the wrong building."*

- Cedric R. Crawford -

As I look back over my life I must admit that I've never seen a person wash or perform maintenance on a rental vehicle. I suspect this is because they don't *"own it."* Such is life... When it comes to our goals and dreams, we must not treat them like a rental car. We have to take "*ownership*" of our goals and dreams and perform routine maintenance on them on a regular basis and make sure that our "*Ladder of Success*" is not leaning against the wrong building.

This maintenance is mandatory and will prevent us from being disappointed once we've climbed to the top rung of our ladder and find that we were duped and our ladder was leaning against the wrong building the entire time. We must make sure our intentions, objectives and motives are clear and our goals and dreams are worthy of our best efforts.

I invite you to consider the following question today. Is your ladder of success leaning against the right building? Is the ascension to the top of your ladder still for the right reasons and worthy of your best efforts? Don't be afraid to take full ownership today and be sure to perform regular maintenance on those goals and dreams because no one is going to give them the love, care and attention they need like you. Check that success ladder today and let's all make it GREAT!

November 4

FALLIBILITY

A Fallible Human Being

"To fail, falter and fumble is to be human."

- Cedric R. Crawford -

I have a secret that's strong enough for a man and also made for a woman and I invite you to consider it as you traverse the days ahead.

Have you ever been riding along in the vehicle of life and was suddenly blindsided by something that reminded you that you're a fallible human being? Well, SURPRISE! YOU'RE STILL HUMAN! The moment when you think you're not vulnerable to mistakes and short-comings is the moment you become most vulnerable, so stay ready. Take comfort in knowing that you're not alone. From the top to the bottom of society and all ages and races, colors and creeds in between, we must all pass through the gauntlet of fallibility.

The reality is our imperfections and fallibility is actually a solid marker and litmus test for what makes us human. I'm convinced that our past faults, failures and faux pas are actually prerequisites for future greatness and becoming better at anything we do.

So don't be so quick to throw in the towel on your relationship, your goals and dreams or your God just yet. Let's continue to get up again and again and again and dust ourselves off and keep going. Yes, to fail, falter and fumble is to be human. So let's keep getting back up and continue to make it GREAT!

Sandra S.   *Aw, thank you for your encouraging words this afternoon, you have no idea how this is right on time today. Be blessed :-)*

November 5

POWER OF WORDS

Un-Spoken Words Can Be Magical

"One of the biggest art forms to master in the area of the spoken word is knowing when <u>not</u> to use them."

- Cedric R. Crawford -

I was asked a question today by a friend that provoked the following helpful response: Every since that glorious day our Creator first demonstrated the incredible power of words by stating the now famous words *"Let there be light,"* the power of the spoken word has been making itself known repeatedly down through history.

There's absolutely no doubt in my mind that our spoken words can be under-rated and the power generated by them is often times overlooked by many. Make no mistake about it, our words have the power to build up or tear down and the words we choose to speak to each other should always be chosen wisely so as to avoid irreparable damage to our fellowman.

Considering the consequences of our words in advance before we speak them is definitely an art form and rare skill. But even more than that, one of the biggest art forms and skills to master in the area of the spoken word is knowing when <u>not</u> to speak them. I've mentioned this little-known fact before in this book but it definitely bares repeating.

No, I don't believe in magic but I do believe in magical moments and knowing when to shut up can create magical moments of peace and tranquility over and over again in many circumstances and situations. Simply put, the truth can hurt and cut pretty deep sometimes and as a result, it's not always appropriate to share it, just concede to shut up for now. Just a little breadcrumb-for-thought for you today. Hope you're continuing to make it GREAT.

November 6

BIBLE

The Good Book

"Of all the good books you can read regularly, please make the Bible one of them."

- Cedric R. Crawford –

Faith, Hope and Love, and the greatest of these three is _____? If you don't know the answer to this question, you definitely needed to be in somebody's church today. Of all the good books you can read regularly, I encourage you to please make the Bible one of them. There's some good stuff in there for life, empowerment, education, inspiration, motivation, encouragement and good, old-fashioned personal development at its best. It's riddled with stories of how others have managed to overcome adversity and become something great. We can definitely learn a lot from those many dead men and women who selflessly poured out their hearts through their actions in life and their written words in hopes that we may live a better life then they did.

I boldly submit to you today that we ought to make an honest effort to know our history so that we will avoid repeating the mistakes that were made by those who came before us. And, the *"Good Book"* is definitely a great place to start. So, let's make it GREAT!

November 7

DREAM

Answer the Door

"When your dream comes knocking at your front door, turn the television off and go answer it."

- Cedric R. Crawford -

I received a phone call from my best friend not long ago. She was agonizing and torn over a phone call she had just received offering her the partnering opportunity of her dreams. This is the one that she had set a goal to land a few years ago. The position that would give her considerably more time freedom and financial comfort while still doing what she loves. The dream that she's invested more time and money into bettering herself for. The opportunity that would afford her the ability to refocus more on family, friends and personal time.

So why was she agonizing over this offer? Well, it's because the offer couldn't have come at a more difficult time. She was two days away from leaving one organization and had committed to partner with another different organization in seven days and they were already eagerly anticipating her arrival. To top it off, there was also a few unknowns about the existing partnership being offered at her by the *"dream organization." "Ughhhh!!!"*

She exclaims. *"WHAT DO I DO? If I would've received this offer a couple of weeks ago this would've been an extremely easy 'Yes' to make, but now, Ughhhh!!!"*

After a few more minutes of discussing the specifics and asking a few more questions, I made the following statement based on my experience of what life has taught me. *"When your dream comes knocking at your front door, you should turn off the television and go answer it."*

"Well what does that mean?" she asked.

I explained, *"This is exactly what you had planned for and was working for and everything else was just a meantime motive or temporary fix and filler. Yes, weeks ago your decision would have been easy, but the fact that it is now difficult gives the choice-process more meaning and creates an opportunity to test the true strength of your faith and belief that this is truly for you."* So, I encouraged her to *"GO ANSWER THE DOOR"* and welcome in her dream and step into the face of fear because on the other side is where the dream is realized.

Well, she answered the door and she feels it was a great decision. Congratulations Karen Ice-Crawford!!! You've definitely inspired me today and everyday since you said "*I do.*" You're definitely proof-positive that *persistence*, *patience* and *perseverance* with a *plan* can be a *potent* cocktail for *prosperity* and *progress*. ☺

Would you be able to recognize the distinctive knock of your dreams? Are you preparing and equipping yourself to take advantage of your opportunity to open the door when the time comes? Are you ready to make the tough decisions if need be? These are just a few questions to ponder on your journey. Be encouraged today and stay the course and equip yourself along the way and stay ready as you attempt to make it GREAT!

November 8

WORRYING

Playing the Odds

"Stop giving yourself away to stress and worry because the odds that you will prevail are definitely in your favor."

- Cedric R. Crawford -

Not long ago my dad and I took one of our usual flights over to Las Vegas to enjoy a front row seat at the famous show of the incomparable Gladys Knight. We also managed to take a few risks beating the casino odds at the world famous Venetian Resort Hotel. My game of choice is the infamous Roulette Wheel and I only bet on the color choices which are *red* or *black*. My dad is usually just there to provide moral support and cheer me on and capitalize on any winnings procured as I flip him a chip or two between spins.

It's no secret the house always has a slight advantage at the odds of 49-to-51 for the large majority of games, yet the entire city of Las Vegas was built and is still growing on this slight advantage. In spite of this reality, millions upon millions of people still flock to this world famous city to try their luck. However, unlike most people who just roll the dice, I actually have a strategy and that strategy actually results in reducing my worry and stress-level and appears to tip the odds in my favor more often than not. While trying my luck at the odds, I suddenly realized that there exists an interesting parallel with the odds in Vegas and the odds in *Life*.

Have you ever been guilty of worrying or stressing in advance about something that eventually never happened? I recently read somewhere that studies show that approximately 87% of the things that we stress over and worry about actually never happen. So if this is true, it means that with any given uncertainty or possible event that we're worrying or stressing about, there exist only a 13% chance of it actually ever happening. Now, I don't know about you, but I would never bet on 13-to-87 odds.

Simply put, worrying and stressing in advance over anything is usually a total waste of energy and I've heard studies also show worrying and stressing can shorten your life span. So, be encouraged today and stop giving yourself away to stress and worry because at the end of the day, the odds that you will prevail are definitely in your favor. Let's continue to reduce that level of stress and worry in our lives as we attempt to make it GREAT!

November 9

DON'T QUIT

Fasten Your Seatbelts

"Victory with a cause that is noble and just is inevitable if you don't quit."

- Cedric R. Crawford -

We must fasten our mental seatbelts and put our seat-backs and tray-tables in their upright and locked positions when we're preparing to change to a different altitude in life for we're guaranteed to encounter turbulence for a while. But take heart and be assured that our flight will eventually reach its destination if we resolve to stay the course.

So press-on, for victory with a cause that is noble and just is inevitable if you simply stay focused and don't quit. A short and sweet message today to get you on your way. Take this little breadcrumb and make this day so AWESOME that yesterday gets jealous.

November 10

UPLIFT

Are you a Good Swimmer?

"May our desire to win always prevail over our fear of losing."

- Cedric R. Crawford -

I distinctly remember as a kid in high school on the swim team, I used to be a bit apprehensive about the *"Speedo,"* tight swim-trunks I used to have to wear at our school swim-meets. Although I acknowledge this feeling of discomfort, I didn't ever let the feeling prevent me from competing in a race. My desire to win always prevailed over my discomfort of how I looked in my swim trunks or my fear of losing the race.

In an interesting twist, as an adult I now realize that in the race of life, there are long distance swimmers, middle distance swimmers and sprinters. There are also some people who sit in the bleachers and make jokes about how some of the swimmers look in their swimsuits. Gut check time: Take a close look at your life and determine which one are you.

Dale Carnegie's famous words were we must continue to be careful not to *criticize, complain* or *condemn* others. We must find ways to uplift those around us and as a result, we may find ourselves being uplifted too.

Let's swim through this life with confidence and let the naysayers point and giggle as we push toward winning our race. Keep your head in your own lane and don't criticize, complain and condemn as you continue to make it GREAT!

November 11

MOTIVES AND INTENT

Same Page – Same Book

"If it's just about the M & Ms (Money and Material things)
of life, then you've missed the whole point."

- Cedric R. Crawford -

Ever heard the phrase, *"Let's get on the same page?"* Well, I've discovered it's possible to be on the same page with someone but be reading from a totally different book. Yes, it's possible to share a common goal or mission, but have two completely different underlying motives and intentions.

If it's just about the M & Ms (*Money and Material things*) of life, then you've missed the whole point of why we were all allowed to occupy space on this planet. Such things will never bring you sustainable happiness this side of the universe, guaranteed. I've learned that it's our ability and willingness to serve and create value to enrich the lives of our fellowman that really counts in the grand scheme of things.

So I say to you today on your shared journey with others, be sure the motives and intentions of all parties involved are equally as honorable as the mission. Simply put, being on the *"Same Page"* is just not enough. You have to also be reading from the *"Same Book."* Be encouraged today and be sure to stay on the *"Same Page-Same Book"* with that special someone as you attempt to take these breadcrumbs and make them GREAT!

November 12

Check Your Boot

"Always check your boots for mice before you put them on."
- Cedric R. Crawford -

May I be so bold to offer you just a little breadcrumb of unsolicited advice on this new day. Be sure to always check your boots for mice before you put them on.

I remember as a kid at least once a year my dad would get us all together to do some deep cleaning out in the front and back yard and shed. I would often times be a little excited about the activity and I'd run and get my work clothes, gloves and boots and head on out the door prepared to be productive for a day. This particular time I remember running into the house and grabbing my gloves but my boots were tucked away in the back of our cluttered, hallway closet. So I dug them out and quickly put them on and started running through the kitchen toward the back door of the house.

I was just about ten feet away from the door when suddenly I felt twitching at the tip of my toes. Since we frequently had a small problem with mice taking up residence in our house in the past, my mind quickly associated this twitching with the presence of a mouse in my boot. I began to scream like a little 5-year-old girl and kept kicking wildly until that boot flew off of my foot and landed a few feet away. I was stunned as I watched the mouse quietly exit the boot and run for cover and sanctuary behind the washing machine.

After hearing my blood-curdling screams, my dad and brothers ran into the house and found me in my "Crane" defensive position ready for action, NOT! The truth is, I was actually curled up on the floor like a poor, little defenseless puppy in a state of shock. After telling them what had happened, they laughed uncontrollably out loud for an embarrassing few minutes as if I had just told the funniest joke this side of the universe. Needless to say I was the "comic relief" for not just the entire day, but the entire week.

As I often times look back over my life at stories like this, they not only make me laugh, they also make me think about how they can apply to our lives today. I invite you to consider the following truth: Whenever we're considering a new business venture or relationship or new endeavor, we should make it a point to always "Check the boot for mice before we put it on." Before you get involved, check it out.

This action will surely help reduce the chances of being shocked and amazed by an unexpected *mouse-of-a-surprise* down the road. Haste can sometimes make waste as evidenced in my own personal story. An ounce of prevention is surely worth a pound of cure and a little due-diligence never hurts anyone. Don't miss the breadcrumb today and be sure to make it GREAT!

Laurie A.   *I once met a dad on a field trip who told me that he never put his shoes on without first checking out if anything was in them. He had been bitten badly once by a spider and never wanted to repeat the experience. Good advice.*

Nita T.   *This was too funny!!! But it had the BEST message Cedric. ☺*

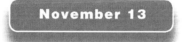

November 13

DON'T QUIT

Going Through Hell?

"If you feel like you're going through hell, don't stop to look for a cup of water."

- Cedric R. Crawford -

I've got a few breadcrumbs and "MILK" (*Motivation-Inspiration-Love-Kindness*) for you today. This "MILK" is sure to do your body good even if you're lactose-intolerant. J

For those of you who feel like you're going through hell today, I invite you to consider the following suggested action: "*Don't Stop! Keep Moving!*" The worst thing you can do when traveling through hell is stop to ask for directions and a cup of water. Keep moving friends and eventually the heat will dissipate.

Your goal is just a little outside your reach right now and it's not what you don't have that's holding you back at this time, it's what you think you need that's preventing you from moving forward and obtaining your goals.

I've learned from first-hand experience that if you just keep moving on your journey down the "*right*" path in the "*right*" direction, the people and the resources you need will eventually show up. So, "*DON'T STOP!*" Keep moving on your journey and continue in your best efforts to make it GREAT!

got milk?

M- otivation
I - nspiration
L - OVE
K - indness

Shaun S. S.   *I approve this message! This is how you win! Keep moving for-ward, and never look back!*

November 14

BULLYING

Mind Bully

*"Our mind can be the ultimate "bully" to our body and get it
to do just about anything we want it to do."*

- Cedric R. Crawford -

I was in the process of dropping my kids off at school the other day and I had one of my *"Hallelujah moments of inspiration."* As a result, I would like to offer a comment and new perspective on how *"bullying"* can actually be a positive thing. I've discovered that our mind can be the ultimate *"bully"* to our body on a regular basis. We can learn to leverage and use our minds to boss our body around and do things that we never thought was possible.

The ability to masterfully leverage this bully is the vital key to being successful in any ambitious endeavor. Some of the greatest men and women to ever walk this earth were ultimate *"mind bullies."* The heights and great feet's they were able to obtain and sustain were no doubt made possible by their ability to leverage their mind over body.

So I say today to all of you *"mind bully's"* out there, keep pushing that body around until it gives you its' lunch money and everything else you want from it. And, if you're not a *"mind bully,"* the good news is you can be one too by simply understanding and embracing this philosophy and utilizing the technique regularly to accomplish your goals. You can start today, right away without delay. Let's all try to bully our body into making it GREAT!

Smile

His Story or History?

*"Are your smile muscles suffering from a severe case of atrophy
because your life is absent of happiness and you've forgotten
how to smile?"*

- Cedric R. Crawford -

I'm definitely a self-proclaimed *"People-Watcher."* I accept the fact that I can always be found guilty of being keenly aware of my surroundings and who's sharing it with me. One of my favorite activities is looking at people and trying to guess what type of life they're living, whether it's happy, sad, frustrated or mad.

While stopped at a stoplight the other day I glanced over at the person in the car next to me and noticed that he had what appeared to be an irreparable frown on his face. You know the kind of face you make when you're sucking on a lemon or bite into a dill-pickle? So as usual, I immediately began to wonder and imagine what his life was like. It appeared that his smile muscles were suffering from a severe case of atrophy because his life was absent of joy and happiness and he'd forgotten how to smile. Maybe the sound of music no longer inspires him or brightens his day. For him maybe the all-familiar sound of children laughing has lost its luster and he had all but given up on the hope that this life could be better for him.

That could've been the end of *"his story,"* but an even better story is that now it's just *"history"* and a thing of the past. Maybe he decided to wake up and take back control of his life. Maybe he decided to shake off the hauntings of his disappointing past and embrace a totally new favorable future. Maybe he was just starting to go through the process of re-familiarizing himself with the action of smiling and has moved himself to a state of *"Gratitude"* instead of *"Bad Attitude."* Maybe he's finally realized that life is really too short to live it with a *"dill-pickle"* face and his face muscles are in the process of catching up with his new perspective and philosophy about life. Yes, I think I like this story better for him.

Change is definitely in the air. Don't be afraid to breathe it in if you need it. Let's keep making these breadcrumbs GREAT! Time for Change?

NOTES

Bonus DAY 11!!!

Change

Memoir of an Average Joe

My dad was a hard working man. He worked from dawn 'til dusk everyday for as far back as I can remember. He did this to provide for our family of six for this was the only way he knew how to spell love. Yes, that's right, he spelled love "w-o-r-k." Seems strange huh. Well, not so strange to me because that's the way I spell it too. After all, that's what my dad did.

I get up everyday of the week, bright and early to that blaring alarm clock at 6:30am. I rush out the door with my coffee in my hand trying to get a head start to beat the traffic. I've traded my dad's hammer in for a computer terminal that's slowly stealing my eyesight. I spend the first few hours of my day handling other people's problems and looking forward to that 30 minute lunch break. Well, that's what my   did.

It's lunch time now, gotta go grab some grub and chit-chat with my buddies to find out who's getting fat, who's sleeping with who and who's pregnant or who's getting fired this week. After 10 years of the same-old, same-old I'm very used to this routine now. I actually like it. Well, most of the time... Well, my times up. I got to get back to work.

Today I have three angry clients that believe the customer is always right. Dang! I don't have the power to solve and settle this problem. Guess I'll take it to the boss. His problem now. Next...

I can't believe what Lisa's wearing today and Mr. Williams sure treats her nice. I wonder if... Nahhh, this is a professional workplace. Of course there's nothing going on. Oh, what's this? My evaluation copy. Another standard score, I guess I'm doing what's expected of me. Maybe I'll get a raise this year. After all, I've been coming in 10 minutes early every day and staying 10 minutes late. That's got to count for something. Not really, I know that they're just paying me enough to keep me from quitting and rightfully so because I'm only working just hard enough to keep from getting fired. So, I guess I'll just roll with it.

Well look at this, it's five o'clock already, I'll just fiddle around for ten more minutes to do my daily impressing of the boss. Well, that's what my dad did... Ok, 10 minutes up, gotta go...

Why are there so many people on the roads these days. Does everybody get off at five? Can't wait to get home. I hope my wife picked up pizza on her way home from work tonight so I don't have to wait for dinner again. Fast, processed food works good for me. Yeah, I know there's almost no nutritional value in that stuff, but it sure taste good.

PIZZA!!! Yeah baby!!! Stuffed crust with sausage and pepperoni, my favorite! Thanks babe. How was school today boys and girls? Great... Finish up and get to your homework. I've got to catch my favorite reality show *"Peek-a-boo ICU"* followed by *"I'm Still Alive."* Ahhh, There's nothing like some good-ole chewing gum for the brain and mind-numbing, pointless entertainment.

What, the show is already over? Man that was fast... Ok, I'm feeling a bit sleepy now, I think I'm going to check in and call it a day. Oh, hi wifey, how was your day at work, anything exciting or different? No? Yeah, I'm tired too. It's been a long day. Good night babe.

Oh there goes that alarm clock again already. Man, I can't wait 'til I'm retired. Just 35 more years to go. Well, that's what my dad did.

(*** *Time for Change?*****)

By Cedric R. Crawford

November 16

PSA(Public Service Announcement)

Modern Day Slavery

"Sometimes the 'hard truth' lives up to its name."

- Cedric R. Crawford -

My PSA (*Public Service Announcement*) for this special day: If we're currently working in an area that has nothing to do with our passion or gift and we have no dream that we're working on to change our situation, I must advise that this existence bares a striking resemblance of the life of a modern day slave. We should use this labor day to reflect on why we're really here and expose our gift to the world for good.

It is my sincere belief that our Creator did not intend for us to spend the best years of our life beholden to our fellowman in an area of discomfort. I urge and encourage you to use this coming Labor day to re-evaluate your current situation and circumstance of employment and ask yourself the serious question of whether or not at the end of the day you're just going home with a paycheck, or are you going home with something more.

By the way, please resist the urge to categorize today's message as being callous or insensitive. Sometimes the *"hard truth"* lives up to its name. Let's all continue to make it GREAT.

November 17

Change

Embrace Change

"Some of us can be found guilty of being seriously NOT serious about improving our lot."

- Cedric R. Crawford -

I've noticed that some of us can be found guilty of being seriously *NOT* serious about improving our lot. For those of us who feel like God is against us and we just can't win, I caution you not to team-up with the Devil just yet. One of my favorite books says, *"For things to change, YOU have to change."* In fact, change is one of the only constants in life and in a lot of cases, change is actually a good thing.

Therefore, I contend that we choose to embrace change and get serious about improving our lot in life rather than resisting change and staying the same. This process is absolutely necessary if our goal is to move to higher and higher levels during our life's journey. Just an FYI... Let's continue to make it GREAT.

November 18

Ready or Not

"READY OR NOT, HERE LIFE COMES!"

- Cedric R. Crawford -

I remember as a kid we used to play the ever-so-popular game called *"Hide and Seek."* The rules were simple. Everybody finds a place to hide while one designated person seeks them out one by one. The seeker's job was to count up to the number 10 or 20 and then yell, *"READY OR NOT, HEAR I COME!"* If we weren't ready we could easily yell out, *"DO-OVER, I'M NOT READY!"* and the seeker would oblige us by starting the count over.

As a seeker I remember having a hard time finding the older kids because they were usually much better at hiding than the younger ones, but in spite of this fact, I still managed to have a load of fun. The actual thought of this childhood memory brings a big *"Cool-aid"* smile to my face and cranks up feelings of nostalgia for me.

The interesting thing is today as an adult I feel like we play a game of *"Hide and Seek"* with life, and once we reach adulthood life becomes a seeker and screams out, *"READY OR NOT, HEAR I COME!"* The only twist is, if we're not ready, we can't call out for a *"Do-Over,"* not this time. Life comes at us fast and furiously and we all have to be ready for it, not just at the beginning of adulthood, but everyday thereafter.

So the question today is, *"Are you ready?"* because ready or not, here it comes again and again and again. Also beware because no matter if you're young or old, rich, poor, big, small, short, tall, hair or bald life is guaranteed to find us all.

My unsolicited advice today is, Don't *Get Ready* for life's ups and down, *Stay Ready* for life's ups and downs because ready or not, here life comes. Let's stay ready as we all attempt to make it GREAT!

Grayson M. *Stay encouraged.*

LuTrina S. W. *Oh I'm ready now!*

Amanda D. K. *Excellent. Some people can not handle life's downs, but are made to handle them whether they are encouraging or a downfall to them. To be open and ready to accept whatever is put before you and to just deal with it the best of your ability is what we need to prepare ourselves for and not to have a nervous breakdown in the process. Excellent words of encouragement Ced. Thanks.*

November 19

TGIM

"Rise-up with the consistency of the rising sun."
- Cedric R. Crawford -

TGIM, *Thank God It's Monday*! Okay, it may or may not be Monday as you're reading this but be advised that any day above ground is a good day. No matter what's on the agenda for the day, we have yet another opportunity to take one more bold step in the right direction. My hope is that in the fight of your life, the comment that defines you best will be, *"No matter how hard he was hit, he just wouldn't stay down."*

We were born to persist and conquer but the average person succumbs to the programming by those around us to say *"uncle"* and give up when things get rough and aren't going so well. But we understand all-too-well that these are the times that define those who are average and those who are GREAT. We declare again that we may be a lot of things in this life, but *"average"* is definitely not one of them. We will continue to persevere and persist and choose to rise up with the consistency of the rising sun today and make it a Magnificent Monday, Terrific Tuesday, Wonderful Wednesday, Tremendous Thursday, Fabulous Friday, Spectacular Saturday or SUPER Sunday! Whatever your day is today, be sure to MAKE IT GREAT!!!

Tiare F. *Thank you Cedric - I needed that one today. Your timing is perfect!!!*

Martha H. J. *Cedric, are you putting all these quotes down in a book? Be a shame to waste them for future generations!*

Cedric R. Crawford *Great question Martha. The answer is "Maybe."*

November 20

SPOKEN WORD

Speak it into existence

"The first one who said, "LET THERE BE LIGHT" was
setting the first example of what the spoken word can do."

- Cedric R. Crawford -

A journey of 1,000 miles doesn't just start with the first footstep, it also starts with the first step in learning how to effectively communicate with those who dare to follow you on your journey.

After years of dealing with people in business and life, I've learned that our ability to affectively communicate is paramount when it comes to achieving a desired result, even if we're just speaking to ourselves. Yes, the ability to both create and destroy exists in the spoken word. After all, I believe the first one who said, "LET THERE BE LIGHT" was setting the first example of what the spoken word can do.

Choose your words wisely and start speaking of those things that are not, as though they were and watch the magic happen. This is a really small breadcrumb today but it definitely has HUGE implications, so be sure to make it GREAT.

Farah N. A.   *It is a great day because I chose it to be! Thanks for the inspiring*
words Cedric!

November 21

GREATNESS

Struggle before Success

"Greatness wouldn't be so Great if we didn't have to endure
struggle to achieve it."

- Cedric R. Crawford -

I t seems to me that greatness, success and significance are all well-protected by struggle, conflict and adversity. This is a good thing because we just can't have the cookies of life without first enduring the fire and heat of the oven in the hot kitchen of living.

I was talking to my wife today and I asked her if she had the choice of winning $10 million in a lottery or building a business that would produce the $10 million, which one would she choose. Without hesitation she chose winning the lottery. I probed more to find out the reason why she responded the way she did and she made the following statement, *"At this stage of my life I wouldn't want to go through the time and struggle to build it. I would just want to win the money and then safely invest it for a reasonable rate of return."*

She then threw the question back at me, and without hesitation I stated that I would rather build a company that would produce the $10 million. My reasoning was that at this stage of my life I would rather have a powerful, inspirational story of overcoming struggle, conflict and adversity to achieve success and significance so that I could inspire others to believe they can too. We both exchanged smiles and continued our visionary, goal-setting conversation.

I've realized that we have to be willing to pay the price to achieve anything that's great or significant in this life, for success and significance without struggle and adversity does not exist, and achievement without reasonable sacrifice is empty and void of any real substance. Simply put, it's the struggle that adds the value to the goal. If this were not so, then things like "*greatness*" wouldn't be so "*Great.*"

So what would be your answer to this hypothetical scenario? Would you take the money or work to create the story of inspiration for others to be inspired too? Hmmmm… Chew on this breadcrumb for a while and be honest with your intentions as we continue in our attempts to make it GREAT.

MARRIAGE

Aim to Please and Aim *too* Please

> "Big things come in small packages and the little things in
> those small packages can amount to BIG things."
> - Cedric R. Crawford -

I've discovered in marriage most women genuinely "*Aim to please*" and one of the few, simple things they ask of us men is that when using the toilet, we will "*Aim too please.*" I'm sure we can all agree that in the beginning of any relationship, it's the little things we do that attract us to that spouse or significant other. However, we must also understand that during the course of the marriage and relationship it's also the little things that may drive us apart if we're not careful and attentive.

The phrase "*Big things come in small packages*" comes to mind here. Beware for this statement also applies in these cases. Little things in those small packages can definitely amount to big things over time, so pay close attention because the relationship you save just might be your own. Make it GREAT.

Dawn G. G.	*Very true, Cedric! That's a two way street. Both parties need to remain committed to other person's happiness!*
Kent P.	*Wisdom speaking*
Sue Watson	*That's not a little thing.*

DREAM

"Minds-Eye Cinemas"

> "The first step toward reaching our Dreams is in our Dreams.
> The second step is to wake up and take some action."
> - Cedric R. Crawford -

S pent all last night watching back-to-back-to-back inspirational movies at my favorite theatre called *"Minds-Eye Cinemas."* There aren't many movies I've seen there that I didn't like. The theatre is always clean, there are no distractions and admission is always FREE. The coolest thing is I always feel like I'm actually in the movie.

I've learned in life that one of the best steps toward reaching our dreams is in our dreams. Then the second best step is to WAKE UP AND TAKE SOME ACTION!   Be sure to take advantage of your own *"Minds-Eye Cinema"* so you can prepare yourself for a *"deja vu"* moment in life when you watch those dreams come true. Dream about then take action to make it GREAT!

November 24

ILL-GOTTEN GAINS

Beware of Ill-Gotten Gains

"Pursuing a source of significance is a noble act, but if our source of significance compromises the boundaries of personal integrity we definitely need to rethink our path."

- *Cedric R. Crawford* -

J ust when I thought I've seen the worst of what human beings are capable of doing for money or fame, someone comes along and restores my confidence in the compassion and loving capability that lies in us all.

The event and individual that I saw the other day on TV was nothing less than awesome as he demonstrated behavior that was indicative of building others up and installing hope. It's funny how that happens right when I need a boost in my confidence in the inherent goodness of mankind the most.

As I look around various industries lately I see over-and-over again the signs of those who are willing to compromise their integrity and good name in exchange for what I call the *"M & Ms"* of life (*Money and Material things*). I do understand that one of our inner-most human basic desires is to be significant in some way whether good or not-so-good. With that said, it appears that the chosen source of significance for many as-of-late exhibits a reckless and even flagrant disregard for morals, ethics and common decency in many cases.

To push the limits and create *"shock value"* appears to be in vogue and more-and-more commonplace now-a-days and it seems the more extreme and risqué the better. Now let me be clear, I'm a huge advocate for being true to ones self and catering to nobody else, but some of these characters and images of individuals being portrayed appear to be absent of any proper and honorable boundaries. Some appear to have even adopted a *"gain significance at all cost"* type of mentality and are sold out to the extreme.

As a result, I invite you to consider the following breadcrumb of advice today. It seems to me that pursuing a source of significance is a noble act in deed, but if our source of significance exhaust and compromises the boundaries of personal integrity, we probably need to rethink our path. It may be necessary to seriously consider a new course of action, for the ill-gotten gains from such behavior won't last, guaranteed. I will always maintain the belief that ill-gotten gains or immorally and unethically acquired gains will always compromise and corrupt the soul of the perpetrator.

The unfortunate reality is, in spite of this truth, there are many who will still choose to turn a blind eye to this fact and hide behind a veil of non-accountability or a trumped up, distorted, shoddy version of justification for their callous actions. Some of their actions may even show a clear reckless disregard for others who would become collateral damage because of their selfish choices. To those people who fit this description, I implore you to please deeply consider what the "*real*" cost is that's associated with your choices and actions and consider a change of heart because somebody's watching you and learning from all that you do.

We may be a lot of things in this life, but let us categorically refuse to be the ones who are easily swayed by things that won't matter much after we're gone. Let us not be the ones who are willing to compromise our values, morals, ethics and integrity in exchange for a crack at riches, fame, popularity or "*making it BIG*," as they say.

Bad decisions come easy but good ones are hard. So, let's agree NOT to take it "*Easy*" through this "*life*" thing, let's take it "*HARD*" as we continue to make those hard, difficult right choices over the easy wrong one's. Making it GREAT can be tough sometimes, but it's surely worth it.

Let's be the example that models the basic human quality of compassion and the ambassadors of goodwill and uplifting encouragement as we build others up in a positive way. Let's keep striving to be the exceptions as we make it GREAT!

November 25

AVERAGE

Average and Mediocre

"Evil will never sit by quietly and let the pursuit of greatness go unchallenged."

- Cedric R. Crawford -

I finally realized years ago that thoughts of living a life pursuing average or mediocrity is not from our Creator. These thoughts originate from the one who wants nothing more than to extinguish yet another life that contains a "*Seed of Greatness*" by convincing us that being average is OK. The graveyards and cemeteries are claiming the unrealized potential and seeds of greatness of thousands of people everyday. The grave is in deed a formidable foe and it is winning the battle against most people, but the war is far from over and we're definitely not "*most people.*"

We continue our unpopular journey to educate "*most people*" so they will know what their Creator has designed them for and what they are capable of. We understand that evil will never sit by quietly and let the pursuit of greatness go unchallenged so we are prepared to persevere through the adversity for as long as it takes. We are designed for GREAT things, so let's go do our jobs and make it GREAT!

November 26

CHANGE

Time to Commit a Murder?

*"I've yet to see someone receive an award for what they've re-
ceived in this life. It's always an award for what they've given."*

- Cedric R. Crawford -

There's been a murder committed and the killer is still at-large. As a result, it's with a heavy heart
I advise you that the *Cedric Crawford* you used to know years ago is no longer with us. It may
sound a bit harsh and shocking to most, but he was murdered and killed-off by the new and
improved version of *Cedric R. Crawford* that you now know and see today. As a result, he no longer
acts the same, thinks the same, walks the same and he definitely doesn't talk the same. He's undergone
a radical make-over of the mind and reconstructive surgery of his goals and dreams and purpose in
this thing called "life."

This new and improved version of *Cedric* is determined to heed to his calling and purpose in this
life. His mission is to wake others up to their potential and expose them to the countless possibilities
if they're willing to use their God-given abilities and gifts and stories to serve and create value for
others.

In all my years on this planet I've yet to see someone receive an award for what they've "*received*"
in this life. It's always an award for what they've "*given.*" So the question today is, "*What are you prepared to give?*" What gifts are you using to serve or create value for others? Is it time for you to reinvent
and redefine yourself. Give it some serious thought and do what you feel is necessary. Even if it means
murder. Start the process today whoever you are and be sure to make it GREAT!

Lakeysha P. A. N.   *I embrace that saying Cedric about killing off the old and introduc-
ing the new. It's just like being a caterpillar before transitioning into
a beautiful butterfly. I say this because I was once a caterpillar but
Thank God I'm a butterfly.... I've been transformed and I've been
reborn and Jesus is the reason why. Thank God we have a choice to
transform our lives and be all that we can be. Keep those uplifting
motivational words coming.*

LuTrina S. W.   *WOW! I'm speechless! I needed to see this! I've been hearing it
for quite sometime now! But this really tapped me on my noggin!
Thanks for being a new you.*

Matt P.   *R.I.P.*

November 27

Make Those Memories

"Snap the photos and record the videos and go to the picture shows and rodeos and watch your kids grow."

- Cedric R. Crawford -

Me and my two boys Cedric Jr. and Chance were out for their first bowling experience with a group of friends a few days ago. Somehow I managed to keep getting beat and embarrassed by one of the girls in the group. Then to add insult to injury, my neighbor's 60+ year-old mother came along and beat me taking what little dignity I had left. Not exactly how I envisioned my boys first bowling experience with their dad. Yes, I stink at bowling because the gutter and my bowling ball seem to have an inseparable relationship, but all-in-all, I still managed to have an awesome time laughing and competing.

Additionally, I'm happy to say in spite of my stinky bowling technique, I still managed to hit a few strikes. To my unexpected surprise this experience reminded me of the following *life-truth.* If you keep trying in life you're eventually bound to score a few strikes and win. Hmmmm… That's a pretty good moral to this story if I do say so myself. ☺

Don't miss your opportunity to make those memories today, for those memories sure will keep you warm during those cold winter seasons of life. So, snap the photos and record the videos and go to the picture shows and rodeos and watch your kids grow. Your active role in your kids and grandkids life is one of the best gifts you could ever give them. I believe this is truly the gift that keeps on giving. While passing through this life, don't forget to *"LIVE!"* Let's continue to make it GREAT!

Erica V.   *Eh don't be crying now that I whooped ya in bowling...... :) hahahahha*

Cedric R. Crawford *Ok Erica, I wished that you would have remained anonymous, but since you've outed yourself, I will have to request a rematch to regain my good name. Or, we can just take it out to the football field. LOL :-)*

November 28

LEGACY

Your Life Legacy?

"If a picture is worth a thousand words, then what one word best describes the picture of your life's legacy?"

- Cedric R. Crawford -

*e*ver heard the phrase, *"A Picture is worth a thousand words?"* If this is true, then what one word would best describe the picture of your life's legacy?

For me, my descriptive word would definitely be *"Relentless."* This one word is also described as unyielding, unremitting and persistent. It is my sincere hope and prayer that such a word will also describe your life's journey to creating your Legacy.

I'm told by some others who are much smarter than me that in life we only get one time through, no do-over's. So, let's pay close attention to what really matters the first time around and remember that life is too short to live it with a smile turned upside down. So let's make a point to make it GREAT!

Chris P.   *Relentlessness is a good word. I like the thought of a single word picture. My word is perseverance - continued steady belief or efforts, withstanding discouragement or difficulty; persistence; Christian persistence is remaining in a state of grace until death. By God's Grace I believe I have this quality. Thanks for challenging me.*

Jami P.   *My word is persevering.*

Moses S.   *One word I would chose to say life is unpredictable since everyday comes with its own fate .*

November 29

DREAM

Even the Wildest of Dreams are Possible

"Our Dreams won't fight for us, we have to fight for our Dreams."

- Cedric R. Crawford -

I'm sure glad someone had a *"wild dream"* that it was possible for a man to fly around the world in a metal box. If not, then I would be doomed to long rides in a boat, bus, train or truck.

Years ago I probably would've been one of the ones who wouldn't have believed it was possible. But, in spite of the naysayers, the Wright Brothers proved that even the wildest of dreams can come true if you believe and stick with it.

Because of their accomplishment and the great accomplishments of many others like them I can boldly say, don't wave the white flag of surrender and throw in the towel on your wildest dream just yet. Our dreams won't fight for us, we have to fight for them. So, keep fighting and take yet another bold step in the right direction today and make this day so GREAT that yesterday gets ticked-off and calls the police. ☺

November 30

ENCOURAGEMENT

Keep Going Through

"While you're going through your problems and challenges,
just remember that you're 'going through' and eventually you'll
reach the other side where a better YOU exists."

- Cedric R. Crawford –

Life is a series of problems and challenges, you're dealing with some now, you're just coming out of dealing with some, or you're getting ready to deal with some more. Your comfort level is not the most important thing, it's the development of your character through these problems that matters most. Problems and challenges are as necessary as the air we breathe.

If you're going through something right now in your life, I've discovered it really doesn't matter what you're going through, the most important thing is you realize you're "*Going Through*." The very words, "*going through*" implies and suggest we will eventually get to the other side. We just have to endure and persist in spite of the discomfort that "*going through*" can cause.

My life experiences have taught me comfort is not always our friend. We have to be okay with going through some uncomfortable stuff from time-to-time in order for us to grow and become better. We can definitely always better our best if we desire.

Be encouraged today and be sure to keep on moving while you're "*going through*" and embrace the thought of who you will become when you reach the other side and overcome. Another breadcrumb for you to make it GREAT!

Valerie F.	*I absolutely needed to come across this quote today! Thank you Cedric, you've helped make my day!! ;-)*
Kristine D.	*After the rain comes the rainbow...Thank You Cedric:)*
Laurel D. H.	*Cedric ~ I just want to say THANK YOU again for all of your inspirational messages! I can't even begin to tell you how many times, on any given day, they have been exactly what I needed to hear. Blessings to you!*
Diane B.	*Thanks for making my day!*

December 1

ASK

Astronaut or "*Asker-Not*"

"Mommy don't let your babies grow up to be 'AskerNots.'"

- Cedric R. Crawford -

Over the years I've spent and wasted countless hours of time with people who seek and ask for my direction and advice. They've enthusiastically listened and agreed with me but fail to alter their behavior and actions in honor of the new-found information. I affectionately call these people "*AskerNots*" because they ask for advice but do not follow it.

It seems to me that the grade level and proficiency of a student should be dictated and determined by ones ability to take what they've learned and apply it to their life. The speed that it takes to go from not knowing to knowing and application is paramount to the learning process because to know and not "*do*" is the same as not knowing.

As a result of the aforementioned, I invite you to consider the following in the days ahead. Whatever you decide to be when you grow up, please make sure you take "*AskerNot*" off the list. Only doer's can play amongst the stars.

Let's continue to make it GREAT!

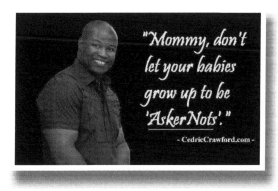

NOTES

December 2

ASK GOOD DEEDS

Doing "*Good*" Results in "*Good Measure*"

"Giving is a tool that when leveraged properly can turn your scarcity into overflowing abundance."

- Cedric R. Crawford -

In terms of doing good deeds in this world, it's unrealistic to think that we can do everything for everybody, but I do humbly submit that we can at least do something for somebody from time-to-time. My Good Pastor Kent Pedersen likes to say it this way, "*Be willing to do for one what you wish you could do for all,*" and I couldn't agree more.

I've come to understand that when giving to others we can't always be sure how people will treat our gestures of kindness. We can't always be sure that the neediness of others is truly genuine and as severe as they may indicate, and we can't always be sure of others intentions with our time, talents and treasures. But one thing we can be sure of is the reward and return we will receive based on the spirit in which we choose to give.

You see, the God-given, universal law of reciprocity isn't specific to and for the "*receiver,*" it's specific to and for the "*giver.*" If we make an honest effort to cheerfully give with a grateful heart out of love and truly good intentions without want or expecting return, then shaken together, pressed-down, overflowing "*good measure*" is sure to visit us in the coming days ahead. Good measure in family, friendship, physical feeling and financials.

So, not feeling like you're experiencing any "*good measure*" these days? I invite you to look for opportunities to give, Give, GIVE and not just out of your scarce and limited treasures, but also of your time and talents. Yes friends, this too is "*good*" and worthy of your best efforts. So let's all commit to do "*good*" for our "*good measure*" as we continue to make it GREAT!

December 3

GOOD VS EVIL

The Outcome Spoiler

"I've never really understood why 'evil' continues to fight so hard when it knows that in the end it will always lose-out to 'good.'"

- Cedric R. Crawford -

Psssst… I know some thing's are better left unsaid but this is not one of them. I hate to spoil the ending of a good book or great movie so cover your ears and close your eyes if you don't want to know because here goes… At the end of it all, WE WIN!!! And they lose. Who are they you may ask? Well, those who choose to live a life exacting evil and chronic negativity upon their fellow man and woman.

I often times find myself scratching my head and wrestling with the question of why "*evil*" continues to fight so hard when it knows that in the end it will always lose-out to "*good*." Hmmm… All I can come up with is that maybe *evil* really doesn't know that it's fighting a losing battle.

Over the years the many stories may change but the end will always remain the same. So for those who choose to instigate and perpetrate evil and chronic negativity in this world rest assure their plight is predictable. Their future fate is a foregone fact, and their outcome and ending is inevitable. THEY LOSE!

So if you're feeling like the shoe fits, by all means please wear it and wise up and join the winning team today because tomorrow just might be too late to make it GREAT!

GREAT DAY!!!

December 4

DREAM

Your Time Will Come

*"Stay the course my friends, in deed all that you do in plain
sight of others and behind the scenes is not in vain."*

- Cedric R. Crawford -

There is nothing more exciting and powerful then a dream whose time for fulfillment has come. This feeling of overwhelming accomplishment is reserved only for those who after several weeks, months or even years have maintained their daily disciplines day-in and day-out not wavering from their belief that one day their applause would come. They've had patience and perseverance and persistent vision in hopes that one day they would eventually have their déjà vu moment in the sun they've dreamed about over and over again. The joy of just knowing their sleepless nights were not in vain. The gratification of knowing their countless hours and commitment paid off and the satisfaction of realizing the many sacrifices made in their life both big and not-so-big were worth it all in the end.

Yes, any and all noble and just, worthwhile goals and dreams acted upon with this type of ferocity and undying commitment shifts the question in terms of success from "*if*" to "*when*." So I say to you today, stay the course my friends, because in deed all you do in plain sight of others and behind the scenes has not gone unnoticed and is not in vain. The time for the fulfillment of your goals and dreams will come soon enough if you resolve today to hang in there with your diligent actions until success shows up and you WIN! So, carpe minutam, diem and vitam (*Seize the minute, day and life*) and use these many breadcrumbs to make it GREAT!

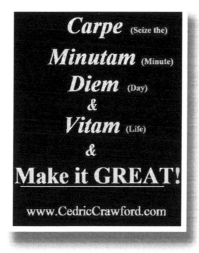

December 5

Mistakes continue until Lessons are Learned

"Lesson repeated until lesson heeded ."

- Cedric R. Crawford -

I consider myself as a person that likes to be nice and welcoming to everyone I meet. I especially like for others to feel welcome in my home but the only visitors that are not welcome back into my home are my past mistakes. You see I've learned over the years that our lessons will be repeated until our lessons are heeded. Our mistakes will continue to visit and revisit us unannounced time and time again until we learn the lessons in them.

Yes my friends, there's a lesson in every mistake and if the lessons not learned, the mistake will continue to ring your doorbell. So I caution you today to not fall victim to allowing the unwanted guest of your past mistakes to return to your doorstep repeatedly. Learn those lessons fast and save yourself from some undue stress and frustration and heartache. Let's tell those mistakes, "YOU'RE NOT WELCOME HEAR ANYMORE!!! I'VE ALREADY LEARNED MY LESSON!!!" Then slam the door shut and move on to the next one.

I also realize we have a lot of mistakes to make in this life so a smart thing for us to do is pick up a CD or good book on a regular basis and learn from some of the mistakes that others have made before us. Experience may be the best teacher but I'd rather learn from someone else's mistakes and experiences whenever possible. Now that's just plain-ole smart.

Let's learn our lessons fast and continue to make it GREAT!

December 6

PERSONAL DEVELOPMENT

The Best Investment Advise Ever

"Money and Material things may come and go, but the suitors
can never take away what you know."

- Cedric R. Crawford -

Over the course of my life, I've discovered that it doesn't matter how far or fast you can run, you can never out run the Truth. I've learned that what you say will always be drowned out by the noise of your actions. And, I've also realized no matter where you go, you can never get away from "*YOU*." Opportunities for a *Better Job*, a *Better Business* and a *Better Life* starts with a *Better "YOU."*

One of the best investments you will ever make in your life is an investment in those things that will assist in making "*you*" better. Money and Material things may come and go, but the suitors can never take away what you "*know*." Let's continue to sharpen our mental ax and commence to chopping down some of those obstacles in our way as we attempt to make it GREAT! I encourage you to be generous with these breadcrumbs so others can make it GREAT too.

December 7

GREED AND FEAR

Pearl Harbor

"Greed and fear are the Bonnie and Clyde of life looking to rob each of us of all that we hold dear."

- Cedric R. Crawford -

I've been doing that *"thinking"* thing again and this time it's about human emotions and I think I've narrowed down the most compelling two. I sincerely believe that these two emotions are absolutely, without question the biggest driving forces in the history of mankind. Every major war and major change in this great world of ours was undoubtedly as a result of one of these two things in some way or form.

I also must admit that my own personal doorstep has been visited a time or two by both of these emotions and have had negative results in the past. I may have shared these to emotional juggernauts before but I think they're soooo important that they bear repeating. What are these two pervasive emotions? *GREED* and *FEAR.*

On this very day, December 7, 1941, our beloved country was attacked by a country whose primary motivation was *greed* and maybe a bit of *fear* also.   Greed and fear is the *"Bonnie and Clyde"* of life looking to rob each of us of all that we hold dear, but a good understanding of how these two work can render them both harmless against us in the future.

So let's make sure that when making decisions in our life we will keep these two emotions in check. If you didn't know this secret before, then now you know. Don't fall victim to the *"Bonnie and Clyde"* of emotions in the days ahead. Keep your mental pistol ready to defend your position as best you can to fend off these two dubious rascals. This is a pretty good breadcrumb so be sure to make it GREAT!

December 8

NEGATIVITY

The Affliction of Negativity

"Sum people r soooo negative that they oftentimes mis the meening of the written n spoken posotive messages because they'r too bizy checking for errors in speling n grammar."

- Cedric R. Crawford -

As I stumble my way through this life I've had the good fortune of coming across people who are sooooo negative that they oftentimes miss the meaning of the spoken and written positive messages around them because they're too busy checking for errors in spelling, grammar and enunciation.

Yes, I think of these casual encounters with these negative people as *"good fortune"* because it reminds me that I can never allow myself to travel down that hill, for it is a very slippery slope indeed. The unfortunate reality is that some individuals have been submerged so deep under the dangerous waters of negativity for so long that they may not even know that they're drowning.

The good news is that people aren't actually born this way. It's a direct result of over-exposure to negativity in their respective environments. The laws of association suggest that it's almost impossible to dwell in a negative environment around negative people for an extended amount of time and not develop into a negative person.

But take heart my friends, if you make an honest effort to change your environment or immerse yourself into positive things and surround yourself with people who are positive and uplifting and encouraging, you can totally reverse the affects of this debilitating disease of negativity. So, yes there is hope for a full recovery from this affliction.

Does this sound like anyone you know? Hmmmm... No need to point fingers or call any names, just make sure you know the rules of the game and stay in the *"right"* lane to avoid unnecessary pain. ☺

One of the best things you can do for a friend, family member or foe is to place this book in their hands. You never know, it just might change their life. So pick up another copy today and place it the hands of a worthy individual and let's all do our part to help others make it GREAT too!

December 9

MODELING AND SERVICE

Don't be "Too Busy"

"Avoid the 'too busy' syndrome like the plague because it can be equally as deadly."

- Cedric R. Crawford -

*D*on't be *"Too Busy"* to read this post today:

My observation of my group-home boys has afforded me the ability to witness first-hand the power of Association. Each one of the boys entered the group-home system at no fault of their own and before entry each one of them could've been defined as *"decent"* kids. But after entering the system they were exposed to the consistent, negative behaviors of the group and over-time they too have slowly assimilated and adopted the same negative behaviors.

This comes as no surprise to me because the Law of Association is an incredibly powerful law that affects all of us. The good news is that this law can also be leveraged for *"positive behavior"* too. A boy that grows up in the absence of an adult, positive male role-model in his life will have a dramatically increased chance of becoming the common denominator of his surrounding environment, good or bad. But a boy who has that consistent male figure around to model positive behavior will have a dramatically increased chance of growing up with some positive behaviors to withdraw from his mental memory bank as he gets older.

As a result, I'd like to issue a *"Call to Action"* for you positive, male role-models out there. Our country is littered with boys that are attempting to grow-up in the absence of men like you. We can continue down this dangerous road and choose to turn a blind eye to the facts and harsh reality of the eventual outcome, or we can commit to do our part, however big or small it may be, to collectively pick up the slack in our respective neighborhoods and communities.

Our young men are constantly becoming victims of what I call the *"Too Busy"* Syndrome. Our decision or in-decision to take action today will affect their decisions and in-decision and actions tomorrow. Simply put, we can no longer afford to be *"Too Busy." "Too Busy"* is costing, not only our country, but our global society as a whole too much. How will our young men ever learn appropriate male behaviors unless we model it for them? Not to shout it to them, but show it to them. I'm not asking you to change the world, I'm just asking you to help shape and change theirs.

They need us now more than ever before, so don't let 'em down. These boys in need closer to you than you probably realize and making a positive difference in their lives is both simple and easy. They're in your neighborhood, on your street, next door to you or maybe even inside your own home. They're quietly calling and counting on you to get this written message. They need desperately for you to loan them that *"time"* stuff and include them in some of your activities with your family. Don't worry, they can repay you by paying it forward.

So what are you waiting for? What are you prepared to do? Today is not a good day to start, it's a GREAT day to start. Too busy? Well, that's the convenient statement for *"Most People,"* but as we discussed many times before, we're anything but *"Most People." "Most People"* didn't even read to this paragraph of this article/post today because they were probably *"Too Busy."* Hmmmm…

Let's be the exception on our journey through this *"life"* thing. It doesn't take a whole lot to do a whole lot. So let's do our part to make it GREAT!

December 10

GIFTS

Squeeze Those Talents and Gifts

"You should make every effort to squeeze the juice out of your talents and gifts to get the maximum 'you' out of 'you' before your days are over."

- Cedric R. Crawford -

A short conversation today with an acquaintance reminded me that one of the most lucrative lessons I've learned over the years is you should make every effort to squeeze the juice out of your talents and gifts to get the maximum "*you*" out of "*you*" before your time is up on this side of the universe.

So many have undoubtedly been found guilty of leaving so much of the best of themselves on the table of life then checking out of this life with the best parts of themselves still lodged dormant and untouched inside. We should all make a point to apply the proper disciplines today like most don't so that we can live tomorrow at our full potential like most won't.

So I invite you today and everyday here forward to press-on and push forward and work to live, love, listen, learn and earn at your full potential in this life. And when the clock strikes twelve, let it find us climbing yet another new hill of challenge and not sliding down an old one.

As I've always said, we only get one time through this life thing, so let's invest our time attempting to make it GREAT!

SQUEEZE THE JUICE OUT OF THOSE GIFTS!!!

December 11

MARRIAGE AND RELATIONSHIPS

"I-Me" vs. "Us-We"

"In marriage and relationships, 'Us-We' is greater than 'I-Me' everyday of the week and twice on Sundays."

- Cedric R. Crawford -

A s I've said before, I don't believe in magic, but I do believe in magical moments and I've realized the minute you come into agreement with that marriage spouse or significant other and make your personal "*I*" needs and wants secondary to a common cause and shared "*We*" goals of the team, a magical moment is created.

Over the years I've had the awesome privilege of visiting with several other couples who had at one time been in crisis and were ill-affected by what I call the "*I-Me*" Syndrome, but later cured the affliction with the "*Us-We*" Formula. This "*I-Me*" Syndrome is really subtle at first, but if left untreated and unchecked it can eventually grow into a full-blown, stage-4 relationship killer.

Many relationships have fallen victim to this not-so-silent killer and there's absolutely no doubt that there's many, many more to come. But there is hope. So, take heart today and know that the "*Us-We*" Formula is capable of eradicating and eliminating this disease without prejudice.

So I invite you today to find something that you and that special someone can do together and make sure that you're not just on the same page in this "*life*" and "*relationship*" thing but also reading from the same book.

"*Us-We*" over "*I-Me*" is the key to increasing your chances of winning together. Oh, and this concept is not limited to just relationships, it is equally as impactful in every facet of business and the business of life. This unsung formula can and will deliver phenomenal results if you just commit to apply it in and on the infected areas of your life, guaranteed.

So why don't "*We*" go out and create our magical moments by applying this "*Us-We*" Formula in our lives as we attempt to make it GREAT! Yes, this is a breadcrumb that maybe small in size but it's big in results.

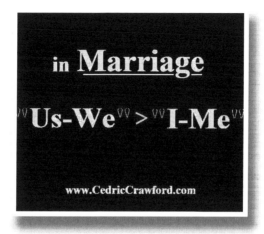

December 12

The High Cost of being Misunderstood

"Choose your words wisely before releasing them out into the unforgiving realm of cyberspace."

- Cedric R. Crawford -

I was having a casual conversation with my friend Michelle recently about some of the inherent perils of the information-driven internet and other content-driven mediums of today. I absolutely love having adult conversation "*Power-Chats*" with like-minded people who are seeking to get better because it always helps me to get better too.

During our conversation I suddenly had one of my "*Hallelujah moments of inspiration*" and realized something we should all be aware of. So I invite you to consider the following breadcrumb today as you go about your daily, content-creating life.

What we say is not always what other people hear and what we write is not always what other people understand when they read it. It's clear to me that every verbal word we speak and written word we write is at the mercy of the interpretation of the reader. The person on the receiving end of your spoken or written words will ultimately draw their own conclusions (*good or not-so-good*) based on their prior experiences and current mental mindset.

As a result, I feel compelled to offer you a bit of unsolicited advice today. It would be wise for us to take the time to choose our words wisely before releasing them out into the unforgiving realm of cyberspace. And as my friend Leta Mae Rhodes would say, "*Make your words sweet because you may have to eat them.*" Not many things can cost you more in this life than the price you could pay for being "*Misunderstood.*"

Don't *"misunderstand"* the words and meaning of my message today as you continue in your efforts to make it GREAT.

December 13

FOCUS

The Curveballs of Life

*"When life throws you a curveball, make the necessary adjust-
ments and knock it out the park."*

- Cedric R. Crawford -

When life throws you a curveball, make the necessary adjustments and knock it out the park. We all should know and understand by now that life is a major-league baseball pitcher throwing missiles down range at us in the form of challenges and changes and they're not always straight and predictable. Sometimes they're knuckles and curveballs. These unexpected challenges require adjustments in order for us to make bat-to-ball contact.

So my word to you today is to keep your eyes on the ball and what's important and make the necessary adjustments and knock those suckers out the park! Our homeruns can only come if we commit to keep swinging the bat. Let's keep making it GREAT!

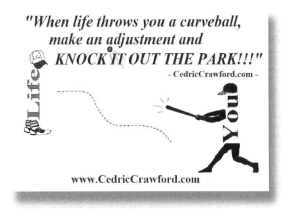

December 14

EDUCATION

Self-Inflicted Education

*"We Know-not because we Read-not and we Hear-not
because we Listen-not."*

- Cedric R. Crawford -

I've observed over the years that the poorly educated are often more easily manipulated, violated and victimized due to the lack of the knowledge that would afford them the ability to make better choices and decisions. I too used to be a part of this group so when I discovered this little-known fact, I was a bit upset at first but I later realized that it doesn't have to be this way. Our fate really is what we make it to be and if we choose not to educate ourselves we're setting ourselves up as a big target for scandalous, scheming, scamming opportunist in every area of life.

I may have referenced this before but it's so important that I feel it bears repeating that "*most people*" believe education stops with graduation, but I believe this couldn't be further from the truth. For years this belief has been the show-stopper for advancement in the lives of many across the globe. And many, many more will continue to subject themselves to manipulation and victimization by those who have made it their business to prey on the poorly educated. There is no doubt that to continue down this slippery slope will ultimately lead to the undoing of once-stable communities all around the world. So what is the antidote? Well, it's quite simple. Continued, Never-Ceasing, Self-Inflicted Education.

In many cases it may not be entirely our fault that we've received inadequate education in the past but I believe it is solely our fault if we don't intentionally seek out more education for our future. I believe that we *Know-not* because we *Read-not* and we *Hear-not* because we *Listen-not*. Knowledge and education doesn't have any feet so it can't walk to us or meet us half-way, we have to get up and go seek it out.

So I invite you today to make the act of seeking out more knowledge, wisdom and education part of your ever-so-important daily disciplines, for the best and most lucrative investment you can ever make is an investment in yourself.

We only get one time through this "*Life*" thing so let's keep seeking the knowledge to make it GREAT!

Better Education = Better Choices = Better Results = Better You = Better LIFE.

December 15

To Plan or NOT to Plan

"A wise man will expect the 'unexpected' part of the plan."
- Cedric R. Crawford -

ver heard the phrase, *"If you want to make God laugh just tell him your plans."* Well, this phrase has been echoed by many down through the generations and ages, and while it may be a bit comical, we must not confuse the message of this phrase with suggesting that planning ahead is unnecessary.

As I look back over my life I realize that all of my biggest accomplishments and successes never happened quite like I planned them, however, they did happen because I planned for them. Simply put, sometimes the best part of a plan wasn't actually a part of the original plan at all, it was unexpected.

So I say to you today, go ahead and make your plans and follow your plans but fully expect for things NOT to always go exactly as planned. Life is fraught with twist and turns and hairpin curves so buckle-up because you never really know what's coming around the corner up ahead.

I invite you today to consider replacing the old aforementioned phrase with my new one. *"God smiles upon the wise man who expects the 'unexpected' part of a plan."*

Make your plans and let's continue to lean forward as we attempt to make it GREAT!

NOTES

Bonus DAY 12!!!

The Creed of Greatness

Times are tough but our will to overcome is tougher. The words normal, typical and usual do not describe us. We are indeed a strange breed and a little bit different than the "Average Joe" in the way we think and act.

In the midst of chaos and uncertainty our natural "fight-or-flight" instincts are prepared to kick-in, but we choose not to flee. We will stand strong and fight our good fight of faith everyday of the week and twice on Sundays.

In spite of what we see with our physical eyes, our resolve remains strong because our mind's eye reflects a clear picture of total and complete victory. Our imagination has securely lodged a favorable vision of unquestionable triumph on our internal movie screen.

In pursuit of that which we seek, we will categorically refuse to retreat or back down. Instead, we will stand firm and demand the unconditional surrender of anyone who dares to stand in the way of us and our ultimate goal, for we know that our fight is indeed noble and just, and absolutely worthy of our best efforts.

Today we make this decree that until we draw upon our last breath in these fallible vessels, we will choose to stay the course in whatever God-ordained endeavor we undertake until success shows up. We smile and rejoice in advance for we know that God has given us unfair favor and our respective battle is already fixed for us not just to win, but to WIN BIG!

We continue to achieve because we continue to believe. We will be encouraged today and boldly move forward with the highest degree of certainty and make this "*good*" day GREAT!!!

by Cedric R. Crawford

Please view the video on:

www.YouTube.com

<u>Search Code:</u> Cedric R. Crawford – (4)

December 16

My Shameless Plea for HELP

"*Not 'I think I can, I think I can,' it's ' I know I can, I know I can. Change your perspective.*"

- Cedric R. Crawford -

Living in a world where *"sex"* sells, *"drama"* dominates, *"chaos"* is a cash-cow, *"profanity"* is profitable and *"raunchy"* and *"risqué"* rules the airwaves and cyberspace, one of my biggest struggles and challenges has been trying to attract and maintain the attention of the masses.

I must admit that it's becoming harder and harder to compete with video games and internet-cyberspace. The mind-numbing TV shows, radios, picture shows and videos are managing to seduce most of the general public into accepting a mediocre mindset. Yet I fight-on.

I fight on because I know my cause is noble and just. I fight-on because my mission is worthy of my best efforts. I fight-on because I was created for a task such as this. I fight-on because evil can only prosper and grow if good men/women stand by and do nothing. I fight-on because my boys want to be like me and they're watching my every step. I fight-on because someone, somewhere is unknowingly waiting to be Inspired, Motivated or Educated by my message, my content and my story of *"You Can Too…."*

In spite of the existing challenges, my #1 goal hasn't changed a bit. I still aspire to remain relevant and produce positive, life altering content in a very competitive market that's not big-on personal growth. *"I think I can, I think I can, I think I can."* was the famous words spoken by the *Little Engine that Could*, but my emphatic word-phrase is, *"I know I can, I Know I Can, I ABSOLUTELY KNOW I CAN !!!"*

Today I have no shame in admitting that I need all the help I can possibly get from my friends both on and off-line. So I say to you today, if you've ever been blessed by any of my work, writings or content, feel free to refer others to my website and blog regularly @: www.CedricCrawford.com and www.MrBreadCrumb.com.

I'm on a mission to help others to Make it GREAT!!! It just gets better from here. So be sure to keep spreading the Word!!!

> **Please view the video on:**
> **www.YouTube.com**
> **Search Code: Cedric R. Crawford – (19)**

December 17

Thankful

"It's not about the hand we're dealt in this life, it's about having the ability to play our hand well."

- Cedric R. Crawford -

I was asked by a friend and fellow author, Ernie "E.L." Lansford, today to reach into my *"bag of blessings"* and pull out something that I am thankful for. And so I write.

I woke up this morning with the sun shining on my face and ready for a crack at life again. I've always been thankful for the sun but I used to have problems with being thankful for the face that it shines upon.

Growing up in the mean streets, inner city of Dallas, Texas in the 1970's and 80's taught me a lot about dealing with struggle and adversity. My environment and the people in it started to rub off on me and I eventually began to believe that my complexion would hold me back from connection and achieving my biggest goals and dreams. I believed that being a poor, inner city, black, male gave me one extra thing to contend with in this life, so for that reason I was not very thankful.

But thank God my story doesn't end there, that was just the beginning. As I grew in stature I also grew in knowledge and wisdom and started to realize that it's not about the hand we're dealt in this life, it's about having the ability to play our hand well.

Eventually I started to pursue developing myself personally by reading good books and listening to inspiring and empowering tapes and CDs and intentionally surrounding myself with positive people who were doing the same. It wasn't long before I had a complete mental *"about-face"* and turnaround. I realized that in spite of all the things around me I can't control, I can always control my attitude and emotions. Now my complexion makes me smile and I am indeed grateful for the God-given ability to play my hand well in this life.

If there's something in our life that we want to change for the better, it starts with making ourselves better. Stay committed to working on the most important factor that makes your life what it is "YOU." Congratulations in advance to you who choose not to settle for those unwanted things in your life.

My bold statement to my Creator for this week is, "Thank you for making me who I am and for your gift of 'free will' and the opportunity to make this life GREAT!" Let's all choose to play our hand well as we attempt to make it GREAT!

December 18

LIVE LIFE

Expiration Date?

> *"Milk-Cartons we're not. Our shelf-life and spoil date remains a mystery, so get to living today because tomorrow may never come!"*
>
> *- Cedric R. Crawford -*

From the moment we're born, with every precious heartbeat we move closer and closer to our expiration date. Some of our dates are sooner and some of our dates are later. Some may expire by the hands of another and some may expire by their own hands. Some will leave a mark on this world and some will just *leave* this world. But no matter the cause or the affect, none of us are like milk cartons with a visible expiration date stamped on our foot or forehead. Our shelf-life and spoil date remain a mystery to all that walk this earth without exception.

As a result, I invite you to join me in committing today to live everyday as if there's no tomorrow because one day we'll be right. So, don't sweat the small stuff because in the end we all eventually discover that life really is too short and we only get one time through. Our expiration dates are all rapidly approaching so don't wait. Start today. It's never too early and never too late to start making it GREAT.

December 19

LIFE

Read the Fine Print

"The following words carry the highest point value in the game of life: 'Thank You', 'Please', 'I'm Sorry' and 'I Forgive You'."
- *Cedric R. Crawford -*

The most important words and phrases in most contracts can usually be found written in fine print at the bottom of the page. After thoroughly reviewing the contract of life I've discovered that the fine print on one of the pages states the following:

"Whoever wants to become great among the masses must be your servant, and whoever wants to be first must be your slave. You were created to be free but do not use your free-will to take advantage or harm and abuse and enslave others, but use it to serve others in love."

Furthermore, in order to win at the game of life you must understand how to score points and one of the ways to score big points is to use the most important words spoken in any language. The following words carry the most point value: "Thank You," "Please," "I'm Sorry" and "I Forgive You." They don't sound like much but when used properly they can make a huge difference in the game of life. So, be sure to use them honestly and often and light up the scoreboard.

As I've always said, we only get one time through this "life" thing so let's continue in our best efforts to make it GREAT! Don't forget to read the fine print.

(All points are ONLY redeemable in the hereafter. Contest rules never change. Children under 18 are admitted without parents and this offer isn't void where prohibited.)

December 20

SERVICE

Service = Happiness

"We have to make sure that our daily job activity gives us more than just a paycheck."
- *Cedric R. Crawford -*

O ne of our greatest fears should be that we will go through life trying to succeed at something that doesn't really matter in the grand scheme of things. Our fear should be that we get to the end of our journey only to find that we were climbing the wrong hill. Gut check time. We must ask ourselves the hard question, "*is our daily activity geared toward something that really makes a difference in people's lives, or, are we just in survival mode trying to take care of our own family and numero uno?*"

I've come to the realization that we have to make sure that our daily job activity gives us much more than just a paycheck at the end of the week. Because if that's all we're receiving for our efforts, then our jobs, careers and overall life will be empty and void of purpose and real accomplishment that matters. We have to find a way to positively affect lives around us on a regular basis because true, sustainable joy and happiness can only be attained and sustained by serving others. This is a truth that isn't always welcomed or received well, but it's absolutely necessary. I encourage you to take this breadcrumb wisdom today and Make it GREAT!

December 21

JOY AND HAPPINESS

"*Joy-Stealers*" You Lose

*"Keep your joy and peace under lock and key away from the
'Joy Stealers' and refuse to allow anyone to steal it."*

- Cedric R. Crawford -

I was talking with a friend not long ago and she was agonizing over a recent encounter she had with a fellow team member that was extremely rude and insensitive to her. You know the type. The kind of person that's quick to get loud and obnoxious and give you a piece of their mind when they really need to hold on to as much of it as they can. I call these people "*Joy Stealers.*"

The incident that took place was totally unexpected and over-the-top in its inappropriateness for the time and place it took place. My friend was emotionally shaken by this event and I quickly reminded her not to be so quick to forfeit her joy and peace because of the callous act of a rude, crude, bad mood "*Joy Stealer*" on a rampage. "*You still have power over the way you choose to respond. Don't give that up.*" I said.

We can all make a point to keep our joy and peace under lock and key and refuse to allow anyone to steal it. Fending off "*Joy Stealers*" can be a full-time job and daily battle that's definitely worth fighting over and over again. Fortunately my friend got the message quickly and regained her joy in the moment and vowed to stay on track in the days ahead. YEAH!!! "*JOY STEALER*" YOU LOSE!!! Crisis averted once again.

I invite you to adopt the same philosophy today and everyday along your way to making this life GREAT! No needless stress inflicted by "*Joy Stealers*" over here. Not today. Just another small breadcrumb to making it GREAT! ENJOY!!!

December 22

CHEER

The Gift Given

"The Christmas season is not about the gifts given and received, it's about 'The Gift' given and received."

- Cedric R. Crawford -

As a kid I remember Christmas seeming to take forever to come around, but as an adult I'm probably not alone in my belief that the Christmas Holiday season appears to come faster with every passing year. All-in-all, it still is my favorite time of year. The time of year where I get the chance to cozy up next to the fireplace and hear the crackle of the gas logs. The time of year where the Christmas tree lights light up the house at night. The time of year where my kids glow with anticipation of the famous day of reckoning. I must admit that I find myself living vicariously through their excitement for the season.

While on your journey through this Christmas Holiday season I invite you to consider the following: Although many have twisted this time of year into somewhat of a *"Consumer Fest,"* I would caution you to truly remember the original reason for the season. No matter what your faith is or spiritual understanding or religious beliefs are, one thing we can all probably agree on is this season is a time of gratitude, kindness and EXTRA-Patience.

I regret to say that over the years I've witnessed time and time again where many people allow this season to cause more stress and frustration when it really should be just the opposite. Don't miss your opportunity to model the appropriate behavior for this season to those around you both young and not-so-young. Simply put, I believe this season is not about the gifts given and received, but it's about the *"Gift"* given and received. Hmmmm… Don't miss the message with this one today.

This holiday season I invite you and challenge you to commit several random acts of kindness to a friend, a foe or even a perfect stranger or two and be as creative as your brilliant mind will allow you to be. Smile more and you'll find that you'll want to smile more. Laugh often and you'll find that you'll want to laugh more often. Shake a hand or hug a neck and make a new friend. And, be quick to ignore an idiot and disregard the reckless *"Joy Stealers"* that are on the prowl even more so this time of year. Just smile, wave and move on quietly singing your song, *"Oh Happy Day."*

"Cheer" is of little use unless you spread it around a bit, so do your part in spreading some holiday cheer this year and making someone else's day GREAT. After all, life is greater when you're trying to help make other peoples life great. So let's keep making it GREAT!

December 23

FAMILY

Family Jewels

"You can pick your friends, but family is just part of the deal."

- Cedric R. Crawford -

Back today with a renewed perspective after visiting my huge family in Dallas, TX. No question about it, you can pick your friends but family is just part of the deal. My mom and dad have 25 brothers and sisters between them, which makes for one of Texas' biggest families I'm sure. To date, I've never attempted the daunting task of trying to determine the number of first and second cousins I have. I'm sure that number changes monthly if not weekly now.

Backyard barbecues are our favorite and we really don't need much of a reason to do one. A few phone calls are all it takes to spread the news and get the gang together. Loud music, spontaneous laughter and idle chatter fills the air and the atmosphere is electric and inviting. Domino's, cards, basketball on the court and football in the street are just some of the most popular activities. Domino's is one of my favorites. After years of being beat by my uncles and aunties, I've finally learned enough to pull out a win or two. Ahhhh… the nostalgic feeling keeps me craving to come back again and again to create more memories and seeing the new generation of second and third cousins coming up makes me smile. My prayer is that their memories of these days will be just as fond as they were for me when I was their age.

I realize that our personalities are as diverse as the species in the Amazon Rain Forest. However, in spite of all of our flaws, faults and fallacies, we sure know how to have a lot of fun, eat some goooood food and love-on each other. We may not all get along all the time, but time and genuine love eventually brings us all back together. Yes we're not immune to having our fair share of black sheep and closet freaks but all-in-all, at the end of the day we love each other like no other. Big, small, short, tall, hair or bald we have them all. Yep, family is just part of the deal. Yours may have it all figured out with no habits, hurts or hang-ups, but I think I'll keep this one.

My message and prayer for you today is to be sure to enjoy your families, not just this season, but all the seasons of life. Create many memories for we'll never know which season will be our last. Let's take this breadcrumb and share it with our respective families as we continue in our efforts to make it GREAT!

Chris P.   *Amen Cedric. LoL! Sometimes the hardest ones to love are those in our family, but I think love should start at home. Good practice if nothing else. And great rewards to those who can get past the hurdles. Merry Christmas!*

December 24

PROBLEMS

Problems: To Solve or NOT To Solve

"Most people's problems don't necessarily need to be solved they just need to be heard."

- Cedric R. Crawford -

On this Christmas eve I feel the overwhelming need to offer you the following breadcrumbs of knowledge for the days ahead. I've discovered over the years of interacting with people during the ups and the downs of life that most people's problems don't necessarily need to be solved they just need to be heard.

Our natural tendency as human beings is to want to solve the problems of our friends and loved ones but I caution you that attempting to solve the problems of others can in some cases do more harm to a person or relationship than help.

The surprising reality is the solution to the most complex problems often times lie within the host itself. So the best things you can do for a friend or loved one sometimes is absolutely nothing but listen and give that friend an opportunity to work through that problem by wrestling with their own words and thoughts.

Being allowed to fully articulate in their own words the problem they're facing can oftentimes be both therapeutic and cathartic and more importantly can reduce the level of stress and anxiety for many situations. Just being willing to lend what I call an *"affirmative ear"* or be an *"encouraging listener"* can go a loooong way sometimes.

So I invite you to consider shutting up and listening sometime and just let the venting process run its course. You just might find yourself being a hero to that friend or family member in distress. Sure couldn't hurt to find out for your self rather or not this really works. Don't take this breadcrumb of wisdom lightly this season.

Let's all continue to make it GREAT

December 25

Spread some Christmas Cheer

"Go out and R.A.K. (Random Act of Kindness) a perfect stranger today and make it GREAT!"

- Cedric R. Crawford -

I was startled awake this morning by the words, "DUDE, NO WAY!!!" coming from the living room area. As my eyes popped open, I then realized that it was Christmas morning and that sound was coming from my third born child, Chance, getting a head-start on seeing what he got from "*Santa*." I glanced over at the clock and it was exactly 7:11 am. Lucky numbers. Yes indeed, this will be a GREAT day. Seconds later the rest of the crew sprang into action and for the first hour of the day, all I saw was teeth and wiggling booties of joy.

Later, Black Santa and his trusted reindeers all got mounted up and headed out on our quest of spreading Christmas cheer on roller blades through the great city of Bakersfield, California. Yes, it's true, I've successfully found a way to workout while making other people smile. This is just another one of our many annual traditions in the Crawford household. We love making you show your teeth around us especially during the Christmas holidays. Horns honking, dogs barking and kids screaming as we dash away, Dash Away, DASH AWAY ALL!!! Over 100 peppermints handed out this year. WooHoooo!!!

What traditions will you create to spread cheer to this world? What one thing will you do different this year to make someone else's Christmas season great? No need to answer out loud or raise your hand, just understand and make your plans. Go out and R.A.K. (*Random Act of Kindness*) a perfect stranger today and make it GREAT. And if someone asks you *how can they pay you back*, tell them that these types of actions aren't to be paid back, they're to be paid FORWARD! And, if they ask you who sent you, just point to the sky and wink an eye.

DISCLAIMER: This random act of kindness may not only make the target person's day brighter, it may just make your day a little bit better too. Let's go out and make this a Christ-filled Christmas and a HAPPY NEW YEAR!

Rob S.   *You da man Santa!!!*

December 26

TRIUMPH

Homemade vs. Store-bought Triumph

"True Triumph is as authentic as Mom's oven-baked, home-made cookies."

- Cedric R. Crawford -

As I was walking through the house not long ago being led by my nose into the kitchen where I found a batch of my wife's freshly baked cookies cooling on the counter, I suddenly had a spark of inspiration so I grabbed my camera and snapped a shot to capture the moment.

Have you ever noticed that store-bought, boxed cookies always fall just a little bit short of giving you that warm and fuzzy feeling you get when you eat Mom's oven-baked, homemade cookies? Those homemade cookies that mom invested her sweat, time and tears into preparing. Mom's cookies may not have been the best according to the world's standards, but for you they were first to few and second to none.

There's an interesting parallel here as it relates to accomplishment. Overtime I've also realized that you can't experience the true elation and feeling of accomplishment that comes with achieving a worthwhile goal or dream if you didn't have to work and struggle through some form of adversity for it. As I've said before, it's the adversity and struggle that actually gives the goal and dream value.

Simply put, the feeling of winning and achieving true triumphant victory is as authentic as mom's homemade, oven-baked cookies and you can't side-step or fake the feeling. So let's continue to be willing to pay the price with an investment of our sweat, time and tears and make it GREAT.

Ana S.   *I really enjoy your daily thoughts. When are you going to write a book that includes this stuff?*

Cedric R. Crawford *I haven't given it much thought, but I'm sure I'll write a book one of these days Ana.* ☺

December 27

PASSION AND PURPOSE

Purpose and Passion Pursuers UNITE!

"The quiet yearning of your true purpose and passion and unfulfilled dreams won't ever let you be fully satisfied with anything less than their complete fulfillment and satisfaction."

- Cedric R. Crawford -

Those who have ears, don't just hear this message, but be moved to take action. I invite you to consider this following truth today. The quiet yearning of your true purpose and passion and unfulfilled dreams won't ever let you be fully satisfied with anything less than their complete fulfillment and satisfaction. They will quietly continue to call for your attention and consideration until your days are no more.

No amount of money will ever be enough to quiet the ever-so-quiet beckoning call of your true purpose. No occupation will ever be able to quench the thirst of your unrealized and unrecognized passion. The "good" is just a creative, cunning distraction from the "GREAT" and many the world over have fallen victim to settling for it time-and-time again. Don't let it be you. I implore you to realize and recognize this unfortunate truth and reality and commit today that you will not be counted amongst this group of individuals who are comfortable with settling for "good."

Many will cast this message off as just another rambling of meaningless content and carry-on with their lives and tolerate the yearning of their unfulfilled purpose, but not you. Many will discount and discard this message and quietly live out their lives becoming more and more accustomed to turning a blind eye and deaf ear to their passion, but not you. Many will allow themselves to be duped yet again by that internal whisper that says, "*You're okay, just continue this way,*" but not you.

Yes my friends, we are indeed a different breed that will refuse to be satisfied until that quiet voice of unfulfilled purpose is silenced. We will refuse to ignore the yearning of our passion that's calling us to give it our undivided, complete and consistent attention. We will categorically reject the notion that a "good" life will do at the expense of compromising the pursuit of creating a "great" life in service to others. We will not neglect our duty and obligation to leverage our passion and purpose in service to our fellowman and strive to make this world a much better place than when we found it.

Be encouraged today and know that I'm extremely proud of you for being the exception to the unwritten rule of settling for a life in pursuit of comfort and average. I'm proud of you for committing to make it GREAT!

BRAVO!!!

December 28

MODERATION

The Law of Moderation

"Too much of anything is not a good thing."

- Cedric R. Crawford -

I just recently heard on the news how the snow was ravaging major cities on the East Coast of the United States this week. After hearing this news, I found myself calling up my college memory of how avid skiers would rave about how beautiful the snow flakes looked when they were falling from the sky on a cold winter morning as they prepared to hit the slopes minutes away in the mountains of Park City, UT. I guess it really does depend on your location and perspective of things.

It's interesting how on one hand, just a few snow flakes can wake an entire city up and bring it to life making adults and kids alike smile with joy and laughter. And on the other hand, how too many snow flakes can shut an entire city down and cause major catastrophes and death. Either way, the flakes sure are beautiful when they're falling from the sky.

It's sure interesting how nature continues to remind us of the term "*moderation*" and that too much of anything is not a good thing. You know of anyone in need of this breadcrumb of wisdom today? Hmmm…

Suffice to say today that moderation is a great creation for our entire nation to alleviate some of our frustration and mental constipation. So start making your preparation. Go play in the snow and let it serve as a constant reminder of "*not too much, but just enough*," as you attempt to use these breadcrumbs to make it GREAT!

December 29

SERVICE

What have you done for me lately?

"There's nothing shorter in life than the memory of those who spend it with their hands out asking for favors."

- Cedric R. Crawford -

I was having a great conversation with my dad this morning and he reminded me that in the eyes of many we're only as good as our last favor. My dad is always good for making statements like this so I wasn't really surprised when he said it. But I was surprised how shocking this can be in the moments you experience it first hand. I must admit there's nothing shorter in life than the memorys of those who spend it with their hands out asking for favors. The last favor tends to fade from their memory rather quickly. Hmmmm…

I'm reminded of the words of the late, great 35th President, John F. Kennedy when he said, "*Ask not what your country can do for you, but what you can do for your country.*" Profound words that were so simple yet carried so much weight. I believe we shouldn't stumble through this life looking for favors, hand-outs and for what others can do for us, but we should find ways to do for others, for it is true that it is far better to be a giver than to be a receiver from those who are willing to give.

Yes, I understand that most people tend to have short memories and are oftentimes stuck on a "*What have you done for me lately?*" mode of thinking. But, the statement and belief that, "*We're only as good as our last favor,*" should never be acceptable. So, don't make the mistake of letting your actions justify this statement and belief.

Our communities are in dire need of servant-leaders who aren't afraid to step up and step out to lead the charge in showing and modeling to others what it means to be a giver of ones time, talents, treasures and tears. Let us not be guilty of "*knowing it*" but not "*showing it.*"

So, what have you done for someone else lately? What are you prepared to do today to make someone else's day great? No need to answer out loud, just "*show me*" and make me proud.

This is definitely a breadcrumb to making it GREAT!

December 30

NEGATIVITY

Join the "No-Negative" Team

*"Don't be **NEGATIVE**, a Naysayer Eager to Get At The Internal Values of Everyone."*

- Cedric R. Crawford -

I invite you to consider the following simple reality today. Either we're sowing "*negativity*" into this world or "*positivity*" into this world.

Being exposed to a world that's fraught with negativity and naysayers around every corner and on every news station and TV show can be extremely taxing at times. Maintaining a positive attitude everyday despite the negativity around us can be a struggle, but it's definitely worthy of our best efforts. The actions of those who are attempting to do good in this world will almost always be overshadowed by the negative, but we must commit to continue doing good anyway. We must never resign ourselves to concede to negativity ruling the day.

For this reason I am in recruitment mode and my networking company of choice has no product or service to offer. We just need a few good men or women who will make a lifetime commitment to deliver large doses of positivity into this world on a regular basis. A few good men or women that will refuse to sit by idly and let negativity go unchallenged. A fearless few good men or women who will make the bold statement of, "NOT ON MY WATCH WILL NEGATIVITY PREVAIL!"

There's no income potential or fast-start bonuses and rank-advancements here, just the great feeling of knowing that you'r e doing good for your fellowman or woman by planting seeds of positivity with your random acts of kindness.

So, dare to join our fast-growing network by becoming a member of my website at www.Cedric-Crawford.com. Our goal is to reach a million strong over the next 24 months and we're already well on our way.

An epidemic of positivity is our goal and no single one of us is better than the group of all of us. Together we can and will make a difference daily. It's FREE and it's easy to join so do it NOW. The world needs us now more than ever, so let's not let 'em down, not today.

Welcome to the team in advance. Let's keep making it GREAT!

> Please view the video on:
>
> www.YouTube.com
>
> <u>Search Code:</u> Cedric R. Crawford – (12)

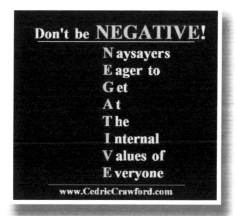

December 31

A Year in Review

"Only a fool will try to take 'it' with him."

- Cedric R. Crawford -

The strangest thought came to me today as I was looking back over this past year. I couldn't help but to consider the question of if I were to die tonight, could I honestly say that I was satisfied with the contribution that I've made to the planet thus far. At this very moment in time as I am writing this entry, I would have to answer that question with a disappointing "No." In fact, my answer would be more of an "*ABSOLUTELY NOT*." I've come a long way, but I still feel that I have so far to go.

Out of all the money I've made over the years from building a once successful real estate investment business and building and developing dozens upon dozens of properties for people, that contribution is short lived at best. Making a more worthwhile contribution from a mental and spiritual perspective to the world and the billions of people that are in it will definitely prove to be a much more arduous task. However, this type of contribution can never burn up, fall down or rot away, so as I've said before, I am convinced that this task is definitely worthy of my best efforts.

I've shared this before, but I think that it deserves being mentioned once more. Looking back at the great history of mankind, the great Pharaohs and Kings of Egypt got it all wrong. They attempted to take their best servants and worldly possessions with them at death, but this action is foolish at best. Be advised that we entered this world with nothing and we take the same with us when we leave, NOTHING! However, we can leave our positive mark with the message of our life-knowledge and wisdom-gained that we are able to successfully poor and sow into those other souls that occupy this great planet with us.

A great man once coined the phrase, "*Service is the rent we pay for occupying our space on earth*," and I couldn't agree more. I've always believed that any day above ground is a good day and an opportunity to be a little bit better today than we were yesterday. If you haven't noticed by now, I've been careful and intentional about using words like, "*let's, we, us* and *our*" throughout this book because the advise and suggestions contained herein are for me too. Yes, I am indeed a self-proclaimed *work-in-progress* that will never be completed.

Finally, in thinking about the timeless story of events surrounding the crucifixion of Jesus Christ over 2,000 years ago, there was a defining point of His journey that shed a huge light on what we all are expected to do this side of eternity. This pivotal moment came while he was hanging on the wooden cross in agony from his strips and wounds. It was the unforgettable moment He looked up and uttered the words, "*It is finished*." With these three words His spirit was released from His body. I don't believe there's a better example of a life that was lived with a fulfilled purpose and mission accomplished. What's most important to note here is, His "*it*" was finished so there was nothing left for him to do here. As a result, I'm convinced this is irrefutable evidence that if we're still alive and breathing, our "*it*" has yet to be completed. Our purpose has yet to be fulfilled. Our "*why*" for living is still pending completion.

So "*let's*" remember that as long as "*we're*" living and breathing, our "*it*" is not finished and "*we've*" still got business and work to do. "*Let's*" seize the opportunities to share our time, talents, treasures and tears with the world at large while "*we're*" here. Oh, and "*we*" must always remember so that "*we*" will never forget to Carpe Diem and take these breadcrumbs and spread them around so we can all **Make it GREAT!**

My Viral Quotes
Feel Free to SHARE

"If you get an unwanted text message from your checkered past, press delete and keep-on moving."

"It's hard to bend a tree when it's two feet thick, so discipline it while it's young."

"The path of least resistance leads to Average Avenue."

"Anger is like a guy with a fat belly. You can hold it in for a while but eventually you have to let it all hang out."

"Passion is intensified in the trenches of troubles and struggles."

"Don't let the stress and strain of your life bully you into a bad attitude."

"You can't please them all because even if you please them all, you're still bound to run into someone that doesn't like the fact that you're pleasing them all."

NOTES

*** NEWS BULLETIN ***

You Can't Take it

With YOU !!!

So, leave the BEST parts of you

here in others and for others.

CONGRATULATIONS for being one of the few who made it to this point in the book! You're definitely not "Most People."

Now that you've completed this book, GO tell a friend about the best parts of what you've come away with.

Don't make the common mistake of giving your brain too much credit in the memory-recall category. Our brains were built for speed and not for retention and easy recollection. So, be sure to keep this book close by for referencing later and little reminders and encouraging thoughts in the days ahead.

More books to come:

In case you were wondering… This book is the first of a multiple book series. My biggest challenge was forcing myself to stop taking content from Book #2 and putting it into this book.

So… The saga of life continues…

This next book will contain even more valuable content, meaningful conversations, events, defining moments, inspirational thoughts, real life stories and nuggets of knowledge that will continue to inspire, motivate, encourage and educate you on your journey.

Everyone has a story and even more of those stories will be shared in this next book to bring these normal, ordinary people to life by sharing their extraordinary journey of struggle, adversity and triumph.

Don't delay in any way. Pre-Order your copy today at: www.CedricCrawford.com

May your family continue to grow in love and knowledge with every passing day.
May you enjoy many moments where life takes your breath away.

May the sun rise and fall on your face without a frown.
May you deposit many good memories for your ups and your downs.

May others gaze upon your family and say "Now that's a sight to see."
And find that loves the lock and kindness is the master key.

Perfect we're definitely not and perfect we shall never be.
But our faults and failures is what makes the perfect imperfect family.

We know our destiny and fates not set, it's based on what we choose.
But with God on our side in the absence of pride we know we cannot lose.

So press-on through your day He'll show you the way through every trial and test.
Now take all that you know to the world and do show and we wish your family the best.

- The Crawford's -

Me, Karen, Monique, Cedric Jr, Chance and Chayse are all counting on you to make this good life a GREAT life.

Make it GREAT!

> **Please view the video on:**
>
> **www.YouTube.com**
>
> **Search Code: Cedric R. Crawford – (27)**

Keywords

To inquire about Cedric speaking or partnering with you or your organization at an upcoming event, please log onto **www.CedricCrawford.com** and click on the "*Book Cedric*" link, or send an email to **Crawford@CedricCrawford.com** (Subject: *Booking Inquiry*)

CedricCrawford.com

I would love to hear from you:

Please feel free to drop me an email at **TheBook@CedricCrawford.com**

OR

You can drop me a letter to:

CedricCrawford.com
9530 Hageman Rd. Ste. #222
Bakersfield, CA 93312

I'd love to hear your opinion about what you liked best
about the book and how you think I could make
it better. My sincere intentions are to
provide great value to you in
the days ahead.

Thanks in advance for helping me to get better.

For more tools:

Books, CD's, DVD's, Downloads, Dream Reminder Novelties, etc.
to help you make it GREAT, please log onto my official website,

www.CedricCrawford.com

and click on the *"Online Store"* and *"Products"* link.

Yes, the saga continues in the Bread Crumbs series. Education in deed
does not stop with graduation. Keep growing and going and

Make it GREAT!